Red Brethren

Red Brethren

THE
BROTHERTOWN AND
STOCKBRIDGE INDIANS
AND THE PROBLEM OF RACE
IN EARLY AMERICA

David J. Silverman

Cornell University Press, Ithaca and London

First published 2010 by Cornell University Press

First printing, Cornell Paperbacks, 2015

Printed in the United States of America

Library of Congress Cataloging-in-Publication Data

Silverman, David J., 1971–

Red brethren : the Brothertown and Stockbridge Indians and the problem of race in early America / David J. Silverman.

p. cm.

Includes bibliographical references and index.

ISBN 978-0-8014-4477-7 (cloth : alk. paper)

ISBN 978-1-5017-0075-0 (pbk. : alk. paper)

1. Brotherton Indians—History.   2. Brotherton Indians—Religion.
3. Stockbridge Indians—History.   4. Stockbridge Indians—Religion.
5. New England—Race relations—History.   6. New England—History—
Colonial period, ca. 1600–1775.   7. New England—History—1775–1865.   I. Title.

E99.B7S56   2010

974'.03—dc22

2010013373

Cornell University Press strives to use environmentally responsible suppliers and materials to the fullest extent possible in the publishing of its books. Such materials include vegetable-based, low-VOC inks and acid-free papers that are recycled, totally chlorine-free, or partly composed of nonwood fibers. For further information, visit our website at www.cornellpress.cornell.edu.

Cloth printing   10 9 8 7 6 5 4 3 2 1
Paperback printing   10 9 8 7 6 5 4 3 2 1

Contents

Acknowledgments

I managed the personal and professional challenges of writing this book with the generous financial support of several institutions, the collegiality of my scholarly community, and the love of family and friends. My gratitude extends wide and deep.

I began this project during a year as Mellon Postdoctoral Fellow at the American Antiquarian Society; two years later, the AAS invited me back for a month-long stay. As ever, the AAS was the ideal incubator for my work. Two other research grants were also critical to this work in its initial stages: one, from the New England Regional Fellowship Consortium, allowed me to visit the Massachusetts Historical Society, the Rhode Island Historical Society, the Connecticut Historical Society, and the Mystic Seaport Museum; another, from the American Philosophical Society's Phillips Fund for the Study of Ethnohistory, sent me to the Special Collections of the Hamilton College Library. Later, several timely summer grants from George Washington University enabled me to visit a host of archives in the Northeast and Midwest: the Special Collections of the Haverford College Library, the New-York Historical Society, the New York Public Library, the New York State Archives, the Onondaga County Historical Association, the Special Collections of the Cornell University Library, the Special Collections of the Vassar College Library, the Newberry Library, the Indiana Historical Society, the Wisconsin Historical Society, the Connecticut State Archives, the Special Collections of the Mashantucket Pequot Museum and Research Center, the Indian and Colonial Research Center (Mystic, Connecticut), the Beinecke Library of Yale University, the Rauner Library of Dartmouth College, the Harvard University Archives, the Phillips Library of the Peabody Essex Museum, the Congregational Library (Boston), the Boston Public Library, the Stockbridge (Mass.) Public Library, the Stockbridge Town Clerk's Office, and the National Archives of the United States. I thank the staff at all these institutions for their courteous assistance. I finished writing this book during a year of academic leave funded by an Oscar Handlin Fellowship from the National Endowment of the Humanities and a semester sabbatical from George Washington

University. I owe special thanks to my department chairmen, Tyler Anbinder and William Becker, for going to bat for me time and time again and to the G.W. administration for its support of my research.

I vetted the ideas for this book at several conferences, in a handful of articles, and in stimulating exchanges with colleagues. I presented portions of my work to audiences at the annual meetings of the Omohundro Institute of Early American History and Culture, the Organization of American Historians, the American Historical Association, and the American Studies Association. I am indebted to commentators Nancy Shoemaker, Seth Mallios, Joel Martin, and William Hart, and the audiences at these sessions, for their constructive criticism. I also discussed portions of this book with the seminar of the Johns Hopkins University Department of History, the Washington Area Early American Seminar, Harvard University's Atlantic History Seminar, and, not least, several of my classes at G.W. I benefited tremendously from the feedback I received at these sessions. Articles related to this project passed through the unparalleled editorial process of the *William and Mary Quarterly* and a riveting symposium of scholars working on Indian Mission History gathered together by Mark Nicholas and Joel Martin. In these contexts, I received the counsel of Daniel Mandell, Rachel Wheeler, Tracy Leavelle, Mark Nicholas, Hillary Wyss, Douglas Winiarski, and Scott Casper, among many others. Perhaps the most essential advice of all came from Wyss, Winiarski, and Jon Parmenter, in their responses to a draft of my first four chapters. I feel fortunate to have such generous and knowledgeable friends.

Members of the Brothertown, Stockbridge, and Mohegan Indian communities have profoundly shaped this book. Caroline Adler of Brothertown, Cindy Jungenberg of Stockbridge, and Melissa Tantaquidgeon-Zobel of Mohegan all provided invaluable comments on the first full draft. Adler has unfailingly answered my many queries ever since, and Tantaquidgeon-Zobel also helped me to secure the image of the story box which opens chapter two. On my visits to Wisconsin, I received warm hospitality from Adler and Dennis DeGrass of Brothertown, Dorothy W. Davids and Ruth A. Gudinas of Stockbridge, and the Stockbridge-Munsee Educational Committee. Numerous other people from these communities have shared their thoughts with me in passing. I hope my work does justice to the legacies of their ancestors.

Permissions to reproduce the illustrations for this book came from the Bowdoin College Museum of Art, Connecticut Historical Society, Hood Museum of Art at Dartmouth College, Mohegan Tribe, and Wisconsin Historical Society.

William Keegan, my cartographer, was a pleasure to work with in the design of the maps.

It would take a poet to express the ways in which my family has sustained me throughout this project. Aquinnah and Bela Silverman are my inspirations, and Julie Fisher is my strength. I will forever associate this book with their loving encouragement. My parents, Richard and Julia Silverman, have come through for me time and time again when I have needed them most. I dedicate this book to them as a modest but heartfelt memorial of my love and gratitude.

Abbreviations

Ayer Ms.	Ayer Manuscripts, Newberry Library, Chicago, Ill.
CHS	Connecticut Historical Society, Hartford, Conn.
Connecticut Records	
	Charles J. Hoadley, ed., *The Public Records of the Colony of Connecticut,* 15 vols. (Hartford, 1850–90).
DHNY	*Documentary History of the State of New York,* comp. E.B. O'Callaghan, 4 vols. (Albany, 1849–1851).
Dean Family Papers	
	Dean Family Papers, Indiana Historical Society, Indianapolis, Ind.
Harvard Grants	Records of Harvard Grants for Work among the Indians, Papers, 1720–1810, 1 box, Harvard University Archives, Cambridge, Mass.
Iroquois Indians	Francis Jennings, William N. Fenton, and Mary A. Druke, eds., *Iroquois Indians: A Documentary History,* 50 microfilm reels.
Johnson Papers	*The Papers of Sir William Johnson,* 14 vols. (Albany: State University of New York, 1921–1965).
Kirkland Journal	Walter Pilkington, ed., *The Journals of Samuel Kirkland: 18th Century Missionary to the Iroquois, Government Agent, Father of Hamilton College* (Clinton, N.Y.: Hamilton College, 1980).
Kirkland Papers	Samuel Kirkland Papers, Hamilton College Special Collections, Clinton, N.Y.
LROIA	Letters Received by the Office of Indian Affairs, 1824–1880, M234, National Archives, Washington, D.C.
LRSW	Letters Received by the Secretary of War Relating to Indian Affairs, 1800–1823. M271. Microfilm rolls 1–4. National Archives, Washington, D.C.
Marsh Papers	Cutting Marsh, Papers, 1802–1860, 2 reels, Wisconsin Historical Society, Madison, Wisc.
MHS	Massachusetts Historical Society, Boston, Mass.

MHSC   Massachusetts Historical Society, *Collections*

NEHGS   New England Historic Genealogical Society, Boston, Mass.

New York Assembly Papers

New York State Archives, Record Series A1823–78, 8 boxes, Assembly Papers, vols. 40 and 41, Petitions, Correspondence, and Reports regarding Indians, NYSA.

NYCD   E. B. O'Callaghan and Berthod Fernow, comps. and eds., *Documents Relative to the Colonial History of the State of New York,* 14 vols. (Albany, N.Y., 1856–1883).

NYHS   New-York Historical Society, New York, N.Y.

NYSA   New York State Archives, Albany, N.Y.

Occom Papers   Samson Occom Papers, 1710–1792, Connecticut Historical Society, Hartford, Conn.

Occom Writings   Joanna Brooks, ed., *The Collected Writings of Samson Occom* (New York: Oxford University Press, 2006).

PYMICR   Philadelphia Yearly Meeting Indian Committee Records, 1745–1983, Quaker Collection, Haverford College, Havertown, Penn.

Rauner Library   Rauner Library, Dartmouth College, Hanover, N.H.

Rauner Ms.   Manuscripts, Rauner Library, Dartmouth College, Hanover, N.H.

RIHS   Rhode Island Historical Society, Newport, R.I.

SPGNA Recs.   Society for Propagating the Gospel Among the Indians and Others in North America, Records, 1752–1948, 23 boxes, MHS

Stockbridge Indian Papers

Stockbridge Indian Papers, Huntington Free Library Collection, Cornell University, Ithaca, N.Y.

Wheelock Papers   *The Papers of Eleazar Wheelock, together with the Early Archives of Hanover, New Hampshire through the year 1779,* 16 reels (Hanover: Dartmouth College Library, 1971).

WHC   *Wisconsin Historical Collections*

WHS   Wisconsin Historical Society, Madison, Wisc.

WMQ   *William and Mary Quarterly,* 3d series.

Writings of Joseph Johnson

To Do Good to My Indian Brethren: The Writings of Joseph Johnson, 1751–1776, ed. Laura J. Murray (Amherst, Mass., 1998).

Red Brethren

That Overwhelming Tide of Fate

T HERE was no way for Lyman C. Draper to know that the manuscript delivered to his desk in the late summer of 1855 had been penned by an Indian. Its author, Thomas Commuck, possessed an Anglophone name and wrote in English with a clear hand and proper grammar; his mailing address was a small town in Wisconsin's agricultural heartland, an area few people still associated with Indians. On the surface, Commuck appeared to have been a simple country farmer or shopkeeper. Yet Draper knew that sometimes the most unassuming bumpkin could recount from first-hand experience the drama of continental explorers, fur traders, Indian fighters, or pioneers.[1] A source with a local story that could be published in Draper's *Collections of the Wisconsin Historical Society* was even better. Commuck was just that, for he offered "a small sketch of the Brothertown Indians, who, as you probably are well aware, are now enjoying all the rights, privileges, and immunities of citizenship, and who now, are a part and parcel of that heterogeneous mass of human beings, of almost 'all nations, tongues, and kindred,' who have happily chosen Wisconsin as their 'Home, Sweet, Home.'"[2] This was precisely the kind of yarn that made Draper love his job.

The Brothertown Indians were indeed an interesting case. Their people, formed from several New England and Long Island tribes during the Revolutionary period, moved from the coast to Oneida country in upper New York in the 1780s, relocated to Wisconsin in the 1820s, and then in the late 1830s became the first Indians as a group to become full citizens of the United States. Yet the most striking feature of Commuck's manuscript was the identity of the author, for he himself was a Brothertown Indian of Narragansett descent. Shrewdly, Commuck did not introduce himself until well into his account, by which time most readers would have assumed he was white. He "passed" as white not only through his command of English but by using the racial clichés of Manifest Destiny to explain Indian decline. For instance, he conceded that Indians had a tendency to mimic the worst examples of their "white brethren," particularly when it came to consuming "Fire Water." He attributed Indian land loss, poverty, and alcohol abuse to the amorphous "mighty rush and bustle consequent upon the planting and consolidating [of] a mighty Republic," rather than to lawless white expansion or actual government policies. Whites familiar with this history generally assumed that Brothertown's constituent tribes, such as the Narragansetts, Mohegans, Pequots, and Montauketts, "have become now entirely extinct." "If not," Commuck wrote, "they ask, Where are they?"[3] Having disarmed his readers and insulated himself with plenty of rhetorical cover, Commuck revealed his identity and then proceeded to answer that question with a damning critique of white Americans' historic mistreatment of Native people.

In Commuck's telling, Brothertown's history could only be understood in terms of race in America, in terms of whites using every means at their disposal to make Indians disappear, even when the Indians made every concession to white demands that they adopt Christianity and civility. Commuck's answer to the question "Where are they?" was *We are here*—small and weak, certainly, but here—despite your ceaseless efforts up to this very day. He explained that the Brothertown Indians' ancestors were once powerful, but after the Europeans arrived, "fierce and bloody wars" combined with the "number, wealth and enterprise" of the "civilized and christianized conquerors" reduced the Natives to "insignificance." Commuck was being subtle here, juxtaposing the terms "civilized and christianized" that whites used to describe themselves, with "conquerors," a label that white Americans stubbornly rejected, all evidence to the contrary. The nation thought of its devastation of Indians not as conquest but as a fulfillment of God's plot, destiny, or nature. American history, by this telling, was a heroic morality tale in which savage pagans gave way to a religiously, culturally, and even biologically superior people, thus fulfilling God's dictate to subdue the wilds. Commuck was having none of this. Focusing on the case he knew best, he told of how the Brothertowns, "Red Brethren" as he called them, left Long Island Sound decades earlier for Oneida country, in the vain hope that "they would be more free from the contaminating influence, and evil example, etc., of their white brethren" (note the contrast here between his use of the uppercase for "Red Brethren" and lowercase for "white brethren").[4] Yet "the genius of the ever-restless pale face" contrived one scheme after another to harass the Brothertowns and their Christian Indian neighbors, the Stockbridge Mohicans and Oneidas, off their lands, involving brazen trespass, liquor-induced land sales, false treaties, and threats of violence. "Annihilation began to stare them in the face, as it had formerly done on the Atlantic coast," Commuck recalled sadly. Desperate, the Brothertowns and Stockbridges appealed to their "red brethren of the West," the Miamis and Delawares, for permission to settle along the White River in Indiana, but this plan failed too, as the United States bought the land from under their feet on the very eve of their relocation in 1818 even though it had encouraged them to go there in the first place.[5] By any measure, it was a crushing betrayal. Still, the New York Indians (as the Christian tribes were by then collectively known), resourceful and determined as ever, rebounded by successfully negotiating with the Menominees and Ho-Chunks (or Winnebagos) of Wisconsin for land along the Fox River west of Green Bay. In theory, this place was to be the New York Indians' last stop, a sanctuary far away from whites where they and their offspring could finally live in peace and prosperity. Yet there was no refuge for Indians in America. No sooner had the New York tribes migrated to Wisconsin in the 1820s and early 1830s than droves of "pioneers" followed in their wake, determined to seize the fertile lands on which the Natives had already built their communities. Pressured yet again by Washington to pull up stakes, the Brothertowns and Stockbridges retreated to the east side of Lake Winnebago, some forty miles inland from Green Bay. Though they were civilized Christians and steadfast friends of the United States, their status as Indians guaranteed that this would not be their last displacement.

Commuck redirected his narrative from tragedy to comedy only by glossing over why the Brothertowns decided to petition for citizenship shortly after arriving on the lake. He did not tell his readers that the Brothertowns had barely unpacked their things before they faced the threat of still another government removal, this time to Kansas, which led them to conclude that their best chance of surviving as an Indian community in Wisconsin was to shed their legal Indian status and divide their land into tracts of private property. Instead, Commuck plotted the Brothertowns' citizenship as the dénouement of their civility. He explained, "Having no laws which they could enforce, for the protection of their lives and property, and having, in all their ways, manner of living, appearance in dress, and speech (not having spoken or known anything of their own tongue for one hundred years), become perfectly assimilated to their white brethren, they concluded to petition Congress for citizenship."[6] Sharing a pathetic list of six Narragansett-language phrases, "all I know of the language of my tribe," stressed the point. Commuck wanted his readers to believe that the Brothertowns were a people divorced from their Indian heritage, accustomed to white ways, and thus qualified for full membership in the republic.

Commuck's final remarks addressed the paradoxical nature of the Brothertowns' quest to survive as an Indian people even as they adopted United States citizenship, which many Americans, including Indians, referred to as "becoming white." Equally paradoxical was the manner in which Commuck framed this subject, for he resorted to the very tropes of white progress and Indian disappearance he had spent the better part of his narrative challenging. In sentimental, haunting prose, he wrote:

> Here, then, are the Brothertown Indians on the east side of Winnebago Lake, in Calumet County, trying to imitate our white brethren in all things except their vices. Here we have taken our last stand, as it were, and are resolved to meet manfully, that overwhelming tide of fate which seems destined, in a few short years, to sweep the Red Man from the face of existence. The thought is a sad and gloomy one, but the fiat seems to have gone forth, and we must submit. Already, has intermarriage with the whites so changed the Brothertowns, in complexion, that three-quarters of them would be readily considered as white, where they were not known, and in another generation our Indian blood will probably become so intermixed with the general mass of mankind, that if the inquiry is made, Where are the Brothertown Indians? echo will answer, *Where?*[7]

Commuck might very well have agreed with his white readership that the prospect of Indians disappearing through assimilation into the American body politic rather than disappearing through violent dispossession was perhaps the best future for which Native people could hope. After all, the Brothertowns' endless travails seemed to prove that it was God's will for whites to prosper at the Indians' expense. Yet in all likelihood Commuck's language was designed to cloak his people's true goals. "Red Men" might have been on the path to extinction, but what of Indians who became legally "white"? Might they not sustain their community ties, cultural values, and sense of Indian identity while otherwise abiding by white rules? The very formation of Brothertown was premised on this kind of adaptation. What Commuck might have been saying, then, in terms that his readers would have barely understood, was *forget we are here, assume we will fade from existence, and leave us alone.* Allowing that question, "Where?" to echo without a direct answer was a survival strategy in a white nation determined to "sweep the Red Man from the face of existence."

More than two centuries earlier, Commuck's Narragansett ancestors participated in their own discussions about the differences between their people and Europeans, differences that later generations came to define as race. Rhode Island's founder, Roger Williams, wrote in his 1643 publication, *A Key into the Language of America,* that the Narragansetts "have often asked mee, why wee call them Indians, Natives, &c.," because they did not recognize the existence of such a group.[8] To be sure, they had general terms for humankind, such as *Nínnuock, Ninnimissinnûwock,* and *Eniskeetompaûog,* meaning "Men, Folke, or People." They identified with town-sized sachemships like Pawtuxet or Chaubutick, larger cultural and political groupings like the Narragansetts or Mohegans, and, when traveling in the interior, a broad family of Algonquian-speakers known to inland tribes as the Wabanakis (meaning "easterners" or "dawn land people"). However, before Europeans arrived they never had any reason to conceive of themselves and their aboriginal neighbors as a distinct category of humankind. Williams did his best to explain why his own nation, the English, thought of them in this manner, and the Narragansetts, he claimed, "understanding the reason, [say] they will call themselves Indians, in opposition to English, &c."[9] Indigenous people would henceforth interpret their struggles with colonialism by continuously refining their understanding of this new term, *Indian.*

The Narragansetts who dealt with Williams were no more familiar with describing people as white than as Indian. They referred to colonists as *Awaunagrss, suck* (these strangers), *Englishmánnuck* (Englishmen) and *Dutchmánnuck* (Dutchmen), but usually their names for Europeans cited their remarkable material culture. According to Williams, Narragansetts generally called the English *Cháquaqock,* or "knife men," and, at other times, *Waútacone-nûaog,* or "coat men."[10] The Mohawks and Oneidas of the Iroquois League similarly referred to the French as "makes an axe."[11] Not until the mid- to late eighteenth century, after New England colonists had adopted the color categories of Britain's plantation colonies and after New England Indians began speaking the English language in greater numbers, did the Narragansetts and other coastal Indians begin to use the term *white* to refer to Europeans. This is not to say that the Narragansetts took no heed of skin complexion. Drawing on the Narragansett word for "black," *Suckêsu,* their word for an African, *Suckáutacone,* meant "a cole blacke man."[12] Unfortunately, we have no idea how the Narragansetts accounted for Africans' dark color or what meaning, if any, they ascribed to it.

If we understand race in its American setting as the categorization of people according to their complexion and the unequal treatment of those groups according to their supposed qualities, then the Narragansetts of the mid-seventeenth century cannot be said to have thought racially at all. They had already held debates, however, about the fundamental differences between indigenous North Americans and Europeans that contributed to such thinking over time. For one, they believed that their people and the English had different creators. Williams explained, "Although they deny not that English man[']s God made English Men, and the Heavens and Earth there [in old England]! yet their Gods made them, and the Heaven and Earth where they dwell." The people's gods explained their basic differences. The Narragansetts conceived that "the God that made the English men is a greater God, because Hee hath so richly endowed the English above themselves" with items like "Clothes, Bookes, &c."[13] By comparison, the main creator of the Narragansett world, Cautantowwit, provided his people with corn and beans, which were their staples. Englishmen and Narragansetts could learn and borrow from each other, the Narragansetts believed, but their basic differences were a matter of divine will and thus to be respected.

This book bridges the span between the Narragansetts' exchanges with Roger Williams in the 1640s and Thomas Commuck's letter to Lyman C. Draper in the 1850s by examining why and how Indians came to interpret their struggles with colonialism racially. More specifically, it is interested in the ways in which Indian people understood, employed, and constantly redefined the categories of Indian, white, and black. At the center of this story are two neighboring multitribal, Christian Indian communities. One of them, Brothertown, was comprised of Narragansetts, Mohegans, Pequots, Niantics, Tunxis, and Montauketts from both sides of Long Island Sound. The other community, Stockbridge, included Mohicans, Housatonics, Wappingers, and Esopus from the New York/Massachusetts border region and, later, Delawares from New Jersey. Brothertown and Stockbridge were inextricably linked from the late colonial period onward. During the early 1730s and 1740s they jointly embraced Christianity; in the late eighteenth and early nineteenth centuries they moved in tandem from New England to New York to Wisconsin; and, finally, in the mid nineteenth century they confronted the momentous question of whether to discard their legal Indian status and become citizens or "whites." Focusing on these groups sheds new light on Indian racial thought and expression in a number of respects. First of all, Brothertown and Stockbridge left behind a voluminous paper trail created not only by whites but also Indians themselves, especially leaders such as Brothertown's

Samson Occom and Joseph Johnson and Stockbridge's Hendrick Aupaumut, Joseph W. Quinney, and Austin E. Quinney. These documents include diaries, sermons, psalms, covenants, letters, petitions, town meeting minutes, and more. Historians necessarily depend on written sources to ply their trade. The rich archival record pertaining to Brothertown and Stockbridge allows the story of these people, including their thoughts about race, to be told with some (though certainly not all) of the detail it deserves.

The Christian status of Brothertown and Stockbridge also provides a rare opportunity to explore the dynamism of Indian racial thought and expression during a critical historical period. The overwhelming majority of scholars who have included Indians in America's racial history have focused on what whites thought of Indians.[14] The few investigations of the Indians' own role as racial thinkers discuss militants from the Ohio River Valley, the Great Lakes region, and the Southeast, who rose up in the 1760s and then again in the 1810s, inspired by their prophets' calls for Indian racial unity.[15] It is now time to explore other, quieter, developments in American Indian racial history in order to appreciate that history's variety and complexity. For the Brothertowns and Stockbridges, Indian racial identity emerged as a unifying force, with whiteness as a negative reference, just as it did among the militants. At the same time, they strived to live alongside whites as civilized Christians, an irony that has been neglected by their previous historians.[16] The Indians' struggle with this tension speaks directly to the story of race in America writ large, for America's religious idealism and racial ideology have always coexisted uneasily. These people met almost every demand the whites imposed on them: they adopted Christianity, literacy, the English language, male plow agriculture, fences, and democratic government. Yet wherever the Indians moved, white civilians, backed by their governments, did everything they could to force them out again, amid public calls to promote Indian civility. To the extent that whites justified this hypocrisy, they dismissed Christian Indians as being "almost" like whites, "but not quite," usually citing the Indians' poverty and struggles with alcohol.[17] The Indians' critics rarely considered the pivotal role that white discrimination had played in those very developments.

Just as American racial history cannot be told simply in terms of black and white, the racial story of Brothertown and Stockbridge is triangulated in nature, for generations of Natives wrestled with the question of whether to allow blacks with Indian spouses or Afro-Indian children to join their communities. The Indians' struggles with racial discrimination at the hands of whites did not preclude them from trying to ban their people from intermarrying with blacks or from denigrating their indigenous political opponents as black "mongrels." They knew the negative connotations of blackness in the white racial regime. Nevertheless, many Native people refused to allow their leaders or the fear of ostracism to control their romantic choices. Afro-Indian relationships continued in greater or lesser degree throughout the history of Brothertown and Stockbridge. The subsequent politics of "miscegenation" was as central to the Indians' self-definition as it was to that of the whites. Creating and defending race was, at its core, a process of drawing lines around interconnected people.[18]

Roger Williams could see this story beginning to unfold as early as the 1640s, and it offended his principles mightily. He appealed to his mostly puritan readership, "Nature knowes no difference between Europe and American in blood, birth, bodies &c., God having made all mankind...and all by nature being children of wrath." To emphasize his point, he composed some original verse that read:

> Boast not proud English, of thy birth & blood,
> 　　Thy brother Indian is by birth as Good.
> Of one blood God made Him, and Thee & All,
> 　　As wise, as faire, as strong, as personall.
> By nature wrath's his portion, thine no more
> 　　Till Grace his soule and thine in Christ restore
> Make sure thy second birth, else thou shalt see,
> 　　Heaven ope[n] to Indians wild, but shut to thee.

Williams, and doubtless some of his Narragansett contacts, could already tell that few Englishmen were truly committed to Christianize the Indians and to treat them with justice. Even Williams himself would eventually preside over the sale of Narragansett prisoners as slaves in the aftermath of King Philip's War of 1675–76.[19] Thomas Commuck, who might very well have been the descendent of one of those slaves, had become too cynical after his people's several displacements by whites to look for a moral principle in Brothertown's history. The lesson he drew from that sad chronicle was that race did matter, that race had dictated the sweep of American history, and that there was nothing he and his people could do about it. This fatalism came from a man whose people once found purpose in winning God to their side and creating a civilized, Christian Indian community as a monument to the possibility of Indian-white coexistence. Within the story of the rise and fall of the Brothertown Indians' dream is a deeply human lesson about the dark power of race in the history of America.

A Note on Terminology

The very act of writing from the vantage of the twenty-first century about the historic emergence of racial thought and expression reveals yet another problem of race: we still use terms such as white, black, and Indian, yet today there is rough consensus among scientists and social thinkers that race is a cultural construct rather than a biological reality. By "construct," they mean that society creates and reinforces categories such as white, black, and Indian for society's purposes, and while those categories might be based on phenotypical (or outwardly physical) differences such as skin tone, they do not reflect substantive genetic differences.[20] Quite simply, a scientist cannot use genes to identify someone as belonging to one or another race. Even the use of physical characteristics to demarcate race is problematic, since the differences between neighboring human populations blend into each other almost seamlessly, making any attempt to determine where one race begins and the other one ends a futile exercise. Thus, while it is wholly appropriate to examine how historical actors came to view themselves and others in terms of race and to act on that worldview, it problematic for us in modern times, cognizant of the illogical status of race and the horror that racialist ideology has propagated, to continue to use racial terms in our discussions. It can be and has been argued that scholarly use of the categories white, black, and Indian serves to perpetuate these mistaken, damaging human divisions.

I write generally convinced by this critique but without an effective way (at least of which I am aware) to apply it. My answer is not to place racial terms in quotation marks. Readers should take as given my awareness that all uses of racial terminology, even my own, are faulty. I follow the counsel of my Indian friends and colleagues in using specific tribal names as often as possible when referring to America's indigenous peoples. As for those tribal names, I follow the lead of modern Stockbridge people by referring to them as Mohicans rather than as Mahicans or Muheconnuck, yet I call the Six Nations the Iroquois rather than their own designation, Haudenosaunee (People of the Longhouse), in order to avoid confusing readers who are generally more familiar with the first term. I refer to America's indigenous peoples collectively as Indians, Natives, or indigenous people rather than as Native Americans or First Nations, terms I find unwieldy and furthermore that have not been taken up by most of the Indians with whom I have associated. I call historical actors of African descent blacks rather than Negroes, a term that today is loaded with prejudicial connotations. I avoid the term *African Americans* because I find it cumbersome and, more to the point, anachronistic in discussing the colonial era, when a portion of the black population had been born in Africa or the West Indies and did not—indeed, could not—yet identify themselves with an American nation. I refer to Euro-American colonists as English, Dutch, or French, as appropriate, and as whites when discussing periods in which that term was in circulation because it is still commonplace today. My contradictory capitalization of Indian and Native but not of white and black is based simply on current editorial and colloquial trends rather than any assertion of my politics.

Amid these tensions, my hope is that books like these, which illustrate the historic emergence of racial thought and action, will encourage continued critical awareness of how our own racial consciousness and modes of expression are the legacy of a colonial agenda. Race is a problem indeed.

CHAPTER 1

All One Indian

S HORTLY after the Rev. John Eliot began his missionary work in the mid-1640s, Indians around Boston told him that "in forty years more, some Indians would all be one English, and in a hundred years all Indian here about would so be." Eliot hoped as much, responding that "they [the Indians] and we [the English] were already all one save in two things, which make the only difference betwixt them and us: First, we know, serve, and pray unto God, and they doe not: Secondly, we labor and work in building, planting, clothing our selves, etc., and they doe not: and would they but doe as wee doe in these things, they would be all one with English men."[1] Colonial-Indian relations in New England were still young enough for Eliot and his Native charges to be optimistic that their peoples could and would live side by side, first as neighbors and eventually as something resembling a single community. They assumed that their differences were cultural rather than innate.

Yet this shared principle did not mean that Eliot and the Massachusett Indians possessed identical dreams for the future. Eliot wanted the Indians to adopt Christianity, English manners, and English laws until they were finally ready to enter the colonial state. Certainly this is not what the Indians meant by becoming "all...one English." They pictured reciprocal trade, military alliance, intermarriage, and perhaps even their adoption of some English religious beliefs and practices in light of the expanding colonial population. Acquiescing to English domination, though, was quite another matter.

The colonial foreground to Brothertown and New Stockbridge involved Native people and Englishmen developing a sense of themselves and each other as Indians and whites in the context of negotiating these competing visions. Englishmen were surprised that most Indians refused to adopt colonial culture wholesale or to accept colonial authority over them even after witnessing the purported superiority of colonial life. Though Indians willingly borrowed what they most admired about the English and even conceded to some colonial influence in their affairs, generally they insisted on political and cultural self-determination. The Indians' stubborn autonomy fed into the colonists' growing insistence that Indians were inveterate savages incapable of becoming civilized members of provincial society. According to this view, civility was a feature of whites alone, thereby rendering America theirs for the taking.

Indigenous people, for their part, defined white and Indian through two related processes. First, beginning in the seventeenth century, Indians throughout the Northeast generated a critique of colonialism that whereas their people had extended the hand of fellowship to the English when Indians were strong and colonists were weak, colonists refused to reciprocate once they held the balance of power. Instead, colonists used their strength to exploit and dispossess Indian people, even allies. Eventually, Indians came to attribute this menacing feature of colonialism to the colonists' fundamental character. Second, Natives explained their peoples' inability to resist colonial expansion by evoking the spirits. The colonists' power, Indians argued, stemmed from the Christian God. As for the source of their own weakness, Indians agreed that it extended from a spiritual power of some sort, but they were uncertain as to whether it was witchcraft, a curse by Jehovah, or punishment from an Indian god for straying from time-tested ways. Though neither Indians nor colonists spoke of their differences in the biological sense of being passed from generation to generation through the blood, by the mid-eighteenth century they had begun to think of their differences as permanent. Experiencing and conceiving of a social structure premised on the division of people according to their complexion went hand in hand.

Few Indians had the opportunity, and apparently none the inclination, to express their nascent racial ideas in print. After all, the vast majority of Indians were illiterate and those who had received formal education had no precedent and little incentive for musing on such theoretical issues through a foreign medium. Yet occasionally the surviving record does contain Indian ideas about the nature of Indians and Europeans, many of them generated by the forerunners of the Brothertown and Stockbridge communities. Tracing the evolution of those statements and the contexts in which they were made provides a backdrop for the Christian Indian migration to Oneida country, for that event involved discrete and even historically antagonistic Native communities making common cause as Indians against the threats posed to them by whites. The racial ideas at the foundation of that movement had a genealogy extending back in time to the earliest years of the seventeenth century.

Creations

From their earliest contacts, Indians associated Europeans with spiritual power, which Algonquian-speakers in the Northeast called *manit*.[2] Only spiritual power could explain the newcomers' stunning technology, such as ships, firearms, knives, woven cloth, magnets, magnifying glasses, compasses, and more. According to one sixteenth-century account, these sorts of items "so farre exceeded [the Indians'] capacities to comprehend... that they thought they were rather the works of gods than of men, or at the leastwise they had been given and taught us of the gods."[3] But for the Indians, wielding spiritual power was not the same as being a spirit. When Indians shouted "*manitou, manitou*" at Europeans, they probably meant "you have *manit*, you have *manit*" rather than "you are a god, you are a god," which was how colonists preferred to interpret these words.[4] The Europeans' possession of *manit* did not make them fundamentally different from spiritually potent Indians such as *pawwaws* (shamans), though the manifestations of their power were novel. In any case, regardless of whether Indians initially believed Europeans to be gods, it is clear that they did not subscribe to such thinking for long. The Indians' views of Europeans and, reflexively, of themselves, experienced a long evolution that began rather than ended at this time.

Coastal Indians attempted to harness and appropriate English power through trade and military alliances framed as kin relationships. Indians expected allies to treat each other as family in almost every respect by protecting, feeding, and counseling each other, quickly forgiving each other's wrongs, and being slow to claim injury. As such, their protocol included activities that one would find in any Native home. Foreign diplomats exchanged presents, feasted, smoked, sang, and danced together, told stories recounting the two groups' shared history, exchanged marriage partners, and, not least, addressed each other using metaphorical kinship terms like *father, son, brother, uncle,* and *nephew*.[5] The storied "Thanksgiving alliance" between Plymouth and the Wampanoags makes the point. As the Wampanoag sachem Philip told it from his perspective in 1675, his father, Massasoit, "a great man," had treated the first colonists of Plymouth "as a little child," or as a father would treat his son, giving them food, diplomatic intelligence, protection, and even land.[6] He expected mutual treatment as the colonists grew in power. The assumption here was that peaceful, productive relationships rested on making two peoples more like one people. Yet even as Indians pursued these alliances, the reality of disease, Christian missions, Machiavellian politics, and war forced them to reconsider whether their interests were compatible with those of the colonists and even if the two groups were fundamentally similar.

The most obvious difference between Indians and Europeans was that epidemics new to America but old to Europe devastated Indian populations, while Europeans went relatively unscathed. Smallpox, measles, scarlet fever, chickenpox, bubonic plague, the flu, mumps, and whooping cough, all of them a regular part of life in the crowded places of Europe, were entirely unknown and horrifyingly lethal to Indian populations. In Europe, most adults carried lifetime immunities to some of these diseases after having suffered them in childhood. But in America these ailments attacked populations with no inherited defenses to them. Thus, almost everyone in Native villages got sick simultaneously once they came into contact with the imported microbes. Parents, children, grandparents: everyone fell together. The sick, who otherwise might have recovered with a bit of warmth, food, and water, died miserably, as nobody was available to care for them. In the outbreaks that struck coastal New England in 1616–19, 1622, 1633, 1643, and 1645, and Long Island in 1622 and 1659, death rates of over 50 percent were common, and Indians sometimes reported losses of 90 percent.[7]

Watching these mysterious ailments whipsaw through the Native population while colonists remained relatively unscathed raised profound questions, among colonists and Indians alike, about the cause of the disparity. The English generally attributed their health and the Indians' misfortune to Providence, as when James I, in his patent to Plymouth colony, marveled that "Almighty God in his great Goodness and Bountie towards Us and our People hath thought fitt and determined, that those large and goodly Territoryes, deserted as it were by their naturally Inhabitants, should be possessed and enjoyed by such of our Subjects and People."[8] Indians also sensed the spirits at work.[9] For instance, in a 1637 conversation with Roger Williams, the Narragansett sachem, Canonicus, "accused the English and myself for sending the plague amongst them and threatening to kill him especially."[10] Williams's answer was that "the plague and other sicknesses were alone in the hand of the one God, who made him and us" and that God was just as liable to smite the English as the Indians if he saw cause. Indians remained skeptical, particularly about God's impartiality. As late as 1750, Oneidas were reluctant to travel to Philadelphia because they feared "the evil Spirits that Dwell among the White People are against us and kill us."[11] Though Indian sorcerers and Indian gods caused their own share of trouble in the world, the disastrous scale of the post-contact epidemics suggested that the colonists and their God were so different in degree as to be different in kind. According to the Native view, it was an entire people's relationship to the spirits that defined them.

The colonists' insistence on a broad gulf between their civility and the Indians' savagery reinforced these early notions of difference. As Englishmen defined it, civility referred to an array of social characteristics that marked humankind's ascension from wildness. Those qualities included literacy, codified law, monogamous marriage, highly graded social classes, sedentarism, plow agriculture, private property, steady work, and sophisticated technology. Though a people could be civilized without being Christian (such as the Chinese), Europeans generally thought of civility and Christianity as mutually reinforcing, as of a piece. By contrast, Europeans associated savagery with human baseness: anarchy, laziness, nakedness, polygamy, blood thirst, nomadism, and paganism. Eventually, Europeans would come to think of themselves as inherently civilized and of Indians as permanent savages, but in the meantime their spokesmen claimed that bringing the Indians to civility was among their foremost goals. The Massachusetts Assembly followed through on this principle with a 1652 statute that encouraged towns to allot land to Indians "brought to civilitie" so they could live "amongst the English."[12] According to this thinking, the gap between civility and savagery, not complexion, was what divided Indian and English peoples.

Christian missions were among the first sites for Indians and Englishmen to compare ideas about their peoples' similarities and differences and to test the English commitment to coexistence. The experiment began in the mid-1640s among the Wampanoags of Martha's Vineyard and the Massachusett Indians around Boston, then gradually extended through English and Indian missionaries alike to the Wampanoags of Cape Cod and Nantucket and the Nipmucs of central Massachusetts.[13] The Narragansetts and Niantics of Rhode Island and the Mohegans of Connecticut generally rejected missionary overtures during the seventeenth century, which colonists attributed to their sachems' fear that Christianity was a wedge for the spread of English jurisdiction.[14] Nevertheless, given the tight network of Indian communities throughout the region, they knew about the discussions that took place within the missions, many of them centered on defining Indians, Englishmen, and their relation to each other.[15]

The missionaries' agenda was to define customary Indian behaviors, or Indianness, as sinful and savage, and English behaviors, or Englishness, as godly and civilized.[16] Yet simply establishing the terms of discussion was fraught with difficulty. Aside from the monumental challenge of trying to interpret theology across a broad linguistic and conceptual divide, Native people found the categorization of them as Indians curious. Echoing the earlier discussion between Roger Williams and the Narragansetts, John Eliot, in just his third meeting with the Massachusett Indians, faced the question, "Why the English call them Indians because before they [the English] came they [the Indians] had another name?"[17] Eliot did not record his answer, but in all likelihood he explained that Indians were a group insofar as they all lived sinfully in ignorance of the Word of God. The concepts of Indian and sin were so firmly linked in the evangelistic mindset that one missionary, William Leveritch of Cape Cod, told his Wampanoag charges that there was no difference between them and "those looser sort of English," that "they are all one Indians."[18]

The most heated topic within the missions was how the English could argue that they and the Indians shared a single creator and that Christianity was universal if the Indians' forefathers had no knowledge of such things. Eliot's response was that the Indians' ancestors "were stubborne and rebellious children, and would not heare the word, did not care to pray nor to teach their children, and hence Indians that now are, do not know God at all."[19] Many Indians were unconvinced. In 1714, the Mohegans politely rebuffed the missionary Experience Mayhew, maintaining that "as several nations had their distinct way of worship, so they had theirs; and they thought their way was Good, and that they had no reason to alter it." In any case, the Mohegans believed that "the difficulties of the Christian Religion were such as the Indians could not endure."[20] The implicit point here, one that Indians in the eighteenth century would repeat over and over again in explicitly racial terms, was that Christianity was meant for whites, not for Indians.

Missionary work, by its very nature, rejected this premise, yet in critical ways the English ghettoized Christian Indians and reinforced the notion of an unbridgeable divide between peoples, even in the early days of the mission. Tellingly, throughout the seventeenth century, colonists and Natives alike called the Christian Indians "praying Indians" rather than just "Christians." Indians themselves had introduced the term *praying Indians* to highlight the mission Indians' distinctive ritual practices. For Englishmen, though, a praying Indian was a hyphenated or qualified Christian. To be simply Christian was to be European; a praying Indian was, by inference, someone between savagery and civility, someone who measured up "almost, but not quite" to the colonists' godly standard.[21] The same divisive principle underwrote the creation of fourteen Christian Indian praying towns in Massachusetts and one each on Cape Cod and Martha's Vineyard from 1650 to 1671. These praying towns were supposed to be permanent reserves where Christian Indians could live apart from the negative examples of non-Christian Indians *and* Englishmen. The praying town land was guaranteed to the Indians by colonial authorities and was, theoretically, subject to colonial jurisdiction, to protect against English trespass and liquor sales because Englishmen could not be trusted to treat Christian Indians like kin.[22] A Christian Wampanoag raised this issue when he asked his missionary, "why doe not English church men let Indi[an] church men rest in th[ier] houses seeing th[ey] must all rest with God," a question made all the more pointed by the emphasis Indians placed on extending courtesy even to strangers.[23] English violations of their own principle of Christian fellowship signaled that they were making *Indian* a degraded category of the colonial social order, one that indigenous people could not escape.

Unity

The fears and tensions underlying the colonists' hypocritical treatment of praying Indians took dramatic shape in their relations with the formidable Narragansetts, Niantics, Pequots, and Mohegans whose descendants would make up the majority of people in Brothertown. Though each of these tribes attempted to forge reciprocal alliances of trade and protection with the English, the colonies' treatment of them as subordinates by attempting to dictate their foreign relations, extracting tribute from them, and even punishing them for capital crimes, ensured that the period from 1636 to 1676 was filled with tension and war. The final conflict, King Philip's War, permanently broke the back of Indian power in southern New England and reinforced English suspicions that Indians were irredeemable savages. It also set the terms for a postwar racial order in which repeated wars and war scares on the frontier and the colonists' subjugation of New England's surviving Indians hardened racial identities.

If there was ever a sign that New England Indians had misjudged their colonial future, it was the Pequots' 1634 invitation to the English of Massachusetts to trade and settle around what is now Hartford, Connecticut. The Pequots, who for years had been consolidating their control over the Dutch trade in the Connecticut River Valley and expanding the number of Indian communities that paid tribute to them, had recently seen their fortunes reversed. A smallpox epidemic in 1633 reduced their numbers by three-quarters or more to just some three thousand people, while at the same time they found themselves at war on two fronts: first with the Dutch, who ran a small post on the Connecticut River, and then with the Narragansetts, apparently over access to the Dutch traders. Surrounded by enemies and facing the prospect of losing their supply of European goods, the Pequots needed friends—and fast. In their desperation, they turned to the English, aware of the colonists' track record of supporting Massasoit's Wampanoags against Narragansett incursions.[24]

Unfortunately for the Pequots, their overtures barely had a chance to succeed, because Pequot hands were already stained with English blood. In 1633, Pequots had attacked and killed the eight-man crew of a trading vessel tacking up the Connecticut River under the command of a ne'er-do-well captain named John Stone. The Pequots claimed that the assault was a case of mistaken identity, for they thought the crew was Dutch. "We know no difference between the Dutch and the English," the Pequots appealed, "they are both strangers to us, we took them all to be one."[25] Moreover, the Pequots assumed that they had "covered the dead," or compensated for the murders, by presenting Boston authorities with a valuable gift of furs, wampum, and land on which to settle. Indians expected allies who accepted official gifts to set aside their grievances in the interest of continued friendship. Yet the English did not consider the matter closed, for presents did not satisfy murder according to their customs. Instead, the English demanded that Pequot leaders turn over the murderers to be tried and punished according to English standards, something Pequot sachems simply did not have the power to do, whatever their inclinations. The English might have been content to allow the Pequots to handle the affair themselves had they judged them to be civilized, but they did not: they viewed the Pequots as savages, as a people without the laws, morality, and authority to prosecute criminality. Moreover, the English viewed this case as an important precedent for their relations with other tribes. They imagined any failure to deal harshly with the Pequots would "cause all the Indians in the country to join to root out all the English."[26] The 1636 murder of a crew from another English trading vessel by the Manisee Indians of Block Island seemed to prove the point. The English then unleashed total war on the entire Pequot population, hoping to send a message to the rest of Native New England about the bloody consequences for "savages" who dared to trifle with Christians.

The carnage, which involved colonial forces systematically hunting down and killing thousands of Pequots and enslaving most of the rest, sent shock waves throughout the region. Initially, the Narragansetts supported the English campaign, for the Pequots were their enemies. But they equivocated after witnessing the English torch the Pequots' Mystic Fort with hundreds of women, children, and elderly inside. "*Mach it, mach it*"—"It is naught, it is naught"—cried one Narragansett, "it is too furious, and slays too many men."[27] Awestruck and terrified, even Native communities that had nothing to do with the Pequots clamored to profess their fealty to the English in exchange for assurances that they were not next.[28] It was precisely the effect the colonists desired.

On the eve of war, the Pequots appealed to their Narragansett rivals for aid, warning that "the English were minded to destroy all Indians."[29] Another account had the Pequots reasoning that "the English were strangers, and began to overspread their [the Indians'] country, and would deprive them thereof in time, if they were suffered to grow and increase; and if the Narragansetts did assist the English to subdue them [the Pequots], that did but make way for their [the Narragansetts'] own overthrow."[30] Yet the Narragansetts rejected these pleas. Their hostility toward the Pequots—centered on competition for control of the wampum trade and tribute payers—was acute. The English had never shed Narragansett blood, not yet, but the Pequots had. Why then, would the Narragansetts oppose an English campaign to dispatch the tribe's greatest enemy? The fallout from the Pequot War would answer that question in spades.

The Pequots' defeat left the closely related Narragansetts and Niantics as the most powerful Indian nations in southern New England and the greatest threat to the interests of Massachusetts and Connecticut. Both colonies craved the rich lands bordering the Pawcatuck River on the Connecticut/Rhode Island border, yet the Narragansetts refused to surrender their claims to this territory. Boston wanted to subjugate Rhode Island's unruly population of English religious dissenters, but the Narragansetts helped to foil these plans by lending their name to the dissenters' efforts to enlist the king's protection. Indian tribute payers formed yet another point of contention, as the Narragansetts and Niantics, on the one hand, and Boston and Hartford, on the other, competed to dominate the region's weaker tribes. Finally, the English wanted to force the Narragansetts to use English arbitration to settle their disputes with the Mohegans over the fate of Pequot captives and Pequot hunting grounds. The Narragansett sachem, Miantonomi, refused to accept such interference in his people's affairs, particularly when he knew that the English would favor the Mohegan sachem Uncas in their judgments. Years after the fact, he saw the prescience of the Pequots' warning: the Narragansetts and Niantics had indeed become the next English targets

despite their contribution to the colonies' war effort. This epiphany inspired Miantonomi to begin waving the banner of Indian unity he had once rejected.[31]

By the 1640s, Miantonomi was trying to organize a multi-tribal resistance
against his former English allies. Most of the sachem's activities, by their very
nature, eluded colonial scrutiny, and many accounts of him that do survive are
suspect because they came from his enemy, Uncas. Nevertheless, there is strong
corroborating evidence of Miantonomi's plotting. The first notice came in 1642
from the Montaukett sachem Wyandanch, who told colonist Lion Gardiner that
Miantonomi had called on him to contribute warriors for a strike against the
English and the Dutch. As Gardiner understood it, Miantonomi argued that Native people needed to become "all Indians as the English are...otherwise we
shall be all gone shortly" and thus, "all the Sachems from east to west" should
"fall upon them [the colonists] all, at one appointed day."[32] Similar reports came
from authorities in New Netherland, who heard that Miantonomi was "passing through all the Indian villages soliciting them to a general war against both
the English and Dutch."[33] Indian whistleblowers foiled Miantonomi's plan in
New England, and the sachem's execution by Uncas with the colonies' blessing prevented him from reviving it, but his message appears to have resonated
with Native communities in the lower Hudson River Valley.[34] The Dutch and the
surrounding Indians were already engaged in low-level hostilities when Miantonomi visited the area, but after his tour their conflict exploded into a full-scale
war that nearly destroyed New Netherland. The power of Indians cooperating
across political lines had become starkly clear.[35]

Just as Miantonomi called for Indians to rally together against their shared
colonial enemies, so too did the colonists, in response to Miantonomi's threat,
unite as never before. In 1643, Massachusetts, Plymouth, Connecticut, and New
Haven formed an alliance called the United Colonies of New England to manage
Indian affairs and raise a common defense. This development was remarkable
given the colonies' previous difficulties getting along, mostly over Indian-related
issues such as control of the fur trade and the spoils of the Pequot War. Yet the
danger of Indians banding together as Indians against English expansion was
enough to trump these differences. New England's puritan colonies shared a
faith, a language, a heritage; the Indians were not their only common enemy, for
they also struggled in tandem against the Crown, the French, the Spanish, and
internal dissidents; but only the colonists' nightmare of besiegement by savages
had the power to force them onto common ground.[36]

Near-constant rumors of war ensured that the terms *Indian* and *Englishman* remained salient even in times of peace. In 1647 the Commissioners of

the United Colonies heard that the Narragansetts and Niantics were conspiring with the powerful Mohawks of the Iroquois League to attack New England.[37] The sachems denied the charge and temporarily defused the crisis, but colonial fears were unabated. Six years later, English authorities believed that the Narragansett sachems Pessacus and Mixam and the Niantic sachem Ninigret were fomenting a pan-Indian strike against them in league with the Dutch, prompting the United Colonies to send a show of force into Niantic country.[38] Apparently the display was ineffective, for in 1669 rumors swirled again that Ninigret and the Narragansetts were drawing the Indians of Long Island into a confederation.[39] The colonists' fear of encirclement only intensified as the Wampanoags too were said to be plotting Indian revolts in 1662, 1667, and 1671.[40] Such threats, real and imagined, encouraged the English to think of Indians not as redeemable savages worthy of evangelism but as predatory wolves. Roger Williams, certain as he was of the Indians' humanity, shuddered to write, "How often I have heard both the English and Dutch...say, These *Heathen* Dogges, better kill a thousand of them then that we *Christians* should be indangered or troubled by them."[41] Native people, for their part, were learning that the English, thinking of them as a single Indian threat, treated them as such, often on flimsy evidence. Yet perhaps the English had good reason to fear. If just some of the rumors were true, a number of the most powerful sachems in the region were promoting a sense of Indian identity to raise opposition to colonial expansion.

Tensions behind the emergent English and Indian identities exploded in King Philip's War of 1675–76. The conflict began when the Wampanoag community of Pokanoket under the sachem Philip (or Pumetacom) took up arms, after years of brooking English provocations, to protest an outrageous breach of its sovereignty: Plymouth's trial and execution of three high-ranking Wampanoags for the supposed murder of a Wampanoag within Wampanoag country. Colonial bungling then turned this isolated local dispute into a regional war. Mainland Wampanoag communities began to join Philip's cause as the English militia stormed into their territory in search of hostiles and after Plymouth magistrates enslaved unarmed Wampanoags who had surrendered themselves in hope of protection. Colonial authorities then turned the Nipmucs in central Massachusetts and the "River Indians" of the Connecticut Valley into enemies by attempting to confiscate their arms despite the Natives' avowals of friendship. Praying Indians near Boston tried to prove their loyalty to the English by volunteering against Philip, but colonial mobs still terrorized their communities based on the charge that they had aided and abetted the enemy. Boston authorities, partly out of a desire to protect the Christian Indians and partly out of distrust of them, addressed this dilemma by interning the Natives on a barren, frigid island in the middle of Boston harbor. Even "down east" Maine degenerated into bloodshed after colonists provoked the Wabanakis by gratuitously drowning a prominent sachem's children. Only in Connecticut, Cape Cod, and Martha's Vineyard did English leaders entrust local Indians to serve as a guard throughout the course of the war. Not coincidentally, these were the only areas where the peace held fast. Elsewhere, the longstanding colonial fear that "the plott is generall (if not universall) among the Indians, and strikes at the interest of all the English in New England," became a self-fulfilling prophesy.[42]

King Philip's War was not a "race war" per se, since the Mohegans, the Pequots, the Massachusetts praying Indians, the Mohawks and even many Wampanoags supported the English and ultimately tipped the scales in their favor, yet the English conceived of it as such by treating many of their Indian allies as wolves in sheep's clothing and casting all Indians as cruel barbarians. From the earliest stages of the war, "the English were so jealous and filled with animosity against all Indians without exception," as the Indians' advocate Daniel Gookin put it.[43] The colonists' perception of Indians as "children of the devil" found proof in the growing number of "friend Indians" who sided with Philip, if only after English provocation.[44] And then there were the printed accounts of the conflict—twenty-one published in eight years—most of which systematically ignored or downplayed the critical role of the colonists' Indian allies during the war, while simultaneously using graphic scenes of violence and inflammatory epithets to depict Indians as bloodthirsty, godless savages.[45] Increase Mather, the most prolific chronicler of the war and the leading puritan spokesman of his era, gripped readers with scenes of "barbarous Creatures" who "barbarously murdered both men and women" and revealed their "inhumanity" by "stripping the slain" and tearing off "the hairy Scalp of their enemyes."[46] The most popular publication about the war, a captivity narrative by Englishwoman Mary Rowlandson, was even more adamant about Indian savagery. The preface set the tone with its appeal that "none can imagine what it is to be captivated, and enslaved to such atheistical, proud, wild, cruel, barbarous, brutish (in one word), diabolical creatures as these."[47] In Rowlandson's telling, Indians were "roaring Lions, and Salvage Bears, that feared neither God, nor Man, nor the Devil."[48] The "merciless Heathen" left "so many Christians lying in their blood, some here, and some there, like a company of Sheep torn by Wolves. All of them stript naked by a company of hell-hounds, roaring, singing, ranting and insulting, as if they would have torn our very hearts out."[49] "Christian" and "English," on the one hand, and "hell-hounds" and "Indians," on the other, were natural pairings for Rowlandson and her readership, even though it was praying Indians allied with Boston who negotiated Rowlandson's release. Natives might cut their hair, don European clothing, and learn to recite a catechism, but war and the accounts of war taught Englishmen that base savagery was the essence of Indian people.[50]

King Philip's War was over in southern New England by the summer of 1676, but the legacies of the conflict extended beyond the final shots. Colonists had shattered Indian power in the region by wiping out some 70 percent of the people who had warred against them. The luckiest survivors fled to the margins of the region, particularly the Hudson River Valley and the Jesuit missions of New France; many others—possibly as many as twelve hundred—lived out their lives as slaves to their English conquerors.[51] As a result, the Indian presence was either severely diminished or eliminated completely in places such as the upper Connecticut River Valley, the Merrimac River Valley, the Buzzard's Bay watershed, and much of Rhode Island. Overall, the Indian population of southern New England was cut nearly in half. The English, though victorious, had plenty of their own wounds to tend. Indian forces had attacked more than half of their towns, destroying sixteen of them outright. Somewhere between eight hundred and three thousand colonists out of a total population of fifty thousand or so lost their lives. The colonial economy was in tatters: thousands of head of livestock had been killed, maritime trade was dormant, and colonial governments were deep in war debt. Not the least of all, King Philip's War attracted unwanted royal attention to the colonies' mismanagement. Four decades of uneasy peace between Indians and colonists, nearly unchecked colonial growth and prosperity, and freedom from London oversight had effectively come to an end in New England.[52]

Perhaps the most important legacy of King Philip's War was the hardening of Indian and English identities, in the minds not only of colonists but of Indians as well. In the summer of 1675, puzzled Narragansetts questioned Roger Williams why the other New England colonies had taken up arms against the Wampanoags and "left not Phillip and Plymmouth to fight it out." Williams's answer was that "all the Colonies were Subject to one K[ing] Charles and it was his pleasure and our Duty and Engagement for one English man to stand to the Death by Each other in all parts of the World."[53] The English abided by that principle throughout the war by maintaining a united front against their various Indian enemies. Indians also rediscovered the English tendency to treat them as a single hostile group despite their many divisions. According to one account,

Philip tried to recruit other sachems as allies by predicting that "the English had a Design to cut off all the Indians round about them, and that if they did not Joyn together, they should lose their Lives and Lands."[54] The conduct and, for that matter, the settlement of the war showed Philip to have been something of a sage.

Vicious Inclination

The context in which Indians and Englishmen constructed their own and each other's identities shifted dramatically after 1676. In the prewar era, English fears of a savage uprising were counterbalanced by the hope that Indians would become civilized Christians, while Indian fears of subjugation were measured by visions of kinship and alliance. King Philip's War was the realization of each group's nightmare and effectively the death knell of their romantic views on identity. Aside from missionaries and a handful of elites, most colonists abandoned any expectation of making Indians like themselves and instead used their enhanced power to relegate Native people to landlessness, debt peonage, and political impotency. They no longer feared local Indians as "bloodthirsty savages"—those from the interior were another matter—but they did hold that the Indians' supposedly savage nature meant that they were incapable of civility and thus suited to degradation within colonial society. Indians, by comparison, cast the English as hypocrites who proclaimed their commitment to Christian brotherhood and their friendship for Indians when Indians held the power but exploited Indians, including Christian Indians, at every turn once the balance shifted. As this postwar order took shape, New Englanders of all complexions increasingly used "white" to refer to Europeans previously known as Christians, coat men, knife men, and Englishmen, and "Indian" to refer to people whose elders never thought of themselves as such. This language, in and of itself, did not signify people's adoption of racial thinking; one could use "white" as shorthand for a political or cultural community without assuming that "white" naturally corresponded to certain characteristics. Yet a social system that afforded manifold privileges to whites, and that routinely exploited Indians, encouraged New Englanders to ascribe racial meaning to these categories. Put another way, racial ideas and a racial social system mutually reinforced each other until colonists reflexively associated whiteness with civility and social superiority and Indianness with savagery and social inferiority. The growing power of colonial society included forcing these terms and their logics on indigenous people until they too routinely spoke of Indians and, eventually, whites. Whether Indians assumed that these categories were natural, god-given, or otherwise is uncertain given the limitations of the written record. What can be said conclusively is that Native people found no justice in the colonists' racial hierarchy.

It stands to reason that as Indians fell subject to colonial law, they grew familiar with the racial assumptions that shaped it. Colonial authorities certainly did little to disguise those sentiments. In 1709 Massachusetts justified restrictions on colonial creditors suing Indians for debt because, it argued, Indians had "an aversion for industry and labor" and an "insatiable thirst" for alcohol.[55] The growing presence of Indian workers in postwar colonial cities and towns inspired one legislature after another to subject them, alongside African slaves, to special curfews, liquor bans, and restrictions on bearing arms and assembling.[56] Connecticut issued special penalties against any servant of color who "shall Offer to strike any White person" because it judged that "Indian, Negroe, and Molatto Servants and Slaves are very apt to be Turbulent; and often to be Quarreling with White People, to the great Disturbance of the Peace."[57] The goal of such legislation was not to control the laboring class generally, for it did not pertain to whites, even of the lowliest status. Rather, the purpose was to degrade people of color in all their varieties and, by extension, to confer privilege on whites. To accentuate the point, between 1696 and 1716 Massachusetts changed the tax status of Indian and black servants and slaves from that of polls subject to the same head tax as white servants to that of personal property, like livestock.[58] Indians, by this reasoning, were "things." Not coincidentally, during the same period Massachusetts debated a bill "against fornication, or marriage of White men with Negros or Indians," for "the Better Preventing of a Spurious and Mixt Issue."[59] A bare majority of assemblymen eventually struck the Indian portion of the bill in acknowledgment that it would discourage Indians from adopting Christianity, but only after intense lobbying by the esteemed Indian advocate Samuel Sewall. Perhaps they also knew that legal bans on intermarriage were superfluous, because by custom alone no respectable white New Englander would bear the stigma of wedding an Indian.[60]

Contemporaneous with these measures, English creditors, courts, and lawmakers worked in tandem to reduce Indians to landlessness and debt peonage. Colonists did not need to resort to arms to wrest land from the Mohegans and Narragansetts, as the Eastern Niantics of Rhode Island became known following their absorption of the Narragansett survivors of King Philip's War. Supporting the right of the Uncas and Ninigret lines of sachems to sell land regardless of the wishes of their people was sufficient because the sachems viewed these sales as a symbol of alliance, a source of personal profit, and a guarantee of their people's safety. Whereas immediately after the Pequot War the Mohegans claimed some 800 square miles of territory, by the time Uncas died in 1682 they held only forty square miles; in 1721 it was down to 5,000 acres.[61] The Narragansett sachems nearly kept pace, quitclaiming four-fifths of their people's land to Rhode Island in 1709 in exchange for a reservation near Charlestown measuring sixty-four square miles, then following up that cession with sales amounting to 1,690 acres between 1742 and 1748.[62] Colonists adopted cruder tactics when dealing with smaller Indian communities such as the Pequots, Western Niantics, and Tunxis of Connecticut and the Montauketts of eastern Long Island. Intimidating the Indians by releasing livestock into their cornfields and then prosecuting any-one who harmed the animals, building fences across Indian territory, or bluntly threatening to "beat [their] Brains out" was often enough to induce a sale.[63] At other times, provincial legislatures answered Indian complaints by offering a devil's bargain: Indian reservations with protected territory—superintended by English guardians.[64] Yet legislators never expected the Indian reserves to be permanent. When Connecticut ruled in 1721 that the Mohegans would "for-ever" enjoy a five-thousand-acre reservation already reduced to a quarter the size promised to them "forever" forty years earlier, it added the qualification that "when the whole nation, or stock of said Indians are extinct... [the reser-vation] shall forever belong to the town of New London." It was the anticipa-tion of Indian disappearance that made reservations palatable for land-hungry Englishmen.[65]

The Indians' loss of land compromised their ability to make a living by their traditional means of hunting, fishing, horticulture, and gathering, forcing them to turn to English merchants for their needs. Indians tried to meet these costs through a combination of wage labor and the sale of venison, furs, goose feathers, baskets, mats, and wooden utensils, yet many of them fell into such des-perate debt that they had no choice but to sell themselves and even their children into indentured servitude. Some Indians signed indenture contracts voluntarily (in the strictest sense of the word), having judged bonded service as the only way to feed and clothe their children. Too often, though, Indians became ser-vants by the order of their guardians or the courts. Lay colonists did their part by slapping Indians with frivolous lawsuits or extending credit lines that they knew the Indians could not pay. Courts provided the Indians with no relief, routinely levying disproportionately high fines and jail fees on impoverished Indians and then forcing them to pay off the balance with years of indentured service. They even seized the children of Indian parents deemed to be incompetent and sold them into bondage. Thus, by the early eighteenth century many Indian communities were populated mainly by the very old and the very young, with a sizable portion of the able-bodied population forced by poverty and English machinations to live among and work for the very people who were exploiting them. There was no more painful symbol of the Indians' status as a subjugated, colonized people.[66]

The interlocking trends of Native land loss, poverty, and servitude at once redefined and reinforced the colonists' perception of Indians as an inferior group of people. Before and certainly during King Philip's War, New England colonists had thought of Indians as savages with independence and clout. Yet the colonists' subjugation of Indians after the war led them to correlate Indianness and degradation. The English highlighted their restriction of Indians to small, isolated tracts of land by calling those places by such names as "Indian neck," "Indian Hill," or "the Indian town," which assumed that all of the surrounding territory belonged to Englishmen.[67] Just as race and place designated where the Indians lived, race and occupation defined the Indians' public status, for English officials typically identified Native people by terms such as "Indian laborer," "Indian husbandman," "Indian washerwoman," or "Indian spinster." The creation of Indian reserves, appointment of Indian guardians, and passage of special laws designed to address Indian debt and liquor consumption, signaled the colonists' belief that Indians needed protection from themselves and their English neighbors, like children or wards. Most poignantly, the colonists justified their exploitation of Indian labor and forced separation of Indian families by arguing that Indians would not work unless forced to do so and that they were incapable of raising their own children properly. This is not to say that colonists thought of all Indians as subjugated, marginalized, and incompetent; strong, autonomous Indians such as the Eastern and Western Wabanakis continued to menace colonial towns in the upper Connecticut River Valley and Maine, and colonial writings, predictably, continued to paint those groups as vicious, wild animals.[68] Yet Indians in the thick of English settlement no longer posed such a threat. Colonists saw them as domesticated savages, shiftless and lazy like most savages but additionally pathetic for having fallen into dependency. As Massachusetts Lieutenant Governor Thomas Hutchinson acknowledged in 1764, "We are too apt to consider the Indians as a race being by nature inferior to us, and born to servitude."[69]

Evidence of Native people using racial terminology between King Philip's War and the mid-eighteenth century is problematic but suggestive. Indian words usually come to us through Englishmen who might very well have taken poetic license in their translations; to take a hypothetical example, an English interpreter or scribe might very well have translated the Narragansett word for "people" as "Indian." Yet it is telling that Native language writings by the literate Christian Indians of Natick, Martha's Vineyard, Nantucket, and Mashpee often contain the terms "ingon," "Engunn," and "Indiansog" for Indian. There are far fewer examples of southern New England Indians using the term *white* until they began speaking English in large numbers in the mid- to late eighteenth century. English translations of Indian statements typically have the Indians referring to colonists as "English" or "Christians." Native language writings by the Christian Wampanoags use the terms *chogquagqunnat* or *chaquaquassog* (sword men), *wattuchkonnaut* (coat men), and *Engllishmone* or *inglishmonsog* (Englishmen).[70] There is only one example of an Indian-written, Indian-language document referring to a colonist as "white."[71]

To the extent that New England Indians stated their opinions about colonists in general, usually they referred to their disgust at the colonists' lack of reciprocity for Indian generosity rather than to an inherently foul colonial nature. As early as 1637, Canonicus, Miantonomi's brother, could see that the English had no intention of living like kin alongside Native people. He told Roger Williams of his hopes that "the English and my posteritie shall live in love and peace together" but doubted it would come to pass, using ten pieces of stick as a mnemonic device to mark ten instances in which the English acted treacherously.[72] It was enough to make the sachem wonder, "Did ever friends deal so with friends?"[73] The Wampanoag leader, Philip, made a similar complaint on the eve of the war that bears his name. He railed that colonists not only had failed to reciprocate the Wampanoags' historic friendship toward them, but behaved more like enemies the stronger they became. Several decades later, the Pequot sachem Robin Cassacinamon emphasized the same point while protesting English encroachment on his people's land even after the Pequots had marched alongside them in battle. "The English in ye time of ye war called us brethren: & Esteemed us to be Rational Creatures," Cassacinamon explained, "but behold now they make us as Goats! by moving us from place to place to Clear rough Land: & make it profitable to them."[74] Indians saw colonists as people who extended the hand of fellowship when they needed help, only to turn on allies as soon as they became expendable. There is no way to tell if Indians thought of this characteristic as innate at this early point, but in time they would.

The early prediction that Indians and colonists would eventually "all be one English" never came to pass, yet Natives and newcomers alike did increasingly conceive of indigenous people as "all one Indian." Initially, Europeans defined Indians not as a biological group of people but a cultural one characterized by savagery and paganism. Colonial spokesmen went so far as to declare that transforming Indians into civilized, Christian people and even members of colonial society ranked among their most important purposes. Yet such spokesmen, who expected Indians to voluntarily embrace European culture, were surprised to encounter widespread Indian ambivalence and resistance. They also failed to anticipate their own people's suspicion of Indians who did reform and tendency to interpret Indian defiance as evidence of the Natives' innate savagery. Such beliefs, encouraged as they were by the colonists' incentives to dispossess indigenous people of their land and control their labor, ultimately turned "Indian" into a low caste of the colonial social order. Native people, however, refused to allow this category to become an uncontested means of their subjugation. Instead, they used it as a rallying cry for otherwise distinct Native people to come together in resistance over their dispossession at colonial hands. Movements for Indian unity collapsed in the face of stubborn tribal divisions and colonial pressure, but the groundwork had been established for the indigenous peoples of southern New England and Long Island to search for common solutions to their common problems as Indians. That quest would continue even as Indian military options dimmed after King Philip's War and the main challenge facing them shifted from power politics to coping with lower-class status within colonial society. The Brothertown movement would emerge from this search. And while the prospect of having Indian people unite under the banner of evangelical Protestantism, civilized reforms, and peaceful coexistence with colonists might have set the Miantonomis and Philips of the past spinning in their graves, nevertheless, in significant ways Brothertown would build on their legacy of making Native people "all one Indian."

CHAPTER 2

Converging Paths

A MONG the prized historical artifacts in the possession of the modern-day Mohegan tribe is an elm bark box believed to have been made by Brothertown Indians in Oneida country sometime in the 1780s or 1790s and then sent to their kinswoman, Lucy Occom, who still lived in Connecticut. More than just a simple gift, the box's ornamentation uses interlocking metaphorical designs to depict the Brothertowns' migration from the coast to Iroquia and their sense of purpose. One motif, running along the box's side, is the Beautiful White Path, which Indians used to compare the life journey to the daily course of the sun. Each day, the sun rises in the east (a direction Indians associated with the moon, femininity, and the beginning of life) and sets in the west (associated with the sun, masculinity, and the Land the Dead). Analogously, the life of every individual or community progresses inevitably from birth to death. However, unlike the sun's arc, the human path twists and turns, depending on one's relationships with the binary forces of the cosmos, such as those of the cardinal directions. Here, then, painted on this box, was a statement about the Brothertowns' commitment to longstanding Indian principles: human existence rarely unfolds in a straightforward manner; there is potential for good and bad in any venture; a strong life balances the competing forces of the world; and, last but not least, the individual and the community are defined by their generations across time, each responsible to the other.

Another decorative theme on this box is of multiple roots feeding into a single strong trunk, hearkening to the Indian metaphor (ubiquitous among the Iroquois, including the Brothertowns' Oneida hosts) of the community as a great tree, with branches providing shelter to the people and reaching up to future generations and the roots plunging down into the earth where the ancestors are buried. In this case, the extensive root system feeding the trunk might also

Figure 1. Story Box. According to Mohegan and Brothertown Indian tradition, this "story box" was crafted in Brothertown in Oneida country sometime during the 1780s or 1790s and then sent to Lucy Occom back in Mohegan, Connecticut. It depicts the Christian Indians' journey from the coast to their new home in Iroquoia. It is also a vivid example of the Brothertown Indians' social and cultural connections to the communities they had left behind on Long Island Sound. Courtesy The Mohegan Tribe, Uncasville, Connecticut.

have symbolized that Brothertown was made up of people from several autonomous yet enmeshed communities. Some of their bonds were of ancient indigenous origin. Yet the cross-like three-leaf design at the head of each root hints at the role of Christianity in revitalizing the people's ties to each other and their common values—henceforth, all would grow or wither together. Christianity, in other words, helped the Brothertowns reinvent relationships and principles they had once associated with their various local identities into a new community premised on Indian racial unity.[1]

This transformative process referenced by Lucy Occom's elm box began earnestly with the Indians' adoption of evangelical Protestantism during the Great Awakening of the 1740s. The Awakening is normally thought of as a colonial movement for a more heartfelt religion focused on the indwelling Holy Spirit instead of on external duties. Indian participation, to the extent that it is mentioned at all, tends to be interpreted as a gauge of the Natives' subjugation. There is some merit in this perspective, for it is unlikely that Indians would have had anything to do with the Awakening had they not been suffering body and soul from the vagaries of colonization. Furthermore, the Indians' Christianization did involve them consenting to longstanding English demands that they host missionaries, attend church, and pursue formal education. Yet these reforms, in the context of the Indians' appropriation and transformation of Protestantism for their own purposes, appear not as a surrender to colonial power but as part of an Indian revitalization movement, itself a distinct phase of the broader Awakening.

English authorities expected Christianity to "yoke" or "reduce" Indians to the laws of the colonial state and the rules of civility, but Indians themselves viewed the faith as an assertion of their cultural and political self-determination. For one, they used Protestant institutions to reach out to each other as fellow believers and as fellow Indians and then drew on this base of support to withdraw from colonial churches and form independent Indian congregations with distinctly Indian forms of worship. Next, they turned these congregations into political bases from which to challenge sachems complicit with colonial authorities. Indians allowed colonial missionaries and schoolteachers to enter their communities only insofar as they sought access to these men's specialized knowledge and political connections—provided outside missionary organizations paid the expense. When Indians tired of English outsiders, they did not hesitate to close their doors to them and install their own indigenous preachers and teachers. In so doing, they sent a clear message: their Christianity belonged to them.

The Brothertown movement was the product of a Christian Indian association spanning the Northeast that developed from the mid-1730s onward, especially after the revivals of the 1740s. This network linked Indian communities from Long Island Sound more firmly to each other and to the Delawares of New Jersey, the Mohicans of the Housatonic River Valley, and the Oneidas of Iroquoia. Historically, these groups were divided by space, politics, and, to a lesser degree, language. Yet the Indians' shared struggles with colonialism followed by their common Christianity led them to identify with each other as a race of people and to express that solidarity in the language of Protestantism. Tracing the interactions of these communities during the era of the Great Awakening shows how their various paths, which once seemed to lead nowhere but darkness, eventually converged in the promise of what might be called the Christian Indian movement.

Stirrings

Just as Indian participation in the Great Awakening laid the groundwork for Brothertown and New Stockbridge, so too did less-heralded missionary encounters during the early eighteenth century establish the conditions for the Natives' Awakening. English missionaries had periodically reached out to the Indian communities on Long Island Sound throughout the seventeenth century, only to meet indifference and sometimes outright hostility.[2] Yet by the 1720s and 1730s the shifting balance of power had convinced most area tribes to permit English missionaries and teachers. The usual arrangement was for a tribe to host occasional sermons from local Congregationalist ministers in the part-time pay of the Corporation for the Propagation of the Gospel in New England (or the New England Company). The Narragansetts, for instance, fielded visits by the Rev. Joseph Park of Westerly, Rhode Island; the Mashantucket Pequots and Mohegans received the Revs. Eliphalet Adams and later David Jewett of New London, Connecticut; and the Niantics and Pawcatuck Pequots alternated between the Rev. Nathaniel Ells of Stonington and the Rev. Joseph Fish of North Stonington, Connecticut. The Narragansetts were exceptional in also drawing an Anglican mission, which started in 1720 when the Society for the Propagation of the Gospel in Foreign Parts sent the Rev. James MacSparran to establish a parish church near the reservation.[3] Most of these Indian communities expressed some interest in literacy education and received lessons now and then, but only two of them, the Mohegans and Tunxis, had full-time schools on their reservations. The most striking sign of the Indians' growing engagement with Christianity and English ways—and of their recognition of its political implications—was the decision of Mohegan sachem Benjamin Uncas II in 1728 to have his heir apparent, Benjamin III, raised and educated by the tribe's schoolteacher, John Mason, and preacher, the Rev. Adams. By 1739, Benjamin III was himself teaching school at Mohegan, thereby showcasing his family's ties to the English and special skills and resources. Yet the Indians' purpose in making these concessions remained limited. Certainly they wanted some of their boys to be literate so that they could deal with the colonial bureaucracy, and they wished to symbolize their friendship to the English. Nevertheless, by nearly all accounts the general Indian population—even most of the Indian children who attended school—remained apathetic about Christianity even as they grew more familiar with it. Not until the Great Awakening of the 1740s did large numbers of them become enthusiastic about the faith.[4]

The Oneidas, who would eventually host the Brothertown community, also had a long history with missionaries that informed their later interest in evangelical Protestantism. The Oneidas were one of six tribes of the Iroquois League (along with the Mohawks, Onondagas, Cayugas, Senecas, and, after 1721, Tuscaroras), inhabiting a three-hundred-mile swath of territory across what is now northern New York state. This location gave the League access to nearly every major waterway in the Northeast and to the French, English, and (until 1664) Dutch colonies. These advantages, combined with an elaborate ritual ceremonialism that kept peace among the League's member tribes while projecting violence outward, made the Iroquois the preeminent military, commercial, and political force of the region during the seventeenth century. In turn, the European powers competed with each other for influence with the League, largely through trade and diplomacy but also Christianity. The French were the first Europeans to attempt a religious alliance with the Iroquois when, from the 1660s through the 1680s, Jesuits fanned out through Iroquoia as part of a peace pact. Even after this campaign ended with the resumption of hostilities in 1683, Jesuits maintained a presence among the Iroquois through the creation of several mission towns in the St. Lawrence River Valley, such as Kahnawake and La Montagne, which eventually boasted hundreds of League residents. Nonresident Oneidas routinely passed in and out of these mission towns to visit relatives, trade, and pursue their spiritual interests. Though they often chafed at the Jesuits' attempts to enforce Christian morality and collect tithes, they were still deeply impressed with the power of Christian ritual, particularly baptism, to seal partnerships with Europeans and to encourage public morality.[5]

Intermittent Dutch and English missionary campaigns among the Oneidas' eastern neighbors, the Mohawks, also left a strong impression, and not always a positive one. The Iroquois never forgot how one of the Mohawks' first Dutch missionaries, Gofridius Dellius, joined a scheme in 1699 to bilk his charges out of their land, even after years of proselytizing them from Albany.[6] At the same time, the Oneidas watched enviously during the early to mid-eighteenth century as the Mohawks used Anglican missionaries stationed at Fort Hunter and Albany to cultivate powerful English advocates, including the English queen herself, and to gain access to formal schooling. In conjunction with the Jesuits' work along the St. Lawrence River, such developments showed the Oneidas the possibilities of using Christianity to meet the challenges of colonialism.[7]

Of all the Christian stirring that anticipated the Indians' Awakening, none was more influential than the emergence of the praying town of Stockbridge among the Mohicans in the Housatonic River Valley of western Massachusetts. That place soon became a model for other missionary enterprises, a training ground for some of the most committed missionaries of their generation, and, above all, a key node in a Christian Indian network that would span the Northeast. Stockbridge's host people, the Mohicans (or Muhekonnucks, as they called themselves), accepted a mission in the 1730s in recognition that their people were at a historical crossroads. Like many other Indians of their era, the Mohicans were a composite group formed in the cauldron of disease and colonial displacement. They included Housatonics from the river valley of that name, Mohicans from the Hudson River Valley around Albany, and Wappingers and Esopus from downstream. These tribes, especially the Mohicans, had been formidable powers in the early to mid-seventeenth century, but epidemics, hostilities with the Iroquois and Dutch, colonial expansion along the Hudson, and alcohol abuse exacted an increasingly steep toll as the colonial era wore on.[8] As one Mohican, Ebenezer Poohqoonuc, observed in the 1730s, his tribe had become "great[ly] diminished; so that since in my remembrance, there were Ten Indians, where there now is one."[9] Amid these losses, the Mohicans' salvation had been that French-Indian raids and jurisdictional rivalries among New York, Massachusetts, and Connecticut kept the English from expanding into their territory. Yet a lull in the cycle of imperial warfare between 1713, the end of Queen Anne's War, or the War of the Spanish Succession, and 1740, the start of King George's War, or the War of the Austrian Succession, emboldened New Englanders to press into this contested zone. In 1719, Connecticut began purchasing Indian titles to the lower Housatonic Valley, and five years later Massachusetts secured a Mohican deed to create two towns further upriver, Great Barrington and Sheffield.[10] Mohican indebtedness to colonial traders and alcohol abuse rose in conjunction with these developments. Under these dire conditions, a Mohican sachem named Konkapot, a "temperate … very just and upright Man," approached colonial leaders about hosting a mission. He knew his people needed to be better prepared to engage with colonial society.[11]

Konkapot found eager partners among the close-knit English ministers of the Connecticut River Valley, but convincing the rest of the Mohicans was a formidable task. Some of them were so opposed to a mission that Konkapot and his supporter, the sachem Umpachenee of Scaticook, feared that they would be poisoned merely for suggesting it.[12] Dutch traders, who had no interest in promoting Indian temperance, stoked this resistance with warnings that the English "design in the End … to make Slaves of them and their Children, and the like."[13]

Even Umpachenee himself retained some strong reservations, for he wondered "if the Christian Religion was so true and good…how there should be so many Professors of it, that liv'd such vicious Lives, and so contrary to what he was told were the Rules of it."[14] Nevertheless, Konkapot's determination, combined with pressure from Massachusetts Governor Jonathan Belcher, swayed enough Mohicans to win tentative approval from the tribe for the experiment. The New England Company then agreed to sponsor two young men to carry the work into Mohican country: John Sergeant, a determined Yale College tutor, would cater to the Indians' spiritual needs; Timothy Woodbridge, the great-grandson of John Eliot, would serve the Indians as a schoolteacher.[15] The missionaries took up this assignment flush with religious conviction but also apprehension about what awaited them among supposed "savages" in the "howling wilderness." For their part, the Mohicans hosted these men anticipating a profitable alliance with the English and their god yet fearful that they had let in a Trojan horse. Both parties' concerns proved to be warranted. Throughout the forty-year history of this mission, English exploitation of the Mohicans tested the Christian convictions of missionaries and missionized alike.

Within two years, the striking progress of the mission, combined with Boston's intent to strengthen its hold on the Housatonic River Valley, spurred a colony plan to create a new Christian Indian town called Stockbridge. The idea was that Indians would be attracted to this settlement by the lands guaranteed to them by the colony, and a permanent base would facilitate the Indians' Christianization. These were the same goals that had influenced the creation of praying towns among the Massachusett and Nipmuc Indians in the years before King Philip's War. Yet the colony's altruistic declarations barely cloaked its self-interested motives. Though the plan for Stockbridge involved the colony restoring thirty-six square miles of land to the Mohicans, it also required the tribe to give up another tract of fifty-two square miles. The deed for Stockbridge pledged that the land would belong to the Mohicans forever, but there was no guarantee other than colony statutes requiring official permission for Indian land sales, a safeguard that had already proved faulty in other parts of Massachusetts.[16] Nor would the land belong to the Indians alone, for the proposal was to bring four English families into town to keep Sergeant and Woodbridge company and to provide models of civility. Finally, Boston wanted Stockbridge to serve as a frontier bulwark against the French and their Indian allies, whether by discouraging raids from Canada or by drawing them away from English communities. Given these features, it is not surprising that Stockbridge ultimately functioned not as a barrier to Mohican dispossession but a mechanism for it.[17]

In the short term, however, Stockbridge emerged as a vital center of Indian Christianity and civilized living. As early as 1739, the town contained some twenty-five Mohican families who began to erect English-style houses; clear, fence, and plow their fields; graze livestock; and promote sobriety. They also constructed a framed meeting house for a congregation that already boasted fully sixty baptized souls.[18] Despite these developments, Stockbridge was no Christian utopia, even from its earliest days. The four supposedly godly English families who moved into town were led by Ephraim Williams, a part-time speculator in Indian lands from one of the most powerful families in western Massachusetts; his presence did not bode well for the Mohicans' tenure. The Indians grew even more suspicious when Sergeant married Williams's captivating teenage daughter, Abigail, whereupon he moved from his river-bottom cabin among the Indians to a hillside seat by the Williams estate. Predictably, Sergeant's interest in his charges diminished once they were out of view. The first Stockbridge town meeting involving both Mohicans and Englishmen only thickened the Indians' resentment. The Mohicans, unfamiliar as they were with this form of English government and wary of any colonial interference with their lands or jurisdiction, "made some talk and difficulty" during the proceedings including, Sergeant noticed, "talking against me and Captain Williams and in general against the English."[19] The missionary callously dismissed the Mohicans' agitation as an instinctual response to "every new thing," for he could not see the potential for abuse like they did.[20] Nevertheless, on average the Indians looked favorably on developments at Stockbridge, as evidenced by the leading Mohican sachem moving to the praying town in late 1743 or early 1744.[21] In the years to come, this community would also become a hub in the region-wide association of Christian Indians.

David Brainerd and Soul Concerns among the Delawares

As Stockbridge took shape, Protestants throughout the British Atlantic began experimenting with bold new forms of preaching, spiritual expression, and church affiliation to address their collective fear that they were not among the elect. In New England especially, people were anxious that they had strayed from their forebearers' mission to purify the Anglican Church and had instead settled for a tempered, respectable, and often apathetic Christianity that promoted godly behavior over spiritual introspection. Sensing the mood, preachers in some of the most isolated corners of the region made a newfound effort to speak to their parishioners' hearts as well as their heads. They stressed, in sometimes graphic terms, that Christians needed to throw themselves prostrate before God in order to be saved instead of focusing on their outward piety, that *they* needed to be moved instead of trying to move God. The laity's response to this message was nothing short of staggering. People wept, groaned, and wrung their hands in reaction to their terrible destiny without grace, then swooned at mention of the generosity of God's offer of salvation, as if they had been touched directly by the Holy Spirit. Afterwards they reinvigorated the listless rituals of their congregations by giving public accounts of their encounters with grace, confessing their sins, presenting themselves for the Lord's Supper, and bringing in their children for baptism. Such reforms made the people feel like a community of saints again, as in the heady days of New England's founding. Yet what made these parish revivals "Great" was the way they fed on each other locally and throughout the empire. Leading preachers like Jonathan Edwards of Northampton, Massachusetts, New Jersey's Gilbert Tennant, England's George Whitefield, Long Island's James Davenport, and numerous others, toured Britain's northeastern American colonies giving guest sermons to promote the outpouring of grace. As often as not, in the process they converted into evangelicals the ministers of the congregations that hosted them. Word of the revivals also spread through print, whether along the far-flung lines of correspondence of the ministerial elite or through the expanding Atlantic marketplace of books, pamphlets, and newspapers. The people believed that their local awakenings were part of a larger movement, perhaps the most important religious stir in the history of the world. Some Christians prophesied that the Second Coming of Christ was imminent.[22]

The missionary work of David Brainerd was one of the earliest and, ultimately, among the most significant results of the Awakening for Northeast Indians, for his labors helped to build the network of Christian Indian communities that would later converge in Oneida.[23] After getting expelled from Yale College in 1742 for charging that one of the tutors had "no more grace than a chair," Brainerd, in need of a job, determined that his calling was to evangelize Indians.[24] In preparation for that work, in 1743 he took a temporary position as minister to the English congregation of East Hampton, Long Island, and part-time preacher to the nearby Montauketts.[25] Afterwards, while awaiting approval from his sponsors to launch a mission to the Delawares, he spent a year evangelizing the

Mohicans of Kaunaumeek, some twenty miles west of Stockbridge.[26] Though Brainerd made only brief stays in these places, his work helped to establish the Christian bonds that eventually drew these communities together. For instance, a number of Brainerd's former charges from Kaunaumeek eventually relocated to Stockbridge.[27] It is easy to imagine their descendents swapping stories about Brainerd with Montauketts who took refuge at Stockbridge during the Revolution. Other Kaunaumeek Mohicans left for the Susquehanna River Valley. Doubtless they influenced the decision of the Susquehanna Oneida community of Onaquaga to host Protestant missionaries in the mid to late 1740s, a development that laid the groundwork for the coastal Indians' migration to Oneida country in the 1770s and 1780s. Brainerd was an essential part of the shared Christian legacy of these peoples.

Brainerd left his post among the Kaunaumeek Mohicans in early 1744 to evangelize the Delawares at the Forks of the Delaware River, only to face a more daunting task than he ever imagined. The Forks Delawares (near the modern town of Easton) had been close to a war pitch ever since the so-called Walking Purchase of 1737 in which Pennsylvania swindled them out of twelve hundred square miles of land. Many Delawares associated this scheme and others with the Christian faith of their antagonists.[28] The Delawares' gradual retreat from the Forks westward to the Susquehanna River Valley added to Brainerd's difficulties, for that part of Pennsylvania was filled with Indian refugees from throughout the East who had concluded that coexisting with Europeans was impossible. These refugees drew from the Tuscaroras of North Carolina, the Tutelos of the Virginia/North Carolina border, the Nanticokes and Piscataways of Maryland, the Shawnees of Ohio, and others.[29] They came from various backgrounds, but all of these Indians had suffered war or displacement at the hands of Christian colonists. Suffice it to say, they did not welcome Brainerd and they counseled the Delawares to do the same. Yet Brainerd embraced the challenge. Several times over the next thirteen months and then intermittently throughout the rest of his abbreviated missionary career, he made the 120-mile journey between the Forks and the Susquehanna Valley Indian towns. His purpose was to convince a skeptical audience that Christians did indeed seek Christian brotherhood with them. At times, however, Brainerd felt as if he was shouting into the wind, preaching to an audience that had already concluded that Indians and whites were incapable of sharing a faith and kinship.

Brainerd's predicament was not only that many of his charges distrusted colonists entirely but that they also believed that Indians and whites were separate peoples with fundamentally different natures. Brainerd was probably familiar from his time among the Mohicans with the common Indian refrain that they had "never been call'd together by the *white* People upon any other Occasion, but only to be treated with about the Sale of Lands, or some other secular Business."[30] His reply was that he had no designs on their land whatsoever, and though there were evil whites, they did not represent colonial society any more than wicked Indians represented theirs. Yet Brainerd struggled with the argument that Indians and whites were "not of the same Make and Original," that "their God" had "expressly prescrib'd for them" a distinct way of living, and that they risked divine punishment if they drifted from the sanctified path. Christianity, according to such thinking, was "no ways proper for them" but only for "the *white* People." Eight years later, Brainerd's younger brother, John, undertook his own mission to the Susquehanna, where he confronted a similar "revelation" by a "young squaw in a trance." This seeker proclaimed that the "Great Power" had created "the Indian, the negro, and the white man" separately, and since whites were "the youngest brother...therefore the white people ought not to think themselves better than the Indians." Her vision also taught that the Great Power expected these groups to adhere to their own particular customs. For example, he had given the book and Christianity to whites but not to Indians and blacks, "therefore it could not be right for them to have a book, or be any way concerned with that way of worship." Brainerd tried to answer all the Delawares' objections, but still they "would give me no liberty to preach to their people."[31] The Delawares believed that by obstructing Brainerd, *they* were doing God's work.

There are unmistakable similarities between, on the one hand, the exchanges involving the Brainerds and the Delawares and, on the other hand, the conversation a century earlier in which a Narragansett told Roger Williams that his people and the English were created by separate gods for separate purposes. The critical difference, however, is that the category of "Indian," so odd to the Narragansett, had by the 1740s grown basic to the various tribes on the Susquehanna through their shared struggles with colonialism. "White" had entered their vocabulary too, perhaps in the mid-Atlantic colonies earlier than in New England, for whereas New England whites were for the most part homogeneously English, colonies such as New York, New Jersey, and Pennsylvania were sites of "multifarious intermixing" among the English, the Dutch, Swedes, Scots, Irish, Germans, and French. Though these groups all fell under British rule, their various appearances, languages, and customs did not fit neatly within the category of "English."[32] They might be called "Christians" with some accuracy, though they were of various denominations, but that term did not distinguish them from Christian Indians, whose numbers had increased substantially over the years. These features of mid-Atlantic life suggest why the Indians of Pennsylvania, ahead of many of their Native peers, began to call Europeans "whites" as a euphemism for their shared light complexion. The meaning Indians attributed to that complexion came from their prophets, who declared that the Europeans' color was a sign that their way of life was meant for them alone. From this perspective, David and John Brainerd were not offering a sacred gift. They were violating the sacred order of things.

David Brainerd was nothing if not determined to become a martyr, but the intransigence of the Susquehanna Indians finally convinced him and his employers that he would be of better use among the Delawares remaining in New Jersey. Though most Delawares had left New Jersey over the course of the seventeenth century, a few hundred remained scattered in small pockets, cobbling together a livelihood through a combination of wage work, hunting, fishing, and horticulture.[33] In June 1745, Brainerd began visiting one of their communities, Crosweeksung (or Croswicks), about ten miles south of Trenton, and there he found a receptive audience. The Jersey Delawares' close proximity to colonial settlements had exposed them to the evangelical fervor radiating from the pulpits of the Tennent brothers Gilbert, John, and William Jr. in New Brunswick and Freehold. The excitement not only piqued the Delawares' curiosity but put them under serious "soul concern." Brainerd appeared at Crosweeksung at just the right time to stoke that anxiety into a full-fledged revival. In the months that followed, Delawares from miles around began moving into Crosweeksung to participate in the religious stir until the community numbered some 150 people.[34] Brainerd could only marvel, "What a difference is there between these and the Indians I had lately treated with upon the Susquehanna!"[35] Yet Brainerd was shocked to discover that neighboring whites were hostile to his work, for, as Indians on the Susquehanna might have predicted, the last thing they wanted on their doorstep was a growing body of sober and civilized Indians capable of making a permanent claim to the land. Nearby colonists told the Delawares that "there was no need of all this Noise about Christianity:—That if they were Christians they would be in no better, no safer, or happier State, than they were already in." Some whites even charged that Brainerd "was a *Knave, A Deceiver,* and the like."[36] Such "abusive behavior" made it impossible to continue the mission at Crosweeksung, so in the spring of 1746 Brainerd and his growing flock

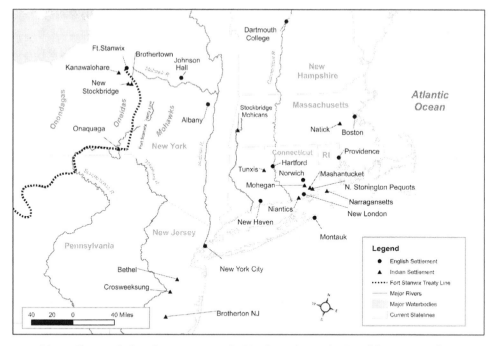

Map 1. Christian Indian Communities in the Northeast during the Era of the Great Awakening. During the Great Awakening of the 1730s and 1740s, Indians throughout the Northeast adopted Christianity in ever greater numbers, culminating in the decision of Christian Indians on Long Island Sound and western Massachusetts to migrate to Oneida country in the 1770s and 1780s. The Oneidas placed these newcomers along the 1768 Fort Stanwix Treaty line in the hopes of making them a buttress against white encroachment. In 1802, Christian Delaware Indians from the Brotherton reservation in New Jersey (distinct from the Brothertown community in Oneida) joined the Stockbridges in New York.

moved fifteen miles northeast to Bethel, New Jersey (near Cranbury), where the spirit continued to flow.

While Christianity thrived among the Jersey Delawares, Brainerd's own life was coming to an end as the result of tuberculosis, which had plagued him for years. In March 1747, he left Bethel for New England haunted by the sense that he would never return, and indeed he would not. Poignantly, he died in the Northampton house of the Rev. Jonathan Edwards, who is often credited with sparking the Awakening that had inspired Brainerd to pursue his missionary career in the first place. The connection between these men would continue even after Brainerd's death, for within three years Edwards would take up the missionary post at Stockbridge, where he tended to a number of Brainerd's former charges. Brainerd's role among the Jersey Delawares was filled by his younger brother, John, for the next thirty years.[37] Along the way, he sustained and extended the Christian ties to Northeast Indian communities that his brother had nourished, by corresponding widely with other missionaries and colonial advocates for the Indians, visiting Delaware communities throughout New Jersey and Pennsylvania, and sending some of his most promising charges to study at the Rev. Eleazar Wheelock's boarding school in Lebanon, Connecticut, alongside Indian pupils from New England, Long Island, and Iroquoia. These actions, which seem so minor when considered in isolation, helped lay the groundwork for Jersey Delawares to join the Christian Indian movement of post-Revolutionary Oneida country.

Awakening Native New England

Like their Delaware cousins, the Indians of southern New England could not help but feel reverberations from the Awakening, given their participation in colonial society. One of Brothertown's founders, the Mohegan Samson Occom, recalled that as a teenager in the 1740s, he learned of "a Strange Rumor among the English, that there were Extraordinary Ministers Preaching from Place to Place and Strange Concern among the White People."[38] Rumor soon gave way to the reality of Whitfield, Tennant, and Davenport sweeping through southern Connecticut and Rhode Island, including occasional stops in the Indians' own villages. The Indians found Davenport particularly captivating, for he was like nothing they had ever seen or heard before from Christians.[39] He was, however, strangely akin to an Indian *powwow* seeking contact with his supernatural guardians. Davenport believed he was a vessel for the Holy Spirit, so he preached as his soul moved him, without notes or preparation. At his most inspired, he gestured, shouted, and sang whatever came to mind, "as if he had aimed, rather, at frightening people out of their senses," as one critic put it.[40] Whereas people of moderate religious temper accused Davenport of being "wild" and "extravagant," his admirers gushed that "the dread Majesty of GOD seemed to fill Heaven and Earth" when he preached.[41] Davenport was all the more compelling because of his challenge to the established clergy. He titillated audiences with his charge that the ministers who droned on week after week, even year after year, without moving their parishioners, were "blind guides" and even "unconverted hypocrites" who might themselves be damned. What Christians needed to be saved, Davenport heralded, was not staid learned discourses by Harvard men in powdered wigs but preaching infused with the spirit, preaching that opened the heart to God's grace. Inspired by this message, local ministers such as Joseph Park of Westerly and Andrew Croswell of Stonington adopted the evangelical, or New Light, style and doubled their efforts to reach neighboring Indian people. More important, Davenport thrust open the door to Indian lay preaching by providing spiritual assurance to people of all walks, including those on the margins who seemed to have so little control over their fate.[42] Unordained, sometimes illiterate, Indian preachers would become central to the evangelization of Native people on Long Island Sound.

Worldly crises are often the bases for spiritual ones, and the uprooted state of Indians certainly made them fertile ground for the Awakening. By the early to mid-eighteenth century, virtually every coastal Indian community had been hemorrhaging land for two generations. A century earlier, these people had commanded vast territories that permitted them to move seasonally among interior hunting grounds, riverine and coastal fishing stations, and well-watered planting fields. Yet by Occom's day each Native community held at most a few thousand acres of land. They all had easy access to good fishing, but hunting now required them to cross English territory, where colonists often treated them as hostiles. Their planting grounds were increasingly exhausted because of their inability to move onto fresh tillage, and what they did grow was constantly at risk of being consumed by trespassing colonial livestock. Even building and heating their homes was difficult because colonists routinely poached on their shrinking wood lots. It followed that poverty stalked most Indian families and hunger crept in when times grew tight. Connecticut's anticipation of the day "when the whole nation, or stock of said Indians are extinct" was more than just macabre wishful thinking; it was a real possibility for the Native people watching their lands and bellies shrink before their very eyes.[43]

The Natives adjusted as best they could, such as by pasturing small herds of livestock, cultivating apple orchards, and performing wage work for colonial farmers and sea merchants, but their reforms were never enough. The more similar the Indians became to the English, the more determined colonists became to "strip us of every thing we possess," as the Stonington Pequots phrased it, lest the Natives strengthen their claim to the land by dint of "improving" it.[44] Colonists usually justified their aggression on the basis of longstanding joint-use agreements or unregistered land deeds—though sometimes they acted out of sheer gall—but their tactics routinely violated the law. Goading the Indians to resist, Englishmen tore down the Indians' fences, enclosed their cleared lands, impounded their livestock, and carted off their wood, often in broad daylight.[45] It would have been suicide for Indians to have taken up the dare, for their communities numbered no more than a few hundred people apiece, whereas the surrounding colonial population had reached the tens of thousands, so they were reduced to filing petitions, sometimes with authorities who were already complicit in fleecing them.[46]

The Indians' protests consistently emphasized a number of themes. They claimed status as fellow subjects of the Crown and veterans of New England's campaigns against the French.[47] They reminded colonists of their earlier pledges to defend Indian land. They claimed to be pursuing civilized reforms such as animal husbandry, just as missionaries has always encouraged them to do, only to have their land stolen. Most poignantly, in a refrain to the Wampanoag sachem Philip, they recalled that when Indians held the balance of power, they treated the English as brethren only to have their kindness go unreturned now that colonists were mighty. These appeals were designed to awaken the colonists' sense of morality. Instead, authorities usually referred them to legislative committees or the Indians' colony-appointed guardians, where they tended to wither from neglect.[48] On the rare occasions that the Indians' lobbying produced legislation for their relief, the measures either went unenforced or lacked sufficient punitive power in the first place. Over and over again, colonists who had seized Indian land argued that it was unfair to remove them after they had invested so much sweat and treasure to "improve" acreage that had previously lied in "waste" under Indian tenure. They found a receptive audience in colonial magistrates, whose typical response was to redraw reservation boundaries minus some or all of the contested territory, promising all the while that these lines would remain permanent.[49] Such men spoke with forked tongues.

Repeatedly disappointed in their appeals to colonial magistrates, the Mohegans turned to the Crown for help in 1704. Their position was that in 1659, the sachem Uncas had placed his land under the guardianship of the Pequots' conqueror, John Mason, and that in 1671 Mason had reserved a thirty-two-square-mile area between the riverside town of Norwich and the port of New London for the Mohegans' exclusive use; these were known as the "sequestered lands." Connecticut's seizure of this tract, the tribe and Mason's descendants charged, violated these legally binding agreements. Connecticut's rebuttal was that Mason had dealt with the Mohegans as the colony's agent and that therefore Hartford could do as it wished with the Indians' territory. The colony considered itself magnanimous for having permitted the Mohegans to remain on any land at all even though they were "not only few but miserable pore [poor]."[50] However, it was not going to allow Indians to control a vast expanse of unbroken "wilderness" amid a colony of thriving farms. It had become a truism among American colonists that their land grabs against Indians were justified by their own more intensive agriculture, so it was much to Connecticut's surprise when the Crown sided with the Mohegans out of concern that Indians would throw their allegiance to the French if their land was seized with impunity. Yet for the Mohegans, this was a hollow victory; though Whitehall ordered Hartford to restore their lands to them, the colony simply ignored the order. A visit to England in 1735 by the Mohegan dissident leader Mahomet II produced a similar result. London agreed to reopen the case, only to find for the colony in subsequent hearings. The Mohegans' appeals finally ran out on the eve of the Revolution. Anxiety over the outcome haunted Samson Occom and his people for decades.[51]

The Indians' troubles found expression in the Great Awakening. Indians believed that the world would become a better place if the throngs gathering to hear revivalist preachers could learn to treat each other as Christian brethren. They also appreciated that the most radical New Lights prized religious expressions such as dream interpretation, ecstatic visions, and speaking in tongues that were part of the Indians' own shamanistic traditions.[52] Particularly resonant was the idea that anyone touched by the spirit of God was not only qualified but perhaps even obligated to share that gift with others, whoever and wherever those others might be. Indians could become not only Christian followers of the English but also Christian leaders of their own people regardless of their poverty, lack of education, and social stigma. Feeling the hot wind of God at their backs, Indian evangelists took to the byways linking the various communities that would someday comprise Brothertown. Pequots preached to Narrgansetts, Mohegans to Montauketts, Niantics to Mohegans, and vice versa.[53] The Indians' Christian ferment was nothing short of "wondrous" to religiously minded colonists.[54] The Rev. Joseph Park, who had struggled for years to draw the Narragansetts to Christianity, wrote in wonderment, "the Throne of GOD's Glory, in his earthly Temple here, is among the *Indians*."[55] Evangelical Christianity was becoming a means to forge an assertive, positive sense of Indian identity in counterpoint to the English association of Indianness with destitution and despair.

The revival also imbued Native people with a renewed sense of cultural direction and political empowerment. Following the Awakening, Indians discovered a "Great Inclination to Live more like Christian English people," as the Western Niantics phrased it, both to symbolize their newfound Christianity and to adjust to diminished territory.[56] Park wrote with delight of the Narragansetts that "there is among them a Change for good respecting the *outward* as well as the *inward* Man. They grow more decent and cleanly in their outward Dress, provide better for their Households, and get clearer of Debt."[57] Archaeological evidence confirms these observations. Pequot sites from the mid-eighteenth century show signs of the Indians' increasing consumption of domestic animals like cows and pigs and English crops such as wheat, barley, and radishes. There is also evidence that Indians were beginning to construct English-style houses and barns and to enclose their fields with stone walls.[58] Such reforms were less thoroughgoing than the Indians' English critics would have liked, but it was beyond debate that many Natives were pursuing a new way of life.

At the same time, the distinctive shape of the Indians' civilized reforms reinforced old divisions between them and colonists. Englishmen complained that only a portion of Indian families pursued colonial-style agriculture and, even when they did, tended to keep only a handful of domestic animals and to cultivate only a few acres of land.[59] The Indians' fields struck outsiders as disorderly because there were no clear boundaries between family plots and different varieties of crops mingled promiscuously. Instead of adopting the colonists' private property ethic, reform-minded Indians tended to share expensive items like plows and draft animals and to graze their livestock in common, thereby turning their innovations into a new expression of communal solidarity. Sometimes their men helped with planting and tilling, traditionally women's work, but they also continued to fish year-round and to take long-distance hunting trips that kept them away from home for weeks at a time. These jobs had defined Indian manhood since time out of mind. Women, for their part, not only gardened but also gathered wild foods, medicines, and craft materials from secret, often sacred places known only to tribal matrons and rising doctresses. Perhaps half of Indian families lived in colonial-style framed houses or cabins, but just as many, if not more, continued to reside in traditional *wetus* (wigwams), albeit with additions such as stone chimneys, tables, and tea sets. The Indians' reforms, in short, were measured and gradual, informed as much by a cherished communitarian ethic and an indigenous gendered division of labor as by Christianity and the demands of colonial authorities. Yet the English did not understand the Indians' behavior in this way at all. They defined the difference between the Indians' agriculture and their own as a shortcoming and attributed it to a lazy, wandering nature. Indians and colonists were becoming more alike in important ways, but that trend seemed only to accentuate the differences that persisted between them.[60]

In a parallel development, the Indians' creation of independent congregations, in which they held the pulpit and their traditions shaped the service, meant that a shared Christianity served to redraw and reinforce the colonial/Indian boundary. Colonial revivalists expected Christian Indians to join English congregations and to defer to English religious leadership, and during the early days of the revival they were cheered by what they saw. A dozen Mohegans joined David Jewett's New London church between 1741 and 1743, including the future preacher Samuel Ashbo and Samson Occom's mother, Sarah. During the same period, Benjamin Uncas II and his family offered themselves for baptism at the New London church of the Rev. Eliphalet Adams.[61] In Stonington, Connecticut, between April 1741 and November 1742, some ninety-five Indians, most of them Pawcatuck Pequots, suddenly affiliated with one or another of the town's three parish churches through baptism, communion, or marriage.[62] After Davenport appeared in Lyme in 1741, thirteen "hopefully converted" Niantics entered "into the communion of the church."[63] The Narragansetts' participation in the Awakening occurred a bit later, but in the fall of 1743 they too felt the Spirit through the preaching of some visiting Pequots. From then on, they "flocked more to the House and Worship of God" at Park's Westerly congregation, with some sixty-four of them becoming full church members by February 1744.[64] These trends reflected the unprecedented sense of religious community that had formed between Indians and whites at the height of the Awakening. Many of them vowed henceforth to treat each other as brethren regardless of the worldly distinctions between them.

Yet sustaining this ethic proved difficult as Indians gravitated toward radical New Light practices that resonated with their shamanistic traditions but chafed against mainstream English standards of propriety and order. It also made the English uncomfortable when their new Indian co-religionists questioned their designs on Indian land. These tensions and doubtless others quickly led Indian evangelicals to break away from colonial churches and establish their own independent meetings headed by their own preachers. They then turned these congregations into headquarters for factions opposed to the sachems' land sales.[65] Colonists who had once championed Indian Christianity as a means of bringing Native people under the English yoke could hardly believe what had happened in just a few short years: Indians had not converted to English Christianity but rather converted Christianity to their own needs. They had taken a mechanism intended for their colonization and turned it into an expression of autonomy.

The Narragansetts' assertion of congregational independence was the most dramatic among the Long Island Sound Indian communities. For years the Narragansetts had worshipped at Park's Westerly chapel, and as long as they remained passive participants the English churchgoers welcomed them there. However, the two groups split on the issue of a former Narragansett *powwow*, Samuel Niles, "exhorting in the Congregation."[66] When the English tried to censure Niles, a hundred Narragansetts walked out to form their own tribal church with their own pastorate on their own land. Generally it was unexceptional for New Light factions to form Separate churches—schisms of this sort were part of what defined the Great Awakening in New England. This split was remarkable because it divided New Lights along racial lines rather than predominantly theological ones. Quite simply, the Narragansetts would not suffer discrimination in their own house of God. Nor would they accept colonial interference in their religious affairs. Two years later, the Narragansett congregation was split over whether to keep Niles as minister or replace him with the Pequot James Simon. They requested advice from neighboring colonial Separatists led by Stephen Babcock but recoiled when those outsiders tried to install Simon unilaterally. For the Narragansetts, this breach of their congregational independence sealed the matter: Niles would remain as their minister and they would ordain him themselves. When "white people" at the swearing-in ceremony left midway through, "disgusted" at the "Confusion" of Indians' "prayers and Tears to God," the Narragansetts shrugged off the insult and broke bread with the attending Pequots and Mohegans.[67] These Indians took literally the Awakening's message that the Spirit alone authenticated their Christianity. They did not need English approval. One Narragansett's response to an English critic said it all: "This is the way that we Indians have to get to Heaven. You white people have another way. I don't know but your way will bring *you* there, but I know that our way will bring *us* there."[68] That principle directed the Narragansett congregation for years, eventually leading it into the Brothertown movement.

Other Indian groups were quieter if just as determined as the Narragansetts to establish their own meetings. The rate of Pequot participation in Stonington's three churches, which rose so dramatically in 1741 and 1742, fell off just as suddenly beginning in 1743, and ceased almost completely after 1750. Groton minister Jacob Johnson thought he knew why. The Pequots, he explained, "have mett together among themselves, & Carried on Religion in their own way on Lords Days; and have Some Shadow of a Form among 'em." Johnson attributed this defection to the Pequots' "Old Natural fondness for Liberty, & Jealosie lest in Some way or other they Should lose it & become Slaves & tributary.... they imagine the White People are Scheming...And have got Possession of Some of their Land & hold them out of their rightful Possession, & design to dispossess them of all their Lands & so turn them adrift, or make Servants of 'em."[69] The Pequots could not help but notice that their churchgoing had done nothing to slow English encroachment on their tiny reservations or exploitation of their indebtedness. As such, there was no drawback but many benefits to worshipping alone. The Niantics agreed. Even though several members of the tribe had joined Lyme's town church, the English continued to deny the Niantics the right to pasture livestock on their own land, even as the colonists' herds picked the grass clean. "We...Don't know how to Defend our Selves," the Indians appealed to Hartford, having once assumed that taking up Christianity was the answer.[70] No longer were they so naive. Shortly they decided to gather their own congregation, run by the lay preacher Philip Cuish (or Ocuish) in the house of Gideon Qequawcom.[71] In this setting, at least, they would no longer have to brook the hypocrisy of Christian fellowship with the English.

The Mohegans had the greatest cause to be bitter about Christianity's limits, for English manipulation of their political divisions and encroachment on their land reached its pinnacle during the era of the Awakening. The Mohegans' factionalism extended from two consecutive disputes over the line of sachem succession. Ben Uncas I came to power in 1723 despite the stronger candidacies of his half brother, John Uncas I, and great-nephew, Mahomet II; three years later, with the death of Ben I, Ben Uncas II seized the mantle of leadership over the rival claims of his cousins Mahomet II and John Uncas Jr. Pressure from Hartford made the difference in both contests, with the colony favoring the candidate most likely to cooperate in its ongoing arrogation of Mohegan land. That fact alone meant that a Mohegan opposition party would endure. The supporters of Ben Uncas I and II clustered in a village known eponymously as Ben's Town, whereas the dissidents lived another settlement a half mile to the south named John's Town.[72] The two groups then squared off year after year over the Mason case and control of the tribe's common lands. Ben Uncas II's strategy was to support Connecticut's claims to Mohegan territory in exchange for the colony's continued recognition of him as sachem, including having the tribe's colony-appointed guardians pay him directly from the profits of their leases of Mohegan land. His interest in Christianity derived at least in part from a desire to strengthen this relationship. Uncas's opponents, with the support of John Mason Jr., rallied around Mahomet II, sending him to London in 1736 to have the tribe's grievances addressed by the Crown. They even went so far, on September 10, 1736, as to publicly disown Uncas in favor of Mahomet II and install Anne, the daughter of their former sachem, Caesar Uncas, as interim sunksquaw (or female sachem) until Mahomet II returned from England, even though they were well aware that it would irritate the English to have a subjugated Indian tribe choose a woman as leader.[73] Mahomet II's death from smallpox while overseas and Connecticut's intimidation of Anne's supporters managed to keep Ben Uncas II in office, but the Mohegans had made a bold declaration of their political and cultural independence and of their resolve to defend their lands.

The Mohegans continued to express that will through their church affiliation as the Mason case wended its way through the imperial bureaucracy. Mahomet II's visit to London succeeded in convincing King George II to form a royal commission made up of colonial elites from outside of Connecticut to hear the Mohegans' complaints. Hartford won the first hearing, which was no surprise given that the commission was packed with Rhode Island officials justifiably concerned about the Narragansetts mounting their own challenge to the Ninigrets' land sales. Mason and the Mohegans immediately appealed, leading to another commission and another hearing in August 1743. This panel's subsequent decision in favor of Connecticut forced dissident Mohegans to realize the weak political value of their Christianity when it came to contesting English designs on their land. Nevertheless, they appealed this ruling as well and then waited another twenty-five years to learn, finally, that their cause was in vain. In the meantime, however, they showed their repugnance by abandoning the parishes of Eliphalet Adams, who had baptized Uncas's family shortly before the commission met, and the Rev. Jewett, who had tacitly supported Connecticut in the Mason case. Henceforth they would worship at their own meetings on their own reservation, run and attended by people they knew were brethren in fact as well as in name.

Over the next few decades, the Mohegan meeting emerged as a wellspring of leadership in the association of Indian congregations that produced the Brothertown movement. The Mohegan church, like those in other New England Indian communities, was purposefully decentralized to encourage lay participation. Among the first people to step forward was Samuel Ashbo, a member of the Mohegan elite and a former student of the reservation schoolmaster Jonathan

Barber. Born in 1718, Ashbo would spend most of his adult life after the Awakening in a pattern of on-again/off-again religious service, including preaching, school teaching, and occasional missionary work as far away as Oneida country.[74] Eventually, he was joined at Mohegan by a number of other lay preachers, including his son, John Ashbo, and fellow tribesmen John Cooper, John Quaquaquid, and John Nanepome, plus visitors from neighboring communities such as the Pequot James Simon, the Niantic Philip Cuish, and the Narragansett John Shattock Sr. All of these men were unordained, unlicensed, and short of the university education that most colonists expected in their ministers.[75] Far better known to history are two Mohegans who did manage to achieve a high level of formal schooling and to secure English approval for their religious activities: Samson Occom, who during the mid- to late eighteenth century served Indians throughout the Long Island Sound region and Oneida country as a preacher, teacher, and missionary; and Joseph Johnson, who taught in Oneida country during the 1760s before becoming schoolmaster to the Tunxis of Farmington and an itinerant preacher in his own right. Their prominence in the historical record can leave the mistaken impression that Indian Christianity along the Sound was more orderly and deferential than it was. In fact, all of the Indians' meetings, including those served by Occom and Johnson, were doggedly egalitarian, often animated in their encounters with the spirit, and always fiercely independent. These characteristics arose from the intersection of two dynamic approaches to the spirit world: traditional Indian shamanism and New Light, especially radical New Light, Christianity, both of which emphasized spiritual seeking and charismatic expression. When Indians discovered that they could not comfortably practice their own version of Christianity within English congregations—particularly when they realized that their English co-religionists continued to view them as subordinates rather than as brethren—they left to form their own meetings. Certainly the Indians were disappointed by this split, for, as they repeatedly emphasized in their petitions to English authorities, Christians were supposed to treat each other as kin. Yet the Indians' Christianity was more to them than a diplomatic tool. It made them feel like they had the Spirit on their side once again after years, perhaps even generations, of hurt. It gave them an impetus to reform their lives when customary practices, however valued, were unable to meet their needs. It was the doorway to the skills of reading and writing at a time when account books, court documents, and land deeds could determine the fate of individuals and communities. It provided a political home and a voice for people tired of having sachem placemen sell the land from under their feet.

Not least of all, it became a new means to reach out to other Native communities to socialize, compare experiences, and design common strategies as fellow Christians and Indians.

"An ornament to the Christian Religion and the Glory of the Indian nation"

No one was more important in the forging of this Christian Indian network than Samson Occom. Though Occom is well known today for his trailblazing writings—he was the first published American Indian autobiographer, poet, and hymnist, an avid letter-writer and diarist, and author of a best-selling execution sermon—initially his reputation derived from his tireless evangelization of Native peoples. English missionary promoters cited his life story as their best evidence that Christianity could refine Indians, with their ultimate goal being to eliminate Indians as culturally and politically distinct communities. Yet that was not Occom's intent at all. Though he believed wholeheartedly that Christianity and civility represented the future for Indian people, his purpose was to use those reforms to strengthen Native people's political and religious autonomy, claims to land, and relationship with God. Building Christian ties among Native communities was central to this vision.

Born in 1723, Occom was ascendant within the Mohegan community by his late teens, even before he embraced Christianity and launched his missionary career. His father, John Ockham, was one of Ben Uncas's councilors, and his mother, Sarah Sampson, had descended from the great sachem Uncas. Thus, the expectations for Occom among his genealogically minded tribesmen were high. In preparation for his future responsibilities, Occom studied as a youth with the Mohegans' schoolteachers John Mason and John Barber, for some Mohegans could already tell that they needed leaders who could work *through* the colonial state rather than futilely struggling *against* it. Occom, for his part, considered his education a gift he was obligated to share with the people. As he explained in his autobiography, he developed "an uncommon Pity and Compassion to my Poor Brethren According to the Flesh, I us[e]d to wish, I was Capable of Instructing my poor Kindred, I use[d] to think if I Cou[l]d once Learn to Read I Wou[l]d Instruct poor Children in Reading,—and used frequently to talk with our Indians Concerning Religion."[76] Occom's comment, "According to the Flesh," can be read two different ways, perhaps deliberately: first, as a personal critique that at this point in life he was more concerned about worldly than spiritual matters;

and, second, as an allusion to his sense of Indian racial solidarity. Whatever the case, the Mohegans clearly appreciated his efforts, for in 1741 he was chosen to sit on Ben Uncas's council.

Occom's educational work became a religious calling after Davenport's revival. In December 1743, Occom's mother arranged for him to be taken in and educated by the Rev. Eleazar Wheelock of nearby Lebanon, who tutored local boys in addition to serving as town minister. Since Samuel Ashbo was already attending Wheelock's congregation, it was probably his influence that led Occom to Wheelock's doorstep. Occom already would have known Wheelock as one of the most ardent revivalists in Connecticut and as Davenport's brother-in-law. Yet Occom could not yet fully appreciate that when it came to the subject of Indian education, Wheelock toed the orthodox line that Indians needed to be "civilized" in order to be "Christianized," which meant killing the inner as well as the outer savage.[77] Only when Indians had learned to yoke the will, such thinking went, could they discover the joy of freeing the spirit. To a certain degree, Wheelock applied this principle to all Christians, Indian or white, for a believer's life was supposed to be a constant war against that mix of sloth, envy, anger, lust, and pride within every soul. Nevertheless, Wheelock reasoned that Indians bore an especially heavy burden because they had supposedly been "inured" to their "savage and sordid practices ... from their Mother's Womb, and from ... the Influence of the Parents['] Example."[78] Put another way, Wheelock believed that both nature and nurture were responsible for Indian savagery. Nothing could be done about nature—that was God's Providence—but Wheelock did intend to nurture Occom and the Indians scholars who eventually followed him within a regiment of discipline and obedience. Day in and day out, the school clock kept a tight schedule while Wheelock monitored his pupils' appearance, demeanor, and, through confession, even thoughts, with the goal to have the students internalize such restraint.[79] The teacher also insisted on students performing rituals of subordination whenever they addressed him in print. Occom nearly always closed his letters to Wheelock as "Your Most Obedient Indian Son," "your true tho' unworthy Servant," "your worthless servant," and "your Good for Nothing Indian Sarvant."[80] It was a hierarchical exercise that, at its extreme, led Joseph Johnson, himself a Wheelock pupil in the late 1750s and early 1760s, to characterize himself as "a Despicable Lumpt of poluted Clay, as is inclosed in this tawny skin of mine" and a "good for nothing Black Indian."[81] "Black," in this case, referred both to cultural savagery and to the social category of blackness that American colonists applied increasingly, if inconsistently, to all subjugated people of color. Wheelock's Indian students spent every day struggling against both kinds of blackness, believing, in vain, that if they defeated the first they could escape the second.

Occom's work as a schoolteacher among the Montauketts of Long Island beginning in 1749 was the first test of his dream of using Christianity and civility to create a better future for Native people. Occom took this job only because his troubled eyesight precluded college study and he was unable to find work among Indians closer to home. Nevertheless, he brought remarkable energy and creativity to the position. Whereas the Montauketts' English schoolteachers routinely struggled with student truancy, which they attributed to Indian wildness, Occom built a steady base of some thirty scholars. One explanation for Occom's success was that, instead of subjecting his pupils to the rote memory exercises of English schools, he introduced an innovative pedagogy of teaching spelling using alphabet cards written on cedar chips and encouraging older students to assist younger ones. It would be decades before white American schools adopted similar methods.[82] Knowing the importance of communal song in Native traditions, Occom also made psalm singing part of his curriculum.[83] As a result, the children made "considerable proficiency" in reading, writing, and Christian doctrine.[84] Eventually, Occom began working with adults too, leading prayer groups, preaching, and conducting services, even though he was not yet ordained. Neighboring ministers credited him not only with promoting Christianity among the Montauketts but also with discouraging them from embracing "wild enthusiastical Notions" of "some foolish Indian Exhorters" from the extreme New Light camp.[85] The Montauketts' English missionary, Azariah Horton, was so impressed with Occom that he redirected his sights to the Shinnecocks and other small Indian communities on Long Island.[86] Occom's public duties mounted year by year until he was also serving as the Montauketts' judge, scribe, herbalist, diplomatic host, and counselor, or, as he put it, "their Ear, Eye & Hand, as Well as Mouth."[87] Occom, in short, had become the Montauketts' leading public figure by transforming himself into a sachem and shaman rolled into one. He gained an even greater stake in the community when he married one of the Montauketts' own—and not just anybody but Mary Fowler, a descendant of the historic sachem Wyandanch. The couple would raise twelve children together in a home already buzzing with public activity.

Occom's hands were more than full with the Montauketts, but his sense of missionary calling compelled him to preach itinerantly to Indians throughout Long Island Sound. To a certain extent, Occom's preaching circuit was merely a round of visiting relatives.[88] His mother was of partial Pequot descent. His aunt, Hannah Justice, lived among the Niantics, and his in-laws, the Fowlers, were one of the most prominent Montaukett families. One of his brothers-in-law, David Fowler, was married to a Pequot woman, Hannah Garret, who had been raised among the Narragansetts. His other brother-in-law, Jacob Fowler, was married to Esther Poquiantup, a Mashantuckett Pequot whose father, Samson Poquiantup, was a church deacon who occasionally hosted Occom's religious meetings.[89] These are just Occom's relatives for whom documentation exists; doubtless he had many more in other nearby communities. Christianity was revitalizing such ties and making them part of a burgeoning Indian identity, for the Indians' Christianity within the colonial setting was seen by the English and experienced by the Natives as just that: *Indian* Christianity, something related to but also distinct from the faith practiced by whites. A comment about Occom's preaching by his friend and fellow minister, Samuel Buell, indicated as much: "His Manner of Expression, when he preaches to the Indians, is vastly more natural and free, clear and eloquent, quick and powerful, than 'tis wont to be when he preaches to others. As an Instructor of the Indians, he makes frequent Use of apt and significant Similitudes, to convey and illustrate Truth: Such a Method of conveying Ideas is natural to Indians in general, and therefore, doubtless, as pleasing as 'tis natural."[90] Native people certainly appreciated Occom's style, but they were equally drawn to the substance of his message. One rare eyewitness account of his preaching suggests that he framed Christianity as a means for Native people to adapt to their times rather than as a sharp break with their past. In this instance, Occom spoke "somewhat at length of what he called a traditionary religion; and he told an anecdote by way of illustration. An old Indian, he said, had a knife which he kept till he wore the blade out; and then his son took it and put a new blade to the handle, and kept it till he had worn the handle out; and this process went on till the knife had had half a dozen blades, and as many handles; but still it was all the time the same knife."[91] Occom was showing the indigenous people of Long Island Sound that Christianity could be their "traditionary religion" too. The faith he inspired during his repeated visits to the communities of his relatives would eventually become the creative force behind Brothertown.

Occom's career at Montauk crystallized yet another, though darker, inspiration for Brothertown—colonial New Englanders' discrimination against even Christian Indians. Occom entered the missionary field with better qualifications than most of his English peers. In particular, his knowledge of the Mohegan language made for easy communication with other Algonquian-speakers, such as

Figure 2. Portrait of Reverend Samson Occom, ca. 1751–56, by Nathaniel Smibert. Unlike the portrait of Samson Occom on page 84, which depicts him in formal English clothes, this one, of a younger Occom, shows him in everyday dress, donning the combination of a manufactured shirt and woolen mantle typical of many Indians of his time. Seeing Occom in vernacular style offers the important reminder that his Christianity and formal education did not preclude his participation in Indian life. Rather, Occom and a number of his Indian peers saw Christianity and civilized reforms as a means of strengthening Indian autonomy and a number of Indian traditions and values. Courtesy Bowdoin College Museum of Art, Brunswick, Maine, Bequest of the Honorable James Bowdoin III.

Brothertown's constituent tribes. No one could legitimately argue that Occom had wasted this potential, for his results at Montauk exceeded those of any other missionary who had ever operated along the Sound. Nevertheless, Occom received scant financial support from the New England Company, just £15 a year. Even far less accomplished English missionaries received several times that amount.[92] The Montauketts' poverty prevented them from making up the difference. Thus, even though Occom was a highly educated man with religious credentials working in a society that typically awarded whites with such qualifications, "I was obliged to Contrive every way to Support my Family."[93] Every way indeed: in addition to his public duties, Occom planted crops, raised hogs, fished, fowled, bound books, stocked guns, carved wooden utensils, and more. Not coincidentally, he seemed to be "almost worn out with Labour" every time Wheelock encountered him, yet still he fell far short of meeting his personal and public expenses.[94] "I Can't Conceive how these gentlemen would have me Live," Occom complained of the New England Company commissioners.[95] He wished he could "Impute it to their Ignorance," because he cringed at the thought of being discriminated against by Christian divines.[96] Yet Occom could not escape the truth. "What can be the Reason that they used me after this manner" he asked rhetorically. Like the hero of his faith, Occom burrowed to the heart of the matter with a parable. He wrote of a "Poor Indian Boy" who toiled as an indentured servant for an English farmer. The boy worked as hard as he could, yet his master beat him every day, sometimes just "because he is mind to beat me." However, the boy understood that "He Beats me for the most of the Time because I am an Indian.'" Occom suffered at the hands of fellow Christians for the same reason. He could only respond, "I can't help that God has made me so; I did not make myself So."[97]

Discriminatory treatment from his fellow believers frustrated Occom to no end, yet he and his tight-fisted missionary sponsors still agreed that Christianity and civility represented the best hope for Indians—and that Occom was the best person to set that change in motion. Calling Occom "an ornament to the Christian Religion and the glory of the Indian nation," white religious leaders consistently ranked him among the top candidates to spearhead new missions into the interior.[98] Occom's example even revived the English commitment to train Indians themselves as missionaries. Wheelock found Indians like Occom to be "at least four times as serviceable" as their English counterparts, since they were half as expensive to maintain, adjusted more easily to the rough life of interior tribes, and showed less contempt for their charges.[99] Anticipating the question of whether Indians had enough discipline to follow instructions, Wheelock proposed that Indians would be more compliant than Englishmen, if only because they recognized that English prejudice limited their job opportunities. "There is no likelihood at all that they will, though ever so well qualified, get into Business, either as School-Masters or Ministers among the English," he sneered, "at least till the Credit of their Nations be raised many Degrees above what it is now, and consequently they can't be employed as will be honorable for them, or in any Business they will be fit for, but among their own Nation," by which he meant Indians generally.[100] Funds raised by these appeals enabled Wheelock to transform what had been an English school with just one Indian student, Occom, into "Moor's Indian Charity School," named after one of Wheelock's benefactors. From the late 1750s through the early 1770s, Wheelock took in forty-nine Indian boys and eighteen Indian girls in the expectation that the boys would become missionaries and teachers to the interior tribes and the girls would become their wives and helpmeets.[101] It was a major step toward the fulfillment of Occom's goal to educate his "Brethren" in Christianity and civility.

Little did Occom and Wheelock know that their missionary work was laying the groundwork for a major exodus of Christian Indians from the coast to Iroquoia. Though Wheelock's students hailed from a variety of northeastern Indian groups, the majority were from communities that eventually participated in the Christian Indian movement to Oneida country: some thirty-one were Narragansetts, Niantics, Mohegans, Pequots, Montauketts, or Tunxis, the constituent tribes of Brothertown; at least eight were Oneidas; and seven were Jersey Delawares, whose people would eventually merge with Stockbridge.[102] Moreover, nearly all of Brothertown's future leading men and a few of its leading women were educated by Wheelock. In addition to Occom, they included the Mohegan Joseph Johnson (Occom's future son-in-law), the Montauketts David and Jacob Fowler (Occom's brothers-in-law), the Tunxis David Mossuck, Elijah Wampy, John Adams, and Samuel Adams (the future father-in-law of one of Occom's daughters); the Narragansetts Mary Seeketor, her brother John, James Niles, John Tukie, Roger Wauby, John Skeesuck, and Emmanuel Simon; and the Pequots James Sampson and Hannah Garrett (the wife of David Fowler). Christianity and civility were supposed to subjugate Indian students to the kind of English authority represented by Wheelock. Instead, they became a driving force for Indian unity and migration beyond the colonial pale.

Wheelock's school, like Occom's relationship with his missionary sponsors, provided Brothertown's rising leaders with powerful lessons about their shared lot in colonial society. After all, they were lorded over by a schoolmaster who insisted that Indians were a single, savage group of people. The school's very mission assumed that Indians were a "Nation," that a Mohegan and a Mohawk shared a natural affinity regardless of their vast differences in language, culture, and history. Lest any of his Native students forget the meaning of Indian identity in colonial society, Wheelock insisted that they accept subordination to him specifically, by confessing their sins and abiding by his discipline, and to whites generally, by hiring them out as servants and refusing to allow them to dress above their supposedly lowly station.[103] Many of Wheelock's Indian students would embrace his teachings on the value of Christianity and civility, and still more of them would accept the premise that they shared something fundamental in common with other Native people. However, they would not concede that they were inferior. They embraced Christianity as source of strength and inspiration, not as a vehicle for their colonization.

Onaquaga and the Grand Design

Whereas Indians were drawn to Wheelock's school by the promise of advancing themselves, their families, and their communities, Wheelock and his colleagues saw them as an advance guard for the British Empire. British colonists, particularly those within easy striking distance of Canada, were acutely aware that the French relied on Indian support to offset their severe numerical disadvantage in North America, and that the common bond of Catholicism was critical to that support. The extent of French influence among Indians was already disconcerting to the British when, in the 1750s, the French began to extend their line of posts into the Ohio Country, which was also claimed by Virginia and Pennsylvania. As elsewhere, the French strategy was less to occupy territory than to forge alliances with Indian peoples—the Miamis, Shawnees, Delawares, and Mingos in this case—but that did not soothe British nerves. Everyone from Whitehall to Williamsburg feared that if New France earned the loyalty of the Ohio Indians, it could turn the British frontier into a bloody ground of terror and halt British westward expansion at the Appalachian Mountains. The British response included invigorating their own generally lackluster missions, particularly among the Iroquois, who, colonial authorities insisted, had the ability to dictate to the Ohio tribes.[104] That urgency remained even after France's loss of Canada in 1763 following the Seven Years' War. More migrants—free and enslaved—would enter the British colonies in the fifteen years after the French defeat than the total number of Indians east of the Mississippi. Their aggressive forays into Indian territory threatened new rounds of frontier warfare, especially in the Ohio Country. Wheelock and his missionary peers believed Indians on the front lines of this expansion had to learn how to make do with less land or else fight a losing battle for it. "The Savages of this Land must be cultivated," Wheelock proclaimed, "or be destroyed and perish, and that very soon."[105] Missions were supposed to be the key to that cultivation, and the Iroquois were supposed to be the doorway to the interior.

Occom was the point man for Wheelock's "Grand Design" of evangelizing the Iroquois, soon to be joined by a growing number of other Moor's Charity School scholars. Talk of sending Occom on missions to the backcountry had begun as early as 1751, when the New York correspondents of the Society in Scotland for Propagating Christian Knowledge proposed stationing him with John Brainerd in New Jersey to make forays to the Susquehanna.[106] The threat of war ultimately quashed this plan, but ambitions for Occom remained. In 1756, the New England Company commissioners recommended ordaining him as "minister at large to the Indians," and in 1759 Occom completed the qualifying examination and received the blessing of the Long Island Presbytery.[107] The idea was for Occom to ride the momentum of his accomplishment to a mission among the Cherokees, but war between that tribe and South Carolina derailed this project too.[108] Occom finally received his opportunity in 1761, when the New York correspondents decided to fund a mission to the Oneidas, who at fifteen hundred people were the most populous nation of the Iroquois League after the Senecas and a force the English desperately wanted to win over to their side.[109]

The path of Occom and his fellow Charity School alumni to the Oneida capital of Kanowalohare had been cleared by a twenty-year Christianization campaign among the Oneidas of Onaquaga, a community some seventy-five miles to the south on the Susquehanna River. Onaquaga was a multiethnic place in which Oneidas were a plurality amid Tuscaroras, Delawares, and a smattering of Mohicans, Shawnees, Miamis, Tutelos, and Nanticokes. Its polyglot character reflected Iroquois policy after 1675 of taking in displaced Indians from all corners of the eastern woodlands and placing them on the edges of League territory most at risk of colonial encroachment or enemy attack, such as the northern reaches of the Susquehanna. As the Moravian missionary Frederick Post understood it, the Iroquois "settle these New Allies on the Frontiers of the White People and give them this as their Instruction. 'Be Watchful that no body of the White People may come to settle near you. You must appear to them as frightful

Men, & if notwithstanding they come too near give them a Push. We will secure and defend you against them.'"[110] The Oneidas were in charge of overseeing
this strategy, for the Iroquois considered them keepers of the League's "southern
door," as the Susquehanna was known. Yet as early as the 1740s, the Onaquagas
showed an interest in hosting missionaries, in part, perhaps, to distinguish themselves from their tribesmen to the north. As British Superintendent of Indian
Affairs Sir William Johnson understood it, the impetus for Oneidas settling in
Onaquaga in the first place was that they were "disgusted with the ruling Politics
of their People," specifically the rivalry between the new capital of Kanowalohare and the old capital of Old Oneida.[111] The Onaquagas might have seen Christianity as a means to assert some independence from these communities while
carving out a special role for themselves as mediators between League nations
and New England. At the very least, Christianity promised to help the Oneidas
adjust to the expanding colonial order gradually making its way toward Iroquoia
westward along the Mohawk River Valley from Albany and northward along the
Susquehanna from Pennsylvania.[112]

Onaquaga's engagement with Christianity began largely through contacts
with the mission at Stockbridge, probably via Mohicans who had settled on the
Susquehanna and married Oneidas. In the 1740s, a handful of Oneida families
sent their children to be enrolled in John Sergeant's Indian boarding school in
Stockbridge. They did not stay long, but a new basis for relations between the
communities had been established. Indeed, Sergeant, accompanied by a handful
of Stockbridge Mohicans, made a brief visit to Onoquaga in 1744, and it appears
that he was followed the next year by David Brainerd.[113] These face-to-face meetings permitted a lengthier mission of two years' duration by Elihu Spencer, a
Yale graduate from the class of 1746 whom Brainerd had handpicked as his successor.[114] His trust was well placed. Spencer's main accomplishments included
educating Isaac Dekayenensere, an Onaquaga sachem, and Peter Agwelondongwas (or Good Peter), sachem of the Eel Clan; they would serve as the pillars of
Onaquaga Christianity for decades to come. Under these men's influence, by
December 1751 some twenty-one Oneidas lived in Stockbridge so that their
children could attend school there. This experiment lasted only a year due to
the Oneidas' disgust at infighting among Stockbridge's English leaders, but the
Onaquagas' interest in Christianity remained strong. None other than Jonathan
Edwards praised them for making "religion their main concern, rather than war,
or any other worldly affairs."[115] The Oneidas gave Edwards even more encouragement in the years that followed. In 1753, they welcomed into their community

the missionary Gideon Hawley, a young Harvard graduate who had recently left his post as schoolteacher at Stockbridge to escape the town's bitter factionalism.[116] By all accounts, Hawley made a favorable impression on the Onaquagas, as did the Oneidas on him, until the Seven Years' War ended his mission in 1756. Over the next several years, the Onaquagas sustained their Christianity without the English. Good Peter and Isaac Dekayenensere ran the Onaquaga congregation throughout the war, assisted periodically by the Mohegan Samuel Ashbo, who visited Onaquaga and the nearby community of Chanango (or Jeningo) in 1760 and again in 1761, the first two of several missionary trips he took to the Susquehanna during the early to mid-1760s.[117] It is uncertain what guided Ashbo to this area. The meager historical record says nothing about the distinct possibility that he had friends or relatives in these neighborhoods; or perhaps he was motivated by a pure desire to work in one of the most exciting theaters of Indian evangelism. Whatever the case, the reports he gave of the community led Hawley to note proudly that "they have improved in husbandry, civility, morality, and Christianity since I left in 1756. . . . I think they need no further instruction, and were Isaac or Peter ordained, they would be contented without an English missionary."[118] Nevertheless, other English and Indian missionaries would follow, including Eli Forbes, who visited in 1762 and returned to New England with four Onaquaga boys for Wheelock's school, and the Delaware Joseph Wolley, who taught school there in 1764 before dying of tuberculosis.[119] Clearly, by the time the Oneidas of Kanowalohare decided to host Occom and other missionaries in the early 1760s, there was already a critical mass of Oneidas to the south well versed in Protestant Christianity and linked to the Christian Indian network spreading throughout New England and New Jersey.

Kanowalohare's interest in the mission derived from a number of factors, including its people's envy of the changes at Onaquaga. Like the colonist Richard Smith, who visited Onaquaga in 1769, the northern Oneidas could see that their Christian tribesmen were "civil and sober" and thriving economically with rich crops of corn, beans, potatoes, and fruits, two plows, and a variety of domestic animals. These conditions stood in marked contrast to other Oneida communities, which were reeling from alcohol abuse and the decline of the fur trade and facing the imminent danger of English encroachment. Thus, when Kanowalohare leaders first met with Occom, they emphasized wanting to learn "the right way of God" by putting "all our sins and all our heathenish ways & customs . . . behind our Backs," setting up an English-style school, promoting sobriety, and soliciting colonial protection of their lands, "that none may molest or incroach upon us."[120]

Britain's victory in the Seven Years' War made these reforms particularly urgent, for it robbed the Oneidas of the threat of going over to the French if the English colonies did not treat them respectfully. In all likelihood, a final consideration was Kanowalohare's ongoing rivalry with Old Oneida; both communities wanted the ear of British authorities, and Kanowalohare judged that a mission was one way to earn it.

Yet the Oneidas were hardly united on this front, for many of them and their fellow Iroquois believed that the spirits did not intend Christianity for Indian people or, as some of them framed it, that Christianity was incompatible with Indians' nature. As early as the 1740s, an Oneida named Shickellamy living on the Susquehanna told a visiting Moravian missionary, "We are Indians and don't wish to be transformed into white men. The English are our Brethren but we never promised to become what they are. As little as we desire the preacher to become Indian, so little ought he to desire the Indians to become preachers."[121] Twenty years later, a Seneca named Onoonghwandekha used similar words to oppose the Wheelock-trained missionary, Samuel Kirkland. He implored his town council:

> If we...receive the white man & attend to the Book which was made solely for White people, we shall become a miserable abject people. It has already ruined many Indian tribes.... How many remnants of tribes to the East are so reduced, that they pound sticks to make brooms, to Buy a loaf of Bread or it may be a shirt[?] The warriors, which they boasted of before these foreigners, the white people, crossed the great Lake, where are they now? why their grandsons are all become mere women!
>
> Brothers attend! This will be the condition of our children & grand-children in a short time if we change or renounce our religion for that of the white people. We shall soon lose the spirit of true men. The spirit of the brave warrior & the good hunter will no more be discovered among us. We shall be sunk so low as to hoe corn & squashes in the field, chop wood, stoop down & milk cows like negroes among the dutch people.[122]

The beliefs that the Creator or different Creators had made Indians and whites distinct and that Indians' attempts to become like whites drew divine punishment grew in popularity during the mid- to late eighteenth century at an even faster rate than Indian Christianity.[123] Discussions about the origins

of Indian and European peoples and their separate natures had been taking place back and forth along the trails and riverways that connected Native
America since early contact, but they took on newfound urgency in the interior,
as Indians confronted a future as colonized people.

During the course of this conversation, the Iroquois not only embraced the
term *Indian* but *apparently* began to refer Europeans as whites with greater regu-
larity. This shift cannot be proved with certainty, given the paucity of Native-
language records. Yet in all likelihood some, if not most, translations of Indians
calling Europeans "white" are accurate. By the early eighteenth century, Indians would have become accustomed to hearing Europeans refer to themselves
as whites.[124] Doubtless Indians throughout colonial America could see the logic
of referring to light-complexioned people as "whites," particularly in opposition
to the darker-complexioned "blacks" who toiled for them. It is more certain that,
over a lengthy process, Native people increasingly thought of Europeans as a
single category of people marked by their skin tone rather than as a series of national or religious groups. For instance, in 1757 an Iroquois delegation to Mon-
treal admonished the French that "the English your Brothers and you are the
common disturbers of this Country. I say you white people together...you both
want to put us Indians a quarriling."[125] The British victory in the Seven Years'
War made it even easier for Indians to characterize as "white" people from more
than a dozen different national backgrounds, religious denominations, and languages. To Indians, the differences among these groups became less important
than their shared membership in the British polity and their shared agenda vis-
à-vis the indigenous population. The Iroquois explained to Gideon Hawley that
they were "sensible to the grasping disposition of the white people. They say now
that the white people have surrounded them and they have[,] as they express
it[,] only an Island left & by & by they are quite afraid they be quite drove off
from their Lands."[126] Clearly Occom and his missionary companion, his "very
promising" twenty-year-old brother-in-law David Fowler, had their work cut out
for them trying to convince the Iroquois to take up the religion of those same
"white people."[127]

No sooner had they arrived in Oneida than Occom and Fowler discovered
that a shared Indian identity meant very little when it came to everyday relations with their hosts. The missionaries' knowledge of the Mohegan language,
an Algonquian tongue, was of no use among the Iroquois-speaking Oneidas,
and therefore initially they had to preach to them in English through an interpreter. This process was so difficult that when the Delaware Hezekiah Calvin

followed Occom and Fowler into the mission field, he complained of feeling
like "a dumb stump."[128] It was probably just as well, for the missionaries' words
had the potential to alienate at least as many Oneidas as they persuaded—
unless presented with skill and sensitivity, as Occom learned the hard way.
Reportedly he irritated the Oneidas by demanding too much too fast, such as
that "they must not cut their hair, but let it grow as the English do; that they
must not wear their Indian ornaments, as wampum and the like: but put them
off and burn them in the fire—That they must not feast at Weddings, as at the
Birth and Baptism of their Children, &c. &c."[129] Occom's sternness reflected the
differences between Indian life at Oneida, which was crude compared to what
Occom had known, and Indian life in New England, which had been shaped by
years of civilized reforms. Fowler, fresh from school, found the transition particularly hard. He characterized Oneida men as "lazy and sordid Wretches" and
"Drunk half their Time."[130] He endured "hunger, cold, health, and weariness"
unlike anything he had ever experienced, and still his school was half-empty
most days.[131] Oneida domestic life offered no comfort, for as Fowler lamented
in a paroxysm to Wheelock:

> I am obliged to eat with Dogs, I say with Dogs, because they are continu-
> ally licking water out of the Pails & Kettles, yea, I have often seen Dogs
> eating of their [the Oneidas'] Victuals when they set their Dishes down;
> they'll only make a little Noise to shew their Displeasure to the Dogs and
> take up the Dish and finish off what was left. Their Cooks are nasty as
> Hogs: their Cloaths are black & greasy as my Shoes; their Hands are dirty
> as my Feet, but they clean them by kneading Bread. their Hands will be
> very clean after they have kneaded 3 or 4 Loaves of bread. I'm obliged to
> eat whatsoever they give me for fear they will be displeased with me.[132]

Such moments crystallized the tension between Native missionaries' claims to
be "Indian brethren" of the Oneidas, even as they attempted to purge the Oneidas of their supposed savagery.

Nevertheless, Occom pressed on, believing that his Oneida mission was the
start of a much bigger movement. Occom's goal was not only to spread Christian
knowledge among the Oneidas but also to lobby Iroquois families to send their
children to Wheelock's school. In this task, at least, he fared relatively well, in
no small degree because he had the backing of Sir William Johnson, Britain's superintendent for Indian affairs in the North. By the 1750s, Johnson had become

the most influential Briton among the Iroquois by virtue of his years as a trader, diplomat, and military leader, and his many Mohawk kin ties, to the point that his mansion, Johnson Hall, in the middle of Mohawk territory, became the de facto British embassy in Iroquois country. Though Johnson possessed an Anglican's distrust of New England's reformed Protestants, he supported Occom as a favorable alternative to French Jesuits. Johnson's endorsement helped Occom recruit three Mohawk boys for the school on his first trip to Iroquoia, including Joseph Brant, the brother of Johnson's common-law wife and a rising star among his tribe. By 1770, some thirty Iroquois had passed through Wheelock's school, mostly for brief stints.[133] While these students were being trained to evangelize their own people, a dozen other Wheelock students ventured to Iroquoia to pursue the Grand Design. Occom returned for visits of a few months in 1762 and 1763 until the danger of Pontiac's War drove him back to New England.[134] Samuel Ashbo, who studied with Wheelock after his return to Connecticut from the Susquehanna, also joined Occom in Oneida country for a spell in 1762. Then the pace picked up in the mid-1760s with the onset of peace. Wheelock's prized colonial student, Samuel Kirkland, began proselytizing the Oneidas in 1766 after a short-lived mission to the Senecas and, with the exception of a few brief periods, he spent most of the next forty years with them.[135] Accompanying him for short stints was David Fowler, who taught school among the Mohawks and Oneidas; Delaware schoolmasters Hezekiah Calvin and Joseph Wooley; a Narragansett teacher named John Matthews; and several young assistants (or ushers), such as Narragansett Abraham Simon, Montaukett Jacob Fowler, and the Mohegan Joseph Johnson.[136] This cohort achieved noticeable gains within a few years despite their many struggles. By 1767, Gideon Hawley could write of the Oneidas, "They are near or quite all of them baptized and profess christianity," though he admitted that most of them as yet "do not practise it."[137] The Grand Design seemed to be under way.

What's in a Name?

The Grand Design never met all of Wheelock's lofty goals, yet it was critical in building a Christian Indian association that was grand in its own right. The Indian peoples who comprised this regional community—Mohegans, Pequots, Niantics, Tunxis, Narragansetts, Montauketts, Mohicans, Delawares, and Oneidas—had ties to each other stretching back well before the colonial period, yet it was Christianity that provided those relationships with direction and meaning for the challenges of the mid- to late eighteenth century. These Indians suffered from the ravages of colonialism no less than their counterparts in the interior, and they too used that experience to assign meaning to the category of Indian that the colonists introduced among them. Yet, for the moment, the Christians disagreed with their Nativist counterparts in the Susquehanna and Ohio River Valleys that the Creator had made Indians and whites with fundamentally different natures and destinies and that, therefore, Indians needed to unite to resist white expansion. Instead, they envisioned promoting Indian unity and defending Indian autonomy around an agenda of Christian and civilized reforms. Their experience following the Great Awakening taught them that it was false to assume that Christianity turned Indians into colonial lackeys ripe for dispossession and enslavement. After all, their Christianity was spread and sustained primarily by other Indians. They worshiped in independent meetings in which they not only filled the pews but even typically held the pulpit. To the extent that they hosted colonial missionaries, it was usually only on a periodic basis, always paid for by outside organizations and largely for the purpose of giving their children a formal education. Christian literacy enabled them to monitor the documents that so profoundly affected their communities, to correspond with outside authorities in moments of need and to stay in touch with each other. Finally, the multi-tribal character of the Indians' meetings, of the Christian schools they attended, and even of the agendas of their colonial missionaries, made Christianity a key component to the people's sense of themselves as Indians.

Brothertown and New Stockbridge were born out of the personal and intercommunity ties of this Christian Indian association and the racial and religious sensibilities it promoted. Samson Occom acknowledged as much when he qualified his praise for the Brothertown movement as "the most Glorious work of God amongst the Indians, that ever was seen anywhere" by adding "except the Jerseys some Years back."[138] He and his colleagues raised this point again when they chose "Brothertown" as the name for their new multitribal Christian Indian community, for its namesake was the reservation of "Brotherton" formed in southern New Jersey after the Seven Years' War by Brainerd's Delaware flock. The name "Brothertown" also spoke to the New England Indians' aspiration to recapture the spirit that had once animated Brainerd's mission among the Delawares. Yet another purpose might have been to attract the Delawares. Indeed, the Jersey Delawares would become the Brothertowns' neighbors in Oneida country in 1802 when they merged with the Mohicans of nearby New Stockbridge.

Certainly, the New England Indians hoped to live like "Brethren," free of the political divisions over their sachems' sale of the land which so plagued their natal communities. But to them "Brethren" also meant something more. The Algonquian term they used for "Brothertown," *Eeyawquittowauconncuk*, intentionally employed the word for "commons," *conncuk*, instead of the one for "town," *otan*, thereby hearkening to the Indian metaphor of the community as a "common pot" into which everyone contributes and from which everyone draws. The message was that they intended Brothertown to be a bastion for communal values that they now saw as both Indian and Christian or, more properly, as Christian Indian. Increasingly over the course of the colonial period, colonists and Indians alike had used the terms *Christian* and *Indian* as if they were antithetical. Yet the Christian Indians of New England, Long Island, New Jersey, and Oneida country knew better. By proselytizing each other, worshipping together, and supporting each other as they took charge of their own congregations and communities, they learned that Christianity belonged to Indians too. Their grand design, their Beautiful White Path, was to promote that message at home and abroad in Indian country so that it could become a rallying point for indigenous people threatened by colonial expansion. The nagging question was whether white Christians would be their brethren in that enterprise.

CHAPTER 3

Betrayals

B Y the 1770s, Samson Occom had concluded that the Rev. Eleazar Wheelock was a boldfaced hypocrite no better than the English society that had produced him. Occom had resisted this suspicion for years despite ample evidence for it because Wheelock had been a towering presence in his life as a teacher, advocate, and spiritual guide. In return, Occom met and even surpassed Wheelock's highest expectations. After excelling as Wheelock's student, Occom went on to perform tireless Christian work among Indians on both sides of Long Island Sound and eventually among the Oneidas of the Iroquois League. As whites took notice, Occom's reputation as a "civilized savage" became part of Wheelock's fundraising pitch for his Indian Charity School. Occom even went so far as to go on a speaking tour of Britain between 1766 and 1768 to solicit donations for Wheelock, braving the dangers of the oceanic voyage, the virulent disease environment of crowded cities and towns, and audiences who mocked dark-skinned Christians as apish imitators. He returned home with an impressive £12,000 in donations. For so many reasons, Occom deserved the respect of his English peers. He certainly merited Wheelock's. Yet he got little aside from the friendship of a few exemplary Christians. Worst of all, while Occom was toiling overseas for Wheelock's benefit, Wheelock neglected his promise to attend to Occom's wife and children and then, adding insult to injury, took the money Occom had raised for Indian education and used it to build Dartmouth College primarily for whites. This duplicity proved to Occom once and for all that Christian Indians would never enjoy any justice in New England, all promises to the contrary. As the wound festered, Occom sat down at his desk, put pen to paper, and composed his declaration of independence from the man who had spent thirty years trying to colonize his mind.

His rage notwithstanding, Occom cut down Wheelock with fluid, learned prose, which in and of itself refuted the old teacher's assertion that even Christian Indians were savages underneath it all. After luring in Wheelock with the traditional honorific address, "Reverend Sir," Occom quickly shifted the tone by asserting, "I am obliged to you So far as it is agre[e]able to god," which Wheelock would have taken to mean: I am obliged to you *only* so far as it is agreeable to God.[1] Occom was being deliberately provocative here, for Wheelock had always insisted to his Indian students that *he* should interpret the Lord's will *to them*. And Occom was just warming up for the centerpiece of his criticism: Wheelock's misuse of the charitable donations. With a pointed flash of Latin, Occom rebuked Wheelock: "I am very Jealous that instead of your Semenary Becoming alma Mater [our mother], she will be too alba mater [white mother] to Suckle the Tawnees, for she is already aDorn'd up too much like the Popish Virgin Mary." This statement was a shot across the bow. Nothing stung a Calvinist clergyman like Wheelock as much as being compared to the Catholic Church—prideful, ostentatious, and power-hungry, or as New Englanders often described Rome, devilish.

Beyond the damage Wheelock's scheme had done to Indian education generally was the embarrassment it heaped upon Occom himself. Occom reminded Wheelock, "I was quite willing to become a Gazing Stock, Yea Even a Laughing Stock" when fundraising for the school, because he saw "a most glorious Prospect of Spreading the gospel of the Lord Jesus to the furthest Savage nations in the Wilderness, thro[ugh] your Institution." Occom had done his part despite warnings that Wheelock was using him as "a fine Tool to get money." Though he would not believe it then, "I am ready to believe it Now," he declared. The thirty-year bond between these two men was broken, a bond premised on bringing Indians and Englishmen together through Christianity.

The kind of betrayal suffered by Occom was experienced by Indians throughout southern New England in the decades preceding the founding of Brothertown. Like Occom, one Indian community after another met the challenges of their day by adopting evangelical Protestantism and a host of civilized reforms, the very changes English authorities had been demanding of them for generations. And, as with Occom, the Indians' efforts won them precious little relief. English contempt for Native people became even greater as Indians narrowed the cultural gap. Indians might have been able to live with such bias if it had been limited to the colonists' refusal to invite them to their dinner tables, but the English seemed intent on driving them out of the region altogether. By the time Occom wrote his letter to Wheelock, all of the coastal communities where he had preached were on the verge of losing their remaining lands.

The limits of Christian fellowship taught Occom and his "Tawnee brethren," as he sometimes called them, the meanings of Indian and white in colonial America, but Indians did not respond by abandoning their Christianity—quite the contrary. Instead, they rallied around their shared faith to unite as Indians.[2] This development was not what Miantonomi had envisioned more than a century earlier when he called for Indians to rise up en masse against the colonies. Yet his campaign had come too soon for Native people whose divisions ran deep and who were still years away from seeing colonization as a common danger. By the mid-eighteenth century, the Indians' perspective had changed. Their collective misery at colonial hands, the colonists' insistence that they were Indians, and the revitalization of their intercommunity ties through Christianity led them to begin to think of themselves as Indian. However, the opportunity to take up arms had passed. The drive for Indian unity among coastal groups no longer belonged to militants but rather to ministers like Occom. Such men would have preferred to take their work even further by promoting Christian fellowship across the color line. Reluctantly, though, they conceded that the faith of whites did not transcend or even significantly challenge the colonial racial hierarchy. Rather, it was constitutive of that division. In the early years of the Awakening, neither Occom, nor his fellow Christian Indians, nor the colonial leaders who encouraged them could have predicted this outcome, yet all of them played a critical role in its unfolding. In that sense, Occom's story is also the story of the people he led, a story of Native people gradually conceiving of themselves as "Christian Indian Brethren" within the "alba mater" that had become colonial New England.

"Insults and abuses"

The eventual migration of Christian Indians to Oneida country happened because whites were seizing their lands and because the Indians had come to recognize that Christianity offered them little help. Yet the stark lesson that Indian-white coexistence was futile, even for fellow Christians, did not emerge suddenly. The evidence accumulated bit by bit until the harsh light of the Seven Years' War cast it into relief.

White persecution of two small communities of Mohican Moravians presaged these dark trends. The Moravians (or Unitas Fratrum), a pietistic sect from Saxony, made their way to Mohican country in 1740 through a chance encounter in New York City between one of their newly arrived missionaries, Christian Hendrick Rauch, and two Mohicans, Shabash and Tschoop, who were there to complain to the governor about white encroachment on their land.[3] The Mohicans had almost no practical incentives to grant these people an audience, for the Moravians had little wealth and no political leverage with English authorities. Nevertheless, the missionaries managed to endear themselves to the communities of Shekomeko (in Dutchess County, New York) and Pachgatgoch (in northwest Connecticut) and build up a small but committed following, just as they were doing contemporaneously among the Shawnees and Delawares in Pennsylvania and Ohio.[4] The Moravians' commitment to Christian fellowship was perhaps their greatest draw.[5] For instance, the Moravians learned the Indians' languages, sometimes lodged in their homes, helped perform their chores, tolerated their customs, and referred to them as brothers and sisters. They even washed the Indians' feet in ritual "love feasts" that exemplified the humility of Jesus and the participants' willingness to serve. One jubilant Mohican gushed that "she had never before been treated in that manner by white people."[6] Indians also appreciated that the Moravians showed not the slightest interest in acquiring their land. However, the Moravians' work among the Mohicans was short-lived. Authorities in New York and Connecticut, suspicious that these foreign missionaries were undercover Catholics plotting to turn their Indian charges into the pope's warriors, relentlessly harassed the Moravians until they abandoned the mission in 1745 and retreated to Pennsylvania with a handful of Mohican followers in tow.[7] A number of the Mohicans who stayed behind joined the Congregationalist mission at Stockbridge, hopeful that colonists would respond more favorably to Indians who practiced the same brand of Christianity that they did. They were in for a disappointment.

The plan for Stockbridge allowed four white families to settle in town as examples of industry and integrity, but they soon proved more committed to robbing the Indians than improving their morals. The Williams clan, led by its patriarch, Ephraim, and his son, Elijah, set the standard for this exploitation, as their control of the political offices of Indian agent, justice of the peace, and deputy to the Massachusetts General Court, enabled them to wrest thousands of acres from the Mohicans.[8] After the death of John Sergeant in 1749, the family also seized control of the Indian schools and, more important, their funds. The Rev. Jonathan Edwards tried to thwart these schemes once he succeeded Sergeant as the town's Indian missionary and preacher in 1750. After all, another branch of the Williams family had driven Edwards from his previous ministry in Northampton, and he was not about to sit idly by as this crew destroyed yet another godly enterprise. In 1753 he managed to hire the committed and competent Gideon Hawley as Indian schoolmaster over the Williams candidate, Martin Kellog, who was barely literate. Yet his victory was double-edged, for the schoolhouse burned down a short while later amid few doubts over who had set the blaze. Edwards repeatedly alerted officials in Boston and London to the Williams's machinations, but to no avail. Ephraim's influence enabled him to deflect the charges until, finally, a frustrated Edwards left Stockbridge in 1757 to take up the presidency of the College of New Jersey in Princeton. The Mohicans were left behind with few advocates, shrinking power, and precious little land in a town supposedly created for them.[9]

A surge of white Indian hating during the Seven Years' War swept away whatever remained of the Mohicans' hopes for Stockbridge. Though the English had every reason to fear Indians allied with the French, including the nearby Wabanakis and Kahnawake Mohawks, the Mohicans had been nothing but loyal friends over the years. Nevertheless, the English treated them as wolves in sheep's clothing. For instance, colonial troops subjected Mohicans warriors who joined them on the march against the French to "many Insults and abuses...their Lives and Scalps Threatened to be taken." In one exchange, "A gentleman imprudently Cursed an Indian who was passing by his Tent, saying that on our return from Canada we should soon extirpate all of their colour—the Indian (who understood English) soon communicated it to the rest, in consequence of which, they...prepared to leave us, letting us know, that they did not think, they should have been insulted for accompanying us."[10] The Indians did not consider the words of this "gentleman" to be an empty threat, for back in Stockbridge racial tensions were approaching open violence. In the spring of 1754, a white jury acquitted one colonist and found another guilty only of manslaughter for the killing of a Mohican. When the Stockbridges called for the English to cover the dead with presents according to Indian custom, the English refused, based on the hollow excuse that the Mohicans were subject to the same laws as the colonists. Unsurprisingly, some Mohicans began to act "surly," giving rise to English fears that they were plotting with "Strangers," perhaps the Mohawks, to "kill as many of the English in Stockbridge as they could in the Night Time and then...to run of[f] to Canada."[11] For their part, the Mohicans heard rumors that "the English were not friendly, but had an inimical and murderous design upon the Indians." All restraint nearly evaporated after a French and Indian attack on the nearby New York community of Hoosick in August

1754. Colonial authorities responded with a scalp bounty, whereupon "some Vile persons" among the English unearthed a Mohican grave and desecrated the corpse. It was enough to make the Stockbridges wonder "who they have to fear most whether the English or the Com[m]on Enemies."[12] The peace would do nothing to change that view.

The Mohicans' tenuous grip on their remaining tribal lands grew even weaker after the Seven Years' War. The French defeat emboldened thousands of white families to enter the former battle zones of western Massachusetts and the upper Hudson River Valley. Pressure on the Mohicans to cede their territory and suits for debt against the Indians rose in kind. By 1774, the Mohicans held only about twelve hundred acres of the original six square miles of their praying town, and land loss in the Hudson Valley meant they no longer had the option of moving back there.[13] Seeing the writing on the wall, the Mohicans asked the Oneidas for permission to move to the Susquehanna, where some of their Moravian relatives had already resettled, only to have this proposal rejected because they wanted to bring along some of their white allies. Nevertheless, this discussion can be seen as the first step toward the Mohicans' relocation to Oneida country in the mid-1780s.[14] As Gideon Hawley later observed, the founding of New Stockbridge among the Oneidas was "twenty years in ripening."[15]

Christianity served the Jersey Delawares no better in terms of their relations with whites. When John Brainerd arrived at Bethel in 1747 to replace his brother David as the Delawares' missionary, this community appeared to be developing into a model for Indian Christianity. Of the village's 160 or so inhabitants, 37 were full church members, 53 attended school, and 27 could read the New Testament. Outward signs of civility included forty acres of cultivated "English grains," a framed meeting house, and a school building. Yet conditions for the Delawares seemed to worsen with every passing year. Brainerd's tenure began with an epidemic that struck down "a considerable number, and especially those who had been religiously wrought upon." Some Delawares wondered if the cause was their having "forsaken the old Indian ways and become Christians," just as Nativist prophets had warned.[16] At the same time, the Jersey Delawares, like their New England Indian counterparts, faced constant harassment from colonial creditors and the courts who threatened to seize their land and labor for unpaid debts.[17] In 1749, even New Jersey's chief justice, Robert Hunter Morris, sued for the land at Bethel based on an old and possibly fraudulent deed.[18] Thus, the Delawares faced eviction from their Christian community just three years after colonists had driven them out of Crosweeksung.

The Jersey Delawares' troubles, like those of the Stockbridge Mohicans, produced some false starts for the Christian Indian migration to Oneida country. In 1753, Gideon Hawley encouraged the Jersey Delawares to move up to Onaquaga among fellow Christian Indians.[19] The Delawares gave this proposal serious thought, even though they were simultaneously considering another invitation from the Iroquois to relocate to Pennsylvania's Wyoming Valley.[20] Brainerd was so convinced of an imminent move that he temporarily left Bethel for a pulpit in Newark.[21] Yet backcountry violence during the Seven Years' War ruined the Delawares' plans. Five years later, in 1758, the Mohicans invited the Delawares to relocate to Stockbridge with Brainerd, whom they envisioned as a replacement for Jonathan Edwards as minister.[22] Nothing came of this overture, perhaps because conditions at Stockbridge were no more favorable than at Bethel, but after the Revolution the Mohicans would renew the offer, and in 1802 the Jersey Delawares would finally join them in Oneida country.

In the short term, staying in Bethel was the best option for the Delawares, but only on a sliding scale. Local whites were so suspicious of any and all Indians that the Delawares feared "being Destroyed by the English."[23] This was no hyperbole, for in some places white Indian hating trumped all reason. In June 1756, the New Jersey assembly placed a bounty on hostile Indians but did not explain how the remains of enemy Indians would be distinguished from those of friends, thereby putting all Indians within the colony at risk.[24] That danger became disturbingly clear when a band of colonists made a nighttime raid on the home of "a Friend Indian...to murder the Family of Indians, and to take their Scalps, and to carry them to Philadelphia, where they were to swear that they were Enemy Indians, and that they had killed them in the Province of Pennsylvania."[25] Ten years later, Jersey Indians were chilled by two more incidents in which whites in the western part of the colony indiscriminately murdered Indians. Even more disturbing was that in one case a crowd of whites freed the accused murderer from jail and "gave several Huzzas" as a sign of solidarity.[26] "Its Not Safe for any Indian to Come [toward] the frontiers this Way," wrote Indian trader George Croghan, adding, the "Mobb Seems to Rule."[27]

The Delawares appealed to the New Jersey government for help, only to discover that they lacked friends there too. The colony's solution was to require each Indian to give "a Solemn Declaration of their Fidelity" in exchange for a certificate of friendship and a red ribbon to be worn on the head as a sign of allegiance. Any Indian found without a certificate was to be taken into custody until he posted bond for his good behavior.[28] The assumption, of course, was that Indians were enemies unless specifically identified otherwise. Whites saw

Christian Indians as the exception to the rule of Indian savagery—and a weak exception at that.

The Delaware reservation of Brother*ton,* which would serve as the namesake and inspiration for the Brother*town* community in Oneida, was born out of this sorry state of affairs. New Jersey's fear of an attack by Delaware Indians in Pennsylvania led it to call a treaty conference in 1758 to address the tribe's outstanding land claims in the colony. As part of the negotiations, the 270 or so Delawares remaining in New Jersey, including those at Bethel, released of all their claims south of the Raritan River in exchange for a permanent three-thousand-acre tract at Edgepillock, amid the Pine Barrens twenty-five miles southeast of Philadelphia.[29] The government would hold the land in trust for the Indians, the Indians would not be allowed to sell any of it without official permission, and a local magistrate would have the responsibility of removing all trespassers. Within a year of the agreement, the town began taking shape. Governor Francis Bernard visited the place in June of 1759 and "saw a house erected being one of ten that were ready prepared" at colony expense. He praised the quality of the soil, the vastness of the surrounding hunting territory, and the settlement's easy access to the sea and to the Delaware River. The Delawares were pleased too, as far as the governor could tell. "They expressed great satisfaction at what had been done for them," he wrote, "& I assured them that the same care of them should be continued & exhorted them to order, sobriety & industry." Such high hopes were captured in the community's name, Brotherton, for which Bernard took credit but which likely came from the Indians themselves, given their use of term *brethren* to refer to friends, Indian and colonist alike.[30]

This was wishful thinking. Christian Indians might have aspired to live as brethren with whites, but the fact remained that their safety depended on living in a marginal location with "but few white people."[31] The Jersey Delawares would continue to do everything they could to demonstrate their friendship to whites and remain a "quiet inoffensive people," such as volunteering their men for military service and sending three of their boys to study at Princeton.[32] But in the long run these gestures did the Indians little good. Brotherton would merely serve as another way station for the Delawares to learn, yet again, that they would never enjoy brotherhood with whites.

Burden upon Burden

If anyone could empathize with the Mohicans' and Delawares' frustrations, it was Samson Occom. After all, no Indian had done more to meet white standards or perform God's work, and few Native communities had produced a more impressive record of Christian and civilized reforms than his natal Mohegan or his adopted Montauk, with so few benefits to show for it. He returned to Mohegan in 1763 after his third mission to the Oneidas, only to find his tribe as divided as ever between Uncas partisans who favored Connecticut in the "Mason Affair" and Uncas opponents who backed the Masons. Sachem Ben Uncas III then raised the stakes in 1764 by leasing out a large tract of Mohegan land without the approval of his council. A number of his followers, including Occom, abandoned him in protest, even going so far as to join with their rivals from John's Town to formally renounce his leadership.[33] Mohegan factionalism grew so severe that it even infected the people's churches and schools. The tribe's schoolteacher, Robert Clelland, and missionary, the Rev. David Jewett, supported Connecticut in the Mason Affair—Jewett had personal property interests at stake—which naturally disaffected a number of Mohegans from them. Mohegans also resented Clelland for taking in tuition-paying English students at the expense of Indian ones. Wherever they looked, Occom and his tribesmen saw divisions generated by colonial interference in their people's affairs over the selfish pursuit of land and money. The Mohegans' Christian status seemed not to matter at all.

Even Occom was not immune to this kind of treatment, for he soon found himself at the center of a controversy spawned by Clelland's and Jewett's resentment of his influence in the tribe.[34] As Occom understood the matter, these supposed colleagues had tried to get his salary revoked by accusing him of being a "bad, mischievous, and designing man" and a "Serpent."[35] Wheelock, fearing that his meal ticket was about to have his reputation destroyed, called on the three men to settle their differences amicably, which was another way of saying that the burden fell squarely on Occom's shoulders. Despite an investigation that found Occom innocent of Jewett's and Clelland's charges, Wheelock and other leading ministers pressured him to sign a statement that it was "very imprudent in me, and offensive to the Public, that I should so far engage, as, of late, I have done, in the Mason Controversy." Swallowing hard, Occom asked for forgiveness and then shook hands with Jewett. His dressing down managed to quell the affair, but it must have nauseated him. After all, he had always considered it a "duty" to participate in Mohegan public life. What business was it of Jewett's, Clelland's, or anyone else's that he used his influence to protect his people's land? More to the point, why did his supposed "Christian brethren" discourage his ministry and not only fail to support but also actively undermine the Mohegans' attempt to defend themselves? Occom bit his tongue in favor of passive resistance to avoid any further damage to his character: after his staged reconciliation with Jewett, he simply boycotted the man's lectures.[36] As for Clelland, who continued to slander Occom at every opportunity, Occom responded in 1768 with a razor-sharp letter that charged him with being "a Busy Body according to Scripture" and warned him that "You are turning yourself out of the Favour of every Body as fast as you can, Except those that are of your Genus—take Care that you don't turn your Self out of Heaven."[37] These were the words of a man increasingly comfortable in his own skin—and alienated from those of a lighter one.

Occom's mounting frustration coincided with a rise in colonial Indian-hating stoked by the vicious, racially charged bloodletting that stained the backcountry during the Seven Years' War and Pontiac's War.[38] The people of southern New England had nothing to fear from this violence, quite unlike those living in western New Jersey or around Stockbridge, but they participated in it vicariously through word of mouth, personal correspondence, and newspaper accounts that routinely characterized Indians as "a pack of hell hounds! who have no idea of mercy! whose glory is the most horrid barbarities, and whose thirst for blood is insatiable[!]"[39] Thus, in 1763, when Wheelock passed a collection plate around a Windsor, Connecticut, congregation to raise funds for his school, it returned to the pulpit empty except for a bullet and flint.[40] Lest anyone mistake the symbolism, a few years later, one of Wheelock's English students, David Crosby, fell into an argument at a Middletown, Connecticut, tavern with some men he overheard saying that Indians could only be converted by "Powder & Ball." These men cut short Crosby's protest and put him on the defensive with the penetrating question, "In case I was single, could I consent to Marry an Indian Squaw?" The answer, of course, was no, which led the tavern patrons to observe that all Englishmen, even Wheelock's own pupils, despised Indians and would continue to do so as long as the two peoples remained distinct. "For their own parts they could never respect an Indian," Crosby's disputants told him, "Christian or no Christian, so as to put him on a level with white people on any account especially not to eat at the same Table. No—not with Mr. Ocham [Occom] himself be he ever so much a christian or ever so Learned."[41] This denigration was Occom's reward for long years of education, civilized reforms, and Christian service. If a man of his background could find no acceptance in white society, and if whites could not see the benefits of missionary work by virtue of his example, then the prospects for the rest of the Indian population were dim, as Native people were becoming increasingly aware.

Colonial society's lack of support for missionary work and even outright hostility toward Christian Indians had confronted Occom with "Burden upon Burden, Trial upon Trial, Both without and within, far and Near," yet he still had faith that Wheelock's academy would make a difference.[42] Occom proved as much in 1765 when he agreed to go on a fundraising tour of Britain for the benefit of the "Grand Design." He took this assignment despite being utterly exhausted from missionary work and homesick for Mary and the kids, because he understood that Christian organizations had to do well in order to do good. Yet no sooner had Occom booked passage overseas than enemies began circling like sharks. Some colonists opposed his mission because they suspected that he intended to lobby the Crown for the Mohegans in the Mason Affair.[43] Occom could live with that criticism. However, he was astonished to learn that his detractors included none other than the Boston Commissioners of the New England Company, who resented Wheelock's trespass on what they considered to be their missionary and fundraising turf. In order to undermine Occom's cachet as a Christianized savage, these men spread lies that he had just recently adopted the faith, that his sole language was English, that he was illiterate, and that he was a Mohawk rather than a Mohegan; others charged that he had been raised from birth as a Christian instead of being educated as one by Wheelock. "The old Devil is in Boston," Occom replied sardonically to these attacks by the puritan city's divines.[44] But he did not stop there. Refusing to concede the print arena or the right to judge him to anyone, in November 1765 Occom wrote the first Indian autobiography on record and then published it in the Boston News-Letter. "I was born a Heathen at *Mimayauhekunnah,* alias Mohegan," he shot back at his critics. "My Parents were altogether Heathens, and I was educated by them in their heathenish Notions." He went on to explain that it was the Great Awakening, not a fundraising scheme, that had brought him to Wheelock's school and made him into a Christian man. In several quick strokes he had dispelled all the falsehoods about his background and exposed the mendaciousness of the supposedly godly men of the New England Company. He also served notice that Christian Indians had reputations worth defending too.

Occom's two years in Britain, which included a long stay in and around London followed by shorter visits to Scotland and Ireland, gave him disturbing insight into what colonists meant when they trumpeted civility. After all, Britain, and London in particular, was for most American colonists the epicenter of the civilized world. Yet he was offended by Britain's stark inequalities and the callous indifference of the privileged few to the anguish of the many as blatant contradictions of Jesus' teachings and the communal ethic with which he had been raised as a child at Mohegan. Sharing an audience with King George III dressing for court or attending a lavish birthday celebration for Queen Charlotte, while just outside there were "Beg[g]ers praying, crying, and beg[g]ing up on their knees," only thickened his disgust. As he confessed to his journal, "The Sight of the Nobility put me in the mind of the Diver and the Rich Glut[t]on, and the poor reminded me of Lazerus. What great Difference there is between the Rich and the Poor, and what Difference there is and will be, Between Gods poor and the Devils Rich, &c." Occom was equally critical of the finery of the Church of England. Like New England puritans of old, he judged that the "Bishops, Lord Bishops, and Archbishops...a good deal resemble the Anti-christian Popes." Furthermore, their lack of support for Wheelock's school made him "apt to think they don't want the Indians to go to Heaven with them."[45]

The rude mockery and polite condescension with which the British public received Occom deepened his doubts about whether Christianity was a bridge between peoples after all. Occom was ill prepared for what it meant to be a novelty act in Britain, where a preaching Indian was not only rare, it was unprecedented.[46] He certainly welcomed the crowds that flocked to hear his sermons, but discovering that "the Stage Players, had been Mimicking of me in their Plays, lately," as if he was an impersonator, made him pray for "greater Courage."[47] He would need it, since the following year he became the object of a "low, foolish & malicious" satire in a "Grub-street penny Paper."[48] If all this abuse was not enough to make Occom feel like an outsider despite his Christian credentials, racially loaded (if well-meant) comments by members of British high society were. "Oh! that I may stand near some of you tawny people at the Day of Judgment," wrote one correspondent, as if "tawnies" were rare in heaven.[49] The only safe way for Occom to respond was through his sermons. He opened some of his talks by acknowledging that it might be considered "a Dareing Presumtion" for him to preach to "you that are highly Priviledg'd" given that God "has taken me from the Dung Hill, and from Heathenish Darkness and Gross Idolatry, to this Sacred Desk." Nevertheless, he proclaimed, "If it may be for God's Glory and Honor, I think I am ready to Stand before you all, if it is only as a Spectical and a Gazing Stock."[50] Occom was coming to terms with the fact that the public considered his learning and grace the exception that proved the rule of Indian savagery, rather than the evidence that disproved the theory.

If Occom refused to conform to white stereotypes of Indians, so too did some of his British hosts buck the worst examples of their own society. Occom's patrons, including Lord Dartmouth, the Countess Selina Hastings Huntington, and his hero, the itinerant George Whitefield, treated him as an honored guest.[51] Occom even received the best in English medicine with a smallpox inoculation in March 1768 and nursing during his convalescence in which he "was attended like a Child by my friends."[52] Yet just as the rare example of Occom's civility further confirmed the white public's belief that Indians in general were savage, such kind-hearted treatment showed Occom the staggering gap between what British society preached and what most of it practiced. Whitefield drew Occom's praise because he stood nearly alone in aiding "the poor, the Blind, the Lame, the Hurt and the ma[i]med, the Widow & the Fatherless" who thronged outside of his house.[53] If Britons as a whole ignored such misery among their own kind, what hope was there, in the long run, that they would assist the struggling Indians of America?

Still, Occom did everything he could to win that assistance—more than anyone could have hoped—and in return, Wheelock betrayed him. During his tour of Britain, Occom made approximately four hundred appearances and raised some £12,000. Along the way, he suffered physically, from a long illness punctuated by four days of "delirium," and emotionally, from the pressure of symbolizing an entire race of people.[54] Most stressful of all, Occom worried constantly about his family, about Mary raising seven children alone, about the short finances, about the unfinished state of his house. "I am Sensable of the great Burden and Care that is upon you," he wrote to Mary in a rare burst of emotion, "and I feel your Burden, Cares and Sorrows. My poor Family is near and Dear to me, and you are the nearest to my Heart."[55] All Occom asked of Wheelock was to look after his family while he was abroad and use the donated funds as they were intended. Wheelock did neither. Though he took in Occom's prodigal son Aaron in order to steer him away from an unadvisable marriage and the temptation of going to sea, he did little to help Mary make ends meet. Then he rubbed salt in the wound by using the monies Occom had raised to relocate the Indian Charity School to the town of Hanover in the upper Connecticut River Valley of New Hampshire, where almost everyone knew it would become a white institution. The move in and of itself was not the issue. For several years Wheelock had openly discussed the possibility of relocating his school either to the Susquehanna or Iroquoia, where there were large Indian populations interested in Christianity.[56] The Stockbridge Mohicans had even offered five hundred acres of their land as a new home for the academy.[57] Instead Wheelock chose New Hampshire, which by then had fewer Indians than any colony in British North

America, with the possible exception of Delaware. Clearly he did not pick this location with Indians in mind, something he tacitly admitted by publicizing his newfound conclusion that Indians were naturally unreliable as missionaries.

Wheelock insisted that his loss of faith in Indians extended from the "bad conduct, and behaviour of such as have been educated here, after they have left the school, and been put into business abroad."[58] As examples he cited the Mohegan Joseph Johnson, whose service among the Oneidas had come to an ignominious end when he "turn'd pagan for about a week—painted, sung, danced, drank, & whor'd it, with some of the savage Indians he could find," followed by his shipping out to sea.[59] There was also the Delaware Hezekiah Calvin, another school teacher, who during the late 1760s got drunk several times, publicly accused Wheelock of exploiting his Indian pupils as cheap labor, and then was imprisoned on the charge of forging a travel pass for a slave.[60] In Wheelock's estimation, "no more than half" of the Charity School's Indian students transcended these poor examples.[61] The teacher was equally disturbed that most Indians abandoned the school before becoming civilized enough to backslide. Wheelock attributed these problems to the "Insufferable Pride" and "Contempt of all Authority" supposedly characteristic of Indians.[62] Yet Wheelock's students attributed their so-called disobedience to other causes. These pupils, most of them mere adolescents, were appalled at Wheelock's rules against their wearing fine clothes, which he judged "to[o] good for Indians."[63] Others complained that Wheelock used them as servants on the false premise of instilling a work ethic in them. The Narragansett John Daniel protested this treatment of his son, explaining that "I always tho't your school was free to ye natives; not to learn them how to Farm it, but to advance in Christian Knowledge....I can as well learn him that myself and have ye prophets of his Labour, being my self bro't up with ye best of Farmers."[64] Indian students in the missionary field were disaffected because Wheelock had provided them with far less support than their white counterparts. Conditions grew so bad for David Fowler in the frigid winter of 1766 that he was forced to beg, "Sir, I am almost nacket [naked], my Cloaths are coming all to pieces."[65] Joseph Johnson perceived the racism behind Wheelock's demands that Indians endure their hunger and cold in silence. He cut to the quick: "If I was an Englishman, & was thus Respected by you, I should be very thankful, but much more doth it now become me being an Indian, to be humble & very thankful in every deed." Yet Wheelock refused any responsibility for his students' uneven performances. The problem, he concluded, was the nature of Indians, so he reversed course and turned his attention to the training of white

Figure 3. Samson Occom, by Jonathan Spilsbury, after Mason Chamberlain, *The Reverend Samson Occom, 1768.* This portrait of Samson Occom, painted during Occom's tour of Britain between 1765 and 1768, captures the ambiguous status of Christian Indians in the British Atlantic world. On the one hand, Occom appears civilized, seated at a desk reading and dressed in fine clothes. On the other, the arrows in the top left corner remind the viewer of Occom's "heathen" background. Occom, like other Christian Indians of his day, repeatedly confronted colonial society's insistence that they were innately savage no matter what reforms they made. Courtesy Hood Museum of Art, Dartmouth College, Hanover, New Hampshire; gift of Mrs. Robert W. Birch.

Figure 4. The Reverend Eleazar Wheelock (1711–1779), 1st President of Dartmouth College (1769–1779), by Joseph Steward. As a teacher, mentor, and spiritual guide, Eleazar Wheelock was towering figure in the lives of many leading Christian Indians from Long Island Sound, including Brothertown's organizers Samson Occom, Joseph Johnson, and David Fowler. Yet his treatment of Indians as degraded subordinates and especially his misuse of funds Occom raised for the education of Indian youth had alienated most of his former Indian pupils by the 1770s. Courtesy Hood Museum of Art, Dartmouth College, Hanover, New Hampshire; commissioned by the Trustees of Dartmouth College.

missionaries. Occom could only read Wheelock's duplicity as a personal insult and betrayal. And he did.

Wheelock's duplicity reached a new low when he began gossiping that Occom had gotten drunk. Occom's lapse was no drinking binge but merely a case of his "having Drank a small quantity of Spiritous Liquor after having been all day without food," as investigations by the Suffolk Presbytery and the Scottish Society confirmed.[66] But the damage to Occom's reputation had been done, and Wheelock had been a prime instigator. A full year later, Occom was still shaking his head that "many white people make no bones of it to call me a drunkard, and I expected it, as I have many enemies round about here, yea they curse and damn me to the lowest Hell."[67] Occom had always been cautious of enemies lying in wait for the moment when his supposedly innate savagery would get the best of him, but he never counted Wheelock among them. Yet his teacher had seized on an isolated mistake and magnified it to the fullest, as if it were the coup de grace in his argument to have Dartmouth College favor whites over Indians. Perhaps this episode is what Yale President Ezra Stiles had in mind years later when he wrote of Wheelock, "He had much of the religious Politician in his Make. It is said that amidst a great Zeal & Shew of Piety, he was very ambitious and haughty."[68] Occom might have put it more bluntly. Instead he cut off contact.

Occom's struggle was shared by Indians across southern New England on the verge of completely losing their lands to their so-called white Christian brethren.[69] The Rhode Island Assembly not only brushed aside the Narragansetts' pleas for help but also authorized the sale of however much tribal land it took to extinguish sachem Thomas Ninigret's massive debts.[70] "Threatened with ruin," as the Narragansetts phrased it, the tribe in 1767 joined other Indian communities on the Sound in soliciting Sir William Johnson's aid, for he had been charged by London to manage colonial-Indian relations in the volatile backcountry.[71] Though sympathetic, Johnson claimed that there was nothing he could do since their region fell outside of his jurisdiction.[72] He did, however, suggest turning to the Crown as a final avenue of appeal—the very strategy the Mohegans had been pursuing for the better part of a century. Accordingly, the Narragansetts withdrew brothers Tobias and John Shattock Jr. from Wheelock's school so that they could go to England to lobby the king directly.[73] To the tribe's dismay, in May of 1768, twenty-six-year-old Tobias died of smallpox in Edinburgh, and although John managed to recover from his own bout and make his way to London, officials were too preoccupied with political unrest in the colonies to provide much help. News that the Crown had ruled against the Mohegans in the Mason Affair followed a short time later in 1773. Occom drew an ominous lesson from his people's defeat: "I am afraid the Poor Indians will never Stand a good Chance with the English, in their Land controversies," he wrote, "because they are very Poor they have no Money, Money is almighty now a Days, and the Indians have no Learning, no Wit nor Cuning, the English have all."[74] Repeatedly, Indians received no justice from their colonial neighbors even though they had become "not only civilized, but christianized and are peaceable and orderly, and willing to behave as good subjects to his Majesty King George," as the Montauketts described themselves.[75] They had come to learn that they would never enjoy peace and security in New England unless they turned white.

"The bone of my bone, and flesh of my flesh"

Tellingly, Occom summed up his thoughts on the dilemmas of being Indian in colonial America in a sermon to memorialize the execution of a Christian Indian by white authorities. In the winter of 1771, a Wampanoag sailor named Moses Paul had bludgeoned a colonist to death in a drunken confrontation outside a Bethany, Connecticut, tavern. Before Paul hanged for his crime, he wanted to make some small gesture of contrition, for he had been raised a Christian and was mortified about what he had done. He asked for a minister to edify him and those who would attend his death, and not just any minister but somebody from his "nation," by which he meant another Indian. Occom was just that person, and on September 2, 1772, before a large mixed-race audience, he delivered one of the signature performances of his life.

Occom's text was conventional for an execution. It was Romans 6:23, "the wages of sin is death, but the gift of God is eternal life through Jesus Christ our Lord." His moral was likewise basic: everyone was a sinner in need of redemption. Yet there was a special message just for Paul and the other Indians in attendance: "I am an Indian also, your Brother and you are my Brethren the Bone of my Bone and Flesh of my Flesh. You are an Indian, a despised creature."[76] Occom had no need to apologize to these people for his presumption in speaking to *them*. He knew their pain, and he had sinned their sins. Yet as a man of God, a learned man, a worldly man, he also had a duty to lead them to a better life. His answer involved more than the stock instruction to open their hearts to God's grace. "If we don't regard ourselves, who will regard us?" Occom asked rhetorically.[77] Certainly not the whites who had peddled Moses Paul the drink, who bilked Indians of their land, and who treated even Christian Indians like despised creatures. Indians had no one else to depend on except each other. And if they were going to win God to their side, they needed to join hands and heed Occom's challenge: "O let us reform our lives, and live as becomes dying creatures, in the time to come."[78]

A Sermon, Preached at the Execution of Moses Paul, an Indian went on to become one of the most popular publications of the late colonial era, with nineteen printings and a readership of thousands. A wonderstruck Occom suddenly found himself deluged by invitations to preach to white congregations, whereas just seven years earlier, as he waited in Boston to sail for England, he had received none. Occom, though, had become too jaded toward colonial America to trust his newfound celebrity status. He believed what he had said: Indians had to reform themselves without the expectation of any outside assistance. One betrayal after another at the hands of even god-fearing whites had shaken his youthful faith that a shared Christianity could bring peace to the various peoples of colonial America. As far as he was concerned, Native people would have to determine their own fate with God—beyond the pale of New England.

CHAPTER 4

Out from Under the Burdens

O happy Souls how fast you go,
And leave me here behind,
Don't Stop for me for now See,
The Lord is just and kind.
Go on, go on, my Soul Says go,
And I'll Come after you,

> *The Slow Traveller, or, O Happy Souls*
> *How Fast You Go, by Samson Occom*

I T might seem strange that Samson Occom was busy writing hymns in 1773. After all, the Mohegans and virtually all of their Indian neighbors were on the cusp of losing their lands after failing in their desperate attempts to enlist the Crown's protection. Yet Occom saw redemption in his people's suffering, for if New England had become their Egypt, there was still a potential Israel in the so-called wilderness of Iroquoia. The answer to the Indians' troubles, Occom believed, was for them to band together to form a new community among the Oneidas. There, at the literal border between British and Native America, Occom's "Christian Indian Brethren" would create a model town where the people worshipped God properly, behaved righteously, tilled the earth, and evangelized their fellow Indians. The point of this movement was not to please whites or even to train Indians to compete in white society. Rather, it was to earn God's blessing through pious living, for it seemed as if human effort alone was incapable of reversing the fortunes of indigenous people. Occom, drawing on the Indian tradition of using song to build communal solidarity among people and their spiritual guardians,[1] became a hymnist at this moment to guide his people to their promised land.

Occom and his peers had been singing this movement into existence for some time.[2] Throughout the 1760s and early 1770s, the Christian Indians of southern New England had gathered as often as three times a week, frequently across community lines, to sing hymns "in their Way."[3] Native evangelists like Occom, David and Jacob Fowler, and Joseph Johnson then carried this practice to Oneida by teaching their students Christian principles through song, an approach that endeared them to people whose own ceremonies and sociability often included rhythmic chants.[4] In these exercises the Indians did far more than simply mouth words dictated to them by white outsiders. They sang for themselves, for a sense of community, and for the stirring message that there was a greater purpose to their ordeal. Speaking to the point is an entry from Johnson's private journal written on the eve of removal. In it, he paraphrased Psalms 137:4–6 but replaced "Jerusalem" with "Mohegan" so that it read: "O mohegan O Mohegan—the time is long before I Shall be walking my wonted places which are on thee—once there I was but perhaps never again, but Still I remember thee."[5] Comforting words for a man who had embraced his responsibility to take the Gospels abroad even as he retained a deep attachment to home.

Occom understood as well as anyone the importance of song to Indian life and Indian Christianity, so he turned to hymns to mobilize support for the migration to Oneida. In 1774 he published an anthology of 109 psalms that he had been collecting and editing for years. It included at least one of his own compositions and perhaps others penned by him, the Fowler brothers, or Johnson—it is impossible to tell conclusively because Occom did not identify the composers of his titles. Occom's publication was both the first work of its kind by a Native author and the first interdenominational hymnal in American history. For Occom, though, the purpose of these songs was to inspire and sustain the Christian Indian movement, a mission that kept him composing until the end of his life. Occom appealed to his Indian audience using songs with the kinds of metaphorical images favored in traditional Native prose: paths and trails as connections between people or mountains, trees, and bodies of water as links to the layers of the universe—sky, earth, and underworld.[6] The hymns also treated the Christian experience as a physical and spiritual journey punctuated by sacrifice, themes that were bound to reassure prospective migrants to Oneida. Stanzas two, three, and five of his composition, *A Son's Farewell*, read:

> *Honor'd parents fare you well,*
> *My Jesus doth me call,*
> *I leave you here with God until*
> *I meet you once for all.*
> *My due affections I'll forsake,*

My parents and their house,
And to the wilderness betake,
To pay the Lord my vows.
... Then thro' the wilderness I'll run
Preaching the gospel free;
O be not anxious for your son,
The Lord will comfort me.

Occom and his fellow "Christian Indian Brethren" were inspired, not resigned, to move to Oneida country (the literal "wilderness" in this tune). They were hopeful that they would rise from the depths of colonial exploitation to become God's chosen people and God's messengers, thereby sparing other Indian people their painful history. Given the challenges confronting them, they were wise to seek divine assistance.

Visions

The plan to form a Christian town in Oneida country emerged gradually through discussions involving individuals from several different tribes and a handful of powerful whites. It was not the result of an epiphany or the creation of any one person or group. In the mid-nineteenth century, Brothertown's Thomas Commuck wrote that David Fowler had introduced the idea by asking the Oneidas if they would welcome the Montauketts to Iroquoia.[7] If true, such an exchange might have taken place as early as 1761, when Fowler first visited the Oneidas. The earliest documentary evidence points to Tobias Shattock as the progenitor of the movement. In October 1765, Shattock made a veiled statement to Wheelock that "I have been very Industreous in trying to unite the Indians, and have in good Degree obtain'd my Desire."[8] He might have been referring to the coastal Indians' attempt to enlist Sir William Johnson to protect their lands, but clearly at some point the tribes asked Johnson to approach the Oneidas about taking them in.[9] By the fall of 1767, Shattock was writing about the possibility of the Sound Indians selling what little land they still possessed so that they could "Imbrace Sr. William[']s offer."[10] The following April, Sir William visited New London, Connecticut, and held "four different Meetings...with the Narragansetts, Nahantocks, Mohigans, and Montoc Indians all concerning Lands."[11] This string of events suggests that, though the coastal Indians' migration to Oneida country is often associated with the leadership of Mohegans Samson Occom and Joseph

Johnson, the Narragansett Tobias Shattock and perhaps the Montaukett David Fowler helped launch the initiative.[12]

Eleazar Wheelock encouraged the movement early on but did not play as singular or central a part as some historians have assumed.[13] It is true that as early as 1762 Wheelock had considered moving his school to a number of different sites in Indian country and surrounding it with towns of godly white families as examples.[14] Yet his idea came to naught. Shattock revised the plan by proposing that a Christian Indian town could serve just as well as a white one as a model for Indians. "If we shou'd move to or near Oneida," he submitted, "we shall be of great service to You in promoting your worthy Design."[15] Wheelock agreed, and during his advocacy of the project he left a trail of correspondence in which he disingenuously portrayed the idea as his own. A representative letter to a British sponsor reads:

> I have been trying to collect a town of Christianized Indians, from the New England Colonies, & settle them in some su[i]table place, in ye heart of ye Indian Country. I have some hopes of accomplishing it. This would furnish an Asylum for our Missionaries, set the Savages a pattern, & exhibit to them the advantages of a Civilized life, much secure them from the many Mischiefs of unrighteous dealers, conciliate their friendship to the English; and who knows but the leaven so put into the lump, may gloriously spread.[16]

Wheelock considered a variety of locations for this experiment, including Stockbridge, but his main focus was Oneida country, where whites were still scarce and he and his students already had lengthy experience and strong personal ties.[17] In 1768 he sent the Mohegan Joseph Johnson and the Rev. Jacob Johnson of Groton (no relation) there to scout out locations and take the Oneidas' political pulse, but the mission backfired.[18] During a treaty conference at Fort Stanwix, Jacob was so aggressive in counseling the Oneidas not to cede land to the Crown but instead to set it aside for Wheelock, that Sir William Johnson concluded the Grand Design was nothing more than a land grab.[19] From that time forward, the superintendent was an opponent of Wheelock's schemes.[20] Still, Wheelock pressed on. The following year he encouraged Occom and David Fowler to go on another scouting mission, this time to the Oneida communities on the Susquehanna. Wheelock believed that this visit would "open a Door for the Settlement of a town of our Christian Indians at Charlestown," by which he

meant the Narragansetts, who were increasingly "convinced that they must seek
a better soil, &c."[21] Occom declined the invitation, citing health problems and
domestic responsibilities, but he did what he could to promote the idea close
to home. In January 1770 he wrote to Wheelock that he had conferred with the
Narragansetts about "your proposal of their removing with the School." "They
will consider it," Occom relayed, "and will let you know their minds by and by."
In the meantime, the Narragansetts could only say that they preferred to move
somewhere to the south or west rather than to the frigid north. In Occom's
judgment, if Wheelock found a suitable location for a new Indian town, "there
wou'd be a Number from all the Indian Places round a bout here."[22] Ultimately,
though, Wheelock soured on the idea of wedding his college to Indians and said
as much by choosing cold, stony New Hampshire as the site for his school. A disappointed John Shattock could only remark that his people "have been toward
that countray a Hunting and found the weather harder and colder than it was
here.... we think it best not to pursue that settlement notwithstanding we are entirely thankful to Doct. Wheelock." Just as Wheelock's move to New Hampshire
completed his break with Occom, so too did it symbolize the end of his involve-
ment with the Christian Indians' plans to leave Long Island Sound.

Wheelock's diminishing role in Native affairs placed the Christian movement squarely in the hands of Indians, specifically a group of four tightly knit
men: Occom, David and Jacob Fowler, and especially Joseph Johnson. Seasoned,
educated, reputable, and well-connected, Occom and the Fowlers were obvious
candidates to pick up the leadership mantle. Johnson, by contrast, was initially
a question mark. He was the youngest of the group, having been born in 1751
to a politically influential Mohegan family. Though he had entered Wheelock's
school at age seven and then gone to Oneida at age fifteen to serve as an assis-
tant in David Fowler's school, he fell from grace a short time later under charges
of having "turn'd pagan."[23] Wheelock expected Johnson to confess his lapse and
then get back to work, but Johnson, like many restless young men of his day, took
to the sea instead, not to return to Mohegan until 1771. As it turned out, getting
some critical distance from the pressures of missionary work and Wheelock's
scrutiny was precisely what Johnson needed. At age twenty-one, he had a born-
again experience, after which he recommitted himself to the evangelical life.[24]
By 1772 he had taken the position of schoolteacher among the Tunxis of Farmington and, like Occom twenty years earlier at Montaukett, became this small
community's jack of all trades: teacher, preacher, judge, scribe, and more. Still,
he continued to take on new responsibilities. A year later he married Occom's

daughter, Tabitha, and within three years the couple had produced two sons. Perhaps it was no coincidence that during this period Johnson became, in his own words, "the very first mover of this Design" to relocate the New England Indians to Oneida.[25] Buoyed by his encounter with grace, he saw in this experiment the possibility of creating a better future for the next generation.

The coastal Indians soon focused their search on Oneida country because of its Christian foundation and its stability during a tumultuous period. The Oneidas remained at peace during the Seven Years' War and even during Pontiac's War of 1763, when warriors from a dozen different tribes, inspired by the Nativist visions of the Delaware prophet Neolin, rose up in unison against British forts in the Ohio Country and Great Lakes.[26] Additionally, the Oneidas had a religious affinity with the coastal Indians and a shared commitment to civilized living. The Oneidas' missionary, Samuel Kirkland, who was hard to impress, described his charges in 1770 as "much ingaged in husbandry," and the following year he reported that "the Church here seems to be in a flourishing state."[27] Indeed, shortly before the Revolution the Oneidas built a Christian meetinghouse that stood two stories tall, 36 feet long by 28 wide, with glass windows and a sixty-foot-tall steeple.[28] Increasing numbers of Oneidas lived in nuclear family homes built in the English style as opposed to their traditional longhouses for an extended matriline. Livestock and English crops, once rarities among the Oneidas, were by the 1770s found in all of their settlements in various degrees.[29] That said, Oneida communities had not become New England country towns, nor did they aspire to be. They still had more longhouses and wigwams than framed houses; the people raised livestock but seldom used plows; most glaring of all to European visitors, the vast majority of Oneidas continued to believe that fieldwork was for Indian women and not for Indian men, based on a sacred gender division of labor that ascribed giving life to women and taking life to men.[30] The Oneidas' purpose in their reforms was not to exchange one culture for another or to disavow their traditional values but to adjust to the encroaching colonial order. The Oneidas' future as a people depended on it.

To be sure, the Oneidas' new course was not without its detractors. From the west, the Senecas were reported to be "very Jealous of the Oneidas," largely out of concern that Christianity had made them English sycophants.[31] From the east, Sir William Johnson began to discourage the Oneidas' interest in reformed Protestantism because he correctly believed that it aligned them more with New Englanders and less with the Crown in the burgeoning imperial crisis. He also questioned whether it was in London's interest to support the transformation of Indian fur trappers and warriors into farmers.[32] The Oneidas were themselves divided. Christianity tended to find its male recruits among the "warriors," men on the make who had earned political followings through their accomplishments but who still lacked the formal councilman titles bestowed by Iroquois clan matrons. By contrast, League sachems, who did possess official status and who therefore had the most to lose by any change, generally opposed the mission. It followed that Kirkland drew his support more from the recently established and less prestigious towns of Kanonwalohale and Onaquaga than from the traditional political capital of Old Oneida.[33] The historical record has little to say about the responses of Oneida women to Christianity, but it is safe to assume that they were similarly divided given their prominent role in Iroquois politics and ceremonialism. Yet the mission's supporters were clearly increasing, and that fact above all made Oneida country the best location for Christian Indians from New England concerned with maintaining their faith and promoting the Gospels.

The coastal tribes also knew that the Oneidas had land to spare and a powerful incentive to share it with them. The Iroquois, and the Oneidas in particular, had a history of taking in uprooted Native people and settling them on the League's periphery as way stations for League warriors, as sources of intelligence about distant rumblings, and as shields against attacks from southern enemies like the Catawbas.[34] After the Seven Years' War, the Oneidas looked to the border towns to hold the line against white expansion. After all, the Iroquois stood at only some nine thousand people after more than a century of losses to disease, warfare, and out-migration.[35] The League's eastern nations, the Oneidas and Mohawks, had less than a thousand people each. By contrast, *tens of thousands* of European migrants flowed into Pennsylvania and New York after the war, leading the population of those colonies to grow by more than 40 percent between 1760 and 1776.[36] This trend, combined with an alarming rise in attacks on traveling Indians by frontiersmen made the Oneidas fear that "by fraud or violence they shall soon be obliged to take shelter among the far distant tribes under the setting sun."[37] Their answer began with the Fort Stanwix Treaty of 1768. In it, the Iroquois ceded to the British Crown their claims right up to the very edge of Oneida country, including the strategic portage between the Mohawk River and Wood Creek on which imperial Fort Stanwix was built. Their logic was that most of this land was not inhabited by Iroquois at all but by Delawares, Shawnees, and other displaced tribes taken in by the League; sacrificing these groups was a reasonable price to pay in exchange for the British promise to keep whites from breaching the line.[38] Still, the Oneidas were unwilling to leave this matter to chance because, as they said, "daily experience teaches us, that we can't have any great dependence on the white people, and that they will forget their agreements for the sake of our Lands."[39] As such, the Oneidas' next step was to recruit allies to assist them in defending the line and in adapting to the oncoming rush of white settlement. The Christian Indians of New England were just that sort of people.[40]

That the New England Indians wanted land in Oneida country and that the Oneidas wanted the New England Indians as a barrier against white encroachment should not obscure that they thought of their cooperation fundamentally as a Christian Indian enterprise. Occom's earliest statement on the subject, made to the New York Presbytery, was that a Christian Indian town in the "Wilderness" would be "the likeliest way to bring the Indians hear [sic] [to] Consider the Christian Religion and to bring [them] to Husbandry." He explained that Indians from the interior were "very Prejudice[d] against the English ministers, and all English, but if a number of Regular Indian Christians Went amongst them and Set good Example before them they may think and be Convinced." It was a project in which Occom believed "with all my Heart."[41] Joseph Johnson was even more effusive about the potential for this Christian Indian experiment. In an address to the Connecticut Assembly in 1774, he explained that the coastal Indians' goal was "not only to better our selves, but also to use our Utter most endeavour to civilize and Christianize our Fellow Natives," both by sending missionaries into the field and by providing an example "in the ways of industry, in the ways of husbandry, in the way of Civility, and above all in the ways of godliness."[42] If God blessed these efforts, as Johnson prayed he would, "Who knows, but that even by this Design, will be opened a way of extensive good to those poor perishing nations, that as yet sit in heathenish darkness."[43] Proselytizing the Oneidas would be just the first step. Eventually Christian Indian missions would extend "even to other Nations further Southward, and westward."[44] One of Occom's and Johnson's favorite metaphors for this "Noble employment" was that there was a "door opening for the great good to the western Nations."[45] The two men also expressed their ambitions by referencing Isaiah 35:1, as when Johnson charged his Tunxis parishioners on the eve of their first migration to Oneida country: "Go ye into all the world and preach the gospel to every creature; go and proclaim to all nations, and kindred, and tongues that inhabit this Earth... Behold this north america, once a howling wilderness, a barren wilderness, now blossom like a rose."[46] The Oneida grant represented more than just land to Occom and

Johnson and, presumably, to their followers. It was an opportunity for the Christian Indians of Long Island Sound to help the Natives of Iroquoia and beyond transform themselves from sufferers of God's wrath into his chosen ones. Then, and only then, could Indians as a race reverse their diminishing fortunes.

The Oneidas also thought of their alliance with the coastal tribes in racial and religious terms. Though their differences with the Sound Indians were substantial, as in their speaking of mutually unintelligible languages, the Oneidas saw these people as brethren by virtue of their shared Indianness, their common white antagonist, and their commitment to Christianity. Those characteristics were not enough, however, to satisfy the western Iroquois. They threatened that "Poverty & a still more wretched life is a certain consequence of our embracing the Christian religion" and that coastal Indians' relocation was part of "a design formed by the people of New England to settle in that western country."[47] The Oneidas rejected these arguments because they trusted the coastal Indians as fellow Christians, or more precisely, as fellow Christian Indians.

Spurred by their utopian dream, Occom, Fowler, and especially Johnson toiled endlessly between 1773 and 1775 to realize the vision. Their tasks included convincing and organizing members of seven different Indian communities to move to a place hundreds of miles away, negotiating with the Oneidas to grant them a tract of land, and, last but not least, earning the support or at minimum avoiding the opposition of colonial and imperial officials. Occom took charge of the work along the coast. For instance, in the fall of 1773 he recounted having "been to Visit 6 Small Tribes of Indians this Summer past," and six months later he complained that "last year was very expensive to me, wee had several Congresses at my house about Western affairs."[48] The responsibility of treating with the Oneidas and their superintendent fell largely to the youthful Johnson, who made four trips up the Hudson between the spring of 1773 and the fall of 1774, joined by David and Jacob Fowler at least one time each.[49] These men had spent the better part of their lives tending Indian communities scattered throughout the Northeast because they believed that Christianity held the answer to their people's troubles. Calling in those sheep to flock in defense against colonial predators was a test of their accomplishments, especially whether they had won God over to their side.

Every step of this journey was a challenge. Indeed, the entire project nearly collapsed at the end of 1773 when frigid winter weather led representatives from the seven coastal communities to hesitate about attending a meeting with the Oneidas to seal the bargain. Yet Johnson would not allow the moment to

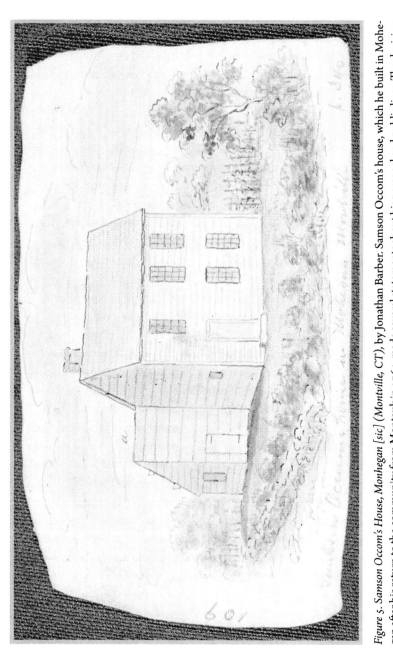

Figure 5. Samson Occom's House, Monhegan [sic] (Montville, CT), by Jonathan Barber. Samson Occom's house, which he built in Mohegan after his return to the community from Montauk in 1764, made several statements about his personal and public lives. The decision of Occom to live in an English-style house announced that he, his family, and even the Mohegans in general were civilized Christians. Its large size was designed to accommodate his large family and the endless stream of visitors who called on him. The public function of the house was never more important than during the organization of the Brothertown movement. Courtesy The Connecticut Historical Society, Hartford, Connecticut.

slip away, not after everything he had done to cultivate the Oneidas' goodwill. In a circular letter, he censured his people that they were about to throw away a precious chance to prove to God and man that they could join the ranks of Christian, civilized people. "Must we let the World know that we are Indians by Nature, and by Practice," Johnson exclaimed, "but we must End beg[g]ing, intreating, and humbly beseeching." Johnson knew that Indians, by nature, were capable of doing better. However, first they had to seize the opportunity in front of them. He implored them to rise: "Do those things which are right, which are praise Worthy. Do those things which become men, so those things which become Christians."[50] The people answered Johnson's challenge. A short time later Occom wrote to Wheelock: "Several of the Tribes round about here, have Join'd to seek for a New Country amongst our Western Brethren.... Four Indians are Just set out again, for Onyda to have further Conference with the indians; Joseph Johnson is gone for Mohegan, Jacob Fowler for Groton & Montauk; Samuel Tobias for Naroganset and Wympey for Farmington—And if the Lord will Continue my Health I purpose to go up in the Spring."[51]

For Johnson, putting this contingent together was only half the battle; he also had to manage the intricacies of Iroquois protocol to deal with the Oneidas. As the Iroquois scholar William Fenton has observed, "There is a principle that students of the Iroquois must inevitably learn: the way a thing is done is often more important than the issue at stake."[52] Participating in an Iroquois council meant knowing when to speak and when to listen, which metaphors to use and which to avoid, what gifts to give and to whom, and so on. The code was elaborate, and there were many opportunities for mistake since these meetings often lasted for days and involved multiple stages of ritual, proposal, deliberation, counterproposal, and then more deliberation. The aim was not to achieve a majority vote—votes were never taken—but to forge consensus and foster a spirit of amity framed in metaphorical kinship terms.[53] Johnson's knowledge of these procedures and principles was put to the test in January 1774 when he trekked out to Kanawalohale to finalize the bargain with the Oneidas.[54] Wisely, he focused less on the specific details of the agreement and more on the spirit of fellowship between the parties. Addressing the Oneidas as "our Elder Brother as a Nation, and beloved Brethren," Johnson began, "We thank you that you look upon us as the same Blood as yourselves, and we thank you that you have received us in your Body. So that we may have one head and one heart & may God keep us united together, indeed untill we both grow white headed."[55] As for Iroquois who were skeptical of the coastal Indians, Johnson responded that his people had important lessons to teach their hosts.[56] He explained, "Whilst our forefathers weare [were] blind and Ignorant, yea drowned in Liquors, the English stripped them, yea they as it were cutt off their Right hands, and now we their Children just open our Eyes and knowledge growing in our hearts and Just come to our senses."[57] All they needed was a place to begin anew so that they could apply this experience and teach their "Indian Brethren" to do the same.

The Oneidas were impressed, as evidenced by their careful affirmation of each of Johnson's points. They agreed that "Now we may say we have one head, one heart, and one Blood.... Now Brethren, our lives are mixed together, and let us have one Ruler, even God our Maker... who is father of us all."[58] These were solid principles for a relationship between the coastal Indians and the Oneidas given their shared Christianity, but for the migrants to deal effectively with other League members they had to enter the Iroquois family. The Oneidas instructed Johnson that they would henceforth look upon his people as "a Brother," and the coastal Indians were to think of the Oneidas, Cayugas, and Tuscaroras of the League, and their dependencies, the Nanticokes and Tutelos, as "elder Brothers." But, the Oneidas emphasized, "as for the Mohawks, Onondagas, and Senecas they are our fathers, and they are your fathers."[59] The Christian Indians of New England, so often treated as unwanted stepchildren by their Christian English neighbors, had become Iroquois kin with a safe place to raise their own families. To be "Christian Indian brethren" was clearly more powerful than just "Christian brethren."

By October 1774 everything was in place. Johnson, Occom, David Fowler, and "some Farmington and other Indians" returned home from Oneida with news that they had secured and surveyed a "very large Tract of choice good land."[60] Choice indeed: this 24,000-acre grant abutting the Fort Stanwix Treaty line and Oriske Creek was considerably more fertile than the stony or sandy ground found along the coast. The game animal population, though in decline, was more plentiful in the woods of Iroquoia than along the deforested Long Island Sound, while fish teemed in local waters. And then there were the generous terms of the Oneidas' grant. The land would belong to the migrants and their descendants, and they would enjoy the freedom to hunt all game except beaver anywhere within Oneida country. There were only two significant restrictions on the coastal Indians' freedom, both of which augured that colonial America was not too far behind. First and foremost, they could not sell their territory to any outsiders, lest they fall into the same trap that had caught their forefathers. Second, their town grant stipulated that the land "shall not be possessed by any persons, deemed of said Tribes, who are descended from, or have intermixed with Negroes or Mulattoes."[61] Even in their new Israel, there were limits to the Indians' Christian fellowship.

Darkness

It is a near-certainty that the coastal tribes rather than the Oneidas included the ban on blacks and Afro-Indians in their agreement. Historically, the Iroquois had had little exposure to black chattel slavery because of their distance from colonial settlement. To the extent that the Oneidas did interact with blacks, it was on rare occasions when they encountered slaves in the company of fur traders or on visits to frontier towns. Iroquois delegations to colonial capitals with large black populations, like Philadelphia, were rarer still. To be sure, there were a handful of blacks who were adopted into Iroquois tribes, apparently as full and equal members given the high political status achieved by some of them.[62] Overall, though, the Iroquois had little contact with blacks. Correspondingly, the occasions on which the Iroquois had anything negative to say about blacks were infrequent. By contrast, the coastal tribes had struggled with how to deal with blacks since the Seven Years' War, and the solutions they reached foreshadowed the racial code of their Christian Indian settlement. For instance, in 1756, a group of Montauketts, including Occom, agreed to a measure that denied community rights to "all Mustees or Molattoes that have Indian Squas to their mothers Natives of Muntock," to any woman paired with a "Negro," and to any children of such a woman.[63] Nine years later, the missionary Joseph Fish observed among the Narragansetts "a considerable Number of mixtures as melattoes and mustees which the tribe Disowns."[64] Finally, on May 12, 1773, forty-four Mohegans led by Occom agreed that any of their daughters who married "strangers" should leave the tribe and that any children descended from "Negroes" would enjoy no rights as Mohegans.[65] The very next day, the Mohegans hosted the first meeting to organize the Christian Indian migration to Oneida country.

These racial codes addressed a spike in Afro-Indian marriages and the disturbing political and cultural repercussions of those relationships for reservation communities. Blacks and Indians were in contact from the earliest days of colonization, but the pace of their interaction quickened throughout the course of the eighteenth century as growing numbers of Indians began working alongside blacks as farm hands, house maids, and especially as sailors, often in the context of indentured servitude. Subsequent friendships and romantic attachments led to a handful of Afro-Indian marriages, with some of the families managing to escape their bondage for the Indian partner's reservation. Scenarios of this kind were rare enough before the Seven Years' War that they hardly ever drew comment, but in the 1760s and 1770s there was a small but conspicuous rise in Afro-Indian pairings, mostly between Indian women and black men. Though every relationship differed in its particulars, the general influences behind this pattern are clear. The main factor was the disproportionate number of Indian women to Indian men. In all likelihood, Indian women had slightly outnumbered Indian men for some time, owing to male deaths in dangerous work like hunting, seafaring, and war, even though women faced their own peril in childbirth. Yet the Seven Years' War was an unprecedented blow to the Indian male population, for Indian men volunteered to fight and died at a remarkably high rate. For the remaining women, marriages with whites were off limits because of white laws and customs, so some of them coupled with the black men they met through work. At the same time, the number of free black men was on the rise. Slave manumissions grew markedly in New England during the 1760s and 1770s as slaves volunteered to serve in the military in exchange for freedom and as white commitment to the institution weakened in light of revolutionary principles and slave resolve. Newly freed black men were drawn by employment opportunities to seaports such as Sag Harbor, New London, Newport, and Providence, which, in turn, were located close to the Indian communities on Long Island Sound. By the same token, Indians who were waiting to ship out or who had recently returned from sea tended to find lodging and sociability in the "colored" neighborhoods along the docks.[66] It was through such ties that an Afro-Indian population began to emerge.

That population posed a stiff challenge to the reservation communities' tradition of sheltering kin in need. After the Seven Years' War, Afro-Indian couples and their children began moving onto the reservations as never before. When such women did not arrive destitute, they often became so when their husbands left the reservation to find work, with the burden of their support falling on communities already stretched thin by their shortage of land. Another trend was for Afro-Indian children, sometimes in the absence of their Indian mothers, to try to claim land in the tribal community even when they were strangers there. Were this an earlier age, when the coastal tribes possessed greater political autonomy and sufficient resources, they might have welcomed such newcomers as sources of manpower and know-how. On the eve of the migration to Oneida country, however, the Indians were fighting to defend tiny reservations in a society shaped by a rigid racial hierarchy. It was incumbent on them to create as much distance as possible between their people and the lowest rung on that ladder.

Afro-Indian relationships threatened Native communities in several respects. Black men, particularly those who had recently achieved their liberty, were often determined to assert their manhood according to the dominant American values they associated with that freedom, including owning land, participating in the market, and receiving public recognition as heads of household. Those expectations clashed with the practices and principles of Indian reservation communities. Indians held land communally, not as privately owned plots, and, given their wares, they would not permit sales without the entire community's permission. At the care of these customs was a communal ethic that prevented anyone from falling too far behind and that kept the people together in one place. It followed that Indians expected their governing councils to be made up of family representatives with long ties to the community and a deep knowledge of its ways. Black men could not meet this standard. There is nothing in the written record to indicate how Indians in Connecticut and Rhode Island addressed this problem, but it is suggestive that among the Wampanoags of Cape Cod and Martha's Vineyard during the late eighteenth and early nineteenth centuries, Native women represented their mixed families in village government even though traditionally Wampanoag councils were made up almost exclusively of men. Another point of tension was that few blacks and their children learned the Native tongue, which was becoming a critical symbol of identity as Indians were adopting so many English behaviors just to survive. This pressure existed even within the family of Samson Occom. Though Occom "wished to live in English style," his wife dressed in the "Indian manner" (which probably meant with a blanket mantle, ample jewelry, and beaded fringe on her skirts), refused to set the table, and, tellingly, answered in Algonquian even when her husband spoke to her in English.[67] If Samson Occom met such opposition within his own house, one can only imagine the Indians' reception of black outsiders unfamiliar with the people's ways.

These problems alone were enough to make Indians resent the surge of black newcomers in their communities, but what made blacks even less welcome was that colonists began to call the offspring of Indian-African relationships, and even entire Native communities, "people of color," which most colonists conflated with black or Negro. The racial double standard of defining simply as black anyone who was of any black descent, while also categorizing the offspring of a mixed Indian marriage as only "part Indian," was designed to promote the colonial goals of expanding the servile black labor force while diminishing the number of Indians on the land.[68] More than just an ideology or a semantics game, such constructions had the potential for real-world impact. Special colonial laws restricting the Indians' rights to sell land and obstructing creditors and the courts from seizing it was all that kept New England's Native communities from completely disintegrating. If whites could deny that the people living in these communities were authentic Indians entitled to protection, it would threaten the communities' very existence. These dangers did not congeal until the early to mid-nineteenth century, but they would have been readily apparent to the Indians by the 1770s.[69] The Christian Indians who planned to move to Oneida country had no intention of opening the door to that risk.

A final influence on the decision of the Christian Indians to exclude blacks might have been the vicious racial politics that had begun to characterize coastal Indian communities on the eve of the migration. Almost as soon as blacks began marrying into Native communities in appreciable numbers, Indian factions began scribbling petitions to colonial authorities in which they accused each other of harboring trespassers or strangers. One of the first signs of this racial politics came in 1768 when the Narragansetts challenged the legitimacy of their sachem, Thomas Ninigret, partially on the basis of his marriage to a "mulatto" woman, Mary.[70] In Mohegan, it was the sachem's supporters, led by Zachary Johnson, who resorted to racial tactics, charging their opponents—the very people behind the Christian Indian movement—with being "Interlopers from other tribes and Strag[g]ling Indians and Molattoes."[71] The sachem party then compiled a "List of the Mohegan Indians, agreeable to the Minds of Zachary Simon and Noah Samuel Tantaquidgeon" that included members of the Uncas, Johnson, Tantaquidgeon, Joyjoy, and Mazzen families, but pointedly excluded Occoms, Ashbos, Coopers, Georges, Horceats, and others.[72] A number of issues were at stake here. Following the death of Ben Uncas III, the sachem party wanted to install his son, Isaiah, as successor, but the "Mason Party" under Occom opposed any settlement.[73] It wanted to get rid of not only the Uncas line of sachems but also the sachem form of government.[74] Without a sachem in place, the parties wrangled for control of the tribal council and, with it, the authority to distribute, lease, and sell the people's land and wood. The people's cultural direction was also in play. As one Connecticut official observed of the Mason Party, "Many of them that have Gone into the English way of Improvement have built houses & barns, and by Industry have acquired Good Stocks of Cattle and Sheep and the poorer Sort complain that they take up more

Land than they have right to[,] which Complaint is not Likely to Cease untill all are Equally Industrious or Equally Indolent."[75] At times, confrontations between the parties grew so heated that Zachary Johnson warned "murder will be commit[t]ed here soon."[76] This contest dragged on for years, and so did its racial tactics. The move to Oneida represented a chance for Johnson's opponents to escape these kind of accusations and, not incidentally, to pursue the "English way of Improvement" without resistance from their neighbors.

The coastal Indians' rejection of blacks was less a violation of their project's utopianism than a central part of it. Their aspiration to win God's favor through a universal religion was, ironically, premised on Indian unity against threats posed by white *and* black outsiders, most of whom were also Christian. Yet it was no more possible for the Christians Indians to shut out blacks than it was for them to escape whites. Both were part and parcel of an expansionist colonial regime that would follow the Indians wherever they went. As long as Indians and blacks continued mutually to suffer poverty, servitude, and racial prejudice under white rule, they would continue to find each other. Native leaders could forbid romances with blacks, but they could not halt these relationships. The struggles of New England's Christian Indians were inextricably linked to those of America's lowest caste.

A Promised Land

The Christian Indians' racial exclusivity reflected their utopian dream of transforming Native people into God's chosen ones. Joseph Johnson shared his belief with Connecticut's governor, Jonathan Trumbull, that "the sins past which our fore fathers and we their children have Sinfully Commit[t]ed, is the Cause of all these heavy Judgments, which my poor Nation is groaning & Sinking under."[77] Leaving for Oneida, where they could pursue Christian lives and proselytize neighboring Indians, was supposed to turn God's curse into a blessing, thereby allowing them to rise as a people. This vision was so intoxicating that on the eve of their migration, Indians on the Sound began to experience "a Religious Stir, and many Hopeful Conversions," as Occom characterized it.[78] Yet fear as well as hope spurred the Indians' revival. After all, they were about to leave places where their people had lived since time out of mind, where they knew the land and all the songs and stories their ancestors had invested in it. Their ancient ones, their loved ones, were buried there. Though Oneida country offered land and opportunity, it was not home. The coastal Indians called the Oneidas "brethren" and thought of them as fellow Indians, but the fact of the matter was that these groups as a whole were virtual strangers. For communities like the Montauketts, Narragansetts, and Niantics, accustomed to the bounty and unique rhythms of the sea, the challenge of adjusting to the northern woods was formidable. These factors alone justified Johnson characterizing the approaching migration as "the day of Trial...when the poor Remnant of Several Tribes Bordering on the Sea Shore shall be tried."[79]

Johnson and his brethren had another concern as well—the imperial crisis between Great Britain and its North American colonies, which had snowballed from a riotous dispute over taxes and sovereignty to the brink of an armed rebellion. Neither the Christian Indians nor the Oneidas had a direct stake in this affair, but they knew from past wars that there would be incredible pressure on them to choose sides if the colonies and the mother country came to blows. They also knew that having to choose might very well spell doom for their experiment, for they had relied on both colonial and royal power brokers to bring their town to fruition, and maintaining that broad base of support was crucial for the future. Joseph Johnson said it filled him with "sorrow" to behold "not only a civilized, but a Christian People Bleeding," but what weighed most heavily on his mind was ensuring that his own people would "have no concern in the bloody Scene which, it is to be feared[,] will shortly Commence in these Parts."[80] The Revolution added immeasurably to the tensions that already filled the Christian Indian movement. As Johnson and his Christian Indian brethren knew all too well, they would need God on their side if they were to have any hope of reaching their promised land.

CHAPTER 5

Exodus

B Y the end of the American Revolution, Samson Occom's pronounce-
ments about making the wilderness blossom like a rose had given way
to exhaustion and dark cynicism. To some degree, his bitterness was a
mere extension of his many physical ills. Occom had already been suffering from
a sore shoulder for years when in the winter of 1780 he also pulled out his hip
while loading a cart, leaving his back and leg in a state of nearly crippling chronic
pain.[1] To add insult to injury, a recurring lesion on his buttocks sometimes grew
too sore for him to ride his horse, his only means of transportation given his
poor health. These mounting ailments could not have come at a worse time.
Occom continued to sire children—ten in all—up to the year 1774 when he
was over fifty years old and Mary was in her mid-forties. With so many mouths
to feed, the couple simply could not afford to slow down, yet Occom was often
bedridden. During those times, everyone suffered. "We were never more needy
than we are now," Occom lamented in November 1783. "Wee are Moneyless,
bare of Clothing, nothing to eat only what wee pick up from Day to Day, by
my Folks makeing Baskets and Brooms."[2] Occom expected his older children to
help pick up the slack, and doubtless some of his six daughters did, but his eldest
son, the teenager Benoni, was of little use. Occom chastised him for falling into
"bad Company...Carousing, Drinking, Fiddling, Dancing, Cursing, Sw[e]ar-
ing, and Blaspheming the Holy Name of God."[3] Unfortunately, these lectures
were no more effective with Benoni than they had been with Occom's first son,
the prodigal Aaron, who died in his late teens in 1771 after burdening his parents with worry.[4] Unwilling to suffer another Aaron, Occom threw Benoni out
of the house, haunted all the while that his own shortcomings as a father were
at least partially responsible for the young man's behavior. And then there was
Occom's continued bile for Wheelock, which poured forth whenever the issue

of the college arose. "If I had Twenty Sons I would not send one there to be educated," Occom told anyone who cared to listen. "I would not do it that Honour."[5] Like the war-torn country in which he was living, Occom was hurting in body and spirit.

Occom's "Indian brethren" were reeling too, which thickened his dejection. Occom judged that the Revolution "has been the most Distructive to poor Indians of any wars that every happened in my Day, both as to their Spiritual and Temporal Injoyments." It is hard to disagree. Oneida country, like much of Indian country, had been reduced to a charred wasteland, and not only by redcoat and Tory forces out to punish the tribe for siding with the Americans but also by other Iroquois who had taken up the Union Jack. There was no chance of building a stable, Christian community under such conditions, so, despite the years of planning, the coastal Indians suspended their migration to Oneida. The harshest blow to the people was the loss of their men in the Continental Army, in which they served at a rate surpassing that of their white neighbors. Their sacrifice left one Indian community after another bereft of fathers, husbands, and sons with strong backs. They were "Stript ... almost Naked of every thing," as the Mohicans put it.[6] If ever the people needed God on their side it was then, yet religion had taken a back seat to war among Americans of all complexions. Even Samuel Kirkland had given up his missionary post among the Oneidas in favor of serving as chaplain to the Continental troops, something that, according to Occom, "prejudiced the minds of Indians against all Missionaries, especially against White Missionaries; Seven times more than anything, that was hear done by the White People."[7] Joseph Johnson's untimely death in 1776 to unknown causes summed up the Indians' tortured state of affairs. No one had been more active than Johnson in promoting the ideal of Christian Indian unity and trying to make it a reality.[8] Now he was gone.

Yet Johnson did not carry his dream with him. Desperation had always been the lifeblood of Indian Christianity, and Indians throughout the East were never more desperate than after the Revolution. As such, once Britain and the United States signed the Treaty of Paris in 1783 ending the war, the Christian Indians revived their experiment for Oneida country. The prospect even cheered Occom, who in 1786 called it "the most Glorious work of God amongst the Indians, that ever was seen anywhere." Hope for the future grounded in religious faith was what carried the Indians through their manifold troubles.

The people's heightened sense of themselves as Indians, as opposed to whites or blacks, also sustained the Christian Indian movement. Although the

Revolution led to a newfound emphasis on white political equality and the gradual emancipation of black slaves in the North, whites counterbalanced these enlightened trends by reasserting their supposedly fundamental differences with people of color, including Indians. White exploitation of Native people, in ways great and small, led the Indians' racial sensibilities to rise in kind. For instance, they began to refer to Euro-Americans as whites to a far greater degree than before. They elevated their own antipathy toward blacks and "race mixing." And they continued to attack their political rivals with racial barbs. It followed that they also clung more tightly than ever to the idea of Christian Indian unity.

"Present troubles"

The threat of war between Britain and the colonies loomed over the Northeast during the early to mid-1770s, unnerving the region's Indians no less than its whites. Since the New England Indians lived in the heartland of colonial opposition to Parliament and were vastly outnumbered and distrusted by the white majority, they knew they would receive no mercy if they so much as hinted at Tory sympathies. By contrast, the Oneidas were surrounded by fellow Iroquois sympathetic to the Crown who had the backing of the British at Johnson Hall to the east and Fort Niagara to the west. The Oneidas leaned toward the colonies out of religious predilection, but they were all too aware of their history of seizing Indian land at every opportunity. As western Iroquois warned, "The white people, particularly the Americans, are in nature treacherous & deceitful, have no true friendship for the Indians—& are not to be depended upon for aid & protections—no sooner have they obtained victory but they turn about, fall upon the Indians."[9] The British track record was not much better. For instance, although the Crown pledged to safeguard the Fort Stanwix Treaty line, its point man on Indian affairs, Sir William Johnson, was an avid speculator in Indian land. Trade offered no clear direction either. Britain ruled the waves, so it controlled the flow of goods on which Indians depended, yet colonists had the numbers to turn the Indians' settlements to dust. Suffice to say, the choice was between Scylla and Charybdis, and most Indians preferred not to choose at all.

Despite the shifting ground beneath their feet, the Christian Indians put their trust in God and continued with their plans to relocate to Oneida country. In May 1774, the heads of the Farmington Indians, Elijah Wimpey, Solomon Mossuck, and Samuel Adams wrote to Connecticut's governor, Jonathan Trumbull, for permission to divide and sell their lands in order to fund their migration, which, they believed, "will be best for ourselves & our Children & also tend to extend & advance the kingdom of Christ among the heathen Nations."[10] The colony eventually followed through by allotting sixty-five parcels at the Tunxis settlement of "Indian Neck."[11] The following February, Joseph Johnson told Eleazar Wheelock that he was about to head to Oneida with "upwards of Sixty young men from the Seven Tribes...who will do their uttermost to get good, and do good."[12] By his count, he had enlisted "from Mohegan 10, from Narragans[e]t 20, from Montauk on Long Island 13, from Nihantuck 5, from Farmington 10."[13] The Pequots of Mashantucket (or Groton) and Pawcatuck (or Stonington) promised to send some of their own the following season if they could free themselves from debt. In the meantime, men from the other communities would serve as an advance party to clear and plant the land and build houses. Women, children, and the elderly were supposed to join them once this base was secure.

Yet, to Johnson's chagrin, the same "White People in New England" who had for so long "wanted to get rid of us" suddenly demanded the Christian Indians to stay put. The reason, they said, was that they wanted the Indians to be available for the patriot cause in the event of war, something that turned out to be just a month away. More to the point, they worried that once the Indians had reached the safety of Oneida, they would join the British and fall on their former neighbors to avenge a long train of abuses. The Christian Indians' white employers refused to pay them back wages "unless they wou'd stay and fight," knowing that without the money the Indians could not afford to leave. Other colonists made the Natives "fear of their Lives for Coming away." In Farmington a mob of "White People" threatened Joseph Johnson that "it wou'd be best to knock all the Indians in the head rather than that they Should go to the Mohawk Country."[14] Johnson, always a quick wit, responded, "It seemed to me [a] Matter of great Surprize that as the People of New England had got almost all our Lands from us, and thereby Oblig'd us to go else where, Shou'd want to Stop us now," but his cleverness got him nowhere. The crowd was alarmed by rumors that Johnson had visited Boston to throw his support to British General Thomas Gage, the newly appointed military governor of Massachusetts. Johnson protested that he had done nothing of the sort, to which the people of Farmington warned him, "It was lucky I did not go there for they would assuredly have cut off my head when I came back." Even Governor Jonathan Trumbull, who had previously supported the Christian Indians, refused to issue a pass for them to leave the colony. He counseled Johnson and Occom that "these were troublesome times, and it was better for us to Stay at home in our own Country, & take Care, for People wou'd think we went up to the Northward to be made Colonels and Captains, and Such like Officers." The Indians' track record of Christianity and military service among their white neighbors made no difference at all.

Though Occom pleaded with his followers that "You cannot possibly die before your time, did you desire it ever so much; and my Advice is that you regard not the Rumours of a discontended People," white intimidation succeeded in shrinking the advance party from its original group of sixty to a modest band of the committed.[15] This unit included only some three Montauketts (David Fowler among them), six Narragansetts (including James and Peter Shattock, John Skeesuck, and Samuel Talman), two Tunxis (Samuel Adams and Elijah Wimpey), and perhaps some others.[16] They were woefully short of funds and supplies, but still they took to the road "rather than it shoul'd be said that not one had Courage enough to come from the Eastern Indians."[17] Fortunately for them, they received the assistance of Guy Johnson, who in July 1774 had taken over as Britain's northern superintendent of Indian affairs following the sudden death of his uncle, Sir William. The party's bare arrival in Oneida should have been counted a success given how dramatically conditions had turned against them in a matter of months. Occom was less sanguine, confessing, "I am Sorry, so few Indians are going up to Onoyda this Spring, yet I hope they will keep moving up more and more."[18]

Occom penned these words just days before the Battles of Lexington and Concord, which marked the opening shots of the Revolution and a temporary end to the Christian Indians' experiment. It took only a few weeks for the fighting to spread to the eastern edge of Iroquoia, which augured that Oneida country would be one of the front lines in this war. Truth was one of the first casualties. Rumors raced back and forth that Guy Johnson was going to raise an Iroquois force to terrorize colonial settlements, that colonial militia were going to seize Johnson Hall, that the redcoats were going to invade New York from Canada, and that the Americans were going to invade Canada from New York. The Indians implored British and colonial officials alike to respect their neutrality, but they knew the chance of that happening was slim. Even their own people became quick to assume the worst about each other. Shortly after the Christian Indians broke ground in Oneida, western Iroquois began threatening violence against them out of fear that the settlement was an advance post for white revolutionaries. It took only until June 1775 for the looming danger of Seneca attack or of getting caught in British and American crossfire to convince them that it was "best for their safety and the Peace of the Country to return for the present from whence they Came, untill the present Troubles shall be ended."[19] That would be some time.

"See how these Christians love each other?"

Throughout the early stages of the revolutionary crisis, Christian Indians defied customary associations of whiteness and Christianity and of Indianness and paganism by admonishing whites (and one another) to heed Jesus' peaceful teachings. In the summer of 1774, Joseph Johnson lectured Sir William Johnson that it grieved him to "see a Brother, taking up arms against a Brother. Is this the fruits of Christianity—what will the heathen Nations Say[?] O Britain! O North America! Can the heathens Say, Behold and See how those Christians love one another?"[20] Occom raised his own questions about the faith of whites in a conversation with the Oneidas. He observed, "If all Mankind in the World, Believed in Jesus Christ with all their Hearts, there would be no more Wars, they would live as one Family in Peace." With whites at each other's throats, it fell unto Indians to preach the meaning of Christian fellowship. "Use all your Influence, to your Brethren so far as you have any Connections to keep them in Peace and quietness," Occom counseled the Oneidas, emphasizing "not to entermeddle in these Quarrils among the White People."[21]

Occom chose these words carefully. In Occom's personal experience and in the fight between Britain and its colonies, self-proclaimed Christians had proven themselves to be anything but Christ-like, whereas the supposed heathens had struggled against formidable odds to create a godly community of fellow believers. It no longer made sense for him to use "Christian" as a shorthand for European and "savage" as a shorthand for Indians, as colonists did. Occom also stopped using "English" to refer to any and all Europeans in the British colonies. This term had been rendered moot by the colonies' fight against mother England and the flood of non-English migrants into the British colonies after 1760. "White" was a more appropriate catchall for the times, particularly given the racial hierarchy that continued to structure American society. The category of Indian had also grown more meaningful than ever for Occom. The Christian Indian movement alone, by its very definition, had imbued him with an enhanced sense of fellowship with Native people and of difference with whites. The imperial crisis reinforced such thinking by spurring whites' heightened suspicion and intimidation of Indians even amid their frequent expressions of enlightened principles to justify opposition to Britain. Whites could proclaim high and low that their revolutionary commitment to equality and justice was going to make the world anew, but for Indians like Occom, the war held little promise regardless of the victor. As Occom explained to one of his British correspondents, "There is a great confusion among the White People yet, between Royalests, Whigs, and Tories, but this is none of my Business. For Indians are neither Whigs nor Tories."[22]

Occom's peers agreed and, in lieu of building their Christian Indian town, did everything they could to promote Indian neutrality. The migrants returned home with a request from the Oneidas to colonial officials to "Let us Indians be all of one mind, and live in peace with one another, and you white people settle your own disputes betwixt yourselves."[23] They also wanted the New England colonies metaphorically to "open the road wide" between the coast and Iroquoia so that the Christian Indians could travel back and forth unhindered. Despite the dangers along this path, David Fowler and Joseph Johnson spent the last months of 1775 on a mission from the Continental Congress to encourage the "back nations" near Fort Pitt in western Pennsylvania to resist British pressure and sit out the war.[24] Johnson, who died around this time, might very well have lost his life in this service, his death a sign of the diminishing prospects for Indian neutrality. Though the western Iroquois rebuffed British entreaties throughout 1776, their resolve weakened as redcoat victories mounted.

Amid the pressures of war, even the Christian Indians turned on each other. Johnson was shocked to learn that rumors of him having become a "high tory" had been planted by none other than his closest Farmington ally, Elijah Wimpey. Johnson could not fathom this betrayal except to say that Wimpey was "a subtle, crafty person" who probably envied "the respect that I receive from white people every where; and more especially . . . that I have so much influence among my western brethren."[25] Yet Wimpey might have had genuine concerns about Johnson's loyalty. Though Johnson insisted that he supported the American cause, in fact he played to his audience. For instance, a message he sent to Colonel Guy Johnson via David Fowler derided Americans' claims of friendship to Indians. "As for friends," Johnson remarked, "these People among whom we dwell, what have they done for us? Any good, or no? they have taken away most of our Lands, and doubtless they wou'd, many of them [like] to have poor Indians as their Slaves."[26] Five years earlier, comments like these would hardly have raised an eyebrow, but in wartime they came to the attention of the New York and Connecticut Assemblies.[27] Investigators quickly exonerated Johnson of any wrongdoing, and Wimpey himself admitted to having spoken "unkind words against the New-England people with indignation." Nevertheless, the sad fact remained that the coastal Indians' migration was only a few months old before a serious crack appeared in their foundation of Christian unity.

The Christian Indians' return to the coast from Oneida brought no end to this factionalism. At Mohegan, those people who had remained at home opposed restoring full political and economic rights to those who had left, however temporarily. These stalwarts, as members of the sachem party, had celebrated the Christian Indians' relocation as a means to rid themselves of their rivals. Yet the migrants had scarcely taken to the road before they were back again, behaving as if nothing had changed. The sachem party's leader, "Old Zachary" Johnson, picked up where he had left off by charging that his opponents had no place at Mohegan as racial and ethnic outsiders.[28] He complained to Hartford that "Original Natives" like him were oppressed by "Strange Indians and disorderly white People," as he characterized them in one petition, and "a Number of Indians and Negros and others now Residing in Mohegan and not proper Inhabitants," as he called them in another. These "strangers" were "headed and assisted by a certain Indian Minister" (certainly Occom) whom Johnson resented for being "determined, as he says, to have the ordering of all the Indian Concerns."[29]

Zachary Johnson's tactics simultaneously drew on a traditional form of indigenous politics while also exploiting the racial sensitivities of the times. New England Indians had a history of defining their communities as a group of people loyal to a particular sachem lineage, and that faction at Mohegan was headed by Zachary Johnson.[30] Indians also defined their communities genealogically. People with deep local roots were considered to be "natural inhabitants," whereas those who had arrived from elsewhere were "strangers," even after a few generations.[31] "Strangers" were welcome as long as they supported the politics of the "native born." When they did not, the oldest families castigated them as unwelcome intruders. For instance, in 1760 Ben Uncas III had dismissed opponents of his rule as "not Mohegans but by marriage indulged to live amongst us," and asked Hartford "to deprive them of the priviledges they enjoy by living amongst us, if they wont be Loyall Subjects to the present Sachem."[32] Johnson's charge that his enemies were outsiders was in the same vein. At the same time, Johnson's employment of racial language in the midst of the Revolution carried more than a tinge of demagoguery. Johnson must have been aware that whites were increasingly anxious about people of color, including slaves, who were boldly claiming that the natural rights trumpeted by revolutionaries should apply to them too.

Moreover, in New England, in particular, growing numbers of blacks were gain-
ing freedom through service in the Continental ranks or manumission after their
masters concluded that slavery was indeed incompatible with republican principles.[33] In this context, Johnson's portrayal of his sachem party as a respectable
community of landowners besieged by lawless racial others was likely to find a
sympathetic audience among Connecticut's governing elite. It was through such
tactics that the language of race became salient and racial categories acquired
practical meaning.

The New England Indians' dark politics paled in comparison to the inter-
necine battles of the Iroquois. Though the Iroquois professed neutrality from
the earliest days of the Revolution, they were also prepared to break this pledge
whenever circumstances required.[34] To the east of the Oneidas, the Mohawks
volunteered to guard Johnson Hall against any patriot attack and protected Guy
Johnson on his retreat from New York to British-controlled Canada. Meanwhile,
the Mohawk parvenu, Joseph Brant, a former Wheelock student, sailed to London to ensure that the Crown would reward Mohawk loyalty, then returned to
Iroquoia to rally his tribesmen "to defend their Lands & Liberty against the
Rebels, who in great measure begin this Rebellion to be sole Masters of this
Continent."[35] To the west, British officers at Fort Niagara showered trade goods
on the Onondagas, Cayugas, and populous Senecas, with promises of more if
those tribes took up the hatchet on the king's behalf. If all this was not enough to
make the Oneidas feel encircled by pressure to go to war, Iroquois from the St.
Lawrence mission towns to the north were fighting in small numbers alongside
the British to turn back the Continental Army's bungled invasion of Quebec.
Even the Continental Congress began to send mixed signals about its respect for
Oneida neutrality. It commissioned two agents fluent in the language and customs of the Oneidas, Samuel Kirkland and the interpreter James Dean, to pledge
the country's friendship for the Iroquois and to explain its case against Britain.
Publicly, both men called for the Oneidas to remain on the sidelines, but in private they worked to ease the tribe into the American camp.[36] Recognizing that
neutrality was impossible to sustain under these conditions, in April 1777 League
sachems extinguished the council fire at Onondaga, the people's ancient symbol
of peace and unity.[37] A few months later, Congress garrisoned Fort Stanwix at
the Oneida Carrying Place and renamed it Fort Schuyler after one of Albany's
leading patriot families.[38] American officials claimed that the fort's purpose was
to protect Oneida country from British incursions and settler encroachment.

In fact, they had created a target that would bring greater devastation to the Oneidas than any war in memory.

Blasted

After a year of plots and posturing, the Iroquois finally confronted each other at opposite ends of the gun during the anticipated British strike against Fort Schuyler in August 1777.[39] From the direction of Fort Niagara, Lieutenant-Colonel Barry St. Leger led some fifteen hundred men, including perhaps nine hundred Indians (mostly Senecas and Cayugas) into Oneida country as part of a two-pronged British invasion of New York from Canada. At Saratoga, this campaign turned into the most significant British defeat of the war with the exception of Yorktown, but that was cold comfort for the Oneidas watching the war descend on their country. After the British lifted the siege of Fort Schuyler, Loyalist Iroquois put the Oneida town of Oriskany to the torch to punish the residents for supporting the Americans.[40] The Oneidas responded in kind, sacking the Mohawk villages of Canajoharie (also known as Mohawk Upper Castle) and Fort Hunter (or Mohawk Lower Castle). For more than two centuries, the Iroquois League had managed to prevent open warfare among its member tribes through shared ritual and open communication. With the Revolution, the great peace seemed to be on the verge of disintegrating.

Moderate sachems scrambled desperately to pull League warriors back from the brink, but they faced steep odds. The Senecas, Cayugas, Mohawks, and portions of the Onondagas, Tuscaroras, and even Oneidas (mostly from Onaquaga) were firmly committed to the royalist cause, while a majority of Oneidas and at most half of the Tuscaroras sided with the rebels. The Onondagas, the central Iroquois nation and the traditional peacemaker, tried but failed to broker a consensus, but they did manage to keep the contending parties from attacking each other directly for almost two years.[41] Instead, League warriors trained their attacks on white settlements, turning the New York and Pennsylvania frontier into a bloody ground of terror throughout 1778.[42] Yet this tenuous balancing act could not last for long given the determination of British and American officials to take the war directly to their Iroquois enemies.

The Continental Army responded to attacks by Brant's loyalist forces with a mission "totally to extirpate all the unfriendly nations of the Indians, to subdue their Country, to destroy their Crops, and force them to seek habitations where they would be less troublesome to us & their allies."[43] The thrust of this campaign took place in the late summer and fall of 1779, when General John Sullivan marched 4,500 men up the Susquehanna River to ravage Cayuga and Seneca country. By the time Sullivan's men were done, they had burned an estimated 160,000 bushels of corn, forty-one villages, and vast amounts of other property.[44] There were few human casualties, since most of the people had fled to Niagara, but Sullivan cruelly calculated that starvation and exposure would stalk loyalist Iroquois during the upcoming winter. Little did he know that his campaign would also heap misery on the patriot Oneidas.

Though the Oneidas had contributed little more than scouts to Sullivan's campaign, they realized that the stakes had been raised and that they could no longer hope to escape the wrath of their Iroquois kin—that is, as long as they continued to side with the Americans.[45] Some of them decided this was too steep a price to pay for their loyalty, so they made the long trek to join the rest of the League nations at Niagara. After Brant's men torched Kanawalohare, most of the other Oneidas headed eastward to the American town of Schenectady, just north of Albany.[46] They were safe from attack there, but in the camp their lives were a pitiful struggle against malnutrition, exposure, and disease, including smallpox. The Oneidas even suffered harassment and at least one murder at the hands of American troops who were supposed to protect them.[47] Predictably, the civilian population treated the Oneida refugees no better. Liquor peddlers appeared in their camp day after day despite the pleas of Oneida leaders that drink was slowly killing them. The environment was ripe for trouble when an unfounded charge of murder led local whites to declare that they would kill any Oneida they happened across.[48] Divided, demoralized, and depleted, the Oneidas had suffered mightily for the independence of an ungrateful people.

Though their homelands were spared direct fighting, the coastal Indians experienced painful losses of their own during the war. At first, military authorities refused to allow Indians to enlist in the Continental ranks, largely out of a fear that the British would respond in kind. Yet as manpower shortages and assaults by Britain's Indian allies escalated, these restrictions broke down and Indian men began joining the army, navy, and privateers in large numbers.[49] The Mohegans, a community of perhaps fifty families, ultimately sacrificed at least seventeen men and probably more, given that the community contained twenty-five widows by war's end.[50] Among the dead were four sons of Samuel Ashbo and five of Rebecca Tanner. They were "all she had," according to Samson Occom.[51] The Pequots lost at least fifteen of their men out of a population of less than two hundred.[52] Nearly every Tunxis man of fighting age marched against the British, as did a sizable portion of the Narragansetts, though precise figures are elusive.[53] The causes of the Revolution meant nothing to these people, for as Indians they had no English rights to fight for, yet they had everything to lose by failing to serve and something to gain by enlisting. With the American economy in tatters, the signing bonus and occasional paychecks of a soldier were practically the only way for a young man to make money. Additionally, the risks were counterbalanced by the opportunity to garner personal prestige and demonstrate the community's support of neighboring whites. Given that "Join or Die" was the slogan of the day, joining was not only the wise choice but also, perhaps, the only one.

Except for the Oneidas, no Indian community sacrificed more for the American cause than the Stockbridges. As war tensions mounted, Stockbridge sent diplomats to Iroquois communities in New York and Canada and to the Delawares and Shawnees in western Pennsylvania to urge them to neutrality.[54] Yet the Mohicans themselves plunged into the American cause as soon as the fighting began, serving alongside white patriots in nearly every battle in the northeast theater, from Bunker Hill to the Brandywine.[55] They attracted the enemy's attention wherever they were, partially because Indians were so rare among the Americans but also because their fighting prowess commanded respect. One Hessian fighter recalled after his unit fought a bloody battle with the Stockbridges in 1778, "No Indians, especially, received quarter." By war's end, Stockbridge had lost as many as forty men, including the chief Abraham Nimham.[56] It was a staggering blow for a community of just some three hundred people. Without their men, the remaining Stockbridges were reduced to begging the provincial government for clothing and selling off more of their already meager lands to keep their creditors at bay.[57]

Even amid their losses, the Mohicans assisted fellow Indians who shared their support for the American campaign. When the coastal Indians decided to abandon their nascent settlement in Oneida, some forty-four of them took shelter with the Stockbridges. Their numbers included the leading Tunxis men, Elijah Wimpey and Samuel Adams, and one of the Christian movement's organizers, David Fowler. The Narragansett Daniel Simons even served as Stockbridge's schoolteacher during the war.[58] Doubtless longstanding ties between these communities facilitated this arrangement; the Tunxis and Mohegans, for instance, already had some people living among the Stockbridges before the Revolution began, and the Stockbridges and Mohegans had served together against the French in the Seven Years' War.[59] The two groups' mutual English contacts also contributed to their alliance. Both Stockbridge and the coastal Indians had sent

Figure 6. A Mohican Warrior in the Continental Army. This sketch of a Stockbridge Indian warrior serving with the American army was drawn by Johann Ewald, a Hessian who fought for the British. The Stockbridges, like their Christian Indian counterparts from Long Island Sound and Oneida, served in large numbers during the Revolution, only to discover that their sacrifice had earned them little gratitude and no refuge from their white American neighbors. *Captain Johann Ewald Diary,* vol. II, Joseph P. Tustin Papers, Special Collections, Harvey A. Andruss Library, Bloomsburg University of Pennsylvania.

children to Wheelock's school, and they had a connection through Samuel Kirkland, who kept a house in Stockbridge for his family while he was away working among the Oneidas, sometimes alongside Occom, Joseph Johnson, the Fowler brothers, and other Indians from the Sound.[60] Adding to the mix, some Oneidas also fled to Stockbridge late in the war. The Mohicans and Oneidas had been involved in each others' histories for centuries as trading partners, confederates, kin, and sometimes even enemies. More recently, the Oneidas had sent some of their children to the Stockbridge Indian school, while the Mohicans had discussed moving to the Susquehanna under Iroquois auspices.[61] The Revolution brought these groups even closer together. Wimpey spoke for all of the Indians in Stockbridge when he bemoaned that his people "for their Fidelity and Attachment to the American Cause have Suffered the Loss of all Things, been compelled to fly from their habitations, leaving those Means of Subsistence behind, with which God had blessed them, and to sojourn where they could find a Place," thus reducing them to "little more than a bare Existence."[62] Companions in their misery, the Oneidas, Mohicans, and coastal tribes held up one another, compared their fortunes, and reopened earlier discussions about building a better future together.

Glorious

Allying with the United States had cost the Indians dearly. At least one young man was missing from nearly every family, and the strain radiated outward from individual homes into every sector of society. The people had also lost vast amounts of property either to enemy forces, in the case of the Oneidas, or to debt and unrelenting encroachment by neighboring whites, especially in the case of the Stockbridges. Divisions that ran deep before the war became more entrenched than ever after it: the politics of the New England Indians had continued to degenerate into charges of race-mixing, while the Iroquois League had split in two, with many Loyalists choosing to relocate to the Grand River Valley of southern Ontario, within the boundaries of British Canada, rather than take their chances with the victorious Americans. The most foreboding sign of all was the widespread American insistence that Indians as a whole had fought against them during the Revolution, and with unrestrained barbarity at that. They conveniently forgot the contributions and sacrifices of the Oneidas, Stockbridges, and coastal tribes to the American cause. It followed that whites also refused to acknowledge the moral debt the nation owed these people.

Instead, the call went up that Indians as a race were bloodthirsty savages inimical to the very principles for which the Revolution had been fought. The Indians' wartime atrocities, real and imagined, were enough to fuel white Indian hating; that Indians possessed lands craved by whites added a practical motivation to the invective. The Oneidas and their New England brethren might have fought for an American victory, but they soon discovered that there was no winning for Indians, whatever sacrifices they made.

In the face of these inestimable challenges, the Indians renewed their plan to transform Oneida into a Christian Indian bastion. To no small degree, this strategy was but an extension of the Oneidas' earlier plan to settle displaced people on territory otherwise at risk of falling into white hands. However, more than ever before, the hope of attaining God's favor for Indian people loomed large in their thinking. The Oneidas' urgency could not have been clearer than in their 1784 appeal to Samuel Kirkland to revive his mission. Their leaders explained:

We have been for many Years attending to the vast differences betwixt white people & Indians. We have laboured much to investigate the cause. We can no longer be idle spectators, for the one are in prosperous Circumstances & have many priviledges, the other are indigent & wretched. The one appears to be the favorites of Heaven & honourable in the sight of men, the other to be despised & rejected by both.

At this moment, at least, the Oneidas knew what they had to do:

We must alter our conduct. We must give up our pagan customs. We must unite all our wisdom & strength to cultivate [in] the manner & civilization of the white people who are thus distinguished by the favour & protection of the great Spirit above, & embrace the religion of the divine Jesus or we Indians shall before many years be not only dispised by the nations of the Earth, but utterly rejected by the Lord Jesus the saviour of the white people.[63]

To achieve these ambitious, even cosmic, ends, the Oneidas renewed their invitation to the coastal Indians to move to Iroquoia and then extended a similar offer to the Stockbridges.[64] Kirkland reported that the Oneidas "expect in the course of two years to have more than 1000 Indians in their vicinity, who will be disposed to attend the word of God & among those, some heart lovers of the religion of Jesus, *to use their own* expression."[65]

The Oneidas were being too optimistic in terms of numbers, but there was no questioning the sense of divine mission behind the project. A group of approximately fifty coastal Indians arrived in Oneida in 1783, followed the next year by another hundred migrants plus an advance party of Stockbridges.[66] By 1785, Samson Occom could report that there were only eight Indian families left at Farmington and that two-thirds of the Stockbridges had already left for Oneida.[67] The migration continued in fits and starts for a decade until by the early 1790s there were more than three hundred Stockbridges and at least half as many coastal Indians in Iroquoia.[68] The two groups planted their communities side by side along Oriske Creek, desperately hoping that this new chapter of their lives would bring them into God's fold. As the Stockbridges expressed it to Occom, "Now it looks Dark upon us[,] all helps from abroad are gone. And we are brought to look about and Consider of our Situation, and we believe that this will be the last, that God will make a Trial with us—if this will not set us to contrive for our own Souls,—God will leave us to our own Distruction."[69] *If* was the critical word here. The Indians were undoubtedly terrified of divine judgment, but the corollary was that banding together to live like Christians would win God's favor. The coastal Indians captured this spirit in the name they chose for their new settlement—Brothertown.

The Indians got off to a promising start even when measured against their own high expectations. This was particularly true with regard to their religious life, as evidenced by the effect of Brothertown's piety on Occom. In October 1785, Occom rode into Brothertown after a long journey from Connecticut in cold, damp weather, the kind of drudgery that made his body ache and his morale droop. Yet as he approached the house of David Fowler, "I heard a Melodious Sin[g]ing, a number were together Sin[g]ing Psalms hymns and Spiritual Song," some of which might have been Occom's own compositions. The music lifted his soul, as did his recognition that he was now among Christian family. The people, he rejoiced, "all took hold of my Hand one by one then they began to Sing again, and Some Time after, I have then a few words of Exhortation and then Conclude with Prayer." After years of suffering, Occom could finally write, "The Lord be praised for his great goodness to us."[70] Meetings such as this, held in barns, cabins, or outdoors and characterized by singing, praying, and lay preaching, were the lifeblood of Brothertown's Christianity. Eventually, the Indians had formal worship too. Kirkland revived his mission among the Oneidas after the war, finding them "greatly waked up to the concern of their Souls," while the Stockbridges were joined in Oneida by missionary John Sergeant Jr., son of the first man to proselytize them.[71] Occom spent most of the 1780s traveling back and forth between Brothertown, where he had relocated most of his family, and the diminished Indian communities of the coast, but finally he agreed to minister to Brothertown and Stockbridge full-time beginning in 1787. Stockbridge welcomed him by proclaiming "the goodness of God, for Raising and lifting one of our own Collour, to be Instrumental to build up the Cause and the Kingdom of the Lord Jesus Christ."[72] The dream of creating Christian towns in the wilderness appeared to be materializing.

The Christian migrants also followed through on their intent to proselytize neighboring Indian people, even though they were busy establishing themselves anew. Their most visible and perhaps most common approach was to host foreign Indians at their religious events. For instance, in the mid-1780s, Occom recorded Oneidas and Stockbridges jointly attending a prayer meeting at the house of Brothertown's David Fowler, Oneidas attending a Christian Stockbridge wedding, Oneidas spending the night in Brothertown for the Sabbath, and more.[73] Additionally, Occom, Kirkland, and Sergeant trekked throughout Oneida country to conduct weddings and funerals and proselytize.[74] By the 1790s, Stockbridge's rising leader, Hendrick Aupaumut, was actively promoting Christianity among the Ohio Valley and Great Lakes tribes. He told them that if they followed the same course as the Stockbridges, "the great and good spirit will bless you that you will become a wise people, and you shall increase, both in number and substance, consequently you will be happy in this life, and the life to come."[75] This was the mantra for the Christian Indians of Oneida country.

The Brothertowns and Stockbridges also expected to have the civilized example of their towns draw neighboring Indians to Christianity. Even though the Indians arrived in Oneida country impoverished, without tools or livestock, within just a few years they had managed to lay the foundation for what could only be called God-fearing farming towns. By the 1790s, Occom was conducting an evening school for young people at New Stockbridge, which included lessons on reading and speaking English, while Brothertown had a school led by an unidentified "sober Indian woman."[76] To this, Stockbridge added a "spinning school" to teach girls how to process wool from the Mohicans' growing flocks of sheep.[77] In 1796, ministers Jeremy Belknap and Jedidiah Morse found that at Stockbridge "two-thirds of the men and nine-tenths of the women are industrious. Agriculture and the breeding of cattle and swine are their chief employment by which they procure a sufficiency of food; and by selling part of their produce they are able to purchase their clothing."[78] Quaker missionaries agreed, judging Stockbridge men to be "sober & well disposed" and the women to contain "some remarkably Religious characters."[79] The Brothertowns struck them as having "made some improvement in agriculture, industry and sobriety," as represented by their "good Cattle, Cows and working Oxen" and their "good disposition…to improve their moral conduct and in agricultural knowledge."[80] It was enough to make the Society of Friends conclude that Stockbridge and Brothertown had no pressing need for their services.[81]

The Christian Indians were able to implement these changes as quickly as they did by virtue of their relative isolation from white society. Before arriving in Oneida, when they lived cheek by jowl with the English, they had complained repeatedly that whites could not legitimately criticize them for failing to become civilized farmers while simultaneously fleecing them of their land. If whites merely afforded them some peace, the Indians contended, they would prove themselves. The early development of Brothertown and New Stockbridge showed them to be right. This is not to say that Brothertown and Stockbridge were utopias—among several problems, their people were wracked by political divisions over governance and land use. Nevertheless, the first decade of the Christian experiment held out hope that the Indians would finally attract God's blessing. That is, until the whites came.

CHAPTER 6

Cursed

I N October of 1784, Samson Occom witnessed the most uplifting spectacle to have crossed his eyes in several years. At the end of a treaty conference at Fort Stanwix, hundreds of Iroquois and American delegates gathered around a freshly dug grave in which "the Indians buried their old Cruel Hatchet very deep in the Ground... and the [Americans] broke their Bloody Sword and lay'd it on the grave of the Hatchet... and the Burying was attended with Great Pompe, Rejoycing, and Shouting." The two groups of former enemies then sat down to smoke from the Indians' "Long Pipe of Peace" to represent their "oneness or Union" and send their prayers up to the heavens. The spirit was still flowing when an elderly chief called on this throng to rise and form a "seven fold Circle" for a dance set to "the Song of Peace of Love." Pounding drums, chanting voices, and hundreds of stomping moccasins and boots created a "Tremble and Rumble" that Occom felt pulsate through his core, like an embodiment of the Indians' precept that allies should share a single heart. Indeed, there was no way to distinguish between dancers in this whirling dervish, for scalp locks and brimmed hats, tailored coats and trade blankets faded into a single tableau. Enraptured, Occom gushed, "Now I think that this Land may truely be call'd the Land of Peace, Unity, Freedom, Liberty, and Independence."[1]

A mere seven years later, Occom's effusive optimism was nearly dead and buried, replaced by the fear that Indians were doomed because "Heaven and Earth, are in Combination against us." After the dancing ended at Fort Stanwix, Indians across New York faced a barrage of schemes by whites to bilk them of their land. Among the victims were the Oneidas, Brothertowns, and Stockbridges, despite their service to the United States and their efforts to live as civilized Christians. By the 1790s, all of the problems that had driven the Christian Indians from the coast were back on their doorstep: land loss, factional battles, poverty, alcohol abuse, and discrimination at white hands. It was enough to make some of them conclude that Indians as a group were literally cursed by God, and not as punishment for their own actions but for the sins of their ancestors. They would rise like the white people when, and only when, God decided they had paid the debt for their forefathers' wrongdoing. The torturous question was whether their people could survive the curse long enough to see it lifted.

"A League of White People"

The Oneidas had begun to feel the pressure of white settlement in the years leading up to the Revolution, but it took the war and its political fallout to direct this expansion energetically toward their country. During the Revolution, the federal and state governments recruited soldiers with land bounties and applied for foreign credit with future land sales as collateral, land that could only come from Indians, enemy or otherwise. With the war's end, it was time to make good on those pledges. Even in peacetime, Indian land remained an invaluable resource for white leaders, for meeting the public's demand for a piece of Indian country was a sure way to drum up votes and raise funds without new taxes. Furthermore, with American federalism more of a theory than a practice at this point and with state boundaries and even the international border with Canada fluid and contested, especially in and around Iroquoia, governments saw their ability to negotiate Indian land cessions as a means of establishing their spheres of jurisdiction. Given such pressures, Congress's promise to the Oneidas in 1783 "that the lands which they claim as their inheritance will be reserved for their sole use and benefit" was pure cant.[2]

A self-serving moral imperative also played an important role in white designs on Oneida country. Whites generally considered it to be God's will that hunting people should make way for farmers, since hunters supposedly left the land in a natural state, whereas farmers abided by the divine order to be fruitful and multiply. The Oneidas' hoe agriculture, performed as it was by women, not men, and without plows, fences, livestock, and fertilizer, did not meet white definitions of farming—few whites bothered to note that these outward signs of civility had been on the rise among the Oneidas before the devastation of the Revolution. It did not help the Oneidas' case that their cornfields usually extended no further than the immediate surroundings of their villages. Most of their country, six million acres inhabited by just six hundred people, was "wilderness" in the view of most whites, displaying little of the human enterprise that whites associated with proprietorship. By contrast, under white American tenure, the forest would be converted into productive farms and buzzing market towns supporting an exponentially larger population. As whites framed the issue, civilized people were going to possess the Oneidas' country one way or another. The only question was whether the Oneidas were going to adopt civilized ways too and thus hold on to part (and only part) of their lands or else recede with the woods. Few whites expected or actively encouraged the Oneidas to pick civility.

Oneida leaders were too desperate and divided to hold out against these pressures to sell. Their people had already lost their homes and farming equipment to the war when famine struck in the late 1780s, leaving them "wretchedly poor" and starving.[3] Sachems were supposed to care for the needy and defend the people's territory, but these responsibilities proved to be incompatible. White authorities were unequivocal that, without land cessions, they would not give the Indians protection from the burgeoning white population or, for that matter, provide them with food and supplies to ease the famine. Oneida sachems had little choice but to consent. Longstanding divisions between Christian Oneidas clustered at Kanawalohare under Agwelondongwas and Skenandoah and the so-called Pagan Party concentrated at Oriskany under the Cornelius and Doxtater families provided an additional incentive for land sales. Lacking any confidence that the other side would put the public good ahead of private gain, these rivals raced to beat each other to the profits of selling tribal territory. Occasionally the Oneidas sold land out of sheer drunkenness, for white land jobbers routinely lubricated them with alcohol before making their offers. Overall, then, for Oneida leaders to refuse to sell land would have required them to forsake their followers to hunger and the mercy of white settlers, to risk antagonizing powerful white governments, to cede valuable resources to political opponents, and to abstain from an addictive drug. The challenge was simply too great, and, in any case, whites were going to use any means necessary to get Indian signatures on their documents.

The corruption underlying the Treaty of Fort Herkimer of 1785 proves the point. The Oneidas arrived at the conference table to protest a land deed in which the speculator and merchant Colonel John Harper—a former Wheelock student—claimed a tract six miles wide by twenty-four miles long in the southern part of their territory. The Oneidas refused to recognize this paper since it had been signed by just one of their sachems and two warriors, all of them drunk with Harper's grog. Furthermore, the Oneidas had repeated assurances from white authorities that, as allies to the United States during the Revolution,

they would never have to part with their lands and certainly not through informal negotiations. Yet whites had made such promises only when they needed
the Oneidas' support. Now they wanted Oneida land, and Harper's deed was
New York's opening to seize it. Though Albany judged Harper's claim to be illegal, it pressured the Oneidas to cede the same area to the state based on the
argument that since whites were already squatting there under Harper's terms, it
was best for everyone to have them living under state law. The Oneidas hedged
that they might be willing to *lease* some lands to whites as "an income to our
Children," but they had no interest in selling. Agwelondongwas explained, "We
look to the Eastward. The Indians who lived there are now settled among Us and
We have been obliged to give them Lands. This will be the Case should We sell
our lands as they have done."[4] Yet New York would not take no for an answer.
Albany bluntly asserted that without a cession it would do nothing to protect
the Oneidas against future incursions by settlers or machinations by speculators.
Given that New York's population had grown to 240,000 people—and was rising
every day—and that land jobbers were swarming around Oneida country like
sharks smelling blood, this was no empty threat. Duly intimidated, the Oneidas
decided to cut their losses, accepting a lump sum of $11,500 for 460,000 acres of
land—which New York then turned around and marketed to whites at ten times
the buying price.

New York's protection was hardly worthy of the name. It took less than a
year before the Oneidas fell victim to another scheme to steal their territory,
this time at the hands of New York's richest man, John Livingston. Prevented
by state law from purchasing Indian lands (a right New York reserved to itself),
Livingston formed a corporation made up of his well-heeled friends to negotiate
leases that amounted to permanent sales. He began with the western Iroquois,
manipulating them into renting nearly all of their remaining estate for 999 years
in return for $20,000 down and $2,000 annually. Then he turned to the Oneidas.
Livingston's tactic of bribing chiefs and offering shares in his company to the
Oneidas' interpreters and cultural brokers, such as Samuel Kirkland and James
Dean, enabled him to acquire another 999-year lease, this one for five million
acres, in exchange for a modest sum.[5] These terms left the Oneidas with only a
250,000-acre reservation on Oneida Lake and some fishing stations. Eventually
Albany declared this lease invalid despite Livingston's tireless lobbying, but the
state's purpose was to thwart a competitor for Indian land rather than to protect the Oneidas. Once again, New York's answer to the problem of whites moving onto Oneida land with false papers was to sit pat unless the Oneidas turned
the illegal lease into a permanent sale to the state. And once again, the Oneidas

relented in exchange for a pittance.[6] The subsequent Treaty of Fort Schuyler spared the Oneidas a confrontation with armed squatters and Albany, which was their greatest concern, yet at the cost of nearly their entire landed inheritance. Moreover, with whites pressing in from seemingly all directions and New York committed to profit from squatter and speculator aggression rather than punish it, the Oneidas were left to count the time nervously before calls came in for another cession.

The Oneidas' losses nearly included the Brothertowns' land too. Pressure from New York led the Oneidas to adopt a new strategy for dealing with white encroachment: instead of ringing their territory with Indian allies, they would set up a bulwark of white lessees they judged to be friendly and useful to the tribe—merchants, interpreters, blacksmiths, and the like.[7] To that end, the Oneidas wanted to free up most of the 37.5 square miles contained in their original 1774 grant to the Brothertowns. Yet Occom and the Brothertown leadership "utterly refused" proposals to reduce their town to just a single square mile or to hold their lands in common with the Oneidas.[8] Undeterred, the Oneidas adopted the same tactic that whites had so often used against them—they plied a few Brothertowns with drink to get them to sign a deed to their people's lands without anyone else's knowledge. The Brothertown leadership managed to foil this "Party Scheam" in October 1787, but there was no doubting the Oneidas' determination, even if it meant acting unilaterally.[9] As expected, the following year the Oneidas pronounced that they would limit Brothertown to an area of three miles by two so they could begin leasing the confiscated lands.[10] However, the Brothertowns' familiarity with white ways, which had convinced the Oneidas to host them in the first place, enabled them to parry this attack as well. Occom, it turned out, had wisely registered the original 1774 grant with Connecticut, thereby giving the paper the authority of white law.[11] New York's subsequent decision to restore Brothertown to its original 24,052 acres confirmed one of the community's founding principles—if Indians were to defend themselves under colonial rule, they would have to appropriate and wield the skills of their conquerors.

Throughout this contest, the Oneidas and Brothertowns charged each other with betraying the Indian race and straying from proper Indian behavior. Louis, one of the Oneida sachems, accused Brothertown of becoming "like the White People; he has long Arms; we gave him a large Piece of Land, and he was not contented with it."[12] Occom shot back that "Our Brothers the Oneidas Mock'd and Deceivd us—They pretended to give us a [Tract] of Land, and we had much Trouble with them about it,—and finally they took it back again, except a little

Spot hardly big enough to Build a Wigwam on—Such a thing never was done amongst the Indians before."[13] Indians agreed that land greed was a distinctively white characteristic and that, by contrast, honesty and generosity were supposed to be essential Indian qualities. The source of their quarrel was what it meant to put those Indian values in practice while defending their borders against white and Indian rivals alike.

The pressure to solve this puzzle mounted as whites streamed onto Indian lands. After the founding of a settlement portentously named Whitestown, the white population of Oneida country grew at a startling rate from less than two thousand people in 1790 to over fifty-five thousand in 1810 residing in two counties (Madison and Oneida) and thirty-two towns.[14] Occom could see this trend emerging as early as the fall of 1787 when he remarked that "this was all a Wild Wilderness in the beginning of last spring & now the People are Settling all along from Whitesborough to Clenton [Clinton]—in a few Years this will be Settled thick as any part of the globe the Land is so good."[15] Yet what whites called "development" and "progress" destroyed the Oneidas' traditional mixed economy. Oneida country's game animal population had been in decline for generations, but nowhere near as precipitously as after the Revolution, when white axemen and livestock encroached on the woodland habitat. Wild fruits, tubers, medicinal plants, firewood, and building materials were lost in kind, and whites obstructed Indian access to what little remained. Fish were the Indians' usual safety net, but a mere decade after the Treaty of Fort Schuyler the local salmon population collapsed due to white commercial fishing and damming of the waterways.[16] This destruction of wild resources forced the Indians to rely more than ever on their harvest, so when famine struck in 1788–89 it brought hardship on an unprecedented scale for peacetime. Thinking back on that season from the vantage point of 1791, Samuel Kirkland shuddered, "No pecuniary consideration could induce me to be even a spectator of another such scene."[17] The Indians of Oneida country had no intent of enduring such misery again either.

The answer for some Brothertowns, no less than for the Oneidas, was to lease out their excess lands to the expanding white population. This strategy made sense from several different perspectives. Brothertown had more acreage than its 150 or so people could hope to farm. Everyone expected the community's demand for tillage to grow over time, but until then white lessees were willing to pay good money to clear the forest and erect fences and buildings on land that would otherwise go unused. White labor would thus prepare the land for Indian cultivation. Furthermore, rent monies would help the Indians meet the costs of starting a new farming community. After all, the people needed to buy plows, harrows, chains, livestock, carts, and all other tools of the trade. In terms of infrastructure, they lacked housing, barns, sawmills, gristmills, roads, fences, and public buildings. Since the people could not produce enough of a marketable surplus to pay for these things, the money had to come either from outside donations or from capitalizing on the community's land. Finally, filling Brothertown with white renters would help counter the standard white argument that the Indians should part with their land because they did not use it productively. Ironically, then, leasing out Indian lands to whites could be seen as a means of protecting the Indian title from whites. At least that was how some of the Indians viewed the matter.

Yet the Brothertowns also knew from hard experience back in New England that leases could easily enflame community disagreements about politics, culture, and race. A handful of Narragansetts from the "Tribe's Council Party" had paid for their relocation to Oneida country and, furthermore, stuck a finger in the eye of the rival "King's Council Party" that stayed behind, by renting out reservation lands to whites.[18] Ultimately, Rhode Island had to step in to arbitrate a settlement: Narragansetts leaving for Brothertown could lease out their own farms, but not communal areas, and for terms of no more than six years, after which time that land would pass to relatives still living on the reservation; additionally, only the Narragansett tribal council could lease out the commons, with no contract to run for more than a year and the profits automatically earmarked for support of the poor.[19] Thus, in 1792, when John Skeesuck wanted to rent out his plot at Narragansett so he could afford "to Remove his Family from this Place to the Oniday," he first had to secure the authorization of the state's Committee to Transact Indian Affairs.[20] The Narragansetts were simply too fractured to manage this business themselves.

In 1790, the Mohegans addressed their own longstanding political divisions with a similar plan to segment their reservation into family-owned tracts that could be leased but not sold to outsiders. However, before the Sachem Party signed on to this agreement, it fired off one last salvo charging that its opponents, including the Brothertown migrants, had abandoned Indian communal values for the selfishness of whites. In a petition to Hartford drenched with resentment and loss, its spokesmen lamented:

The Times have turn'd everything Upside down, or rather we have Chang'd the good Times, Chiefly by the help of the White People. For in

Times past our Fore-Fathers lived in Peace, Love and great harmony, and had everything in Great plenty. When they Wanted meat they would just run into the Bush a little ways with their Weapons and would Soon bring home good venison, Racoon, Bear and Fowl. If they Choose to have Fish, they Wo'd only go to the River or along the Sea Shore and they wou'd presently fill their Cannoous With Veriety of Fish, both Scaled and shell Fish, and they had abundance of Nuts, Wild Fruit, Ground Nuts and Ground Beans, and they planted but little Corn and Beans and they kept no Cattle or Horses for they needed none—And they had no Contention about their Lands, it lay in Common to them all, and they had but one large Dish and they Cou'd all eat together in Peace in Love,—But alas, it is not so now, all our Fishing, Hunting and Fowling is intirely gone, And we have now begun to Work on our Land, keep Cattle, Horses and Hogs And wee Build Houses and fence in Lots, And now we plainly See that one Dish and one Fire will not do any longer for us.[21]

This statement shows how the Indians' very sense of identity was wrapped up in the lease issue. The Mohegan Sachem Party and the Narragansett King's Party defined their respective people according to their maintenance of select traditions. Of particular importance was communal landholding and communal generosity ("one large Dish and one Fire"), sachem authority, and a gender division of labor in which males took life through hunting and fishing and females nurtured it through horticulture, child rearing, and cooking. To conservatives like these, it made all the difference in the world that their families stubbornly held on to these customs and values, compromising them only grudgingly when they had no other choice. They derided their political opponents, like the Brothertowns, for being too enthusiastic to adopt the ways of "the White People." Conservatives particularly resented how their people's embrace of individual allotments, fencing, animal husbandry, and town meeting government had spawned the same contentious land greed for which they criticized whites.

Brothertown's split on the lease question ran along somewhat different lines. The Brothertowns were united in their Christianity and pursuit of civilized reforms. However, they disagreed over whether individuals could lease out their family plots. Most of the town founders, including Occom, said no, for they had created Brothertown as an exclusively Indian place. Yet that principle was not codified, and the opposing faction, led by the ever-contentious Elijah Wimpey, had white law on its side. New York had included in its 1789

restoration of Brothertown land a provision for Indians to make leases for periods not exceeding ten years; no sooner had the ink dried than Wimpey's men
seized the opportunity.[22] A horrified Occom watched leases throw open the gate
to "White People" accompanied by "their Children, Horses, Cattle Hogs, and
Dogs." These intruders, he railed, "begin to threten our Children; and they bring
Rum, to Sell to our Indians too and Some of these Whites will Work on Sabbath Days."[23] The renters seemed poised "to ruin and Destroy our Town," but
there was next to nothing Occom and his supporters could do about it. Brothertown was run by an informal town meeting that depended on consensus and
moral suasion, not force. Outspoken, resolute dissent could grind proceedings
to a halt, as Wimpey's group illustrated by shutting down operations for nearly
two years.[24] Christian peer pressure was no match for this discord, particularly
as political factions began to coincide with religious ones. As early as 1793,
Samuel Kirkland described Brothertown as "rent & torn in pieces" into "methodists, baptists, separatists, & Presbyterians," to such an extent that he predicted
"these divisions & animosities…will eventually prove their ruin."[25] The main
split was between radical New Lights under Samuel Ashbo and moderate New
Lights who followed Occom.[26] In all likelihood, the radicals formed the bulk
of Wimpey's support, for Occom's description of the pro-lease party as acting
"without regard, to old Substantial People, Without any regard to Rule or order"
echoed his critique of the so-called religious enthusiasts.[27] Such overlap between
religious and political disputes, a common feature of Native communities under
colonial pressure, narrowed the already slim chance of compromise over the
lease issue.[28]

Occom appealed to New York for help by employing the same kind of
charges, including racial ones, that the Sachem Party at Mohegan had so often
levied against his faction. "Many of Wampy's party is compris'd of strangers,"
Occom informed Governor George Clinton, "that is, they did not come from
the Tribes, to whom this land was given." Thomas Pechaker, a Wampanoag from
Martha's Vineyard, was among the people he had in mind.[29] Occom was careful
to add that three families of these "strangers" were "mixtures or Mulattoes" and,
by insinuation, not true Indians. Brothertown had admitted these people out of
"Benevolence & Favor," despite its race code, only to have them show their ap-
preciation by "picking out our Eyes."[30] As for authentic Brothertowns among his
opponents, Occom portrayed them as "Crazy…poor Miserable lazy Drunken
Creatures," the very same characterization that generations of whites had used
to dismiss Indian grievances. By contrast, Occom praised his supporters as "the

oldest men and the first settlers, and the most sober and judicious men of the Town," but in making them the civilized exception to the savage rule, he undercut his broader argument that Indians could achieve white standards. This was the unfortunate trend in an Indian politics that required jousting factions to appeal to white outsiders for assistance. Securing that assistance involved using whites' prejudicial language, thereby reinforcing a racial order that oppressed all Indians. Moreover, the assistance itself meant increasing white authority over Indian affairs, including control of the land.

New York's first legislative answer, in 1791, rebuffed Wimpey's party in general, but its vagueness on key issues ensured that the lease problem continued.[31] Under this law, each April Indian males age twenty-one and over would elect three trustees (later called "Peacemakers") to manage the people's affairs, a marshal to execute the trustees' decisions, and a clerk to record their proceedings. The trustees' first order of business was to divide the people's lands into individual plots and manage the remainder as a commons. The trustees could lease out the commons, but they could not issue a contract for more than 640 acres or for a term of longer than twenty-one years, and even then they had to receive the approval of a majority of voters. All proceeds would go toward support of the ministry and the school. The obvious intent of these provisions was to end the Wimpey Party's obstruction of local government and the lease of communal land without public sanction. The law was less clear about the Indians' freedom to manage their private plots as they saw fit. It stated that Indian families were entitled to land for their "separate improvement" but did not define whether that phrase included leases. Wimpey's party believed that it did, while Occom's party held it did not. The two groups petitioned New York for clarification, but to no end.[32] In the meantime, Wimpey's band "went on with all fury to lease Lands to the White People."[33]

In the end, it took the lawlessness of white settlers to produce some consensus in Brothertown on the lease issue. Brothertown's divided government was incapable of keeping the renters from ranging beyond the boundaries of their lots and poaching the community's best timber with abandon. These violations grew so dire that even Elijah Wimpey conceded that something had to be done. So, in the fall of 1794, he joined his former opponents, David Fowler, John Tukie and John Paul, plus twenty-two other men, in a petition calling on the governor to remove trespassing whites from Brothertown.[34]

New York came to Brothertown's aid, only to turn from protector to parasite, just as it had done before with the Oneidas. The process began in earnest when

Governor Clinton ordered William Colbrath, sheriff of the newly created Herkimer County, to expel all whites from Brothertown land. Yet when Colbrath went to the nearby village of Paris to raise a posse, he was met by a crowd of the very tenants he was supposed to evict; they pleaded that they were already settled on the land and improving it, thus giving them a moral if not a legal claim to stay. This line of reasoning had been used for more than a century to justify governmental inaction against whites who occupied Indian territory, and it lost no strength as it aged. His conscience pricked, Colbrath could not bear to carry out his duty against "upwards of a thousand [white] Men, Women, and Children included in the dreadful Sentence."[35] Predictably, given New York's interest in obtaining Indian land for whites, Clinton's heart was also moved, leading him to suspend the evictions until study could be made of the issue.[36]

In the interim, the white tenants developed the argument that removing them would be a grave injustice both to civilization and the Indians, and in so doing they contributed to a twisted racial logic that soon became part of the ideology of white American expansion. Echoing Wimpey, they contended that the Brothertown Indians deserved the individual right to issue leases because "they have been brought up in a civilized life, and...profess the Christian religion...can read and write, and some of them speak the English language with no small degree of grammatical propriety."[37] Yet the tenants had no such regard for Indians who stood in their way. They castigated their opponents as "three or four individuals" who had "many of the vices & few of the virtues of civilized life," including "an inveterate hatred of the White Inhabitants."[38] Here was the beginning of a racial double standard that would plague the Brothertowns and many other Indians for generations to come—whites praised Indian Christianity and civility to justify opening Indian land to the market but denounced as half-savages Christian Indians who defended themselves against white encroachment. The tenants then broadened this formulation to submit that they deserved the land because they and they alone had developed it in accordance with God's dictates and the interests of the republic. After all, they insisted, they had already made more improvements in Brothertown than the Indians ever would, all "to encrease the wealth and promote the happiness and prosperity of a people," by which they meant whites of the United States.[39] By contrast, the Indians, "few in number," clustered languidly in "a small old settlement and that in one corner of the tract." Leases to whites offered the only means of developing Brothertown's extensive waste lands, yet the Indians' "unsteadiness" led them to denounce the very contracts they had made toward this end. To grant the Indians' wishes would be to sacrifice the high purposes of the nation so a handful of Indians could watch rich land lie idle. The best alternative, the white tenants proposed, was to sell them the tracts they were currently renting. This talk placed Brothertown's David Fowler "under fearfull apprehensions from the league that was forming among the white people on their lands," for he knew as well as they did where the state's loyalties truly lay.[40] He had every reason to worry.

New York titled its response an "Act for the Relief of the Indians who are Intitled to Lands in Brothertown," but it was less concerned with helping Brothertown than orchestrating a land grab. Rather than eject the white lessees, as promised, it seized 14,662 contiguous acres of Brothertown land (61 percent of the total) for sale and incorporation in the white town of Paris.[41] This legislation also robbed Brothertown of a critical measure of its sovereignty. The Indian Peacemakers (whose number had been enlarged to five) would no longer be selected by popular vote of the Indians but instead by three white superintendents appointed by Albany. To avoid any future disputes over leases, Brothertown's 149 people would divide most of the community land into individual plots that could not be leased out or sold. Any remaining acreage would be held as a commons for future generations, and it too could not be leased. The superintendents were supposed to make sure of that. This law taught the Brothertowns, like the Oneidas before them, that any request for state assistance was like inviting the proverbial wolf into the hen house. Governments in the new republic were mechanisms of an expansionist white racial regime, not fair-minded arbiters of conflicts between people of different complexions living within their borders. The trouble for Indians was choosing between cutting their losses with these governments or attempting to deal independently with the mobbish behavior of the encroaching white population.

Stockbridge's determined refusal to permit leases to whites illustrates that Indians were capable of retaining control over their lands even under the same pressures that afflicted the Brothertowns and Oneidas. Like their Indian neighbors, the Stockbridges were surrounded by whites who craved their territory. They too suffered from religious factionalism, for a minority of the community led by the sachem Hendrick Aupaumut favored Samson Occom as minister, while the majority wanted to retain John Sergeant Jr.[42] Stockbridge also had a party that favored leases, headed by John Konkapot and his brothers, descendents of Stockbridge's first Christian sachem.[43] Yet Stockbridge's leaders cooperated to defeat this dissident group. Though Aupaumut opposed Sergeant's ministry, the two men agreed that it would be disastrous to lease out land to whites. Thus, at no point did religious factions overlap with one or the other of the lease factions. Equally vital was that Stockbridge women spoke out against leases. When some Stockbridge men tried to lease out community land in the summer of 1794, Sergeant received a "delegation of chiefs and women" who told him to inform Albany that "no such lease would take place."[44] Clearly Aupaumut had a mandate when he declared Stockbridge's intention "never to admit white people on our land, but it shall be for our own use & for the use of our grand children after us."[45] Much to the surprise of white land sharks, even the tried and true tactic of plying Indians with liquor failed to work at Stockbridge. No matter what they did, they found that "they cannot obtain a good title to the land."[46] The key to Stockbridge's success, then, was strong leadership and a rough consensus on the lease issue across divisions of religion and gender. By contrast, white encroachment only widened longstanding fissures among the Oneidas and Brothertowns. Consequently, they were faced with the dark prospect of losing their lands and autonomy so soon after launching the experiment to secure those very things. It was enough to make them question the faith at the very heart of their movement.

"Wo, Wo, Wo"

From the very start, the Christian Indians had seen their communities as fragile experiments. The Oneidas recruited Kirkland back to his missionary post after the Revolution with the promise that they would make "one trial more" of Christianity and that "if there be no encouragement after this that we shall be built up as a people and embrace the religion of jesus he may leave us & we shall expect nothing but ruin."[47] A group of Montauketts visiting Brothertown in the spring of 1790 thought similarly. They told Kirkland that "their whole Nation have it in contemplation to move up into this wilderness" because they saw "a probability that God may build up their Nation." They admitted being "afraid *Indians* would not work like *white people*," but "they farther observed that if they thought they could all be united with regard to religion, they would move up and make one *effort to live like white people,* and leave the issue with that God who governed all the Nations of the Earth."[48] The Indians' assumption was that God rewarded his faithful and punished his enemies in the here and now, not only in the afterlife. The question that plagued Indians in the 1790s was how to account for whites becoming "strong & great" through their low avarice and Indians degenerating into "nothing but a wreck of bones" despite their Christian efforts.[49]

Most Indians agreed that the root cause of their troubles was whites' greedy scheming, something they attributed to whites' basic character. "Indians have been so often deceived by white people," observed Timothy Pickering after several visits to Oneida country, "that *White Man* is, among many of them, but another name for *Liar*."[50] This opinion was so widespread as to be shared by the Oneidas' Pagan Peter (as he was called with no hint of irony), leader of that tribe's Nativist faction, and Samson Occom. Pagan Peter railed that "The White skin race as a body have become proud. And some of you too proud. You glory in your riches, your great & commodious houses, your large fields & your abundance. You wear a white shirt & sometimes it is ruffled. And you despise us Indians for our indigence, our poor huts, our scanty food, & our dirty shirts." Whites touted themselves as Christians, but Pagan Peter found them to be anything but Christ-like. "Brother Whiteskin Man," he asked rhetorically, "do you think that God our Maker...will make such a discrimination by & by or in the end....A foul spirit may be concealed in a body richly clothed & a pure heart may reside unseen in another covered only in rags. God our maker will judge right in respect to the worth of souls, whatever complexion the bodies wear."[51] His words were barely distinguishable from Occom's, whose sermons after the Revolution shifted from the themes of universal Christian fellowship and the need for Indians to reform to a critique of whites in which Indians were the Christian standard bearers. In one of them he wrote that "the Savage Indians, as they are so calld, are very kind to one another and they are kind to Strangers— But I find amongst those who are call'd Christians, Void of natural affection." He admonished any whites who might be paying attention: "It is in vain for any of you to think, that you Love God, when you know, you have no regard for the happiness of you Neighbour, you have no pity and Compassion upon the Poor and distrest." Occom could have pointed to any one of a number of Indian afflictions to make his point, but he used black slavery as his most damning piece of evidence. "You have no more right to keep them as Slaves," he charged, "as they have to keep you as Slaves."[52] Yet Occom himself struggled to reconcile the principle of Christian brotherhood with his increasing hatred for whites. In one essay, he called whites "the most Tyranacal, Cruel, and inhuman oppressors of their fellow Creatures in the World"; in another, he judged white Christian hypocrites to be "worse than the Heathen, Heathen in general manifest more Humanity than such degenerate Christians."[53] No mere rhetorical device, Occom's bile toward whites grew so pronounced that Kirkland judged no Indian other than Joseph Brant "has more inveterate prejudices against white people, than Mr. Occum, altho' his education & professional calling in most cases restrain them."[54] Even Stockbridge complained that he went too far "to alienate the affections of our poor ignorant [people] from White people in general and Ministers in particular."[55]

Kirkland blamed Occom for stoking Indian bias toward whites, but nothing was as responsible as whites' own behavior. First and foremost there was the pattern of whites using force and fraud to secure Indian land sales. "It is just so with your People," Agwelondongwas lectured a delegation from Albany. "As long as any Spot of our excellent Land remains, they will covet it, and if one dies, another will pursue it, and will never rest till they possess it."[56] It did not have to be that way. The Stockbridges, like so many other Indian people, praised the Quakers for donating them expensive farm equipment and spinning wheels in the spirit of Christian charity rather than as a bribe to encourage land cessions. "If our forefathers had received such kindness, such way of help, by their white brothers who got all their country...we might have been able to become useful citizens of this Island," Aupaumut mused in a letter to the Friends of New York City. "But they were not allowed to have such privileges."[57] The rum trade was a case in point. Generations of Indian leaders had pleaded with white authorities to halt this nefarious traffic, with nothing but toothless legislation to show for it.[58] The dreadful consequences were illustrated in January 1797 when a drunk Stockbridge boy froze to death after whites sold him liquor but refused him shelter from the cold.[59] As far as Indians were concerned, the state's indifference toward the liquor trade made it complicit in such tragedies. "You refused to give that Assistance which a brother had a right to expect from another," Stockbridge scolded New York, to which Pagan Peter added, "If we Indians must bear this reproach of loving Rum, the White Man certainly loves money. Which will deserve the heaviest punishment, I presume not to determine."[60] Yet Pagan Peter and his fellow Indians did know. Though they accepted some responsibility for their problems, they would not pretend that the main cause was anything other than white colonialism. With characteristic bluntness, Occom charged, "The poor Indians were in a Miserable Situations before Europians Came; and since...they are more so except a few that have had a little Gospel light."[61] Occom even had doubts about that exception.

White words sapped Indian morale no less than white deeds. A European visitor to the early republic was shocked at how often he encountered whites who spoke of the Indians' "annihilation...with atrocious pleasure."[62] Genteel whites rarely used such vicious terms, but they too generally believed that

Indians were on the road to extinction, based on a theory that innate savagery prevented Indian people from adapting to the white order of things. "I cannot help being of opinion that Indian never were intended to live in a state of civil society," wrote the Presbyterian minister John McDonald in 1792 after touring Iroquoia. "There never was, I believe, an instance of an Indian forsaking his habits and savage manners, any more than a bear his ferocity." Though McDonald was familiar with Christian Oneidas, he judged them to be "Indians still, and like a bear which you can muffle and lead out to dance at the sound of musick, becomes again a bear when his muffler is removed and the music ceases."[63] According to such thinking, Native societies would inevitably recede as white America expanded. "Husbandmen and Hunters, civilized and uncivilized people, cannot generally, live in the same limits," Hartford's *American Mercury* posited in 1795, "or if there be an attempt to incorporate them into the same society, the former will always rise superior, and the latter will sink into a state of dependence."[64] Even the Indians' advocates tended to share these views. The Oneidas' favorite interpreter and go-between, James Dean, told a visiting missionary, "Few know an Indian's Heart, but I do; and I think they are not of the same species which we are."[65] Indians could not help but overhear such talk, coming as it did from all quarters of white society. An Oneida in Kirkland's flock complained that "as he understood, it had become a proverb among the white people to say 'dirty as an Indian,' 'as lazy as an Indian,' 'as drunk as an Indian,' 'lie like Indians.' And we Indians can only say 'Cheat like a white man.' And poor Indians must bear it."[66]

Few Indians pardoned whites for their bigotry and exploitation, but some believed that only God's wrath could account for the staggering depth of Indian troubles. Indeed, the Christian Indians began to ask whether their utopian hopes had been so much naivety and even to suggest that Indians as a race might be cursed by God. Evidence of this conversation first surfaced in September 1789, when Kirkland sat with a group of Oneidas, Tuscaroras, and probably some Brothertowns and Stockbridges to discuss "the character and state of the Indians." The Indians asked Kirkland three questions: First, "whether I did not think in my mind, that the displeasure of Heaven in a singular manner rested upon the Indian Nations." Second, "whether this displeasure of Heaven or curse of God was not inflicted on them for some great sins against God committed by their forefathers?" And then, third, if this was not the case, "what did God mean by what is said in the Second Commandment; that he would visit the iniquities of the Fathers upon the Children to the third and fourth generations?"[67]

The Indians, knowing full well that Kirkland ascribed their plight to "their own wicked, unbelieving hearts and ungodly practices," appear to have been less interested in soliciting his views than in airing their own. A growing number of them, including some of "very considerable abilities," imagined that "the Indians are punished for the sins of their forefathers and the displeasure of the great Spirit is fixed upon them, in consequence of which, they cannot reform and become a prosperous Nation, like the white people, until such time as this curse or punishment should be removed." The missionary consoled himself that these opinions were an excuse of the weak-hearted to follow a "general course of idleness, and intemperance, idleness, stupidity, and ingratitude," but he could not have been more wrong. Even some of the most dedicated Christian Indians were reaching the devastating conclusion that God meant for Indians as Indians to suffer. The worst thing of all was that there was nothing they could do to ease their plight.

The Christian Indians believed that God punished them not so much for their own shortcomings, which would have given them some control over their fate, but for the sins of their ancestors, which left them entirely subject to God's whim. Though no believing Christian could claim to be free of sin, the Brothertown and Stockbridge Indians, if not the Oneidas, held that their Christianity and civility compared favorably with the white communities surrounding them. Even some white authorities conceded the point.[68] Still, God granted the Natives no relief. This pattern pushed the Indians toward a terrifying yet inescapable conclusion: God cursed Indians as a race in the present for their ancestors' sins. Until he decided to take his foot off their necks, there was nothing they could do to improve their lives.

This idea of God's curse drew on a combination of basic Christian principles as well as Christian and Nativist interpretations of colonialism. Every Christian knew of the Curse of Eden, in which humankind was destined to toil, suffer, and die as God's punishment for the transgressions of Adam and Eve. Only God's grace would spare a select few from a worse fate in the afterlife. The Indians also would have been familiar with the genealogical Curse of Ham, in which Noah punished his son Ham for looking on his nakedness by sentencing Ham's son, Canaan, and his progeny to servitude. According to many colonial-era thinkers, Africans descended from Canaan and thus were destined to slavery. In these two cases, Indians had precedents for associating worldly suffering with divine judgment for the sins of ancestors. They also had a longstanding tradition of attributing their collective misfortune to spiritual punishment, as when they questioned the source of their devastation by epidemic disease. This tendency might have grown during the eighteenth century, as white New Englanders increasingly invoked providential judgment to account for the misfortune even of communities that did not have a special convenanted relationship with God, including those that were not Christian.[69] John Sergeant Jr., for instance, chastised the Stockbridges that "the reason why God left Indian churches and Tribes to distruction was because of their national sins of drunkenness, Idleness, and the like, and gave their country to a more industrious and virtuous people."[70] The Christian Indians' lifelong exposure to such thinking manifested itself in the idea of the curse. Since the 1740s the Christian Indians had also heard Nativist warnings that the Great Spirit or Master of Life punished Indians in this world and the next for their dissolute morals and drift from time-worn ways. The prophets' emphasis on sin and an omnipotent sky god, both of which reflected Christian influences, and their promotion of a distinct Indian racial identity and destiny, which clearly did not, likely shaped the Christian Indians' perspectives.[71]

To this discussion, the Christian Indians added yet another strand of thought. Their belief in God's curse was distinctly Calvinist in its origins, consistent with their reformed Protestantism, even as it expanded God's judgment to include Indians as a race of people rather than as separate tribes, reflective of the prophets' stress on a shared Indian destiny. It extended from their failed attempts to quicken their spiritual power and autonomy through ritual and social reforms, which was the prophets' agenda, but those reforms had been Christianity and civility, as their missionaries insisted. In short, the Christian Indians' beliefs were at once colonial and anti-colonial, Christian and Nativist, Indian and white, original and derivative.

Talk about the curse arose in the aftermath of the Revolution and the famine of the mid- to late 1780s, then built to a peak amid the land loss, factionalism, and social struggles of the 1790s. In 1783 Occom became one of the first Indians to voice this gloomy analysis, frustrated as he was by a lifetime of disappointment, including, most recently, suspension of the Brothertown movement during the war. Though he tried to find hope in the Bible, he admitted, "Some Times I am ready to Conclude that [Indians] are under great Judgment and Curse from God."[72] His people's unrelenting misery kept bringing him back to this theme. "It seems to me, at Times there is nothing but Wo, Wo, Wo Written in every Turn of the Wheel of Gods Providence against us," he lamented in 1784. "I am afraid we are Devoted to Distruction and Misery."[73] Seven years later, Occom's view was equally bleak. Living day to day in such a "Deplorable Condition and

Situation" forced him to concede that "Heaven and Earth, are in Combination against us"—this from a man who once saw himself as a Moses leading his people out of Egypt.[74]

Occom's fatalism was widely shared among the Indians of Oneida country. The Stockbridge Mohicans asked Sergeant over and over again about the nature of racial difference, with many of their concerns alluding to the curse. For instance, in a meeting in September 1791 about "God's providence towards Indians," they questioned their missionary, "What were the reasons they had been, and now were given up, to so much evil? How can god be just in making such a difference between Indians and white people? Did it not appear manifest that God never intended Indians should rise like white people?"[75] The Oneidas had a number of similar discussions with Kirkland. One, in August 1793, involved a headman asking "Whether God had not decreed evil to Indians?" He explained, "When he looked only on the side of Indians, all seemed dark, and when he looked on the side of the white people, they appeared to have light and to be the Lord's favorites," even though "the conduct of a great many of them, and of their great chiefs too, was such, that he considered them mere conjurors, and like the magicians of Egypt, of which he had been often told." One unnamed Oneida thought that he knew the source of this disparity. "I sometimes believe God has put his curse on us," he confessed to Kirkland. "It may be for the sins of our forefathers and that is the reason we can't live like white people." Some Indians took this idea so far as to posit that they were descendents of Jews under divine sanction for the death of Jesus.[76] They would continue to suffer in this world, if not necessarily in the next—until God forgave them

Conversations about the curse were ubiquitous during the late 1780s and 1790s, but belief in it was not universal. There were still Oneidas who insisted that "the minds of Indians may become as enlighten'd as the Minds of the White People & that all the difference between us & them consists only in the Colour of the skin."[77] Among them was Agwelondongwas, who "considered the Oneida Indians as approaching the verge of civilized & improved state; & that they would not stop there long; but must go forward or soon come to ruin for the customs of their forefathers."[78] Quakers visiting Brothertown in 1795 encountered an Indian man who "hoped the partition wall that divided nations would be broken down, bigotry and prejudice done away, and all mankind come to live more like brothers."[79]

Nevertheless, the sheer number of conversations about the curse, most of them recorded in journals kept by missionaries for whom this idea was anathema, reflects that a critical mass of the Christian Indians believed that God hated them. At the height of desperation, these people had uprooted their lives because they trusted that God would smile on them if they worked hard, strove against sin, spread his word, and worshipped him honestly. They had done their best to fulfill their part of the covenant, only to realize that they were living a lie. There was no longer any basis for Sergeant to revert to the shelf-worn argument that an angry God chastised Indians because their men refused to farm.[80] Nor could the case be made that Indians suffered because they "would not receive his Gospel," as missionary David Avery had once accused the Oneidas—not with white settlers sometimes attending the Indians' churches for a lack of their own.[81] Though Indians were not wholly obedient to God—no one could be— they could plainly see that they were no more sinful than the whites who sold them liquor, bilked them out of their land, and threatened them with violence merely for being Indian. Indeed, in some Natives' estimation, they were the better Christians. How could anyone claim that God was merciful and just when he granted whites manifold favors even as he "decreed evil to the Indians"? Indians might make their way to heaven, but God seemed intent on destroying Indians in this world for no fault of their own, a conclusion that led Indians discussing the subject with Kirkland, "to mourn and sigh and weep like children in the view of their present miserable state, compared with the white people."[82] Unlike Nativists, whose prophets had definitive answers to their people's spiritual crisis, heartfelt Christians had nowhere left to turn. The Christian God to whom they had dedicated their lives seemed to despise them as much as whites did, and that broke their spirit.

Such demoralization among the Oneidas, Brothertowns, and, to a lesser extent, Stockbridges, weakened their urgency for reform, with a corresponding rise in domestic violence and other self-destructive behaviors, much of it fueled by the very alcohol abuse they had come to New York to escape.[83] In 1793, Brothertown experienced a suicide by a young man distraught at being rejected by his Oneida lover's family. Several years later, Brothertown's George Peters, originally of Montauk, became just the eighth person executed by the state of New York after he was convicted for murdering his wife Eunice, the daughter of Elijah Wimpey.[84] Another murder followed in 1817, when Brothertown's John Tukie, age seventeen, bludgeoned his nineteen-year-old brother after the two got drunk in the town of Clinton during an election day celebration. Symbolic of the racial subjugation that contributed to this culture of alcohol abuse, Brothertown's only role in Tukie's arrest, trial, conviction, and execution, was to hand him over to the white authorities and then retrieve his dead body.[85] Similar crises beset the Oneida reservation with even greater frequency, usually in the context of what contemporaries called "drunken frolicks."[86] These were the actions of people whose present was filled with disappointment and humiliation and whose future held little promise.

The Indians' sense of futility deepened as they suffered the death of their most prominent Christian leaders and a loss of confidence in Kirkland. No one had been more central to the rise of Christianity among the Oneidas than Agwelondongwas (or Good Peter) during his half-century as a deacon, preacher, and political figure. His death in October 1792 left a gaping hole in the Oneidas' Christian community.[87] The stage was set for younger, more energetic Oneidas to step into the breach, yet growing numbers of them were skeptical of the faith, owing in no small degree to their falling out with Kirkland. Kirkland's reputation among the Oneidas had always depended on him fulfilling a promise never to seek any of their land. This "Covenant," he boasted, "has done more to establish my Character among the Indians than perhaps five hundred pounds in presents to them would have done."[88] However, after the Revolution, Kirkland violated this pledge with abandon, parlaying his role as a trusted go-between into one grant of land after another, until he became one of the richest men in the Oneidas' neighborhood. Kirkland added to the Oneidas' disillusionment by neglecting his missionary work and sometimes showing open disdain for his charges, even going so far as to call them "in plain English, filthy, dirty, nasty creatures, a few families excepted."[89] It was a sad but appropriate dénouement of Kirkland's relationship with the Oneidas that when he raised donations of money and land for a school, the Hamilton Oneida Academy, purportedly dedicated to the education of Iroquois in the liberal arts, he then mimicked his mentor, Eleazar Wheelock, by turning it into a school for genteel whites—Hamilton College.[90]

Fortunately for Kirkland, Samson Occom was not there for long to awaken his conscience, for after feeling ill for a number of days, he fell dead in July of 1792 at the age of sixty-nine. Occom's star had been fading during his last years: distraught over Brothertown's factionalism, he moved his family to Stockbridge, where almost immediately he alienated the majority of people by interfering in their civil affairs and attempting to lure away Sergeant's followers. "We consider him as an old man superannuated and try not to resent his ill behaviour," wrote Occom's opponents at Stockbridge, "but we must say that untill we can see an intire alteration in his behaviour we can get no manner of good by his preaching." Perhaps not coincidentally, Occom appears to have slipped into several bouts of drunkenness in the early 1790s.[91] Still, that his funeral attracted some three hundred Indians from a radius of ten miles, followed by a week of discussions focused "principally on the subject of Mr. Occums death," spoke to his abiding reputation as a leader.[92] The people would miss him dearly.

Out of the House of Bondage

Whites who followed the Christian Indians into Oneida country shared the Natives' desire for economic opportunity and Christian fellowship, but that was not enough of a foundation for these groups to coexist. Two factors in particular drove them apart and would continue to divide them for most of the next century. First and foremost, there was the zeal of whites to turn land into private property, a commodity that one bought and developed in order to raise its market value so that it could be sold again at a profit. Christian Indians believed in improving the land in terms of clearing, plowing, planting, and fencing. They even divided their territory into individual plots that could be passed down from a holder to his heirs based on the principle that families were more likely to develop land in which they held a permanent stake. Some Indians even favored leasing out land to whites as a source of income. However, practically none of the Indians approved of allowing their land to be sold to outsiders—of turning it into a commodity—for they knew that it would only be a matter of time before whites discovered the means to wrest that acreage away from them. The Indians saw land less as a resource by which individuals got ahead, as whites did, than as a source of community security and solidarity.[93]

Above all, what divided whites and Indians was the white agenda to establish a racial hierarchy with their own people on top, an agenda that involved appropriating the Indians' land by means fair and foul, extending white governmental jurisdiction over Indian peoples and land, and then either displacing the Indians or reducing them to abject status. It would be too simplistic to argue that there was a single trajectory to this process, since rival white interests sometimes worked at cross-purposes, yet a general pattern did emerge from the fray: Indians seeking income and improvements on their territory leased land to whites despite the protests of their more farsighted tribesmen; as whites invested labor and capital in that land, they pressured state authorities to turn their leaseholds into freeholds; the state, in turn, forced Indians to cede portions of their land to the state for resale to the leaseholders and other whites. Indian communities, even those committed to Christianity and civility, generally sank into poverty and despair in the wake of these losses, but white authorities refused to take responsibility for this pattern. Almost to a man, whites claimed that these land cessions were for the Indians' own good, since clear boundaries would protect the Indians from future land loss, and annuities would provide them with regular income. Furthermore, whites argued, forcing the Indians to do more with less land would encourage their civilized reforms. Most whites also agreed that if Indians continued to struggle despite these advantages, it was due to their own supposedly savage nature, the God-given order of things. Such refusal to call ethnic cleansing by anything like that name would characterize Indian affairs in the United States for more than a century to come.

Christian Indians were not loath to call whites to account for their crimes, but the sheer relentlessness of the Indians' struggles—land loss, betrayal, famine, alcohol abuse, factionalism, and war, over and over again—seemed so cosmic in scale that Native people, much like whites, could only understand it as something beyond human means. After weighing their belief in God's omnipotence against the Nativists' argument for polygenesis and the inescapable misery of Indian life under colonial rule, many Christian Indians determined that race was something created and maintained by God for reasons all his own. They did not subscribe to the idea that supposed racial characteristics passed through the blood from one generation to the next, as white Americans and eventually many Indians would argue in the years following the Revolution. They did not believe that there was anything inherently superior or inferior about whites, Indians, and, by extension, blacks, except insofar as God willed it to be so. God, at his own whim, could overturn the racial hierarchy of the United States and restore Indians to happiness. Until then, whites seemed destined for worldly comfort and dominance, blacks for servility and degradation, and Indians for poverty and dispossession.

The question, then, remained what to do in the meantime as they strived for something better; it must have seemed a futile question, but giving up would only bring more misery. Right before his death, Samson Occom thought he might have an answer. Following the lead of Hendrick Aupaumut, he began to support the Christian Indians leaving Oneida country for Indiana, where they could revive their experiment absent the company of whites. Sergeant wrote of Occom in August 1792 that "for six months past he had been labouring to make a division among the Oneidas" and that "he had determined to move off to the westward with his friends."[94] Occom no longer thought of Oneida country as a new Israel. His people had gone there to escape white America and instead they had brought it with them. Their subsequent exploitation at white hands had nearly destroyed their faith, just as it had nearly destroyed their communities. Unwilling to sit and watch the final, excruciating scenes play out, Occom and his allies recommitted themselves to move west and pursue whatever glimmer of hope was left that they could win God's blessing, in a place, they hoped, where they could finally be free of the white man's republic.

CHAPTER 7

Red Brethren

I F there were any two people whose lives proved that Indians could adapt to the white order of things, they were Asa Dick of Brothertown and Mary Dox-tater of Stockbridge. Dick emerged as one of Brothertown's most important political men during the 1820s and 1830s when many of the community's more veteran leaders were out west trying to find their people a new home. Stepping into the breach, Dick reinvigorated the Peacemakers' oversight of community morals, including punishment of Sabbath breaking, as if he was seeking God's blessing for Brothertowns' next remove.[1] Dick also managed Brothertown's day-to-day business, such as buying and distributing supplies, dealing with guardians from Albany, and assisting less-educated people in court.[2] When Washington seized lands the Brothertowns had secured first in Indiana and then in Wisconsin, Dick was among the men who petitioned the White House for redress.[3] Even in a fiercely egalitarian community, the Indians called Dick "Esquire," and the neighborhood around his two-story, white-painted house became known as "Dicksville."[4]

As one of the only Stockbridge or Brothertown women to assume a visible leadership role in New York, Doxtater was every bit Dick's equal.[5] Educated as a child among Philadelphia Quakers, at age twenty Doxtater began compiling a list of public achievements, starting with her establishment of a spinning and weaving school for Stockbridge women and girls in 1817. In 1820 she helped to found Stockbridge's Female Cent Society, which promoted reading, spinning, knitting, sewing, and sound morals, and the following year she opened another school among the Onondagas.[6] Unwilling to cede the political arena to men, she protested loudly when a Stockbridge faction tried to sell town lands without public consent. Doxtater was unequivocal that her people "are desirous of becoming civilised & christianised: & this they think is in a fair way to be done where they are. But if they sell their land, & remove into the wilderness, they fear that they will remain savages for ever."[7] Doxtater had no intension of meeting such a fate. By the 1830s she lived in a "hospitable Indian mansion" surrounded by "very valuable" improvements.[8]

It speaks volumes about the Christian Indians' predicament that Doxtater and Dick ultimately spent their talents managing their people's relocation from New York to Green Bay, Wisconsin, rather than defending their lands in Oneida. The cost of moving out west required the Brothertowns and Stockbridges to divide and sell their lands, but many Indians were loath to negotiate with whites for fear of being cheated. Instead, they either sold out to Doxtater and Dick or simply gave them power of attorney, so that those two figures could handle the complicated dealings.[9] The Stockbridge and Brothertown tribes even went so far as to make Doxtater and Dick, respectively, their agents for all public business with Albany at a time when other leaders were in transit.[10] The Indians refused to entrust their state-appointed guardians with such responsibility. "We want none of their care," Doxtater emphasized, with equal measures of pride and bitterness. "We are quite capable of caring for our affairs ourselves."[11] Yet providing that care under a hostile white regime required more resources than even these gifted figures could muster. In 1841 Dick put his name on a list of Brothertowns who wanted to migrate to Wisconsin the next year, but, sadly, he died in New York in September of 1843 at age 47, insolvent.[12]

The accomplishments of Dick and Doxtater could have served as evidence that Indians could adjust to life in the new republic, but instead whites either ignored such examples or dismissed them as exceptions to the rule as an excuse to force the rest of the Indians out. Indeed, the decision of the Stockbridges, Brothertowns, and Oneidas to leave New York was voluntary only in the narrowest sense of the word. A tangle of white interests, ranging from legislators and land speculators all the way down to common tenant farmers, pressured the Indians to abandon their territory. When the Indians finally conceded after securing land on the White River in Indiana from the Miamis and Delawares, the federal government snatched that place away from them too on the very eve of their migration, thus forcing them to turn to the Menominees and Ho-Chunks of the Green Bay area for refuge. Whites justified such betrayals by arguing that Indian possession of the land retarded civilization and that Indian exposure to whites invariably produced Indian decline. Yet the Christian Indians' very example exposed the lie. In New York, they had accommodated their white neighbors in practically every way short of disappearing: for the most part, they lived up to the Christian and civilized standards preached to them by white missionaries; they rented land to white settlers at generous rates; and they ceded land to the state whenever it wanted to build roads or canals across their territory. They even premised their westward migration on the promotion of formal education, male plow agriculture, and peaceful relations with the United States among tribes that had resisted white expansion for decades.

Herein lay the Christian Indians' paradoxical dilemma. Over and over again, their inability to convince whites to brook their presence showed that whites wanted them gone simply because they were Indians, leading them to conclude that their best hope for prosperity and quiet rested not among their Christian brethren but among pagans from the continental interior, whom they began to call their "red brethren." Culturally, the Christian Indians no longer had much in common with the Miamis of Indiana or the Menominees and Ho-Chunks of Wisconsin. In terms of religion, material culture, economy, and even, increasingly, language, they shared more with the whites who had displaced them than the Indians who would provide them sanctuary. Yet whites' relentless campaign to displace any and all Indians encouraged Native people to conceive of themselves as sharing a single racial identity and destiny. The question for them was what that destiny would be. The Christians' answer was that if Indians hung on to their ancestral ways of living, they would never secure God's favor or adapt to the colonial order. The old path allowed whites to prey on their divisions and ignorance to seize their land. It invited the scourge of alcohol abuse into their communities. It permitted men who could no longer pursue their traditional duties of hunting and war because of white expansion to grow inactive, alienated, and, too often, dangerous to themselves and others. If Indians continued in this direction, they were doomed. Their only hope, the Christians submitted, was to seek God's blessing and some concord with whites. Though this approach had thus far proved to be only marginally more effective than militant resistance, the Christians could argue that the first principle, Indians reforming as an entire race, had never come close to being fulfilled. Their pursuit of this vision would carry them across half the continent in the space of a single generation.

The Christian Indians used the opening of fresh territory, first in Indiana and then in Wisconsin, to revive their sense of mission despite their many trials. Though their troubled lives provided ample evidence of God's curse, the prospect of an interior homeland free of the corrupting influences of whites, where they could reform themselves and other Native people, lent itself to an alternative view: God was providing his flock with a glimmer of inspiration so that they would persevere even when it seemed that there was no place for the William Dicks and Mary Doxtaters of the world within reach of the white man's republic. Suffering was a redemptive test of faith.

People of My Color

It was difficult for Indians to find peace almost anywhere in the young United States, but the Christian Indians of Oneida country had the special burden of confronting New York, which was expanding at an unrivaled pace. After the Revolution, whites poured into the state from New England and western Europe, both for its fertile land and for its remarkable access to domestic and international markets. Beginning in the 1790s, New York launched a series of internal improvement projects, culminating in the completion of the Erie Canal in 1825, which, by creating a water highway between the Hudson River on the east and Lake Erie on the west, ultimately linked the Atlantic Ocean with the Great Lakes, the Ohio River Valley, and the Mississippi River.[13] This system unleashed entrepreneurial energy throughout the state and the nation as a whole. The rising flow of commerce along dredged and straightened rivers and freshly dug canals gave rise to a host of new cities such as Troy, Utica, Syracuse, Rochester, and Buffalo. It also invigorated old ones, none more so than New York City, which grew from a large town with a population of 33,000 in 1790 to over 200,000 forty years later.[14] Farmers between these nodes and far into the continent thrived from the increased demand for their produce in the country's growing urban centers and from their enhanced ability to reach those places. Not the least of all, they profited from the government's commitment to seize Indian land for them.

It was the unfortunate accident of the Christian Indians that the old Oneida Carrying Place, as the portage at Fort Stanwix between the Mohawk River and Wood Creek was known, served as the lynchpin for New York's planned complex of canals, roads, cities, and farms. Throughout the 1790s and early 1800s, companies underwritten by a roll call of elite New Yorkers—Schuylers, Livingstons, Van Rensselaers, Morrises, and Clintons—put endless pressure on the Indians to cede their lands and then transformed their country into an entirely new landscape. Already by 1797 the Mohawk River was open to continuous navigation, followed shortly by the canal through the Carrying Place, another canal linking Lake Oneida to Lake Ontario, and broad, flat new roads like the Genesee and Seneca turnpikes, all of which connected Oneida country to western New York.[15] The white population along these routes exploded, with Oneida and Madison Counties surrounding the Oneida Indians' territory growing from just 1,891 in 1790 to 28,865 in 1800 and 93,493 in 1825.[16] The Oneidas and their Christian Indian guests, standing at only some twelve hundred people, were outnumbered and overwhelmed.[17]

Whites looking for a justification to seize the Indians' land highlighted the worst examples of Native behavior they could find, ignoring exceptions among the Oneidas and the rule among the Brothertowns and Stockbridges. David Ogden, founder of the Ogden Land Company, which speculated in Iroquois land, charged that Indians were inveterate "alcoholics," "liars," and "prostitutes" as part of his self-serving argument that New York's tribes should be restricted to reservations or forced out of the state altogether.[18] He was seconded by John C. Calhoun, secretary of war responsible for Indian affairs under President James Monroe. Calhoun's position was that "savage customs ... cannot, and ought not, be permitted to exist in an independent condition in the midst of civilized society." He wanted to remove New York's Indians to Arkansas, Illinois, or Michigan Territory.[19] New York governor DeWitt Clinton agreed that the Indians needed to go, but for their own sake rather than to line white pockets. Forgetting that he had once praised the Oneidas' "insipient civilization," he declared, "Their departure is essential to their preservation" because "Indians are experiencing the fate of all savage and barbarous tribes in the vicinity of civilized nations ... constantly deteriorating in character and diminishing in number and before the expiration of half a century will entirely disappear."[20] This judgment included the Brothertowns and Stockbridges, whom Clinton characterized as "the gypsies of our country" in reference to their sale of homemade brooms and baskets door to door.[21] Part of the Indians' trouble was that they depended on such powerful men to shelter them from white yeomen who were even less generous in their assessments. Stockbridge's white neighbors called for an end to state restrictions on the Indians leasing them land based on "a fact of such notoriety as not to need conformation that Indians will not to any considerable extent become agriculturalists. They have an aversion to labor, and will sooner starve then work."[22] There were precious few whites who disagreed, and practically none who could do anything about it.

The power of these beliefs and the profits to be made on Indian land meant that there was barely any lag between New York's promises to protect the Indians and its violation of those pledges. In 1795, just seven years after the Treaty of Fort Schuyler establishing the Oneida reservation, New York convinced the tribe to cede yet another 132,000 acres for just $6,000.[23] Further cessions

followed, particularly as the state cut the Genesee Road through Oneida territory: 30,000 acres in 1798, another 11,000 acres in 1802, and 33,000 more
acres between 1807 and 1809.[24] These transactions reduced the Oneidas'
claims from an area the size of a country to a small village. New York also
pressured the Brothertowns and Stockbridges to give up their lands, albeit in
a more subtle manner. It began in 1807 by permitting the Indians' state superintendents to lease out lands belonging to Indian widows, orphans, or the
indigent, as a way of enabling them to support themselves financially. On the
surface, this measure was compassionate, but given the large number of Indians in need of public help—by 1818, Brothertown had half as many widows
(twenty two) and orphans (eight), collectively, as intact families (sixty)—it
had the predictable effect of transferring a sizeable portion of Indian land
over to whites.[25] Moreover, this act stipulated that the superintendents could
sell or lease up to three hundred acres along the turnpike "for keeping public houses," even though such places were known to sell alcohol.[26] The Indians distrusted the state's intentions, and for good reason. Governor Clinton
pronounced that the Brothertowns and Stockbridges had the mere right to
occupy their lands but did not *own* them since, he argued, New York had purchased the title from the Oneidas in 1788 through the Treaty of Fort Schuyler.[27] If they wanted to sell their right of occupation, they would have to deal
with the state as holder of the preemption right and not with individual white
purchasers. To punctuate this argument, in 1811 New York paid the Oneidas
$1,200 for their remaining claims to Brothertown and Stockbridge.[28] Clearly,
the state believed the time was growing near when the Indians in those towns
would have to sell.

Indians responded to this pressure by revisiting who belonged to their communities and who did not, with Brothertown focused on the policing of blacks
and their families. Brothertown's anti-black policy was difficult to square with
its recruitment of friends and relatives from the coast, for New England Indians
and blacks were becoming so intertwined that one scholar goes so far as to call
them a "single antebellum socioeconomic class, defined by their occupations as
well as color."[29] Additionally, the Indians' white lessees and sometimes Indians
themselves brought blacks into the community as wage laborers and renters, and
inevitably some of these relationships grew personal.[30] Yet the Peacemakers tried
to keep the groups apart, though inconsistently, especially when land claims
were at stake. They began in 1796 by ordering the removal of the Narragansett
Sarah Pendleton, who had married and produced children with James, "descendant from a negro man, and a woman who was part white and part negro." The

Peacemakers justified their decision by citing Brothertown law and "immemo-rial custom" among the coastal tribes.[31] Two years later, fourteen Brothertown men forcibly evicted Nathan Pendleton, whose "Father was a Black Man," from a tract he was subleasing, prompting a lawsuit for assault and battery in which a white court awarded Pendleton $117.25.[32] Presumably the Indians used gentler tactics the next year against Hiram Robins, Samuel Reeds, and Amar Clap, and in 1804 against Isabella Schooner, Jerusha Wells, and William Peters.[33] Certainly a number of these black or Afro-Indian people were hardworking and had rela-tives in the community, but the Peacemakers were not about to risk the people's status as Indians right when the state was grasping for their land. As vulnerable as the Indians already were to white exploitation, they would become even more of a target if whites could call them black.

Whereas the Brothertowns tried to shore up their borders by expelling any-one tainted with "blackness," the Oneida Pagan Party called for a revival of Na-tive ritual and self-determination. The Oneidas, to an even greater degree than the Brothertowns and Stockbridges, were plagued by white encroachment, poverty, and alcohol abuse despite—and, in the minds of some, because of—Christianity. As an alternative, large numbers of them, particularly in Oriskany, turned to two Iroquois prophets who emerged in the late 1790s, the first an un-named Mohawk from Grand River in Ontario and the second a Seneca named Handsome Lake, or Kanyadaligo.[34] Though these prophets had received visions from different spirits (the Mohawk from Thauloonghyauwangoo, Upholder of Skies, and Handsome Lake from the Creator) and emphasized different rituals (the sacrifice of a white dog in the first instance and the four sacred Iroquois ceremonies in the second), both of them saw moral and religious reform as the keys to recovering sacred power and prosperity. Furthermore, even though these movements developed as alternatives to Christianity, both prophets urged their followers to respect Christian moral teachings, especially on the issue of tem-perance, and Handsome Lake advocated certain civilized reforms.[35] The Pagan Party even instituted a ritual of confession and exhortation each Sunday like the Christian Sabbath. The lines between Christianity and Nativism were blurring, but the fact that this new agenda came from Indian spirits through Indian proph-ets made all the difference in the world to the Pagans. More than ever, they saw themselves as the embodiment of true Indianness and the Christians as white lackeys. Whereas in 1793 the Pagans rejected a proposal to divide the Oneida reservation into Christian and non-Christian halves for fear that the Christian district would have "no trait…of the genuine Indian," in 1805 they agreed to a split to preserve their own integrity, with the Pagans receiving the territory east of Oneida Creek containing Oriskany, and the Christians getting the western portion containing Kanowalohare.[36] The irony of blazing a line to mark the two groups' shrinking differences appears to have been lost on everyone.

The Stockbridges were as unwilling as the Pagans to admit their similarities. Though they praised the Nativists' determination to "forsake all wicked practices and to follow the good path," they considered those efforts to be futile under "temptations of the evil spirit."[37] That evil spirit, the Stockbridges implied, was the source of the prophets' visions, for the great deluder Satan often disguised himself in holy garb. Thus, the Stockbridges called on the Pagans "not [to] depend upon that Prophet you speak of…but you and we must depend on the good spirit together, and make our wants known to him every day, or if we neglect this we can[']t expect his blessing." Without Christianity, the Stockbridges warned, "you and I must come to ruin." Faith would determine just what the people's destiny would be.

The Stockbridges, Brothertowns, and Oneidas all agreed that Indian identity was something real and meaningful, but in the context of struggling to defend their communities against the onslaught of white expansion, they developed quite different ways of expressing that sense of self. The Brothertowns' answer was to enforce their ban on blacks and Afro-Indians, lest whites redefine the community as "people of color" or "negroes" in order to deny their Indian land rights. Yet in the process the Brothertowns violated two nearly universal Indian customs stretching back to time immemorial: the tracing of identity through the family and the acceptance of multiple, fluid identities when kin ties extended across community lines. Living under a colonial regime that insisted on hard-and-fast racial identities as a means of determining social privileges had taught the Brothertowns to police the line between Indian and black and thereby, in practical terms, to define true Indianness as the product of an unadulterated bloodline. The Oneida Pagan Party, by comparison, emphasized custom and ritual in their definitions of what it meant to be Indian. The Pagans charged that Christian Indians were not true Indians because their behaviors had been prescribed by the Great Spirit to whites for whites only. The principle here was that Indians and whites were different kinds of people, and thus if Indians were going to recover from the ravages of colonialism, they needed, as a race, to heed their own spirits and sacred ways. The Mohican spokesmen also urged moral reform and Indian unity, but they held that the Great Spirit punished Indians for their neglect of Christianity and civilized reforms, not for their abandonment of ancestral spirits and rituals. Indians were a race of people, answerable as a group for their sins against God, so they needed to band together to encourage their kind, collectively, to change. It followed, perhaps, that once Indians as a whole entered the Christian family and God lifted his judgment, they would cease to be distinguishable as a race. The Stockbridges were determined to spearhead that goal before Indians disappeared though less inspiring means.

A Covenant of Friendship

As early as the 1790s, Samson Occom and Hendrick Aupaumut had concluded that the future of the Christian Indian experiment lay in the Ohio Country; because of the Mohicans' longstanding ties with the tribes of that region, opening that path devolved to them.[38] Mohican oral history taught that fellow Algonquian-speaking peoples, including the Delawares, Shawnees, and Miamis of the Ohio Country, and all of Brothertown's constituent tribes, originated from a common family.[39] Over the generations, the family had separated into individual bands, but they maintained metaphorical kinship relationships to uphold their sense of mutual obligation and to assign each group special roles.[40] The Mohicans, for instance, claimed the historic responsibility of brokering relations between the interior tribes and "white people in the east."[41] They viewed moving to the Ohio as an opportunity to recover that status as the locus of Indian-white affairs moved westward. The Mohicans also looked west because generations of them had considered the Miami country an escape hatch from trouble. The Miamis had invited the Mohicans to join them as far back as the late seventeenth century as a means of enhancing their numbers against Iroquois attacks and epidemic disease. Only a small band of Mohicans accepted the offer at that time, but the Miamis renewed the invitation each time the two groups met in council.[42] It took the whitewashing of Oneida country for the remaining Mohicans to consider it.

Aupaumut took the lead in opening discussions with the interior tribes, venturing to the Ohio Country twice in 1792 and again in 1793 as a paid peace agent of the United States, which he used to further his own people's business.[43] Yet warfare between the young republic and the confederation of Shawnees, Miamis, and Delawares, among others, meant that any relocation of the Christian Indians would have to wait. The nation's victory at the Battle of Fallen Timbers in 1794 and the subsequent Treaty of Greenville then forced the Indians out of most of Ohio. The Miamis and Delawares regrouped along the White River in Indiana, awakened to their need to prepare for life under white dominion even as they were determined not to cede whites another acre of land.[44] It was with these ends in mind that the two tribes renewed their bid for the Mohicans to join them.

In 1803 Aupaumut visited the White River tribes to restate his vision for their collective future. He argued that whereas "all the nations who rejected Civilization and Christian religion[,] ingrained the wicked practices of the white people [and] were poor and finally became extinct from the earth," Indians, like the Stockbridges, "who accept the offer of the good white people were blessed, so far as they were faithfull they prosper and they remain to this day." He was not, he emphasized, calling on the White River tribes to give up hunting or their ancestral customs immediately. He did, however, want them to heed the Gospels and begin learning their "A.B.C.s," as he called them, as first steps toward greater reforms. Sensitive to the Ohio tribes' recent loss of territory, he added, "Be assured that by following this path I and my nation have found many advantages[.] Among other things our white brother can not so easily cheat us now with regard to our land affairs as they have done to our forefathers." His overall point was that if these Indians followed the Stockbridges' course, "the great and good spirit will bless you that you will become a wise people, and you shall increase, both in number and substance, consequently you will be happy in this life, and the life to come."[45]

Aupaumut appreciated the manifold contradictions of what he was saying. True enough, his people had *survived* colonization, largely by using their Christian status to carve out a place for themselves amid white settlement, yet they were hardly thriving; in fact, they had suffered so much land loss and persecution at the hands of white Christians that *they* were the ones preparing to flee their homes. As Aupaumut wrote to Timothy Pickering a decade earlier after his return from the Ohio Country:

> In all my arguments with these Indians, I have as it were [been] oblige[d] to say nothing with regard to the conduct of the Yorkers, how they cheat[ed] my fathers, how they have taken our lands Unjustly, and how my fathers were groaning as it were to their graves, in losing their lands for nothing, although they were faithful friends to the Whites; and how the white people artfully got their Deeds confirm[ed] in the Laws &c. I say had I mention[ed] these things to the Indians it would [have] ag[g]ravated their prejudices against all white people.

Though Aupaumut was right that Indians could never defend their vast hunting grounds in the face of determined white agricultural expansion, whites also disrespected the claims of the Indians who fenced and plowed their lands. The most poignant lesson of Stockbridge's history was that race trumped religion and culture in determining who would enjoy peace and security in white America. Aupaumut knew this point as well as anyone. His agenda, then, appears to have been grounded in the belief that if Indians persevered through their trials, they might attract God's blessing. The stark alternative, as he explained to the White River tribes, was that "you will be dispised by many, and finally you will become extinct from the earth."[46]

As these discussions grew serious, the Stockbridges invited the Jersey Delawares to join them temporarily in New York in anticipation of a future move to White River. This union had been in the making for decades—in a certain sense, for generations. The Delawares and Mohicans thought of each other as close kin and historically had intermarried and cooperated in war and diplomacy.[47] In more recent times, Christianity bound together their communities of Stockbridge and the Brotherton reservation in New Jersey in vital new ways. Their extended kin had worshipped together in the Moravian missions of Pennsylvania and Ohio, their children had studied together in Wheelock's school, and their communities had shared David Brainerd as a missionary. In turn, the Jersey Delawares forged increasingly strong connections to the constituent tribes of Stockbridge's neighboring community, Brothertown. Their children also studied together with Wheelock and then evangelized the Oneidas, and for a time it seemed likely that Occom would join Brainerd's mission. That plan fell through, but the Narragansett Daniel Simon, himself a Wheelock alumnus, fulfilled the promise by replacing John Brainerd at Brotherton, New Jersey, in 1783 after a three-year teaching stint at Stockbridge.[48] So it was something of a natural progression when, in 1797, Simon's former Delaware charges petitioned the New Jersey state legislature for permission to sell their reservation lands "to enable them to remove to their brethren in the state of New York."[49] Five years later, in the summer of 1802, some eighty-five Delawares took to the road for New Stockbridge.[50] They explained that the chance to relocate to White River alongside the Mohicans gave them "some hopes left still to unite all our tribe in one place, & become a good & civilized people like our white brethren, in that can we fully believe that the good Spirit will bless us as he does the whites, & we should increase like them & fill the country & be a happy people."[51] These two groups would never part ways again, but many trials lay ahead.

During 1809, everything for the move to Indiana seemed to be in place. That summer, four Brothertowns—John Tukie, John Skeesuck Sr., Jacob Fowler, and

Henry Cujep—accompanied Aupaumut on a visit to the White River to deliver the Miamis and Delawares a wampum belt of friendship and to survey the country.[52] In the fall, the host tribes laid out a tract of land for the new Christian settlement. Then, in December, Aupaumut trekked to Washington and won President Thomas Jefferson's acknowledgment that this grant "should be the property of said tribe forever."[53] Aupaumut also managed to obtain a federal salary to "superintend Indian affairs on the White River for three years," which included encouraging the interior tribes to form "nucleated settlements," overseeing a school run by Mohican John Jacobs, and promoting male plow agriculture.[54] A move seemed so imminent that a half-dozen Stockbridges and Brothertowns left for White River as the advance party of what was anticipated to become a much larger migration. Even Stockbridge's consensus against leasing land to whites broke down as Indian families sought to make money as quickly as possible so that they could reestablish themselves out west.[55] However, like Brothertown during the Revolution, their plans were derailed by war. In November 1811, the United States marched against followers of the Shawnee prophet, Tenskwatawa, and his brother, the war leader Tecumseh, camped at Prophetstown on Indiana's Wabash River. This Battle of Tippecanoe was the first strike in a renewed frontier conflict that would segue with the War of 1812 between Great Britain and the United States, thus forcing the Christian Indians to postpone their relocation.

It was much to the delight of Christian Indians like Aupaumut that Tecumseh's defeat in 1813, followed by the peace struck by United States and Great Britain in 1814, signaled a permanent end to multitribal Indian militancy in this region and the last opportunity for Indians to use European powers as a counterweight to the republic. Aupaumut referred to Tenskwatawa as "the emisary of Satan" for what he considered to be his suicidal opposition to God and the United States.[56] As such, Aupaumut used the cover of his negotiations for White River to spy on the prophet for the United States and then served in the forces of American General William Henry Harrison at the Battle of Tippecanoe. Back east, thirty-eight Mohican men under the leadership of John Jacobs and Jacob Konkapot, and some two hundred Oneidas under Adam Skenandoah, Jack Antoine, and Pagan Peter, assisted the American army in patrolling the U.S./Canadian border at Niagara, while another Indian force of some 120 men, mostly Oneidas but also some Stockbridges and Brothertowns, played a key role at the Battle of Sandy Creek in May 1814, in which American forces broke a British blockade of the Lake Erie ship-launching port of Sackett's Harbor.[57] When they were done, the time seemed ripe to extend their Christian project to the White River.

Dark Days on White River

After years of talk and more talk, finally, in 1817, the Stockbridges, Jersey Delawares, and Brothertowns began preparing in earnest to remove to White River. Between the late spring and fall, a delegation of Brothertowns, including Thomas Dick, Paul Dick, Jacob Dick, Sarah Dick, Thomas Isaac, Betsey Isaac, Charles Isaac, Rodolphus Fowler, and their white agent Thomas Dean, scouted out locations for a settlement and consulted with everyone who could possibly be concerned with the affair. At Vincennes, they met with Indiana governor Jonathan Jennings and predicted that their future community would rival any other in the area "heretofore purchased and now settled with those who call themselves white people."[58] Later, after they had been joined by Stockbridge's Henry Nimham and Brothertown's Isaac Wauby, they visited with Delaware and Shawnee leaders and obtained approval for the migration.[59] News of this development filled the people back home with productive energy. Stockbridge suddenly launched a "general reformation," while the Brothertowns were said to be "considerably improved...particularly in their buildings, stock of grain, meat, etc."[60] Doubtless the Indians wanted to raise the value of their land before it was sold to fund resettlement. Stockbridge's council, for instance, quickly secured permission from New York to alienate a mile-wide area on three sides of the township.[61] The date of migration seemed near.

A renewed sense of mission was another spur to the people's reforms. The Stockbridges began to recall how "their ancestors have told them that there is a very numerous and powerful tribe of Muhheakens living far beyond the Misisipi [sic], near what is called the White Mountains." From their base at White River, the Stockbridges hoped "as soon as they are able to send messengers to find that lost sheep of their tribe, and recommend civilization in the proper way & time."[62] The Mohicans expected to lift up themselves in the process. Sergeant noticed on the eve of the move that his charges had developed a newfound "desire to rise to glory and importance among the nations to be more happy and numerous than their ancestors on account of civilization and religion."[63] That sentiment rang through loud and clear as an advance party of some eighty people prepared to leave for Indiana in July 1818.[64] In the migrants' final Sabbath in New York, Sergeant preached to them from Acts 22:21: "And he said unto me, depart, for I will send thee far hence unto the gentiles."[65] Though white encroachment had been the main cause of the Indians' decision to leave New York, the Indians had turned this misery into a source of inspiration. They viewed their relocation to White River as a mission from God to save their people, tribe, and race.

The first Stockbridges arrived out west only to have their hopes "blasted," in their words, by the Treaty of St. Mary, in which the Delawares ceded all their claims in Indiana to the United States.[66] The New York Indians had known the risk of such a sale—Governor Jennings had told them as much, and it would have been foolhardy not to believe him given the direction of federal Indian policy and the growth of Indiana's white population, which already stood at nearly seventy thousand in 1816.[67] The Indians considered themselves safe, however, because they had presidential approval for their move and a promise from the Delawares that they would not sell.[68] They had even written to the Delawares on the eve of their migration reminding them of this pledge. Yet Jonathan Johnston, the federal Indian agent in the region, refused to forward the letter. He explained, "You warn the Delawares in the strongest manner not to sell any more land to the white people. You ought to know that as an agent of the United States, I could not be the means of communicating such sentiments to the Indians."[69] But the Christian Indians did not know. Even though white Christians had driven them from their land in New England even after their people's military service and Christian reforms, even though whites had made their lives impossible in Oneida country when all they wanted to do was pursue their reforms in peace, they appear to have believed that life in Indiana would be different. It was difficult to give up the dream. A Stockbridge delegation to President James Monroe appealed that they had gone to live among their "red brethren" on White River only because "GOD called upon us to send among them a colony of our nation in which was built a church of our Lord and Savior, that we might be the means of Civilizing and Christianizing them and doing to them great good."[70] The problem for the Indians was that they were caught up in a power play, not a morality play. The United States was not going to give up this land to Indians, regardless of their mission or any earlier promises to them.

In the short term, the Stockbridges and Brothertowns faced the problem of what to do with community members who had already set out for Indiana after selling their lands in New York. Aside from Brothertown's Isaac Wauby and Jacob Dick, each of whom managed to get 320 acres at White River confirmed to them in acknowledgment of the time and labor they had invested there, these people were left with nothing.[71] About half of them stayed in Indiana in the vain hope that the government would restore their grant, and in the meantime they scratched out an existence on lands to which they no longer had title.[72] The other

half made the long journey back to Oneida, where they faced an equally uncertain future. In a tragically appropriate symbol of their plight, two white men
"wantonly fired upon" one of their bands as it passed through Licking County,
Ohio, killing a pregnant twenty-six-year-old named Rachel Konkapot (who delivered the baby as she lay dying).[73] To be Indian in white America was to be
considered a savage enemy.

Come and Sit Down with Them

The Stockbridges and Brothertowns were committed psychologically and financially to leaving New York regardless of their losses in Indiana, and they were
soon joined by a portion of the Oneida Christian Party, for whom prospects
in the east were no brighter; the only question was where they would go, and
when. White authorities recommended Wisconsin. For years, white leaders
such as the Massachusetts clergyman Jedidiah Morse, Secretary of War John C.
Calhoun, and land jobber David A. Ogden had discussed plans to remove the
Oneidas somewhere out west. Morse favored Green Bay as a location because
he expected the Oneidas' fidelity to the United States "would act as a check upon
the Winnebagos [or Ho-Chunks], the worst affected of any Indians upon our
border."[74] By "worst affected," Morse meant that Indians living in and around
Wisconsin, including not only the Ho-Chunks but also the Menominees, Sacs,
Foxes (or Meskquakies), Potawatomis, Ojibwas, and Ottawas, generally subscribed to militant Nativist ideologies and had contributed warriors to the British campaign in the War of 1812.[75] Furthermore, many of them had relatives
among the French and Métis (French-Indian) families at the fur trading post of
Green Bay, and those people were themselves deeply distrustful of Anglo-American rule. Calhoun agreed that the Oneidas would help introduce the idea of
American dominion to these populations, so in 1819 he instructed the governor
of Michigan Territory, Lewis Cass, to broach the issue with the Menominees.[76]
Calhoun and Morse, in other words, favored uprooting the Oneidas from their
ancient homeland in order to serve the very nation that had victimized them. It
was a cruel calculation.

The main advocate for removal among the Oneidas was not Oneida at all, but
Eleazar Williams, a Mohawk missionary from St. Regis (or Akwesasne) on the
St. Lawrence River.[77] Williams brought an impressive skill set to the Oneidas at
a time when they were hungry for leadership. He was not only fluent in the Mohawk language and Iroquois custom but also conversant with Anglo-American

ways. His remarkable background included a private education in Longmeadow, Massachusetts, a brief stint at Dartmouth College, and ordination within the Episcopal Church. One of his ancestors was a minor celebrity: Eunice Williams, who as an English girl in 1704 had been taken captive from Deerfield, Massachusetts, by a French and Indian force and then adopted into a Mohawk family in St. Regis, where she lived out the rest of her long life. Eleazar capitalized on her well-known story and his own polished talents to establish himself as a link between the Oneidas and white society. His charismatic preaching earned him a devoted religious following, particularly among the Christians of Kanawalohare but also, to a lesser degree, among the Pagan Party, many of whose members later became Episcopalians and renamed themselves the Second Christian Party. Yet Williams had even greater plans. Echoing the Christian utopianism that had long characterized Brothertown and New Stockbridge, he pictured an Oneida community in Green Bay serving as a magnet for thousands of Indians from across the continent who would then adopt Christianity and civility and perhaps even organize themselves into an American state. His idealism, however, did not prevent him from partnering with men the Oneidas considered to be devils. In 1821 he began receiving payments from the Ogden Land Company, a corporation determined to remove the Iroquois by hook or by crook.[78] If Williams's vision was the pull of Oneida removal, scheming by white land jobbers was the push.

The Stockbridges had their own reasons to consider Wisconsin. Just as an ancient covenant linked the Mohicans to the Miamis of White River, so too did they have historic ties to the Indians of the Great Lakes. Tradition held that "over a hundred years ago a delegation from their nation visited the Sauks and Foxes when they resided at Green Bay; and that their grand children (the Sacs &c.) invited them to come and settle down with them then, and as an inducement they said they 'would give them beaver-skins for their bed.'"[79] Such a meeting might very well have occurred during the 1680s, when a group of 110 Mohicans joined the Ottawas for an extended hunting trip through the Lakes.[80] As far as the Stockbridges were concerned, their interest in Wisconsin resulted from this "chain of friendship," not from the directives of white outsiders.

From this foundation, the Stockbridges hoped to turn Green Bay into a center of Indian Christianity, civility, population, and strength, reflective of their former visions for New York and White River. In an appeal to the St. Regis Mohawks to join them in Green Bay, the Mohicans reasoned that whereas they had both once been "powerful nations, which spread from the spring of great Eastern waters, to the western great Lakes…our own extensive Territories is now covered all over with our white Brethren," leaving them with reservations "comparatively no larger than moccasin rags." Wisconsin was a place "where our several Tribes might at some further day sit down together in pace & have an opportunity of cultivating more their friendship which their forefathers had established…whence we can have, once more, an ample room to spread our Blankets, Smoke our pipes, & promote each others welfare, & thereby have our children after us to enjoy the same to the latest generations."[81] The Stockbridges also believed that they would be "of material advantage to our Brethren" of the Lakes "by setting forth to them examples."[82] Their enthusiasm for this venture was so infectious that it gave Sergeant "strong faith that in the Northwest Territory the Lord intends some important revolution in favour of the natives in that country."[83]

The principle of Indian security and prosperity through racial solidarity and civility was a hallmark of the Christian Indians' negotiations for a homeland in Wisconsin. In the summers of 1821 and 1822, delegations from New York led by Eleazar Williams, Solomon U. Hendrick (Hendrick Aupaumut's son), and the Oneida chief Daniel Bread met with scores of Menominees and Ho-Chunks in the council room of Fort Howard, a federal installation built shortly after the War of 1812 near the mouth of the Fox River. Speaking through a series of interpreters (for the Menominees spoke an Algonquian language distinct from the Mohicans', while the Ho-Chunks spoke a Siouan one), Hendrick declared that his people wanted to relocate to Wisconsin "under the direction of the Great Spirit" to teach them white ways like literacy and Christianity even as they defended them against white encroachment. A number of the Wisconsin Indians were persuaded. According to Stockbridge's John Metoxen, some Menominees responded that "you brothers know the ways of the white people better than we do. You know they always want more land—that when a white man puts his finger upon our lands, he has long nails & they go deep, and it is hard to get them out…brothers, you will help us keep off the white man."[84] Later, the Menominees reportedly said that they wanted the "Wapanokas" (or Wabanakis, meaning "eastern or dawnland people") to "teach their young men how to till the land and live like white people," because "they were poor & their game scarce & their crops of wild rice uncertain."[85]

Yet these ideals were difficult to put into practice, because the two sides brought vastly different assumptions about land use and ownership to the council fire. A number of the Wisconsin Indians, counseled by their Métis relatives, were suspicious of the New York tribes' intentions. They sensed that these

Figure 7. Fort Howard dans la grand Baie verte (Ouisconsin), 1842, by Ligny et Cicr., Salle au Compte. Fort Howard, built in 1812 by the federal government at the mouth of the Fox River on Green Bay, was the site several Indian conferences between, on one side, the Oneidas, Stockbridges, and Brothertowns (known collectively as the New York Indians) and, on the

other side, the Ho-Chunks (or Winnebagos) and Menominees of Wisconsin. Though these two parties initially engaged each other in a spirit of Indian brotherhood, land disputes soon drove them apart. Courtesy Wisconsin Historical Society, Madison, Wisconsin.

Wabanakis were angling for fee-simple title to the land, which would give them the exclusive right of use and alienation, rather than just permission to settle down and plant. The Ho-Chunk chief, Oogotheed (or Dog's Head), warned that "as Indian men of our own colour & our species…surely the great spirit would be angry if one Indian should cheat another." In any case, he believed, "the lands are not ours.…They are the property of the Great Spirit.…Do you think God ever intended that an Indian should sell land to an Indian? No." His people were willing only "that you should come & live among us as we live with each other, & if you contemplate giving us anything we repeat to you that we shall not receive it as payment for the lands, but as a token of your love for us, & your desire to assist us."[86] This was the principle of *apēkon ahkīhih,* in which allies were welcome to share in the people's land.[87] The Menominees believed that everyone agreed on this point when they finally signed a treaty with the Stockbridges, Oneidas, and St. Regis Mohawks for 860,600 acres of land along the Fox River stretching between Green Bay and Lake Winnebago in exchange for $1,500 in goods to be paid the following year. The deal, however, was not yet done, for the next summer, when the delegates from New York arrived in Wisconsin to deliver this payment (or present, from the Wisconsin Indians' perspective), they pressed for still more territory, claiming that the original grant was insufficient to support all of their people. After strained negotiations, the Menominees finally relented, granting the New York Indians 6.7 million acres for less than $4,000 in goods. The Brothertowns were confident enough about this title to buy into the compact, assuming the final payment of $950 to the Menominees in exchange for a tract eventually set at thirty miles long by eight miles wide on the east side of the Fox River at Little Kakalin, some twenty miles from the river's mouth.[88] Wonderstruck at their success, the Christian Indians had no idea that in refusing to respect the Wisconsin tribes' understanding of these transactions, they were setting the stage for years of discord and yet another removal.

"Join Our Hands Together"

The New York Indians were far from unanimous in their support for the move to Wisconsin. Some Stockbridges saw no point in trying to outrun their problems, because experience had taught them that "whites and liquor will follow them let them go ever so far as it always has done."[89] The Oneidas' Second Christian Party and the remaining Pagan Party members denounced Eleazar Williams as an intruder who had no right to represent their tribe. Yet pro-migration Indians all but forced their opponents to concede by weakening the already perforated border between Indian and white lands. A number of Stockbridges had begun to rent their lands as early as 1806, despite laws to the contrary, when Aupaumut was negotiating for White River.[90] Twelve years later, there were some two hundred white families residing at Stockbridge, "so that there are now but very few lots that there is not a white family upon," according to the Indians' superintendents.[91] Stockbridges who protested these leases did so to no avail. Quite simply, most of the tribe saw greater benefit in renting out the land than in farming it, given that they were planning to move at any time. The Oneidas faced similar pressures, particularly with the opening of the Erie Canal. Already by 1820, their reservation contained an estimated "three hundred families of white People, besides Negroes & mulattoes" squatting illegally.[92] White encroachment only increased when, in 1824, the state passed legislation permitting Oneida migrants to sell off portions of the reservation to fund their resettlement.[93] Bowing to the inevitable, throughout the 1820s and 1830s, all but a handful of stalwarts grudgingly decided to leave for Wisconsin.

The ideal of Indian racial unity centered on Christian and civilized reforms had carried the Brothertowns, Stockbridges, and Christian Oneidas through their crushing disappointments in New York and Indiana to the banks of the Fox River in Wisconsin. None of them were so naive as to ignore the obstacles in front of them—the certainty of continued white encroachment, tensions with the host Menominees and Ho-Chunks, and their own deep-seated divisions— yet they believed in their purpose. The opening of fresh land, first in Indiana, then in Wisconsin, was the source of their inspiration, for it provided a sign of God's favor, just as their loss of land and plagues of alcohol abuse and poverty seemed to indicate his test of the faithful or even his curse. The Christian Indians' faith in the people they had come to call their "red brethren" gave them additional hope of holding back this flood. It was no pipe dream for the New York Indians to envision thousands of their friends and relatives flocking to join them at Green Bay given their title to nearly seven million acres of land and the dismal prospects for Indians elsewhere in white America. Wisconsin, then, could become the home for displaced Indians from Long Island Sound, Iroquoia, the Ohio Country, southern Ontario, and beyond. Their numbers, combined with those of the Menominees, Ho-Chunks, Sacs, and Foxes, whom the New York Indians intended to evangelize, would, in theory, provide a formidable barrier to white expansion. The idea here was that Indians could turn their common misery into a source of strength and survival if only they united. Yet the very forces of colonialism that spawned this vision fought against its realization. White Americans were not going to wait for the Indians to enact their utopian dreams before they fulfilled their own ambition to seize control of Wisconsin and the lands beyond.

CHAPTER 8

More Than They Know How to Endure

FEW whites ever visited the Stockbridge or Brothertown settlements on the Fox River, which was just as the Indians wanted it, but those who did in the early 1830s were impressed by what they saw. Located at the Big Rapids or Grand Kakalin at the height of the river's navigation, the Indians enjoyed a twenty-mile buffer between their new home and Green Bay, the lone center of white settlement in eastern Wisconsin. Nevertheless, in many ways their new community, which they called Statesburg, resembled the Yankee towns that had forced them out of New York. By 1831, just nine years after the first group of Stockbridges arrived on the Fox, they boasted some 225 people living in forty-five houses, most of them "very ordinary log huts" except for the missionary glebe, which was "a large frame building." There was a sawmill, a school house, a smith shop, and cleared land covered with grazing livestock and crops of wheat, corn, and potatoes extending for four miles along the river and two miles or so inland.[1] "It is evident that they farm better than the French inhabitants at Green Bay," wrote one impressed federal official.[2] The Mohicans' Christianity also caught the attention of outsiders. One of the Indians' guests, David Greene, said he felt "at home" in the Stockbridge church because the Indians conducted part of their service in English, sang with "order and propriety," and maintained strict discipline during worship.[3] Statesburg's day school, with an enrollment of forty-five students, was the region's first free public school and the first to be taught by a woman, Electra Quinney.[4] Then there were the Mohicans' high moral standards, which often surprised whites who had been raised to assume that all Indians were dissolute. The Indians' playfully named missionary, Cutting Marsh, found that "the excellencies of their character are hospitality, kindness, peaceful[ness], not revengeful[ness], readiness to forgive injuries, respectful[ness] to the aged and superiors."[5] The Brothertowns made less dramatic progress on the Fox than the Stockbridges, since most of their migrants did not arrive in Wisconsin until after 1830, but, still, federal officials conceded that their people "are farther advanced in civilization and the arts of domestic life than perhaps most of the borderers on a distant frontier."[6] Federal Indian agents in New York, hearing this news, contended that Brothertown's example should "afford conclusive evidence of the great advantages of their concentration in a position not immediately surrounded as they were here by white settlements."[7]

Yet rather than keeping settlers away, white governments continued to pressure the Indians to make way for them. To the Indians' utter dismay, that pressure arose within just a few short years of their arrival on the Fox River, as Washington teamed with the Menominees and Ho-Chunks to uproot them again, this time to the banks of Lake Winnebago, further up the Fox. As in the earlier removals, this crisis reopened debate about the meaning of race in the Indians' lives and America generally, including the nature of Indianness, the responsibility of Indians to each other, and the place of Indians in the white republic. In turn, the Indians' dilemma in Wisconsin became part of a broader national debate about what to do with Indians in the path of United States expansion or, rather, about how to justify their removal.

Red Brethren, Christian Brethren, and the Racial Politics of Land

Relocating to Wisconsin cost the New York Indians dearly in time, energy, and resources, but they persevered, pushed by their destitution and pulled by the hope that their new home would provide succor to future generations. The first Stockbridge party arrived in 1822, consisting primarily of those who had already gone to Indiana under John Metoxen and who, since the Treaty of St. Mary's, had moved from place to place in the Midwest.[8] By 1829 all the Stockbridges and a number of Brothertowns had left New York for the Fox, followed the next decade by the majority of Brothertowns and Oneidas.[9] The pace was determined by a number of factors, most of all cost, given the steep expenses of nearly every stage of the journey. The migrants needed livestock, wagons, clothes, food, tools, and passenger fare for the steamboat from Buffalo to Detroit and then Detroit to Green Bay.[10] Not surprisingly, these outlays, combined with the work of carving out new settlements in a dense forest, left them in a "truly deplorable situation" during their first years in Wisconsin.[11] To get by, they contracted debts with a merchant at Fort Howard and even resorted to "pawning their guns, Traps,

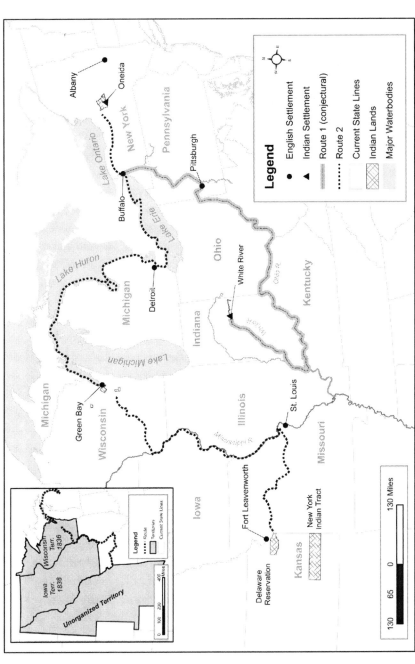

Map 2. The New York Indians' Migrations during the Nineteenth Century. During the nineteenth century, the New York Indians (the Brothertowns, Stockbridges, and Oneidas) repeatedly migrated to new homes under pressure from white encroachment and white governments. These migrations took portions of them from New York to Indiana to Wisconsin (including stops on the Fox River and Lake Winnebago) to Kansas. Their battles over these removals exercised a formative influence on their views about race.

clothing & house hold furniture."[12] That they managed to overcome these obstacles to create a landscape of fields and fences, and a village anchored by a church and school, should have left whites with no doubt about their ability to thrive if given the opportunity.[13]

What easterners saw as progress, the Menominees, Ho-Chunks, and Métis increasingly viewed as a threat.[14] The Menominee chief Grizzly Bear denounced the New York Indians as "dogs" for hunting along the Wolf River northwest of the Fox, far outside the bounds of their original grant. "Was this their agreement?" Grizzly Bear asked rhetorically. "No—they were to cultivate the land."[15] In response, the Menominees poached the Mohicans' livestock, just as the Stockbridges hunted the Menominees' deer.[16] The Wisconsin tribes were also startled by the number of Indian migrants from Oneida. The Ho-Chunk Four Legs explained that the "Wappenekee" had merely asked "for land to sit down upon; to cultivate and raise something to feed their children." No one had discussed just how many eastern Indians planned to move to the Fox or how much land they would plant. "At first a few came," Four Legs recalled, "but since then they are coming yearly, as though they would claim the whole country in spite of us."[17] The Menominees grew so exasperated with this growth that in 1831 they threatened to remove the Brothertown settlement by force.[18] Ironically, their complaints echoed those of the Brothertown Indians' seventeenth-century ancestors, who had ceded land to small numbers of Englishmen in the expectation that the two people would share it, only to confront a veritable swarm of settlers who insisted that purchased territory was their exclusive property.[19]

The Wisconsin Indians also resented the newcomers' air of superiority and sharp territoriality. "These New York Indians are hard to be satisfied," Grizzly Bear complained to Fort Howard's Joshua Bowyer. "They are made like you are. They have education and pride themselves upon it.... When we give them a piece they want more. They have no hearts or souls. And, as I have told you before, they behave so badly that we hate them."[20] Just years before, the Menominees had welcomed the Christian Indians into their country as fellow "Red Men," only to encounter the limits of racial unity among Indians with dramatically different ways of life. The New York Indians remained committed to Christianizing and civilizing their so-called savage brethren and using that shared culture to create an Indian safe haven. However, in the interim they were going to consolidate their own gains to avoid ever being displaced again, even if that security came at the expense of their hosts. That point became clear in 1827, if it was ever in question before, when the Stockbridges and Oneidas formed the "New York Indian

Militia" to assist federal officials in hunting down the Ho-Chunk leader, Red Bird, whose band had risen up against four thousand American settlers in Wisconsin's Lead District near the border with Illinois and Iowa.[21] In such an environment, "Red Brethren" could become hated "dogs" in an instant.

These tensions became particularly acute as the United States began pursuing its racial agenda of Indian removal even in remote Wisconsin. Its wedge came in 1827 at the Treaty of Butte des Morts when the Menominees asked federal commissioners to reject the New York Indians' claims to co-ownership of the Fox River Valley and restrict them to a much smaller tract. The Menominees' intent was not only to punish the New Yorkers for behaving, as they saw it, like ungrateful guests, but also to solidify their own claims to as much land as possible at a time when Washington was pressing for cessions.[22] Accordingly, the Menominees sold the United States a strip of land running southwest along the Fox River from Green Bay to Lake Winnebago.[23] The United States was an eager partner in this assault on the New York Indians' lands because its people were already eyeing the western Great Lakes for expansion. By 1830, Ohio contained nearly one million white Americans, Indiana could boast 338,000, Illinois another 155,000, and Michigan 31,000.[24] Wisconsin's days as an Indian-dominated territory were certainly numbered if this growth continued, as it was certain to do. The Fox River Valley was especially appealing to whites for the same reasons that the Indians had settled there: it contained excellent mill sites, rich soil, and plenty of marketable hardwood, all within easy reach of water transportation. Surveyor A. G. Ellis went so far as to envision turning southern Wisconsin into a "Second Genesee Country," in reference to the part of New York state transformed by the Erie Canal, by cutting a passage through the two-mile portage between the upper Fox and Wisconsin Rivers, thus linking eastern Wisconsin to the Mississippi.[25] The New York Indians seemed to represent the only major obstacle to such development.

The Indians fought their removal in person and in print, both in Wisconsin and in Washington. They wrote to the President, Congress, the secretary of war, the territorial governor of Michigan, and virtually anyone in office who had influence over their affairs. The Brothertowns even went so far as to send their agent, Thomas Dean, and a series of their leading men (Thomas Dick, Eliphalet Mathers, Benjamin Fowler, and David Tukie) to the federal capital three times between 1824 and 1831 to lobby Secretary of War John C. Calhoun and President Andrew Jackson, with the final trip taking place alongside the Oneidas' Daniel Bread and John Anthony and Stockbridge's John W. Quinney.[26] Given the

Indians' utter lack of political power, they had to try to shame the country into honoring its promises to their tribes. They ran up against a national racial ideology that no moral argument could budge.

Federal officials framed their proposal to remove the Christian Indians from the Fox as an act of benevolence rather than tyranny. The government's position was that the Menominees and Ho-Chunks had never intended to sell the New York Indians co-ownership of the Fox River Valley but only the right to settle there, so it would be unfair for them to lose these lands. This logic did not consider that generations of eastern Indians, including the New York Indians' own ancestors, had made similar complaints against white land deeds without redress. The government favored upholding the Wisconsin Indians' joint-use customs only because they dovetailed with the nation's interests. Equally hypocritical was Washington's contention that the Christian Indians, as farmers, could make do with less land than their hunter-gatherer hosts and that, in any case, they were likely to "reconvert…from agriculturalists to Hunters" if they had access to "boundless" territory. The subtext was that whereas white authorities accepted the right of white farmers to hold undeveloped land as a capital investment or in expectation of parceling it out to future generations, Indians were too inherently savage to resist the urge to abandon their fields for the chase. From this perspective, robbing Indian farmers of their land was doing them a favor.

The Stockbridges and Brothertowns would have none of this cant, not after three prior removals and a solid record of Christianity, civility, and loyalty to the United States. Their right to live on Fox River was clear as far as they were concerned: the United States had encouraged them to move to Wisconsin and then given its express approval of the deals they had struck with the Menominees and Ho-Chunks; their negotiations with the Wisconsin Indians had been made in good faith, and everyone at the treaty councils had understood the terms; moreover, their settlements on the Fox River were beacons of civility in an otherwise savage land. Their first point was beyond dispute. Federal officials all the way up to the president were on record endorsing the New York Indians' relocation to Wisconsin.[27] In 1820, the Senate had even refused to ratify a treaty that would have given the United States the Wisconsin Indians' title to the Fox River Valley in part because it recognized the nation's obligation to the Christian Indians who had settled there.[28] The Christian Indians had secured the federal government's backing at every stage of their negotiations with the Menominees and Ho-Chunks because they knew it was their only check on an encroaching white population. "If treaties thus made by us with the approbation of public authority, and confirmed by the same, are to be thus disregarded and trampled on," the Stockbridges appealed to the Senate, "on what can we rely, or where shall we ever rest?"[29] The answers, they knew full well, were nothing and nowhere, particularly in light of the Supreme Court's 1831 decision, *Cherokee Nation v. Georgia,* on the issues of southeastern Indian removal. The court ruled that the Cherokees and other independent Indian tribes were "domestic dependent nations" with a right to their lands and self-government. In turn, the United States was obligated to honor the provisions of its Indian treaties. Yet what this ruling meant in practice, observed the Cherokee chief, John Ridge, in a letter to Brothertown's agent, Thomas Dean, was that "the responsibility is thrown upon the Executive of the U.S. to maintain the political faith of the Union pledged to the Indians."[30] Unfortunately for Indians, the executive in question was Jackson, the foremost proponent of Indian removal. His officers rejected the New York Indians' argument that "if the present administration revokes the solemn acts of a former one, which promised to secure a home in these western territories to them & their posterity, they can no longer have any faith in the Government." Lewis Cass, Jackson's governor of Michigan Territory, denounced such reasoning as a "party question" that, by connecting the Fox River affair with Cherokee removal, was designed "to embarrass the administration."[31] The New York Indians' charge that the administration deserved to be embarrassed for its treatment of them was lost in the exchange.

The Indians also objected that the government had no right to alter an agreement that had been struck fairly between them and the Wisconsin tribes alone. Stockbridge and Brothertown presented one witness after another to testify that they had conducted their negotiations with the Menominees and Ho-Chunks through well-qualified interpreters and that the Menominees had repeatedly welcomed them as brethren whose knowledge of white ways would help guard them against American land grabs.[32] The New York Indians attributed the Wisconsin Indians' cries of foul just years after the negotiations for Fox River to Métis scheming and rising chiefs who were resentful for having been left out of the bargain.[33] As for the issue of whether a fair price had been paid for the Fox River lands, the New York Indians discerned that this question could be used to challenge nearly every land title in the United States: "Ten miles Square—or a hundred Square Miles on Connecticut [River] in Massachusetts taking Northampton for a center—was once sold by Indians to the whites for 20 shillings sterling," one of their petitions pointed out.[34] The deal, however, was done. In the New York Indians' view, so was their deal for Fox River.

The New York Indians' most earnest appeal was to the government's responsibility to them as fellow civilized Christians, longstanding allies, and repeated victims of American Machiavellianism. The Brothertowns pleaded with Jackson that "they never anticipated or intended the purchase of a large tract of country for the purpose of hunting but they purchased the land for themselves & their posterity for agricultural purposes."[35] Their claims to Fox River land were indeed vast, but their need for land could not be judged on the basis of their current numbers since their plan was to attract kin from all over the country to Wisconsin, and that process would take some time. The New York Indians set their overall population at 5,549 people, which, if all of them came to Fox River, would give them 120 to 150 acres each, a comfortable but not an exorbitant amount of land for a farm.[36] Their vision was to "put in practice experimentally the good ways of civilized people" and thus to be of "material advantage to our Brethren in this country"—meaning other Indians—"by setting forth to them examples of this kind & by maintaining & keeping a pacific & friendly intercourse with them to be instrumental of preserving a continued peace between them and the United States."[37] Why would the government destroy such a noble experiment? Did not the government owe the Christian Indians a debt for its prior wrongs against them? "Our own people, as a body, did not wish to come here," John Metoxen protested. "But we were compelled by extraneous influences—by the interest & policy of white men, both in the Government, & out of the Government. And it was to gratify them, and not ourselves, that we came."[38] Moreover, did not the New York Indians deserve some reward for their abiding loyalty to the United States despite their many grievances? After all, as Daniel Fowler, John Quinney, and Daniel Bread put it, "We have been the friends and allies of the United States thro' the old and the last war. The bones of our warriors lie mingled on many grounds with those of your brave men."[39] By contrast, the Menominees had fought against the United States in the War of 1812. How could Jackson and the Congress claim to be "a father, who always attends the cries of his red children" under such circumstances?[40]

Stockbridge's John Metoxen thought he knew the answer: white Americans had fooled themselves into believing that they were inherently civilized and Indians were inveterate savages, so they could rob Indians of their land. The doctrine that civilized people could seize the territory of savages was, he contended, "merely convenient to the parties interested—& by them originated & declared for interested purposes." Metoxen considered it to be natural law that "the Indian title ... is as full & perfect, as that of any other people for all political, civil, & municipal purposes," be they "more or less civilized."[41] As for his own Mohicans, they "profess to be civilized" and were acknowledged by many authorities "to observe better regulations in Society, to have better manners, more virtue & more religion of the Christian name, than some white citizens who now occupy large territories in the new settlements of the United States." To highlight the racial double standards that shaped the country's Indian policy, Metoxen questioned whether his people, as civilized Christians, possessed an equal right to seize the land of frontier whites who had sunk into "barbarism." No was the only answer, which illustrated that the only reason United States felt justified in overturning the New York Indians' title was that they were Indian.

Federal officials were unaffected by these appeals. For one, they charged that the New York Indians could not simultaneously claim to be as civilized as whites while continuing to appeal to the government to protect them from white encroachment, as if they were savage Indians. Jackson's officials, echoing their president, contended that the logical end of civility was full membership in the republic, not a separate community existence as Indians. Put another way, Indians could either lose their community identity by subjecting themselves to the same laws as whites, including a private property regime that routinely forced friends and relatives to scatter in search of opportunity, or they could maintain their communal customs and tribal governments along with the threat of continued displacement by whites. And the reason for that continued displacement? In their more honest moments, federal commissioners admitted that, quite simply, their white constituents wanted the land and the U.S. treasury wanted the profits. Federal agent Samuel Stambaugh realized that if Congress reaffirmed the New York Indians' title, "the Menominees, stript of the largest portion of their country by the New York Tribes, will have no more land to sell: and thus, this extensive, fertile, and delightful country, *worth several millions of dollars,* will be lost to the government, and its rich prospects of soon becoming a flourishing agricultural and commercial country entirely blighted."[42] With such high stakes, the Indians' supplication that "Congress would be pleased to establish this country for their permanent abiding place to them and their heirs forever, so that they need not be disturbed for ages and ages to come," was simply not going to happen.[43]

The government's solution was to set aside five hundred thousand acres on the west side of the Fox River for the New York Indians, with one hundred acres reserved for each of the five thousand people the New York Indians said were going to join them in Wisconsin. After three years, the federal government would reclaim one hundred acres for every person short of that mark. The

Oneidas were the first to agree to this proposal since they had already settled at Duck Creek on the west side of the Fox just outside of Green Bay, so they would remain largely unaffected.[44] The Stockbridges and Brothertowns, however, were vehemently opposed to the plan and lobbied the Senate hard to reject it.[45] Their campaign failed to save their lands on the east side of the Fox, but it did manage to produce a much better deal. The Senate agreed to set aside from its purchase of Menominee land one township for the Brothertowns (or 23,040 acres) and an adjacent two townships for the Stockbridges and Delawares on Lake Winnebago, roughly twenty-five miles to the south of Statesburg. It also pledged to compensate the Brothertowns and Stockbridges for all the improvements they had made on the Fox.[46] Cutting Marsh observed that the Christian Indians found it "exceedingly painful... after so many professions of friendship, so soon to be disturbed in their supposed last retreat.... [it] is more than they known how to endure."[47] Yet they realized that the Lake Winnebago site was the best they could hope for under the circumstances. And so, they packed up their things and prepared to relocate—once again.

Signs

According to Marsh, some of the New York Indians continued to "believe in signs," and in the removal crisis they discerned a number of mixed messages.[48] Just as the promise of taking up fresh land far away from whites had lifted their spirits several times before, so too did the prospect of life on Lake Winnebago. Everyone agreed that the soil there was of "excellent quality & well covered with a thrifty growth of excellent timber."[49] The lake itself was stocked with fish (especially walleye) and also attracted waterfowl. Its marshes were full of wild rice grass, while its shores contained wild grapes, plums, and a variety of berries. Perhaps, then, Lake Winnebago would be the place where God lifted his curse and allowed Brothertown and Stockbridge to emerge as stable, thriving centers of Indian Christianity and civility. Indeed, there was little in the Indians' behavior to suggest that they had lost faith in this dream. Their people continued to migrate to Wisconsin throughout the 1830s despite the loss of the Fox River lands, with bands arriving at Brothertown (initially called Deansburg) in 1831 (forty people), 1832 (forty-four), 1834 (more than ten), 1835 (about six), and 1836 (more than a dozen).[50] In 1832, when violence erupted between white settlers living on the Wisconsin/Illinois border and a Sac and Fox band under the leadership of the chief, Blackhawk, Stockbridge and Brothertown men volunteered

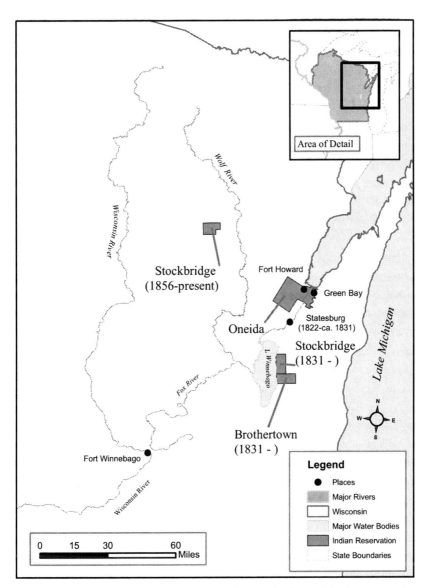

Map 3. The New York Indians in Wisconsin. The Stockbridge and Brothertown Indians first settled on the lower Fox River during the 1820s, then, under pressure from the federal government, moved to the shores of Lake Winnebago, only to have those lands come under assault during the late 1830s and 1840s. The Oneidas, too, suffered the government diminishing their lands at Duck Creek. The Brothertowns' attempt to remain on Lake Winnebago involved becoming citizens and accepting private property in 1839. The Stockbridges, after a three-year experiment with citizenship, gave it back in 1846 and then moved to a reservation on the Wolf River, where they remain today.

for the American force that put down the uprising even though whites had so recently robbed them of their own territory. Their friendship to the United States, this service declared, remained sound. Once the crisis was over, Stockbridge's John Metoxen, Austin E. Quinney, and John W. Quinney, along with Cutting Marsh, visited the Sacs and Foxes to persuade them to host a mission.[51] They still believed that sustaining and spreading their way of life in the face of manifold trials was their best chance to win God and, through him, white America, over to their side.

Yet dark signs threatened to blot out the Indians' rays of hope. Some Stockbridges contended that removal to Lake Winnebago was "a manifestation of God's displeasure against them," the latest stage of a curse that previously had forced them from New England, New York, and Indiana to the Fox River.[52] The Ho-Chunks, Menominees, Sacs, and Foxes still showed little interest in Christianity and civility but instead subscribed to Nativist teachings that "the Gr[eat] Sp[irit] had given them mouths to speak with and they did not wish to learn to talk on paper" and that "the Great Spirit made all things and that He had made two places, for the red and white men to go to after death.... the red man would go to the W[est] but the white to the E[ast] (or South)."[53] The prospects for Brothertown and Stockbridge were very dim indeed if they rested on convincing these Indians to pursue Christian lives. The most ominous sign of all was that the United States seemed determined to force the Indians off their new lands even before the experiment had begun. Already by 1828 the military had strengthened its hold on the region with the construction of Fort Winnebago at the Fox-Winnebago portage, garrisoned by a 110-man force.[54] Then, in three treaties negotiated between 1831 and 1833, Washington acquired the Indian title to the land bordering Lake Winnebago on the north, east, and south, excepting only the Brothertown and Stockbridge townships. Over the next ten years, it would expand its claims to encompass most of the rest of Wisconsin. These transfers took place at a time when the United States was sweeping Indians out of the Midwest by the tens of thousands and relocating them west of the Mississippi, predominantly to Kansas.[55] White expectations that Wisconsin land would open up in a similar fashion attracted them to the territory in ever increasing numbers until they stood at some thirty-one thousand people by 1840, concentrated in Green Bay in the east and the Lead Mining District in the west.[56] Like white settlers in other parts of the country, these newcomers had little intention of allowing Indians to live alongside them as separate polities withholding their lands from the market. It did not matter whether those

Indians were savage or civilized, pagan or Christian. Yet there was an option to removal. George B. Porter, the governor of the Territory of Michigan of which Wisconsin was a part, predicted as early as 1832 that "the advanced state and improvement" of the New York Indians "renders it probable that at no remote period they will become citizens."[57] What Porter meant was that shortly the Brothertowns and Stockbridges, like the Cherokees and other "civilized tribes" in the Southeast, would either have to move west *or* divide their lands into private property, submit to white law, and begin paying taxes. He meant, in short, that they would not remain unmolested on their lands. His words portended sorrowful days ahead.

CHAPTER 9

Indians or Citizens, White Men or Red?

AMERICANS are unaccustomed to people giving back their citizenship once they have received it, for citizenship is usually thought of as a gift, a blessing, or a privilege, representing the height of an individual's public being.[1] Yet that is precisely what the majority of the Stockbridge tribe wanted to do in 1846 after just three years as U.S. citizens. Earlier in the decade, a faction of Stockbridges, following the lead of the Brothertowns, had petitioned Congress to become citizens, believing that this shift would strengthen the rule of law in their community and, more important, enable them to remain on their Wisconsin lands despite renewed government pressure to move west. Washington complied, only for the Stockbridges to realize that their assumptions had been mistaken. As it turned out, citizenship was less of a step toward political equality with whites than a mechanism for whites to throw open Indian lands to the market, for citizenship was accompanied by division of the Indians' communal territory into privately owned, fee-simple tracts subject to sale, taxation, and foreclosure. As soon as Stockbridge's division was made, merchant creditors and the taxman began seizing the Indians' property for overdue bills. Yet, at the same time, Washington refused to pay the Stockbridges monies it owed them in one lump sum because it held that, as Indians, they would squander these funds. The Stockbridges' leading spokesman, John W. Quinney, complained to Wisconsin officials that his people "cannot understand how they can be considered as *citizens* for one purpose," by which he meant taxation and subjection to white law, and "as *Indians* for another," meaning the government's withholding of their annuity. "They do not think they can be both *fish & flesh*." All the Stockbridges wanted, Quinney emphasized, was "that they may ascertain what kind of beings they are, *Indians or Citizens, White Men or Red!!*"[2]

Quinney had come to realize that full citizenship truly belonged to whites only, but for a brief period his fellow Stockbridges and the Brothertowns had gambled that Indianness and citizenship might be compatible. Though their people's recent history was one hard lesson after another that there was no place in white America even for Christian and civilized Indians, they still had two more reforms to make before they would accept that judgment—division of their common lands and subjection to white law. After all, the Anglo-American democratic tradition was premised, at least until the Jacksonian period, on re-stricting the suffrage to land-owning men, based on the assumption that only landowners could be trusted to guard the sanctity of private property against the redistributive urges of the landless masses and to keep a close watch on the government taxing their estates. Whites also judged Indian communalism to be incompatible with citizenship because it subsumed an individual's judgment at the polls to group needs and, by restricting tribal members from capitalizing on their land, discouraged entrepreneurialism. Yet these were not the principles that led the Brothertowns in 1839 and Stockbridges in 1843 to accept U.S. citi-zenship. Their hope was that if they became legally "white," as they called citizen-ship, whites would finally leave their people, as a people, alone.

By 1846, a portion of the Stockbridges, many of whom had never been in favor of citizenship in the first place, had concluded that their strategy was naive. "What are they now," Quinney asked rhetorically about his people. "A weak and dependent Band, half 'citizens,' and half 'Indians,'" subject to all of the liabilities and few of the benefits of each. Stockbridge's "Indian Party" could no longer brook this ambiguity if its only purpose was to destroy their community. Thus, they petitioned to have their Indian status and reservation restored so that they could sell their tribal lands and move west into Indian country, be-yond the reach of whites. "They have all of their lives been called *Indians*," wrote the Stockbridges to Congress, "it is their desire so to continue. While they are willing to adopt, in many respects, the customs of whites, they are unwilling to come under the laws and submit to the restraints of civilized society."[3] The Stockbridges even went so far as to argue that they were incapable of compet-ing as Indians in white society, not because they were inferior to whites but just because they were different. Put another way, they had determined that "their natures and their dispositions can no more be changed, than their skins be made white and transparent."[4] Experience had taught them that race was real, that Indians and whites were so fundamentally unalike they could not live according to the same laws in the same society.

Figure 8. John W. Quinney, by Amos C. Hamlin, 1849. Quinney was Stockbridge's famously eloquent spokesman from the early to mid-nineteenth century. By his own reckoning, he made nine lobbying trips to Washington, D.C., between 1830 and 1852 and still more to Albany and other places. His campaigns to have New York and Washington pay restitution to the Stockbridges for the land white governments had seized from the tribe and his opposition to Stockbridge citizenship were both designed to defend the principle of Stockbridge's existence as Christian, civilized, tribal Indian community *in Wisconsin.* He cultivated a polished appearance as testimony to this possibility. Courtesy Wisconsin Historical Society, Madison, Wisconsin.

Despite the Indian Party's campaign to regain Indian status, most Brother-towns and even some Stockbridges still believed that remaining "white" was the best way to survive as an Indian community in Wisconsin. It was impossible to resist the nation's determination to eliminate sovereign Indian tribes, yet perhaps by empowering Indian individuals to compete as equals in white society, the Indians could maintain neighborhoods with their kith and kin. They understood that dividing the land would sacrifice some people to creditors and the courts, but such losses were acceptable on a sliding scale that included relocating yet again, this time to the "savage" lands of Missouri River Valley, with future removals certain to follow. Better to face the inevitable transition to citizenship while the people still lived in fertile Wisconsin and not in wind-swept Kansas.

The fight over Indian removal and citizenship was the crystallization of the generations-long debate among Indians and between Indians and whites about the meanings of Indianness and whiteness in the republic. Raging from the very moment that the Brothertowns and Stockbridges took up their new homes on the shores of Lake Winnebago, this argument centered on questions of the Indians' capacity to compete with whites in white society, the willingness of whites to give Indian citizens a fair chance to succeed, and the fate of distinct Indian communities in an expanding republic. Land and jurisdiction were the main stakes for the Indians, for cultural as well as economic and political reasons. Indians knew that citizenship would leave them without contiguous tribal territory or exclusive control over their own affairs. In turn, they would lack the social and material basis for their communal ethic in which no one was left behind, which many of them considered to be the consummate expression of their Indianness *and* Christianity. They also knew that the breakup of their reservations and the inevitable scattering of at least some of their families would increase the likelihood of their young people marrying outsiders. Thus, the Indians called their acceptance of citizenship "turning white," not only in reference to the widespread American insistence that full political participation in the republic was reserved for whites only—but also out of concern that their descendants would no longer physically appear to be Indians. The Brothertowns and Stockbridges were confronting their very future as communities and as Indians. The outcome of their ordeal would in many ways presage the future of Indians throughout the nation.

"Why cannot we be left alone?"

The Indians settled on Lake Winnebago as if it was to be a permanent home despite the probability that whites would eventually pressure them to abandon

this site too. By 1836 the Brothertowns had cleared a strip of shoreline from
the dense forest that covered the sloping hills of their reserve. Using their own
water-powered sawmill, they cut basswood planks to construct a series of "water
tight" log cabins, most of them twenty by sixteen feet anchored at each end with
a large fireplace. The Brothertowns also ran a flour mill, which attracted white
customers from Oshkosh on the other side of the lake.[5] One measure of the Indians' achievement was that outsiders actually recognized them as "Indian farmers," a term that many whites considered to be oxymoronic.[6] Nobody questioned
their Christianity. Yet the Indians were concerned less with impressing whites
than living up to their goal of being "more united than they have been...endeav-
oring to assist each other."[7] They put this principle into practice by turning out
en masse to erect the new schoolhouse and to help Jeremiah Johnson build a
new cabin when his burned down.[8] Not coincidentally, migrants from New York
and even New England continued to arrive in the Lake Winnebago communities throughout the 1840s. Brothertown's population rose from 129 in 1835 to
259 in 1841, with more growth to follow since there were still fifty Brothertowns
in New York and others among the Narragansetts in Rhode Island who planned
to come to Wisconsin.[9] Likewise, Stockbridge expanded from some 210 people
in early 1833 to 320 just a year later.[10] These were communities determined to
thrive where they were.

Yet whites would not grant Indians that opportunity, whatever progress they
made. Ominously, the Wisconsin Seal, adopted in 1836, featured the Latin saying "Civilitas Successit Barbarum" ("Civilization replaces barbarism") and de-
picted an Indian hunter retreating westward in the face of a white man guiding
his plow. There was no room for the Brothertowns and Stockbridges in this symbolism, for most whites agreed with the *Wisconsin Enquirer* that "the red man
is doomed to be *exterminated!*—and the white man will not cease to follow in
his footsteps until the last Indian shall have trod to the shores of the Pacific!"[11]
The federal government was committed to do its part. Early in 1836, President
Jackson gave several speeches calling for the removal of all Indians east of the
Mississippi, including the Great Lakes region, which was followed quickly by the
government's acquisition of four million acres from the Menominees.[12] Then, in
May, the Stockbridges got hold of the annual report of the secretary of war and
had their worst fear confirmed: Washington was seeking their relocation too.[13]

By summer, the dreaded treaty conference had been scheduled, and the
federal government signaled its resolve by choosing John F. Schermerhorn as
its agent. Just years before, Schermerhorn had negotiated the corrupt Treaty of

Figure 9. Great Seal of the Territory of Wisconsin, 1838. The seal of Wisconsin Territory (and later state) captures the white racial assumptions that constantly threatened the Brothertown and Stockbridge Indians' tenure in Wisconsin. White Americans tended to conceive of all Indians as savage hunter-gatherers destined to retreat in the face of white farming and industry, hence the Latin phrase that translates as "Civility Succeeds Barbarism." This perspective left no room for Indians, even those who had adopted Christian and civilized reforms. Courtesy Wisconsin Historical Society, Madison, Wisconsin.

New Echota in which a slim minority of Cherokee leaders, intimidated by the government and local whites, committed their entire tribe to abandon its Smoky Mountain homeland for Oklahoma. The subsequent Trail of Tears, in which a quarter or more Cherokee migrants died en route, took place not only despite but also, to a certain degree, because of the tribe's longstanding efforts to use Christian and civilized reforms to defend its sovereignty and territory. As Schermerhorn explained, "History proves that nearby whites are not favorable to the Indians' improvement and civilization," because they did not want to make good on the nation's promise of peace and security in exchange for progress.[14] Schermerhorn applied this principle to Brothertown and Stockbridge as well. "The fixed purpose of the Government," he asserted, "is to remove *all* of the Indians in this country [Wisconsin], and in the state of New York, West of the Mississippi, so soon as it can be done or those lands are wanted."[15] Schermerhorn began by essentially dictating a treaty to the Oneidas in which they ceded 434,600 of their 500,000 acres west of Fox River, exempting only a tract along Duck Creek, in exchange for land in Kansas along the Little Osage River, a payment of $340,000, and the costs of removal.[16] Though the Oneidas judged the treaty to be "contrary to our views of the interest of the Nation," they signed it because they felt they had no choice.[17] Likewise, Schermerhorn bullied the Stockbridges, who were said to oppose removal "all to a man," to examine the Little Osage and to consider selling one of their two townships on Lake Winnebago if some of them decided to go.[18] The Brothertowns' best bad option was to make a similarly half-hearted pledge to explore the western country for a suitable place to live. The Indians could not have been clearer that they wanted to stay in Wisconsin, but it was equally unmistakable that the government was determined to force them out. It proved as much in 1838's Treaty of Buffalo Creek, which established a 1,824,000-acre "New York Indian Tract" in Kansas to which all Iroquois, Stockbridges, Brothertowns, and New York Delawares (or Munsees) were supposed to relocate, even though the Wisconsin bands had not yet consented to go.[19]

Throughout these proceedings, Schermerhorn's insistence on treating Indians as a single race in opposition to whites clashed with the tribes' conception of themselves as civilized people who had earned the right to remain among white society. Though Schermerhorn acknowledged the "improvement" of the New York Indians, still he could not imagine Indians and whites living side by side. "You see the rapid march of the white population," he warned, "and it is not possible . . . that you can remain & improve the country you now occupy, surrounded as you must be in a short time with a dense population." The issue was not the Indians' ability to adapt per se but white intolerance of their presence and the unwillingness of the government to protect Indians from its own people. Still, Schermerhorn insisted that the president's ultimate goal was the "happiness of his red children . . . to preserve the remnant of Indian nations once powerful from becoming extinct" by relocating them "near your red Brethren where you will never be surrounded or intruded upon by the white settlements."[20] It was an argument that the Brothertowns and Stockbridges had heard before.

The Oneidas' eloquent chief, Daniel Bread, seeing this betrayal for what it was, refused to allow Schermerhorn to call it anything but. He charged, "We have hardly laid down our packs on cleared land enough to live on, when word comes for us to go on." No, he pronounced defiantly, "we have gone about far enough." Bread saw no prospect of his people finding a permanent home out west, for, he observed, "Wherever we go whites go also, and to get away from them is impossible." Jackson portrayed Indian Territory as a refuge where savages could prepare to join American society whenever white expansion reached them yet again. But the New York Indians were already civilized. "If you see us improving," Bread implored, "why cannot we be left alone until we cho[o]se to change our residence and go further," adding for good measure, "you are rich enough."[21] Yet the hard fact, the Indians realized, was that there was no such thing as "rich enough" in the white republic. Americans had an insatiable thirst for land and were determined to seize it from Indians regardless of the Indians' civility, Christianity, or historical friendship to the United States.

With the Treaty of Buffalo Creek, the Brothertowns and Stockbridges faced the prospect of their fifth removal in the span of just two generations, but this crisis was different in essential ways from the earlier ones. Each of the previous moves had been premised on three shared factors: whites had overrun the Indians' homes; the land to which the Indians were going to relocate was guaranteed to them both by local Indians and white officials; and the Indians viewed their relocation as an opportunity to reform themselves, evangelize other tribes, and win God's favor. By the 1830s, the negative push factor of white encroachment remained, but the positive pull factors had lost their force. The Indians no longer had any reason to believe white promises that they would enjoy their reservation lands "forever," since "forever" usually meant just a few years. At the same time, the Indians had grown confident that their Christianity and civility could bear the toxic influences of white neighbors. They remained supportive of Indian evangelization, but their zeal for this service had waned considerably amid the relentless American advance. Given these developments, some Brothertowns and Stockbridges wanted to try to remain in Wisconsin by dividing up their lands into private property and accepting white jurisdiction. The hope was that if they "became white," at least in terms of the law, perhaps whites would leave them in peace.

"A Permanent Resting Place"

The Brothertowns raised the possibility of becoming citizens not as a triumphant capstone to their long history Christian and civilized reforms, though they often appealed to that record, but as an alternative to removal. As the Peacemakers informed Thomas Dean, "If we were to sell...and go to the west it would not be 20 years & perhaps half that time before we should be told our title to the Land was not good and we must remove further."[22] From this perspective, staying in Wisconsin by becoming citizens would be no more risky than moving to Kansas, and perhaps a great deal less so. In Kansas, the Brothertowns emphasized, the "inhabitants are almost wholly uncivilized and [it] entirely an Indian country." Whatever solidarity the Brothertowns felt with their so-called red brethren on the prairie plains, they did not want to live alongside them. "We have long since laid aside those arms made for use in war for the peaceful implements of agriculture and husbandry," the Brothertowns emphasized. "We have so far progressed in the arts of civilization...having for several generations past been brot up among in the neighborhood of white people." These developments, combined with the fact that most of them were English speakers, led them to imagine that "they could perhaps be incorporated with their white brethren."[23] Brothertown's Thomas Commuck spoke for the majority when he contended that "the plans of the government of the U.S. are laid, and I think that it is useless to contend with the government. We must go over the Mississippi or become citizens here....all Indian plans are about to be done away with I think."[24] Just months after the Brothertowns had signed Schermerhorn's provisional removal treaty as a stalling tactic, they sent a petition to Congress asking for a patent to their Lake Winnebago lands and "equal privileges" with whites, based on the argument that "they have lost the language of their forefathers and also the manners and customs of the Indians, and acquired those of the white people, and it is believed they will make useful citizens."[25] Their ultimate goal, they explained on another occasion, was to obtain "a permanent resting place for ourselves and posterity"—that is, not to disappear into the white population.[26]

There is little question that the Brothertowns' main purpose in lobbying for citizenship was to protect their homes, but another consideration was that they needed an outside authority to police murders both among Indians and between Indians and whites. By the 1830s, the Brothertowns and Stockbridges had rejected the traditional Indian form of justice followed by the Menominees and Ho-Chunks, in which the family or clan of a murder victim had the right to exact revenge against the perpetrator's kin or to obtain compensation in the form of goods or a human replacement for the dead. By this code, leaders became involved only if revenge killings spiraled out of control or threatened the peace between communities. The Brothertowns and Stockbridges favored the white American system, in which government exercised a monopoly on the arrest, trial, and punishment of murderers and in which the murderer alone, not his family, was answerable for the crime. The problem was that their status as Indians under white law meant that white authorities would not support their legal proceedings. Thus, whenever there was a murder among Indian groups, the Peacemakers had to improvise a solution that balanced their quest for justice with respect for each community's sovereignty. Even murders within Brothertown and Stockbridge were difficult to manage, since there was no consensus on the right of the Peacemakers to punish their own people corporally.

A handful of killings highlighted these difficulties following the New York Indians' arrival in Wisconsin, prompting the Brothertowns to question whether they could function as a civilized community without the firm rule of law. The first case occurred in 1826, when Stockbridge asked James Duane Doty, one of the federal judges for Michigan Territory, for help prosecuting the murder of one of their women by another tribal member. Doty immediately perceived the jurisdictional dilemma. Writing to his superiors, he asked, "Whether an Indian is punishable for the murder of another Indian, by the laws of the United States or of this Territory, when such murder is committed within the Indian country, at a place where the Indian title has not been extinguished?"[27] The government's conclusion was no, thereby leaving the Stockbridges to handle this matter on their own, something they were loath to do. This precedent was upheld in 1830 when Green Bay authorities arrested and tried the Menominee chief, Oshkosh, for executing one of his people who had himself committed a murder, only to have Doty rule that the United States had no jurisdiction over the matter.[28] The danger this power vacuum posed to Brothertown became glaringly apparent in the summer of 1836, when two inebriated Stockbridge men with violent reputations, Peter and Jacob Konkapot, brutally killed Brothertown's Joseph Palmer during a chance encounter on the road.[29] Indian authorities quickly arrested the men and held them in irons but were uncertain about what to do next, in part because Jacob was the son of Robert Konkapot, one of Stockbridge's leading men and a founder of the original Fox River settlement. The blood had barely dried on Palmer's corpse before Robert began calling for his Jacob's release based on the argument that "Our Savior did not condemn the woman taken in adultery, and we ought to be like Him, forgive, &c." Stockbridge and Brothertown Peacemakers tried to deliver the murderers to Green Bay to avoid a schism, only to be turned down because "as they were Indians and the deed was done upon Indian lands, the laws of the U.S. did not recognize such cases." Lacking options, the men of these two communities gathered as a single court and, after proceedings governed by a spirit of "harmony, coolness, and deliberation," on August 5 they rendered a guilty verdict by a margin of forty to two (the dissenting voices belonging to Robert Konkapot and his friend, Thomas Hendrick). Then, after weighing the option of banishing the two men, the court issued a sentence of execution by hanging. Yet the hanging never took place. Less than two weeks later, the convicted men escaped from their holding cell, and though it was an open secret that Robert Konkapot was involved, there was nothing anyone could do about it.[30] It was with this disturbing example in mind that Brothertown asked for citizenship "being fully sensible of the disadvantages they labor under by being placed in the midst of a dense population of white people, and without laws, government, or protection."[31]

The Brothertowns' petition for citizenship hearkened to a little-known feature of Jackson's removal plan for the southeastern tribes that allowed Indians to become citizens of the states in which they lived if they swore off the authority of tribal government, submitted to white law, and took up a portion of their tribe's land as private property subject to taxation and seizure for debt.[32] Only a few southeastern Indians tried to exercise the option; the results, from the Indians' perspective, were disastrous. For instance, no sooner had the Creeks divided their lands than Georgia land speculators began hiring Indians to sell fraudulent claims to their neighbors' tracts. The speculators then sold these bogus titles to white settlers who, in turn, drove the legitimate Indian owners off the land. These confrontations degenerated into all-out war in the spring and early summer of 1836, prompting the federal government to round up thousands of so-called hostiles and march them to Oklahoma. The rest of the Creeks followed, as predicted. Crooked episodes like these, which typified the federal government's removal of the southeastern Indians, portended that whites would never accept Indians as coequal neighbors, that, instead, Indian citizenship and subjection to state law would only release whites to terrorize Indians and seize their lands under the color of law.[33]

Yet the Brothertowns calculated that their situation in Wisconsin was sufficiently different from that of the southeastern tribes that they could turn citizenship into a buttress for their interests. The challenge for the southeastern Indians had been to defend territories as large as some northeastern states, but Brothertown had only to protect a township-sized tract. Whereas the southeastern tribes faced whites numbering in the hundreds of thousands, Wisconsin's population was but a fraction of that amount notwithstanding its remarkable growth. Southern whites had been overtly hostile to neighboring Indians in part due to a long history of frontier warfare but especially because the Indians sat upon prime cotton lands and even gold reserves. By contrast, relations between the Brothertowns and their white neighbors were for the most part mutually respectful, and the territorial government, as opposed to the federal one, showed no particular urgency to have them gone despite the tone of its official seal—its treatment of the Menominees and Ho-Chunks was quite another matter. Finally, whereas the southern states framed their calls for Indian removal in terms of states' rights which, in turn, was proxy for their defense of federal noninterference with slavery, Wisconsin had no such political agenda involving the Brothertowns. Given these factors, the Brothertowns judged citizenship a risk worth taking.

The tribe could hardly have picked a better time to submit its petition. Jackson's successor, his former vice president Martin Van Buren, needed to answer his Whig Party opponents who questioned whether his administration was committed to civilizing Indians in light of Jackson's forced removal of the southeastern tribes. For their part, these same humanitarian critics needed an example to prove that missionary work produced actual results, that civilized Indians were capable of competing in white society and therefore should be allowed to remain on their lands. Finally, most whites in and around Green Bay supported the Indians' proposal. The *Wisconsin Enquirer* editorialized that the Brothertowns "would make good citizens—being generally intelligent, well disposed, and industrious."[34] In any case, it believed that the Brothertowns "have not one trait of aboriginal character about them" and therefore should not be treated as savages.[35] A congressional investigative committee agreed on all counts. It judged that the Brothertowns "have become both civilised and christianized to a higher degree than perhaps any other tribe of Indians on this continent." Moreover, it anticipated that granting the Brothertowns' petition would inspire other Indians to follow their course. Unless Indians had concrete evidence that reform would bring them "all the advantages of civilization," including its pinnacle, citizenship, few of them would ever go down this path.[36] Not that the committee believed that many Indians would or could reach the standard of the Brothertowns. The "onward and resistless march of the Anglo-Saxon race" meant that Indians were destined for "total destruction." The most humane thing the country could do under the circumstances was "to incorporate such of them as may be benefited from it into our free system of government." The rest would be left to their supposed fate.

The Brothertowns' transition from legal savages to citizens took place over the course of 1839. In March, Congress approved the Brothertowns' petition, contingent on the community dividing its lands. By October, the Brothertowns had completed this task, distributing sixty acres to each of the 378 community members to be held in fee simple, with the remainder set aside as a commons for public use and future distribution.[37] The only Brothertowns who did not receive land were women who had married outsiders, regardless of whether those outsiders were black, white, or even other Indians. The Brothertowns understood that men usually controlled family real estate according to white law and custom. Given the tribe's goal of using the division of their territory to keep the community together on Lake Winnebago, it was incumbent on them to restrict landholding to people of "the Nation," as they called themselves.[38]

Yet no sooner had the Brothertowns fulfilled their requirements for citizenship than some whites began questioning whether, as Indians, they should enjoy the right of suffrage. The context for this debate was a contested election in 1840 between William H. Bruce and Albert G. Ellis for a seat in the Wisconsin Territorial Legislature. Ellis barely won with a 34-vote margin from Brothertown, whereupon Bruce's supporters contested the legality of the Indians' ballots. Though Bruce's camp acknowledged that Congress had made the Brothertowns citizens, their position was that the Territorial Legislature alone decided who had the right to vote within its jurisdiction and years earlier it had limited the suffrage to "free white male citizens." Additionally, one of Bruce's partisans contended that "wandering Indians" had no business determining the outcome of elections. Despite this challenge, the legislature decided by a margin of 14 to 10 to count the Brothertown ballots. This decision had lasting consequences: over the next ten years, Indian votes carried three Brothertowns into the Wisconsin Assembly as representatives of Calumet County: William Fowler (1845), Alonzo Dick (1849), and William H. Dick (1851).[39] White Wisconsinites, however, still generally favored racial qualifications at the polls. In 1843, the Territorial Legislature voted 21 to 5 to defeat a bill that would have struck "white" from the qualification to vote. Instead, when Wisconsin drew up its state constitution in 1846, it included as an exception to the white rule, "All Indians declared to be citizens of the United States, by any law of Congress" and "All civilized persons of the Indian blood not members of any tribe of Indians."[40] The Brothertowns' purpose was to use their citizenship to protect their community's existence, but that was not the goal of their white neighbors. As far as they were concerned, Indians had to cease living socially as Indians in order to participate in American society.

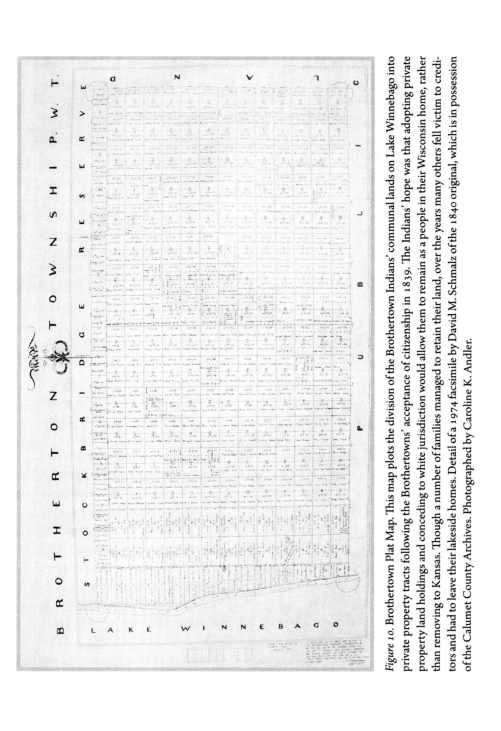

Figure 10. Brothertown Plat Map. This map plots the division of the Brothertown Indians' communal lands on Lake Winnebago into private property tracts following the Brothertowns' acceptance of citizenship in 1839. The Indians' hope was that adopting private property land holdings and conceding to white jurisdiction would allow them to remain as a people in their Wisconsin home, rather than removing to Kansas. Though a number of families managed to retain their land, over the years many others fell victim to creditors and had to leave their lakeside homes. Detail of a 1974 facsimile by David M. Schmalz of the 1840 original, which is in possession of the Calumet County Archives. Photographed by Caroline K. Andler.

"To make white men of them"

Whereas the Brothertowns embraced citizenship to deflect removal, the Stockbridges generally favored remaining in their legal Indian state. They disagreed, however, on whether to take up the government's offer of western lands and, if not, on what reforms they had to adopt in order to stay on Lake Winnebago. One group, known as the Emigrant Party, advocated banding together with Munsee Delawares from western New York and southern Ontario and relocating to Fort Leavenworth, Kansas, where another group of Delawares was already living.[41] It also favored selling off one of the tribe's two townships to fund the migration, even though not all Stockbridges were willing to go. The Emigrant Party's opponents, known as the Quinney Party after its leaders John W. Quinney and Austin E. Quinney, favored the people's right to stay in Wisconsin. It believed that Stockbridge could weather the political storm and strengthen its viability by securing new forms of income, particularly government compensation for outstanding Mohican land claims, and by instituting political reforms on the white model. The rivalry between these groups centered on the question of removal, but there was an even greater issue at stake in their fight. At its heart was the question of what it meant to be authentically Indian.

The Emigrant Party contained some of the most conservative members of the Stockbridge community, who feared it would soon be impossible to live as true Indians in Wisconsin. The group's conservatism is evident in the fact that when it wrote President Van Buren in 1838, only forty of the sixty-five male petitioners signed their names, with the rest leaving marks, a rate well below that of Stockbridge men as a whole.[42] This relatively low written literacy (or at least a low willingness to sign) reflected the Emigrant Party's general attitude toward outside influences. "They want old language, old customs, etc.," observed Cutting Marsh.[43] They also wanted old leadership, favoring men who descended from sachem lineages. They could not imagine preserving such things in Wisconsin. For one, alcohol had already begun to wreak havoc on the community, as was evident in the murder of the Brothertown man. Such incidents were bound to multiply with the increase of white settlement. So too was intermarriage between Stockbridge women and outsiders, which had already seen an alarming spike after the federal government opened up a military road between Fort Howard and Fort Winnebago right along the Indians' lands.[44] Wisconsin seemed primed to become another New York. Yet perhaps the greatest threat to the Indian way of life, as the Emigrant Party defined it, came not from white outsiders but from the Quinney Party itself and its program of reform.

The Quinney Party had a twofold agenda for Stockbridge survival in Wisconsin. Part of it involved seeking financial compensation from the federal government and the states of Massachusetts and New York for their many historic wrongs toward the Stockbridge people. To that end, John W. Quinney made nine lobbying trips to the east between 1830 and 1852, which by his calculation took up more than five years of his life.[45] The second part of the Quinney Party's strategy was to model Stockbridge's polity on white American governments, the better to keep order and, equally important, to enable the people to claim a place amid whites. To that end, in February 1837, Stockbridge men gathered at the community schoolhouse to draw up a "Declaration of Rights" and a new "Frame of Government" for submission to public vote. The Declaration would guarantee liberty of conscience, habeas corpus, and freedom from hereditary government, including the sachemship that had governed Mohican society since time immemorial. In its place, the Frame proposed a "Supreme First Magistrate" (also called sachem) and a council of five members, to be chosen by adult male voters, with age and property requirements for those offices. This government would have the power to adopt criminal and civil laws, manage lands, lay and collect taxes, borrow and remit money, negotiate with other Indian tribes and governments, and judge criminal cases of the highest degree. Lesser matters would be handled by an annually elected Peacemaker. The idea was that the new Stockbridge government would be recognizable to whites and someday even respected by them, just as the Cherokees had attempted a decade earlier when they adopted their own tribal constitution modeled on that of the United States. As the Stockbridges emphasized, "We do not acknowledge allegiance to any power upon earth."[46]

Quinney's faction was willing to see the Emigrant Party go, but it opposed the sale of any tribal lands to fund the migration, an issue that became even more heated as some two hundred Canadian Munsees began to arrive in Stockbridge in late 1837 in preparation for the joint move to Kansas. The Quinney Party charged that though the Stockbridges had always intended to merge with the New York Munsees, these people from southern Ontario were "miserably poor" "British...intruders" with whom the tribe had no relationship.[47] "They ate up a great deal of what we raised," complained Austin E. Quinney, "and now many of our families must suffer for want of provision."[48] Yet the Munsees looked to the Stockbridges for more than just hospitality. They wanted a cut from the proposed sale of the second township, and Quinney's supporters knew that their very presence strengthened the bogus claim of the Emigrant Party to represent the majority view.[49] Contributing to the air of mistrust was that none other than Robert Konkapot and Thomas Hendrick, who had obstructed the legal process in the 1836 murder of the Brothertown Indian, were the very men who had escorted the Munsees from Ontario to Lake Winnebago.[50]

The Quinney Party had ever reason for suspicion. The Emigrant Party was not only determined to sell one of the Stockbridge townships but also, in the meantime, to obstruct the new Stockbridge Constitution.[51] The Emigrants' tactics included accusations that the Quinney Party consisted "partly of negroes, who they have received into their party in order that their party might become stronger."[52] This was the first time that charges of this sort arose among the Stockbridges even though blacks and their Afro-Indian offspring had been residing among and sometimes intermarrying with the tribe for years. That trend began in earnest when the Jersey Delawares joined Stockbridge in 1802 along with a number of their black and Afro-Indian kin. Other blacks and Afro-Indians, such as Nathaniel Pendleton and John Baldwin, had come to Stockbridge after being rejected by the Brothertowns.[53] By all appearances, very few of these people were active in the public life of the tribe, but in New York the Stockbridges did permit them to settle on a portion of tribal land, thus giving rise to a reservation neighborhood known as "New Guinea."[54] Their presence finally became an issue in the late 1830s only because the Emigrant and Constitutional Parties each needed to inflate its own numbers and minimize those of its rival in order to win the support of the federal government.

This "party spirit" infected nearly every aspect of Stockbridge public life, leaving the place "confused and unsettled."[55] Thomas Hendrick believed that the "Quinney Party...would do almost any thing that lays in their favor to prevent us," and he was not far off the mark.[56] The Quinneys' supporters went so far as to excommunicate Hendrick and Robert Konkapot from the Stockbridge church on charges of "*slander, lying,* and *dishonesty.*"[57] In response, Emigrant Party members formed their own Baptist church, thus creating the kind of overlap between political and religious factions that had once characterized Brothertown and that continued to plague the Oneidas. Given the increasingly harsh feelings between these groups, it could hardly have been otherwise. As the Emigrants explained to the commissioner of Indian affairs, "Whatever Quinney proposes, we oppose."[58]

It took very little lobbying for the Emigrant Party to enlist government support, since Washington was already intent on removing Wisconsin's Indians west of the Mississippi River one way or another. To that end, in September 1839 U.S. Indian Agent Albert Gallup convinced the Stockbridges to approve a treaty that arranged for the sale of the eastern half of Stockbridge's two townships and used a portion of the proceeds for the Emigrant Party's relocation. As soon as this was done, eighty people signed up to leave.[59] The Quinney Party had been thwarted to a degree, yet by this point they so desperately wanted the Emigrants gone that they saw a silver lining. Suffice it to say, there was no love lost when the Emigrants left for Kansas, just a month after the signing of the treaty and without even waiting to receive their promised federal aid.[60]

Yet the imminent threat of still more land cessions meant that the Emigrant Party's removal was but an opening phase of Stockbridge's factional battles. After watching the Hendrick band take to the road for Kansas, Marsh predicted a bleak future for those who remained in Wisconsin. "I have never been more disheartened by the prospects of this people than at the present time," he wrote. "My heart aches for them. Poor Indians. I fear they are doomed to total extinction."[61] The Indians shared his apprehension but could not agree about what, if anything, to do about it. One faction, led by the Quinneys and John Metoxen, and including members of the Pye and Turkey families, wanted to leave Stockbridge lands in their communal state and defend the tribe's sovereignty over its people and resources despite outside pressure. As defenders of their people's legal status as Indians, they called themselves the "Indian Party." Their opponents, led by Jacob and John N. Chicks and drawing support from members of the Jourdan, Davids, Gardner, Jaccobs, Yoccum, and Moore families, wanted to follow the Brothertowns' lead by dividing up the reservation into privately owned plots, accepting citizenship and white jurisdiction, and then quietly using the mechanisms of white government to protect Stockbridge interests.[62] Another murder, this one committed by Stockbridge's Isaac Littleman against another member of the tribe, heightened their urgency, for though Stockbridge successfully tried and executed Littleman, that the murder had taken place at all, particularly on the cusp of the killing of 1836, suggested that the people had lost control over their own affairs.[63] As the Citizen Party framed things, the tribe's laws had become a "solemn mockery."[64] Its hope was that citizenship would restore order to their community and spare them from the "uncertainty in which they live, from day to day, as to their future destiny."[65] To that end, in July 1842, the Citizen Party petitioned Congress to act on its agenda. This letter, arriving as it did on the heels of the Brothertowns' transition to citizenship and accompanied by ample white testimony of the Stockbridges' civility, led Congress in March 1843

Figure 11. Austin E. Quinney, by Amos C. Hamlin. Austin E. Quinney ranked with John W. Quinney as one of Stockbridge's foremost leaders in Wisconsin. They shared a political agenda of defending the Mohicans' land and political status as Indians in Wisconsin. Austin Quinney's dress in this portrait asserts the Stockbridge people's Indian identity at a time when they were under pressure to become U.S. citizens and divide their lands. Courtesy Wisconsin Historical Society, Madison, Wisconsin.

to authorize division of the tribe's lands and elimination of the people's special Indian status.[66]

Attempts to put this measure into effect over the Indian Party's opposition raised Stockbridge partisanship and racial politicking to unprecedented levels. The Indian Party accused Congress of passing the act of 1843 against the majority will and pleaded to postpone the division of Stockbridge land until the matter could be reviewed.[67] Yet the Citizen Party made it as difficult as possible to turn back the clock. Its members rushed to elect their own commissioners to divide and distribute allotments without the Indian Party's consent. Subsequent mortgages and land sales to outsiders quickly turned Stockbridge into a patchwork of overlapping Indian and white claims.[68] Equally disruptive was the Citizen Party's attempt to collect taxes on land that Indian Party members refused to recognize as taxable real estate by collectors chosen in what the Indian Party deemed a sham election.[69] When Indian Party members would not or could not pay, most of them being "very poor," the tax collector seized their personal property for auction.[70] The Indian Party responded by excommunicating members of the Chicks family from the tribal church, leading to the formation of a dissident Methodist congregation with close ties to Brothertown.[71] Fellow Christians only in name, Stockbridge's two parties came to view each other as "enemies."[72] John W. Quinney, who had spent most of his adult life laboring tirelessly for the benefit of his tribe, lamented that "Our people have sinned, & God is punishing them, by permitting a factious spirit to rise among them."[73]

Quinney and his followers, however, contributed to this divisiveness by claiming authentic Indianness for themselves and denouncing their opponents as frauds in an effort to convince Congress to overturn the citizenship act. Though Stockbridge, as a community, had always proclaimed its civility, the citizenship fight led the Indian Party to assert the people's special Indian character. Quinney contended that his people's "ignorance" about the value of property meant that they were "not prepared to come under Uncle Sam's laws, & to become one with his ambitious & artful children." He warned that if Congress upheld the division of Stockbridge lands, the Indians "would sell, become landless, yea even homeless, & be as so many beggars or swamp hermits."[74] It was impossible "to make *white men* of them," the Indian Party added, for they had "an abiding faith that we must be a people by ourselves—Our God hath made us distinct from you—We must remain so or perish."[75] The Indian Party was less confident about the immutable Indian character of its political opponents. Members of the Citizen Party "may make *good white men*," the Indian Party conceded, but "some of them have proved to be *faithless and bad, Indians.*"[76]

To some extent, these words were mere political posturing. After all, the Stockbridges had a long tradition of highlighting their Christianity and civility when the goal was to separate themselves from the "savages" that whites were so intent to displace. Once Stockbridge's civility became the main threat to the sanctity of the people's land base, Indian Party members recast themselves as culturally and even biologically wedded to Indian communal customs. At the same time, the Indian Party's rhetoric did reflect heartfelt sentiments. The party drew support from those who tended to "dress in the Indian style and speak their own language."[77] These conservatives included the aged headman John Metoxen, who told Cutting Marsh that "speaking the English language is what has made so many of the Brothertown people infidels," by which he appears to have meant traitors to Indian ways rather than backsliders from Christianity.[78] Likewise, a disproportionate number of Indian Party members were elderly, including several widows. Having already passed through their best working years, these people looked forward to the community supporting them, just as they had once cared for the needy.[79] To them, Stockbridge tradition involved the creative tension between, on the one hand, Christian and civilized reforms and, on the other, the people's maintenance of a commons and adamant refusal to sell their family plots to whites. Managing land for the benefit of the group instead of for individual profit was a quintessentially Indian characteristic as far as the Indian Party was concerned. Indeed, nearly every Indian community with which Stockbridge was in contact, at least until the Brothertowns became citizens, operated according to this principle. The Indian Party feared that suddenly forcing their people to defend individual tracts of private property while surrounded "by a white population larger & apt for acquisition" all but guaranteed that "the generation which shall succeed us would find themselves without a home."[80] What the Indian Party wanted was for Congress to "Let the protection of American law be thrown *around* the Indian Country and not *over* it. Let it be a bulwark to protect us against the incroachments of the whites and not a whirlwind to scatter dissension and discord among us."[81] Without this kind of protection, the Indian Party members preferred to follow their former Emigrant rivals to Kansas. As they explained in a letter to the Delawares near Fort Leavenworth, "If we remain here, we are forced to become citizens (*white men*). Now Grand Fathers, all we have to say is, that, as we have lived Indians, so will we die Indians."[82]

By contrast, the Citizen Party viewed citizenship as consistent with a century's worth of Stockbridge adaptations to white demands. The basic matter, the Citizen Party contended, was that "their own ancient Indian form of Government is wholly inapplicable to their condition of life." At the very least, their military service in every one of the nation's wars had earned them the right to the same political privileges that the same sacrifice had afforded whites.[83] As for the rival party's claim that it was the defender of Stockbridge heritage, the Citizens replied that some of the so-called Indians "have been elected to local offices, under the constitution of the Territory. They have sold land in some cases and exchanged it in others. Can they now be listened to when the[y] call themselves indians, of the pristine unsofisticated red blood stamp?"[84] Charges of being inauthentic cut two ways.

Both parties crafted their racial rhetoric with a white audience in mind, but ultimately the Indian Party's argument that citizenship had been forced on the tribe by a minority faction, combined with the appointment of a sympathetic Morgan L. Martin as Wisconsin Territory's delegate to Washington, convinced Congress in August 1846 to restore Stockbridge to its Indian status.[85] This legislation included provisions to nullify all previous sales of Stockbridge land to whites and to divide the tribe's territory in half, with the northern part to serve as a reservation with land held in common, and the south to remain divided in fee simple. All people had to do was enter either the Indian or Citizen Party rolls to identify where they stood. Yet this legislation, which aimed to end Stockbridge's discord once and for all, instead magnified it.

The act authorized a $5,000 government payout to the tribe as compensation for its former lands on Fox River. Anyone who entered the Citizen roll effectively renounced his or her right to a share of the money, which no one was willing to do. Additionally, since a large number of Citizen Party members had already sold off their private plots, joining the Indian Party ranks would allow them to recoup tribal land. In other words, this legislation allowed Citizen Party members to have their cake and eat it too, much to the chagrin of their Indian Party opponents. At the same time, a portion of Citizen Party leaders asserted that they were under no more of an obligation to declare their citizenship than white citizens, so they refused to enter either roll. They also saw the act of 1846 as wholly illegitimate, which they punctuated by continuing forcibly to seize property from Indian Party members in arrears for their taxes. Blood nearly spilled when an Indian Party posse, with the support of thirty to forty Oneidas, tried to reclaim confiscated property, whereupon the Citizen Party called on the Brothertowns for assistance.[86] This turmoil made John W. Quinney fear that "nothing can stay the final extinction of the Indian race."[87] Echoes of God's curse continued to reverberate on Lake Winnebago.

In this heated environment, the two parties reverted to accusations that their opponents were corrupted by black blood. After the Indian Party seized control of the tribe's general fund for education, it barred the children of certain Citizen Party families from the tribal school on the charge that "they have a littel African blood running in their veins, which taints the whole in the view of the Indians."[88]

The Citizen Party responded by opening its own academy, but the Indian Party denounced it as an "African School" and denied it any financial support from the tribe. Thwarted again, the Citizen Party alleged that the Indian Party itself contained a "Sambo [who] claimed to be a Stockbridge Indian, when in fact he had not a drop of Stockbridge blood in him."[89] And so the racial barbs continued, even though the citizenship question had been settled. The racial bile between factions was becoming more heated as the stakes in their contests became less important.

Another sad effect of this factionalism was that it diminished the community's ability to fight removal. The broken leadership simply could not match the lobbying of former white purchasers of Stockbridge land who were outraged at the prospect of having their titles in the northern part of town nullified under the act of 1846. Exhausted by a decade of chronic infighting and desperate to restore the people's fiscal health after a series of expensive legal battles, John W. Quinney indicated that his people might be willing to relocate if they were adequately compensated for their Lake Winnebago lands. After closely considering a move to Minnesota, in 1856 they finally agreed to a location on Wisconsin's Wolf River fifty miles northwest of Green Bay within the recently created Menominee reservation.[90] According to the subsequent treaty of that year, all members of the tribe unwilling to take up their Lake Winnebago lands in fee simple and live under white government would relocate to the Wolf.[91] Most of the tribe took the latter option knowing all the while that this decision would be a mixed blessing at best because of the land's poor quality. True enough, families on the reservation made their livings either in forestry, which left them vulnerable to exploitation by Wisconsin's rising logging industry, or as wage workers away from home. At the same time, the reservation attracted Mohicans and Munsees from across the broad arc of those tribes' migrations, thus gesturing toward the unification once envisioned by Hendrick Aupaumut. This reservation fulfilled another of Aupaumut's hopes too, for it became a permanent home for the Mohican people. They remain there to this very day.

A New Epoch?

When the Brothertowns received citizenship in 1839, Thomas Commuck, with whom this book began, hailed the development as "a new epoch in the history of our nation" because "already we anticipate a permanent resting place for ourselves and posterity: the tyranny and oppression—that discord and jealousy, which, for the last three or four years have reigned so despotically over us, we trust will then be precipitated from the throne, and the more welcome sovereigns, Justice and Humanity—equal rights and privileges, be seated thereon."[92] Commuck's aspirations were too grandiose for the reality of Indian life in white-dominated America. As early as 1854, some Brothertowns had come to "regret the action of Congress and its consequences," in part because "many white men have bought lots and settled among them."[93] Displaced Brothertowns fanned out in search of work, with the vast majority of them remaining close to home in factory towns like Fond du Lac and Milwaukee or logging camps scattered throughout the Lakes region. Others, determined to remain in Indian places, married into the nearby Oneida and Stockbridge reservations or took jobs near the eastern Sioux reservation in Minnesota. Staying within the orbit of Brothertown meant that they could make periodic visits to the community for picnics, weddings, funerals, and family reunions, especially during the summer. They were able to do so because a core group of more than a hundred people remained in the original Lake Winnebago settlement well into the twentieth century. Similar social patterns marked the Stockbridge reservation, with the critical difference being the security of the Mohicans' lands. By the end of the nineteenth century, some three hundred Stockbridges lived on the Wolf River reservation all year long, while others came and went according to economic demands and romantic attachments.[94] Was this a new epoch? No, it matched neither the utopian aspirations expressed by Commuck nor the disastrous premonitions of the many naysayers. Rather, citizenship for the Brothertowns and the reservation for the Stockbridges afforded them a small measure of the stability they so desperately wanted, but without the resources to thrive as a people.

Perhaps the Brothertowns and Stockbridges took solace that things would have turned out much worse for them if they had taken the option to move west. By the 1850s, there were hundreds of Brothertowns, Stockbridges, and Oneidas in Kansas, most of them on the New York Indian Tract or among the Delawares near Fort Leavenworth. The migrants left for Kansas because of the government's pledge to provide them with food, housing, supplies, and, most important, guaranteed land. Washington fell short in every respect. Passage of the Kansas-Nebraska Act of 1854, with its provision to allow settlers to vote on whether these territories would become free or slave states, led tens of thousands of pro- and anti-slavery men to stream into the area, with many of them primed for a fight. Predictably, this violence spilled onto the Indian reservations. Southern "Bushwackers" seized the Indians' houses while the owners were away running errands, rustled the Indians' livestock, razed their timber, and even shot down Indians in cold blood, all with the aim of terrorizing Native people off their lands and wearing down the government's commitment to protect them.[95] By and large, it worked. As Indians retreated in the face of these threats, the government opened up the New York Indian Tract for sale. Numerous other tribes, such as the Delawares, Shawnees, Wyandots, and Miamis, who had come to Kansas from the Midwest, sold off huge portions of their claims in the hope that smaller reservations would be easier to defend—but they weren't. By the 1870s the government had removed most of these tribes to Oklahoma.[96] It was this very kind of scenario that the Brothertowns and Stockbridges had feared when they refused to go to Kansas in the late 1830s and early 1840s.

To the extent that citizenship represented a new epoch for Commuck's Brothertowns, it was with regard to the issue of intermarriage. Recall that the same Commuck who was hailing the possibilities of citizenship in 1839 was by 1855 writing to Lyman Draper that the Brothertowns had almost vanished as a distinct people through their mixing with whites.[97] The Brothertowns had always made a formal distinction between marrying into the community and marrying out, with marriages between Brothertown men and non-Brothertown women deemed legitimate for the purpose of access to tribal land and those between Brothertown women and non-Brothertown men resulting in forfeiture of the woman's land claims. Yet once the Brothertowns lost their reservation, *all* such relationships carried the tinge of *marrying out,* at least from the perspective of white society. The white public held that Indian blood receded as Indians reproduced with non-Indians, hence the terms "mixed-bloods" and "half-breeds" to refer to people of Indian-white parentage. In later years, the federal government would translate these colloquialisms into the scientific language of blood quantum, which measured Indian identity according to wholes, halves, quarters, and eighths, and would refuse access to protected Indian land and annuities to people at the lower end of the scale. Since the Brothertowns spoke monolingual English, followed a white gendered division of labor, dressed like whites, lived in framed houses, and, after 1839, held private property, there was little else but their complexions to support their claims to Indian identity. As the skin color of the people claiming Brothertown identity faded, so too did the white public's acceptance that they were Indians.

The preeminence of state goals in determining these racial classifications becomes particularly evident when one contrasts white policies toward Indians and definitions of Indianness, on the one hand, and policies toward blacks and definitions of blackness, on the other. Official white encouragement of Indian civility and citizenship stood in marked contrast to public strictures on blacks, who, regardless of their refinement, faced legal segregation and barriers against voting even in most of the states that had done away with slavery. Of course, the white nation reaped material benefits according to this double standard. Indians who practiced male plow agriculture were able to make do with less land than those who did not. Likewise, Indians who became citizens opened their land base to the market. Receding blackness and black citizenship held no such benefit for whites. Rather, if blackness was a permanent legal condition, black people would forever remain a low-wage labor force that whites could exploit. The same goal of enlarging the servile labor pool shaped the idea of black hypodescent (or the "one-drop rule") in which a person with any degree of black ancestry is defined as black. Whites were so accustomed to assuming that blackness polluted bloodlines and that Indianness receded through mixture that they took no notice of the inconsistency of these beliefs. More to the point, they had a firm stake in maintaining these contradictions, for it was in their interest to increase the number of cheap black laborers for white employers and to free up Indian land for white farmers.[98]

Commuck's literary flair aside, most Brothertowns refused to concede that they were fated to disappear, regardless of their reforms, regardless of their citizenship, regardless of their intermarriages. For one, many of them continued to believe that there was something fundamentally different between themselves, as Indians, and whites. Some of them attributed that distinction to God's will, believing he punished Indians for the sins of their ancestors and as a test of their faith. Others were less concerned with the cause of the difference than the effect. Over and over again, they pointed to the restlessness, greed, and scheming of whites and the simplicity, gullibility, and fairness of Indians. They also laid claim to their ancestral identity, even as citizens, by continuing to refer to themselves as the Indians of Brothertown, the Brothertown tribe, or the Brothertown nation whenever they conducted public business involving their remaining parcels of tribal lands, collection and distribution of annuities, or lawsuits against the federal government.[99] They gathered periodically to celebrate their shared Brothertown Indian heritage, sometimes in showy displays of Plains Indian dress adhering to popular notions of Indian appearance. They had changed, yes, but they had not forgotten who they were or where they came from.

Yet with every passing generation these rituals felt like a one-way conversation. Whites generally were unwilling to accept the complexities of Indian identity among people who were Christian, civilized, and, finally, citizens, for over the course of two centuries whites had turned Indian from a cultural category into an essentialized racial one. According to this typology, the basic racial characteristics of Indians included not only innate savagery but also a destiny of extinction, be it through violent displacement, a slow demise on remote reservations, or gradual assimilation into white society. Indians who adjusted to make their people viable for a new era, especially Indians who thrived despite the odds, were incomprehensible according to this schema, so whites ignored them or defined them away as inauthentic, cartoonish, or a sham. This dilemma, so powerfully captured in the question posed by the Stockbridges during their own struggle over citizenship—*Indians or Citizens, White Men or Red*—continues to confront Native people in the twenty-first century. Its persistence is testimony that race is one of the most profound legacies of American colonialism.

"Extinction" and a "Common Ancestor"

I T is not difficult to imagine why the white people of Reidsville, New York, invited John W. Quinney to speak at their 1854 Fourth of July celebration. After all, on a day to celebrate the birth of the United States, Quinney's people seemed like an ideal symbol of nation's enlightened, benevolent principles. Whites credited missionary work with transforming the Stockbridge Mohicans into some of the most "civilized" Indians on the continent. Virtually all of these Indians practiced Christianity. Their men were no longer hunter-warriors but farmers, loggers, artisans, and wage laborers. Their children received formal schooling, and English was generally their first language. Not the least of all, their tribe had written laws and followed democratic procedures. In these respects and more, the Stockbridge Mohicans served as human evidence of America's taming of the savage wilderness.

Quinney's personal appearance also testified to Stockbridge's conversion at American hands, at least in the eyes of whites. Two contemporary portraits show that his hair was short all around and brushed to one side, a cut that could have been found on the streets of any white town or city. He wore a thin mustache to distance himself from the traditional Indian revulsion toward facial hair. Whenever Quinney conducted public business, he dressed in a full suit, including a white-collared shirt, tie, vest, tailored jacket and pants, and leather-soled shoes. Christian in faith and Christian in appearance, Quinney, without even saying a word, was appealing to white audiences that there was indeed hope for reforming the Indians before United States expansion wiped them from the face of the earth. In all likelihood, however, whites read Quinney's image differently. They probably took solace that at least the nation had genuinely tried to civilize Indians even though most Indians had rejected the gift, thus ushering in their demise. To them, Quinney's civilized cast meant that the gift was real. As such, surely the two thousand or so spectators who crowded to hear Quinney speak expected an uplifting, even patriotic message.

Indians across North America insisted that meetings between foreign peoples should begin with a historical recounting of their relationship. How else could the parties grasp their mutual obligations, their relations of power, the customs that structured their interaction? Quinney was by any measure a "civilized" Indian, but he still believed in this protocol. He could perform it because his tribe, for all its reforms, still had a rich oral tradition. Quinney made no apologies that among the Mohicans, oral histories "are as firmly believed as written annals by you." In fact, in his judgment, Indian histories contained fewer errors and many more truths. His people could recount their past, including the history of their relations with whites. It was not what the people of Reidsville wanted to hear.

You people, Quinney began, "occupy by conquest, or have usurped...the territories of my fathers, and have laid and carefully preserved, a train of terrible miseries to end when my race shall have ceased to exist."[1] Anticipating that the startled crowd would dismiss him as an ignorant ranter, he emphasized that he was well educated and well read in the published histories of the United States. His studies taught him that the Fourth of July was supposed to represent the "free birth of this giant nation." Yet to him the rise of the United States was but the "transfer of the miserable weakness and dependence of my race from one great power to another." To Indians, the United States differed from its colonial predecessors only in its capacity to dispossess and subjugate Native people and, as Quinney hinted, to delude itself that it was an apostle for human progress.

Notice that Quinney made his appeal on behalf not of his tribe or his nation but of his *race*. And by race he meant all American Indians, not just the Mohicans. He explained his people's belief that "all the red men are sprung from a common ancestor, made by the Great Spirit from red clay." That was why Indians identified "one another by their color, as brothers, and acknowledge one Great Creator." Yet Indian identity gained contemporary meaning only through indigenous people's shared suffering under the white regime. One of Quinney's goals was to make the people of Reidsville understand that process.

Quinney recalled that the Mohicans had thrived before the arrival of the Europeans. At some distant time, they had migrated to the East from the Northwest with a large family of Algonquian-speakers. Over the generations that family had broken into several lineages, "Delawares, Munsees, Mohegans, Narragansetts, Pequots, Penobscots, and many others." Quinney's ancestors eventually settled down along the Hudson River and Housatonic River watersheds, where they became known as "Mu-he-con-new," meaning "like waters which are never still." Their name wedded them to their homeland, and they flourished in this location. Quinney understood that they once numbered some twenty-five thousand people, including four-thousand warriors. Strong and confident, they had no fear when their shamans began to prophesy the arrival "of a strange race…as numerous as the leaves upon the trees."

The arrival of the "pale-face," however, was the beginning of endless tragedy. The Mohicans' first impression of the newcomers was "our visitors were white, and must be sick." Full of pity, the Indians fed and clothed the Europeans and eventually offered them land and alliance. Yet in return they received "vice and disease, which the white man imported" and which "have done the work of annihilation." Whites also encouraged feuds among the Indians as part of a strategy of divide and conquer. Then, once the Indians were weakened, whites "induced" them through fraud and intimidation "to abandon their territory at intervals, and withdraw further inland." The pattern played out repeatedly until the Mohicans found themselves in Wisconsin. Numerous other tribes had suffered similar fates, with many of them winding up at "those happy hunting-grounds which the Great Father has prepared for all his red children," otherwise known as Oklahoma. Quinney's sarcasm dripped with bitterness.

This was not a story of the triumph of enlightened principles but a case study in the hypocrisy of American values. "The Indian is said to be the ward of the white man, and the negro his slave," Quinney observed, adding, "Has it ever occurred to you, my friends, that while the slave is increasing, and increased by every appliance, the Indian is left to rot and die, before the humanities of this model Republic!" If this admonishment was insufficient to inspire whites to repent, Quinney offered one more consideration: the Creator would judge them before too long. Quinney knew his Bible, and he belonged to a people who for nearly three-quarters of a century had thought of Indian suffering as punishment for the sins of their ancestors. He knew that "national wrongs are avenged, and national crimes atoned for in this world." Quinney might have believed that the day was approaching "when my race will have ceased to exist," but he advised whites in the meantime to grant Indians "justice," if only to save their own souls.

Like Thomas Commuck and so many others, Quinney was wrong that Indians were on the road to the extinction, but there is no questioning the reality of the pain he highlighted or, for that matter, its power to convince indigenous people of the reality of race. Those legacies continue to shape Stockbridge and Brothertown life to this very day, as I learned during my own visits to these Wisconsin communities. There is no mistaking that the Stockbridge-Munsee Mohicans are an Indian tribal nation. Their reservation northwest of Green Bay is clearly marked with signs announcing their sovereignty. Many roads contain Indian names. The hotel on the reservation is called the Konkapot Lodge after a historic Mohican family, and the place is filled with Indian artwork and indigenous architectural motifs. A local general store sells Indian-made goods, T-shirts with Indian logos, and powwow gear. The North Star Casino and a first-rate golf course are unmistakably Indian-run. As for how all this came to be, the tribal library houses a superb exhibit of Stockbridge history from ancient times to the present. The reservation and the tribe's sovereignty allow these people to live and accentuate their Indian identity despite many of them having married non-Indians over the years. They have an answer to Commuck's question, "Where?" They have bucked their supposed destiny.

American society has found it easier to ignore the Brothertowns, not because the Brothertowns have ever ceased to exist but because they confound popular assumptions about what it means to be Indian. No one from the tribe lives on the Brothertown site anymore, though some of them visit it frequently. Many Brothertowns live in or around the nearby city of Fond du Lac at the southern end of Lake Winnebago or in other communities in southeast Wisconsin, though tribal members also can be found in places much farther afield. Without a reservation, the tribe's public presence includes a historical marker on their former Lake Winnebago territory and a storefront headquarters in downtown Fond du Lac. From that location, a group of committed volunteers has worked tirelessly for decades to regain federal recognition of Brothertown as a tribal Indian nation and, with it, benefits in the areas of health care, education, and perhaps even land restitution. The climb has been difficult. For reasons obvious to anyone who has read this book, the Brothertowns' tribal organization since 1839 has remained largely informal and thus has not produced a thick trail of written evidence, though there have been periodic spikes in official tribal activity by headmen who clearly had public support. Brothertown has survived as a community of people less through top-down leadership than via a web of sociability that includes visits, reunions, weddings, funerals, correspondence, and phone calls. The annual summer picnic I attended was a casual yet powerful example of this process. Though most of the people could easily pass as white, many of them had a staggering knowledge of their Indian genealogy and the tribe's history. A large group of them had once organized a bus tour to significant Brothertown sites in New England and New York, including the modern-day reservations of the community's ancestral tribes. Perhaps most important of all, they made sure the young people in attendance appreciated their rich heritage. Socializing of this sort has held the Brothertown people together for well over a century, yet is it possible to *document* the significance of events like a picnic so that the Bureau of Indian Affairs will acknowledge that the tribe exists?[2] As I complete this book, I have learned that the BIA has rejected the Brothertowns' petition for federal recognition. The tribe is appealing the decision.

If the Brothertowns are successful, it will represent a milestone on a journey that began with the community's founding during the Revolution and then forked as the people confronted the question of citizenship. Before 1839, the Brothertowns traveled down a path charted by Samson Occom, Joseph Johnson, and David Fowler toward the goal of living as civilized Christians in their own distinctly Indian community. However, when confronted with removal from Lake Winnebago, after so many other displacements, the tribe decided to risk subjugation to white law and division of the people's lands into alienable private property, two of the very things the founders had created Brothertown to avoid. The Brothertowns accepted citizenship in the hope that it would enable them to remain on their lands as a people, but in the short term the results were mixed; in the long run, the consequences were tragic. While a core group of more than a hundred people managed to remain in or around Brothertown well into the twentieth century and to organize politically whenever the need arose to engage outside authorities, poverty and land loss displaced others from their allotments, particularly as families distributed land to heirs in plots insufficient for profitable farming. Many Brothertowns forced from Lake Winnebago left to find work in white municipalities though they tried to remain as close to home as possible and to live and socialize in neighborhoods with large numbers of Indian people. Others went to live on or near the reservations of fellow Indians such as the Stockbridges, Oneidas, Menominees, or Minnesota Sioux, where they felt a sense of belonging. Eventually, stalwarts at the original Lake Winnebago settlement were forced out too by the Great Depression and a legal debacle. A well-educated Oneida activist, Laura Cornelius Kellog, and her white lawyer husband, Orrin, convinced Brothertowns, Stockbridges, and Iroquois throughout the United States and Canada to hand over their life savings to fund a lawsuit against the federal government seeking compensation for their original lands in New York. Initially, hopes for this suit were high, but eventually many

Native people grew suspicious of how the couple used these monies. Authorities in Quebec even charged the pair with fraud, only to acquit them. In the end, American courts threw out the suit, ending the "Six Nations Movement." Brothertowns who had gambled everything they had on a government payout were left penniless, demoralized, and forced to make a living elsewhere.[3]

Life off the reservation confronted Brothertown people with a terrible choice: assert their Indian identity or protect their livelihoods, even safety. One elderly woman told me about white schoolmates teasing her mercilessly after they discovered her Indian background, which was the last time she ever mentioned it. I heard from people who had spent their working years terrified that they would be fired if their employers learned that they were Indian. There was even a story about white loggers burying an Indian campmate up to his neck in dirt and then leaving him there for hours, just because he was an Indian. It is no wonder that some Brothertowns kept their Indian heritage a secret from their children, at least until the children had grown into adults. Today, some of these children (now well along in years) are among the most active members of the tribe, which gives them a depth of perspective on the dilemma their parents faced.

In the twenty-first century there are far more incentives and far fewer dangers for people to identify themselves as Indian. Consequently, increasing numbers of tribes, thought by the white public to have disappeared, have reorganized and convinced their people to enroll as official members. Likewise, public educational institutions dedicated to Indian themes, such as the Smithsonian's National Museum of the American Indian, have increasingly addressed the complex and often contradictory ways that Indians, the federal government, and the American public have created and continue to create a moving set of criteria for judging Indian and tribal identity. Blood quantum, language, religion, dress, cultural knowledge, material culture—all factor variously in the reckoning of who is an Indian and to what group an Indian belongs. The joint history of Brothertown and Stockbridge teaches that this problem has existed for hundreds of years and is likely to continue as long as Indianness is associated with kinship in a tribal community and access to tribal or federal government benefits—that is to say, indefinitely.

Throughout their existence, Brothertown and Stockbridge have forced people, including their own people, to ask the question: when does an Indian cease to be an Indian? Is there such thing as a quintessentially Indian culture? Can an Indian tribe exist without an actual tribal homeland? Is it possible to be a member of an Indian tribe without outwardly belonging to the Indian race? And, perhaps most important of all, who decides? Brothertowns and Stockbridges have argued these points with white and black outsiders and among themselves throughout their existence, because that very existence was and is at stake in the answers. Therein lies the greatest problem of race for Indians in America.

Notes

Prologue

1. On Draper's work, see "Lyman Draper and the South," *Journal of Southern History* 19, no. 1 (1953), 20–31; and the State Historical Society of Wisconsin's website, www.wisconsinhistory.org/military/draper/draper.asp, accessed Jan. 22, 2010.

2. Thomas Commuck, "Sketch of the Brothertown Indians," *Wisconsin Historical Collections* 4 (1859), 291.

3. Ibid., 293 ("Fire Water"), 291–92 ("mighty rush"), 298 ("Where?").

4. Ibid., 291, 292 ("Red Brethren"), 293 ("white brethren").

5. Ibid., 295.

6. Ibid., 295.

7. Ibid., 297–98.

8. Roger Williams, *A Key into the Language of America,* ed. John T. Teunissen and Evelyn J. Hinz (Detroit, 1973), 85.

9. Williams, *Key into the Language of America,* 84–85.

10. Ibid., 197, 121 ("knive men"), 133 (coatmen), 137.

11. See the discussion of the Oneida term for white person (*oʔslu·ní*) in Karin Michelson and Mercy Doxtator, *Oneida-English/English-Oneida Dictionary* (Toronto, 2002), 324.

12. Williams, *Key into the Language of America,* 132–33.

13. Ibid., 85, 189.

14. Among many works, see Roy Harvey Pearce, *Savagism and Civilization: A Study of the Indian and the American Mind* (Berkeley, Calif., 1988); Robert E. Berkhoffer, *The White Man's Indian: Images of the American Indian from Columbus to the Present* (New York, 1978); Richard Drinnon, *Facing West: The Metaphysics of Indian Hating and Empire Building* (Norman, Okla., 1997); Richard Slotkin, *Regeneration through Violence: The Mythology of the American Frontier, 1600–1860* (Norman, Okla., 2000); Bernard W. Sheehan, *Seeds of Extinction: Jeffersonian Philanthropy and the American Indian* (New York, 1973); Sheehan, *Savagism and Civility: Indians and Englishmen in Colonial Virginia* (New York, 1980); Anthony F. C. Wallace, *Jefferson and the Indians: The Tragic Fate of the First Americans* (Cambridge, Mass., 1999); Brian W. Dippie, *The Vanishing Indian: White Attitudes and U.S. Indian Policy* (Lawrence, Kans., 1991); Anthony Pagden, *The Fall of Natural Man: The American Indian and the Origins of Comparative Ethnology* (New York, 1982); Olive P. Dickason, *Myth of the Savage and the Beginnings of French Colonialism in the Americas* (Edmonton, 1984); Alden T. Vaughan, *Roots of American Racism: Essays on the Colonial Experience* (New York, 1995); Joyce Chaplin, *Subject Matter: Technology, the Body, and Science on*

the Anglo-American Frontier (Cambridge, Mass., 2001); Peter Silver, *Our Savage Neighbors: How Indian War Transformed Early America* (New York, 2008). See also Kathleen Brown, "Native Americans and Early Modern Concepts of Race," in *Empire and Others: British Encounters with Indigenous Peoples, 1600–1850,* ed. Mary Daunton and Rick Halpern (London, 1999), 79–100.

15. Gregory Evans Dowd, *A Spirited Resistance: The North American Indian Struggle for Unity, 1745–1815* (Baltimore, 1992); Dowd, *War under Heaven: Pontiac, the Indian Nations, and the British Empire* (Baltimore, 2002); Joel W. Martin, *Sacred Revolt: The Muskogees' Struggle for a New World* (Boston, 1991); Alfred A. Cave, *Prophets of the Great Spirit: Native American Revitalization Movements in Eastern North America* (Lincoln, Neb., 2006); Daniel K. Richter, *Facing East from Indian Country: A Native History of Early America* (Cambridge, Mass., 2001), 189–236; Nancy Shoemaker, *A Strange Likeness: Becoming Red and White in Eighteenth-Century North America* (New York, 2004). See also Joshua Piker, "Indians and Race in Early America: A Review Essay," *History Compass* 3 (2005), 1–17.

16. On Brothertown, see W. DeLoss Love, *Samson Occom and the Christian Indians of New England,* introduction by Margaret Connell Szasz (1899; Syracuse, N.Y., 2000); Brad Devin Edward Jarvis, "Preserving the Brothertown Nation of Indians: Exploring Relationships amongst Land, Sovereignty, and Identity, 1740–1840 (Ph.D. diss., University of Minnesota, 2006); Franz Laurens Wojchiechowski, "Actors and Actions of the Brothertown Indian Genesis: A Tale of Contradictory Accounts, and a Proposed Solution," *Yumtzilob* 10, no. 4 (1998), 391–413; Anthony Wonderly, "Brothertown, New York, 1785–1796," *New York History* 81 (2000), 457–92. Offering important insights on the racial history of Brothertown are Hilary E. Wyss, *Writing Indians: Literacy, Christianity, and Native Community in Early America* (Amherst, Mass., 2000), 123–53; and John Wood Sweet, *Bodies Politic: Negotiating Race in the American North, 1730–1830* (Baltimore, 2003), 316–28. Important works on Stockbridge include Patrick Frazier, *The Mohicans of Stockbridge* (Lincoln, Neb., 1992); Marion Johnson Mochon, "Stockbridge-Munsee Cultural Adaptations: 'Assimilated Indians,'" *Proceedings of the American Philosophical Society* 112, no. 3 (Jun. 1968), 182–219; James W. Oberly, *A Nation of Statesmen: The Political Culture of the Stockbridge-Munsee Mohicans, 1815–1792* (Norman, Okla., 2005); Rachel M. Wheeler, *To Live upon Hope: Mohicans and Missionaries in the Eighteenth-Century Northeast* (Ithaca, N.Y., 2008); Wyss, *Writing Indians,* 81–122.

17. Homi Bhabha, "Of Mimicry and Man: The Ambivalence of Colonial Discourse," in *Race Critical Theories,* ed. Philomena Essed and David Theo Goldberg (Malden, Mass., 2002), 114.

18. Among many works influencing this discussion are Michael L. Blakey, "Scientific Racism and the Biological Concept of Race," *Literature and Psychology* 45 (1999), 29–43; Barbara J. Fields, "Ideology and Race in American History," *New Left Review* 181 (May-Jun. 1990), 95–118; Patrick Wolfe, "Land, Labor, and Difference: Elementary Structures of Race," *American Historical Review* 106, no. 3 (Jun. 2001), 866–905; Mara Loveman, "Making 'Race' and Nation in the United States, South Africa, and Brazil: Taking 'Making' Seriously," *Theory and Society* 28 (1999), 903–27; Pauline Turner Strong and Barrik

Van Winkle, "'Indian Blood': Reflections on the Reckoning and Refiguring of Native North American Identity," *Cultural Anthropology* 11 (1996), 547–76; Maria P. Root, ed., *Racially Mixed People in America* (Newberry Park, Calif., 1992); Essed and Goldberg, eds., *Race Critical Theories.*

19. Patricia E. Rubertone, *Grave Undertakings: An Archaeology of Roger Williams and the Narragansett Indians* (Washington, D.C., 2001), 16; Margaret Ellen Newell, "The Changing Nature of Indian Slavery in New England, 1670–1720," in *Reinterpreting New England Indians and the Colonial Experience,* ed. Colin G. Calloway and Neal Salisbury (Boston, 2003), 115.

20. See the excellent discussion at www.pbs.org/wgbh/nova/first/race.html, accessed Jan. 21, 2009.

Chapter 1. All One Indian

1. Thomas Shepard, *The Clear Sun-shine of the Gospel Breaking forth upon the INDIANS in New-England* (London, 1648), *MHSC,* 3rd ser., 4 (1834), 50.

2. Kathleen J. Bragdon, *Native People of Southern New England, 1500–1650* (Norman, Okla., 1996), 184–90.

3. Thomas Harriot, *A briefe and true report of the new found land of Virginia* [1588], in *The First Colonists: Documents on the Planting of the First English Settlements in North America, 1584–1590,* ed. David B. Quinn and Alison M. Quinn (New York, 1973), 70.

4. Roger Williams, *A Key into the Language of America,* ed. John J. Teunissen and Evelyn J. Hinz (1643; Detroit, 1973), 191; James Axtell, *Beyond 1492: Encounters in Colonial North America* (New York, 1988), 52–58, 75–96; Karen Ordahl Kupperman, *Indians and English: Facing Off in Early America* (Ithaca, N.Y., 2000); Evan Haefeli, "On First Contact and Apotheosis: Manitou and Men in North America," *Ethnohistory* 54, no. 3 (2007), 407–43.

5. Robert A. Williams Jr., *Linking Arms Together: American Indian treaty Visions of Law and Peace, 1600–1800* (New York, 1999); Russel Lawrence Barsh, "The Nature and Spirit of North American Political Systems," *American Indian Quarterly* 10 (1986), 181–98.

6. John Easton, "A Relacion of the Indyan Warre" [1675], in Charles H. Lincoln, ed., *Narratives of the Indian Wars, 1675–1699* (New York, 1913), 10–11.

7. Alfred W. Crosby, "Virgin Soil Epidemics as a Factor in the Aboriginal Depopulation in America," *WMQ,* 33 (1976), 289–99. On the epidemics that struck the coast, see Timothy Bratton, "The Identity of the New England Indian Epidemic of 1616–1619," *Bulletin of the History of Medicine* 62 (1988), 351–83; Dean Snow and Kim M. Lanphear, "European Contact and Indian Depopulation in the Northeast: The Timing of the First Epidemics," *Ethnohistory* 35 (1988), 15–33; Catherine C. Carlson, George L. Armelagos, and Ann Magennis, "Impact of Disease on the Precontact and Early Historic Populations of New England and the Maritimes," in *Disease and Demography in the Americas,* ed. John W. Verano and Douglas H. Ubelaker (Washington, D.C., 1992), 141–52; Brenda J. Baker, "Pilgrim's Progress and Praying Indians: The Biocultural Consequences of Contact in Southern New England," in *In the Wake of Contact: Biological Responses to Conquest,* ed. Clark Spencer Larsen and George R. Milner (New York, 1994), 35–44; David J. Silverman, *Faith and Boundaries: Colonists, Christianity, and Community among the Wampanoag Indians of Martha's Vineyard, 1600–1871* (New York, 2005), 22–23; Marion Fisher Ales, "A History of the Indians on Montauk, Long Island,"

in *The History and Archaeology of the Montauk,* ed. Gaynell Stone, 2d ed. (Mattituck, N.Y., 1993), 35, 38.

8. Quoted in Patricia Seed, "Taking Possession and Reading Texts: Establishing the Authority of Overseas Empires," *WMQ,* 49 (1992), 208. See also John Winthrop, "General Considerations for the Plantations in New England, with an Answer to Several Objections," *Winthrop Papers,* vol. 2 (Boston, 1931), 120.

9. Generally on this theme, see William A. Starna, "The Biological Encounter: Disease and the Ideological Domain," *American Indian Quarterly* 16 (1992), 512–19.

10. "Roger Williams to Henry Vane and John Winthrop, May 1, 1637," *The Correspondence of Roger Williams,* ed. Glenn La Fantasie, 2 vols. (Hanover, N.H., 1988), 1:72.

11. Conrad Weiser's Journal of a Trip to Onondaga, Pennsylvania Provincial Council Minutes, Oct. 11, 1750, Iroquois Indians, reel 15. See also William M. Beauchamp, ed., *Moravian Journals relating to Central New York, 1745–1766* (Syracuse, N.Y., 1916), 92.

12. *Early American Indian Documents: Treaties and Laws, 1607–1789,* gen. ed. Alden T. Vaughan, vol. 17, *New England and Middle Atlantic Laws,* vol. eds. Alden T. Vaughan and Deborah Rosen (Bethesda, Md., 2004), 105–6.

13. James Axtell, *The Invasion Within: The Contest of Cultures in Colonial North America* (New York, 1985); Silverman, *Faith and Boundaries,* 16–77; Cogley, *John Eliot's Mission;* Kristina Bross, *Dry Bones and Indian Sermons: Praying Indians and Colonial American Identity* (Ithaca, N.Y., 2004).

14. Henry Whitfield, *The Light appearing more and more towards the perfect Day. Or, A farther Discovery of the present state of the Indians in New-England, Concerning the Progresse of the Gospel amongst them* (London, 1651), *MHSC,* 3d ser., 4 (1834), 139–40; Henry Whitfield, *Strength Out of Weaknesse; Or a Glorious Manifestation of the further Progresse of the Gospel among the Indians in New England* (London, 1652), *MHSC,* 3d ser., 4 (1834), 170; Daniel Gookin, "Historical Collections of the Indians in New England," *MHSC,* 1st ser., 1 (1792), 208, 210.

15. On news traveling through Indian country, see John Eliot, *The Day Breaking, If Not The Sun-Rising of the GOSPEL With the INDIANS in New-England* (1647), *MHSC,* 3d ser., 4 (1834), 16; Williams, *Key into the Language,* 135–38.

16. Axtell, *Invasion Within,* 218–41.

17. Eliot, *Day Breaking,* 17.

18. Whitfield, *Strength Out of Weaknesse,* 181.

19. Eliot, *Day Breaking,* 11.

20. Experience Mayhew, "A brief Journal of my visitation of the Pequot and Mohegin Indians...." [1713], in *Some Correspondence between the Governors and Treasurers of the New England Company in London and the Commissioners of the United Colonies in America,* ed. John W. Ford (1896; New York, 1970), 119–20, 126.

21. Homi Bhabha, "Of Mimicry and Man: The Ambivalence of Colonial Discourse," in *Race Critical Theories,* ed. Philomena Essed and David Theo Goldberg (Malden, Mass., 2002), 114.

22. Edward Winslow, *The Glorious Progress of the Gospel amongst the Indians in New-England* (London, 1649), *MHSC,* 3d ser., 4 (1834), 81, 88. On Eliot's concern about Indian

consumption of liquor, see Cogley, *John Eliot's Mission*, 60. On the problem of Indians, colonists, and livestock, see Virginia DeJohn Anderson, "King Philip's Herds: Indians, Colonists, and the Problem of Livestock in Early New England," *WMQ* 51 (1994), 601–24; Robert E. Gradie, "New England Indians and Colonizing Pigs," in *Papers of the Fifteenth Algonquian Conference*, ed. William Cowan (Ottawa, 1984), 147–69.

23. Len Travers, ed., "The Missionary Journal of John Cotton, Jr., 1666–1678," *Proceedings of the Massachusetts Historical Society* 109 (1998), 80.

24. On these events, see Alfred A. Cave, *The Pequot War* (Amherst, Mass., 1996), 49–121; Francis Jennings, *The Invasion of America: Indians, Colonialism, and the Cant of Conquest* (Chapel Hill, N.C., 1975), 186–201; Salisbury, *Manitou and Providence*, 203–20.

25. Underhill, "News from America," 57–58. See also Alfred A. Cave, "Who Killed John Stone: A Note on the Origins of the Pequot War," *WMQ* 49, no. 3 (1992), 509–21.

26. Cave, *Pequot War*, 138.

27. Underhill, "News from America," 84.

28. Pulsipher, *Subjects unto the Same King*, 22; and Silverman, *Faith and Boundaries*, 6–7.

29. Roger Williams to John Winthrop Jr., Oct. 24, 1636?, *Correspondence of Roger Williams*, 1:69.

30. Morton, *New England's Memorial*, 127–28.

31. Pulsipher, *Subjects unto the Same King*, 21–36, 55–59; Jennings, *Invasion of America*, 254–81; Paul A. Robinson, "Lost Opportunities: Miantomomi and the English in Seventeenth-Century Narragansett Country," and Eric S. Johnson, "Uncas and the Politics of Contact," in *Northeastern Indian Lives*, ed. Robert S. Grumet (Amherst, Mass., 1996), 13–28, 29–47; Johnson, "Some by Flatteries and Others by Threatenings"; Glenn W. LaFantasie and Paul R. Campbell, "Covenants of Grace, Covenants of Wrath: Niantic-Puritan Relations in New England," *Rhode Island History* 37 (1979), 15–23; Timothy J. Sehr, "Ninigret's Tactics of Accommodation: Indian Diplomacy in New England, 1637–1675," *Rhode Island History* 36 (1977), 43–53.

32. "Leift Lion Gardiner his relation of the Pequott Warres," in *History of the Pequot War: The Contemporary Accounts of Mason, Underhill, Vincent, and Gardener*, ed. Charles Orr (Cleveland, 1897), 142. Generally on Miantonomi's efforts, see Michael Leroy Oberg, "'We Are All Sachems from East to West': A New Look at Miantonomi's Campaign of Resistance," *New England Quarterly* 77, no. 4 (Sept. 2004), 478–99; John A. Strong, "Wyandanch: Sachem of the Montauks," in *Northeastern Indian Lives*, ed. Grumet 54–55.

33. "Journal of New Netherland, 1647," in *Narratives of New Netherland*, ed. James Franklin Jameson (New York, 1909), 276.

34. John Sainsbury, "Miantonomo's Death and New England Politics, 1630–1645," *Rhode Island History* 30 (1971), 111–23; Michael Leroy Oberg, *Uncas: First of the Mohegans* (Ithaca, N.Y., 2003), 102–7.

35. On this conflict, see Evan Haefeli, "Kieft's War and the Systems of Violence in Colonial America," in *Lethal Imagination: Violence and Brutality in American History*, ed. Michael A. Bellesiles (New York, 1999), 17–40; Allen W. Trelease, *Indian Affairs in Colonial New York: The Seventeenth Century* (1960; Lincoln, Neb., 1997), 60–84; Paul Otto, *The*

Dutch-Munsee Encounter in America: The Struggle for Sovereignty in the Hudson Valley (New York, 2006), 114–26.

36. Harry M. Ward, *The United Colonies of New England, 1643–1690* (New York, 1961).

37. Alden T. Vaughan, *New England Frontier: Puritans and Indians 1620–1675,* 3d ed. (Norman, Okla., 1995), 171–72.

38. Pulsipher, *Subjects unto the Same King,* 33–34; Robinson, "The Struggle Within," 184–85; Oberg, *Uncas,* 132–36; and Vaughan, *New England Frontier,* 174–75.

39. Gentlemen of East Hampton to John Mason, Jul. 1, 1669, Conn. Indian Series, ser. 1, vol. 1, p. 11, Connecticut State Archives, Hartford, Conn.

40. Russell Bourne, *The Red King's Rebellion: Racial Politics in New England, 1675–1678* (New York, 1990), 95–96; Shurtleff and Pulsipher, eds., *Records of the Colony of New Plymouth,* 4:165–66; and Pulsipher, *Subjects unto the Same King,* 98–99.

41. Williams, *Christenings Make Not Christians* [1645], quoted in Alden T. Vaughan, "Tests of Puritan Justice," in his *Roots of American Racism* (New York, 1995), 211.

42. Commissioners of the United Colonies to Anonymous, November 12, 1675, *Further Letters on King Philip's War* (Providence, 1923), 18–19; James Drake, *King Philip's War: Civil War in New England, 1675–1676* (Amherst, Mass., 1999); Pulsipher, *Subjects unto the Same King,* 101–237; Jill Lepore, *The Name of War: King Philip's War and the Origins of American Identity* (New York, 1997); Silverman, *Faith and Boundaries,* 78–120; Christopher William Hannan, "'After This Time of Trouble and Warr': Crisis and Continuity in the New England Anglo-Indian Community, 1660–1725" (Ph.D. diss., Boston College, 1999), chs. 6–7.

43. Gookin, "Historical Account," 434.

44. William Hubbard, *A Narrative of the Indian Wars in New England, From the first Planting thereof in the year 1607 to the Year 1677* (1677; Boston, 1775), 92.

45. Lepore, *Name of War,* 51.

46. Increase Mather, *A Brief History of the Warr with the Indians in New-England* [1676], in *So Dreadfull a Judgment: Puritan Responses to King Philip's War, 1676–1677,* ed. Richard Slotkin and James K. Folsom (Middletown, Conn., 1978), 86, 90.

47. Mary Rowlandson, *The Sovereignty and Goodness of God, Together with the Faithfulness of His Promises Displayed, Being a Narrative of the Captivity and Restoration of Mrs. Mary Rowlandson* [1682], ed. Neal Salisbury (Boston, 1997), 67.

48. Ibid., 107.

49. Ibid., 69–70.

50. See Lepore, *Name of War.*

51. Margaret Ellen Newell, "The Changing Nature of Indian Slavery in New England, 1670–1720," in *Reinterpreting New England Indians and the Colonial Experience,* ed. Colin G. Calloway and Neal Salisbury (Boston, 2003), 106–36; Lepore, *Name of War,* 150–70; Evan Haefeli and Kevin Sweeney, "Wattanummon's World: Personal and Tribal Identity in the Algonquian Diaspora, c. 1660–1712," in *Proceedings of the 25th Algonquian Conference,* ed. William Cowan (Ottawa, 1993), 212–24.

52. Drake, *King Philip's War;* Lepore, *Name of War;* Pulsipher, *Subjects unto the Same King;* Michael J. Puglisi, *Puritans Besieged: The Legacies of King Philip's War in the Massachusetts Bay Colony* (Landham, Md., 1991).

53. Roger Williams to John Winthrop Jr., Jun. 25, 1675, *Correspondence of Roger Williams*, 2:693–95.

54. Nathaniel Saltonstall, *The Present State of New-England with Respect to the Indian War* [1675], in *Narratives of the Indian Wars*, ed. Lincoln, 26.

55. *Early American Indian Documents, New England and Middle Atlantic Laws*, 60, 177.

56. Ibid., 154, 168, 193, 201, 278, 322–23, 341–42, 371, 380–81, 446, 463–64, 538, 665, 681–83, 684–89, 689–90, 692, 716, 718–19.

57. Ibid., 371.

58. Newell, "Changing Nature of Indian Slavery," 127.

59. M. Halsey Thomas, *The Diary of Samuel Sewall, 1674–1729*, 2 vols. (New York, 1973), 532.

60. David D. Smits, "'We Are Not to Grow Wild': Seventeenth-Century New England's Repudiation of Anglo-Indian Intermarriage," *American Indian Culture and Research Journal* 11 (1987), 1–32.

61. *Writings of Joseph Johnson*, 33; Laurie Weinstein-Farson, "Land Politics and Power: The Mohegan Indians in the Seventeenth and Eighteenth Centuries," *Man in the Northeast* 42 (1991), 9–16.

62. John Wood Sweet, *Bodies Politic: Negotiating Race in the American North* (Baltimore, 2003), 15–57; William S. Simmons, "Narragansett," *Handbook of North American Indians: Northeast*, ser. ed. William C. Sturtevant, vol. 15, vol. ed. Bruce G. Trigger (Washington, D.C., 1978), 194–95.

63. Petition of the Pequot Indians, Groton, Sept. 22, 1735, Talcott Papers, *Collections of the Connecticut Historical Society*, vol. 4 (Hartford, 1829), 320–21. Generally, see David J. Silverman, "'We chuse to be bounded': Indian Animal Husbandry in Colonial New England," *WMQ*, 60 (2003), 511–48.

64. Wendy B. St. Jean, "Inventing Guardianship: The Mohegan Indians and Their 'Protectors,'" *New England Quarterly* 72 (1999), 362–87; Amy E. Den Ouden, *Beyond Conquest: Native Peoples and the Struggle for History in New England* (Lincoln, Neb., 2005), 4–5, 24; Daniel R. Mandell, *Behind the Frontier: Indians in Eighteenth-Century Massachusetts* (Lincoln, Neb., 1996).

65. Quoted in Trudy Lamb Richmond and Amy E. Den Ouden, "Recovering Gendered Political Histories: Local Struggles and Native Women's Resistance in Colonial Southern New England," in *Reinterpreting New England Indians*, ed. Calloway and Salisbury, 203.

66. David J. Silverman, "The Impact of Indentured Servitude on Southern New England Indian Society and Culture, 1680–1810," *New England Quarterly* 74 (2001), 622–66; Ruth Wallis Herndon, "Racialization and Feminization of Poverty in Early America: Indian Women as 'the poor of the town' in Eighteenth-Century Rhode Island," in *Empire and Others: British Encounters with Indigenous Peoples*, ed. Martin Daunton and Rick Halpern (London, 1999), 186–203.

67. Petition of Jonathan, Nepash, and John Tauon, Indians of Farmington, Apr. 8, 1738, Conn. Indian Series, 1st ser., vol. 1, p. 171a.

68. Emerson W. Baker and John G. Reid, "Amerindian Power in the Early Modern Northeast: A Reappraisal," *WMQ*, 61 (2004), 77–106; Colin G. Calloway, *The Western*

Abenakis of Vermont, 1600–1800: War, Migration, and the Survival of an Indian People (Norman, Okla., 1990); Kenneth M. Morrison, *The Embattled Northeast: The Elusive Ideal of Alliance in Abenaki-Euramerican Relations* (Berkeley, Calif., 1984); and Evan Haefeli and Kevin Sweeney, *Captors and Captives: The 1704 French and Indian Raid on Deerfield* (Amherst, Mass., 2003).

69. Quoted in Vaughan, "From White Man to Redskin," 21.

70. For Indian use of *chaquaquock* (also spelled *chaquogque, chokquogque,* and *chaquaqussog*), see Ives Goddard and Kathleen Bragdon, eds., *Native Writings in Massachusett,* 2 vols. (Philadelphia, 1988), 1:171, 177, 211. For Indian use of *waû tacone* (or *wattuhkonnawt*), see ibid., 1:329. For Indian use of *Indiansog, inglishmonsog,* and *Englishmansog,* see ibid., 1:364–65.

71. Ibid., 1:451 (*wompessue*).

72. Williams, *Key into the Language of America,* 136–37.

73. Roger Williams to John Winthrop, Aug. 20, 1637, *Correspondence of Roger Williams,* 1:113–14.

74. Robin Cassassinamon to Gov. Gurdon Saltonstall, May 11, 1721, Conn. Indian Series, 1st ser., vol. 1, p. 95.

Chapter 2. Converging Paths

1. Melissa Jayne Fawcett, *The Lasting of the Mohegans: Part 1, The Story of the Wolf People* (Uncasville, Conn., 1995), 37–39; Fawcett, *Medicine Trail: The Life and Lessons of Gladys Tantaquidgeon* (Tuscon, 2000), 135–36; Ann McMullen and Russell G. Handsman, eds., *A Key into the Language of Woodsplint Baskets* (Washington, Conn., 1987).

2. Daniel Gookin, "Historical Collections of the Indians in New England," *MHSC,* 1st ser., 1 (1792), 191, 208; John Eliot, "To the worshipful Mr. Steele," Dec. 10, 1652, *New England Historic Genealogical Register* 36 (1882), 294.

3. Wilkins Updike, *A History of the Episcopal Church in Narragansett, Rhode Island,* 3 vols. (Boston, 1907), 3:64, 65, 66, 68, 70, 73, 74–75, 81; Joseph Park, "An Account of the late Propagation of Religion at Westerly and Charlestown in Rhode-Island Colony," *The Christian History,* no. 26, Aug. 27, 1743, 203; William S. Simmons, "Red Yankees: Narragansett Conversion in the Great Awakening," *American Ethnologist* 1 (1983), 260–61; John Wood Sweet, *Bodies Politic: Negotiating Race in the American North, 1730–1830* (Baltimore, 2003), 134–36.

4. This work among the Indians of Rhode Island and Connecticut can be traced through Corporation for Propagating the Gospel in New England, Records, boxes 1 and 2, NEHGS. See also New England Company Records, MS 7955/2, pp. 15–16, 22–23, 24, 30, 40–41, 74, 132–33, Guildhall Library, Corporation of London; John D. DeForest, *History of the Indians of Connecticut* (Hartford, Conn., 1852), 343–46, 370–71, 383–84, 430–31; William Kellaway, *The New England Company, 1649–1776: Missionary Society to the American Indians* (New York, 1961), 250–56; James Axtell, *The Invasion Within: The Contest of Cultures in Colonial North America* (New York, 1985), 186–89, 243–47; Margaret Connell Szasz, *Indian Education in the American Colonies, 1607–1783* (Lincoln, Neb., 1988), 173–90; William De-Loss Love, *Samson Occom and the Christian Indians of New England,* introduction by Margaret Connell Szasz (1899; Syracuse, N.Y., 2000), 24–33, 198; Linford D. Fisher, "'Traditionary

Religion': The Great Awakening and the Shaping of Native Cultures in Southern New England, 1736–1776" (Ph.D. diss., Harvard University, 2008), 24–80.

5. Daniel K. Richter, *The Ordeal of the Longhouse: The Peoples of the Iroquois League in the Era of European Colonization* (Chapel Hill, N.C., 1992), 105–32, 167–68, 197–99; Christopher Vecsey, *The Paths of Keteri's Kin* (Notre Dame, Ind., 1997), 77–123.

6. Richter, *Ordeal of the Longhouse*, 165, 178, 192.

7. William Bryan Hart, "For the Good of Our Souls: Mohawk Authority, Accommodation, and Resistance to Protestant Evangelism, 1700–1780" (Ph.D. diss., Brown University, 1998); Richter, *Ordeal of the Longhouse*, 225–35; Richter, "Some of Them…Would Always Have a Minister with Them: Mohawk Protestantism, 1683–1719," *American Indian Quarterly* 16, no. 4 (1992), 471–84.

8. Amy C. Schutt, *Peoples of the River Valleys: The Odyssey of the Delaware Indians* (Philadelphia, 2006), 40–51.

9. Rachel M. Wheeler, *To Live upon Hope: Mohicans and Missionaries in the Eighteenth-Century Northeast* (Ithaca, N.Y., 2008), 25, 36–37.

10. Shirley W. Dunn, *The Mohican World, 1680–1750* (Fleischmanns, N.Y., 2000), 75, 127–29.

11. Patrick Frazier, *The Mohicans of Stockbridge* (Omaha, Neb., 1992), 1–17; Wheeler, *To Live upon Hope*, 25, 33–34; Samuel Hopkins, *Historical Memoirs, Relating to the Housatunnuk Indians: Or, An Account of the Methods used, and Pains taken, for the Propagation of the Gospel among that heathenish Tribe, and Success thereof, under the Ministry of the late Reerend Mr. John Sergeant* (Boston, 1753), 35.

12. Wheeler, *To Live upon Hope*, 37, 38.

13. Hopkins, *Historical Memoirs*, 15.

14. Ibid., 49.

15. Kellaway, *New England Company*, 270–72.

16. Daniel R. Mandell, *Behind the Frontier: Indians in Eighteenth-Century Eastern Massachusetts* (Lincoln, Neb., 1996); Jean M. O'Brien, *Dispossession by Degrees: Indian Land and Identity in Natick, Massachusetts, 1650–1790* (New York, 1997); David J. Silverman, *Faith and Boundaries: Colonists, Christianity, and Community among the Wampanoag Indians of Martha's Vineyard, 1600–1871* (New York, 2005).

17. Frazier, *Mohicans of Stockbridge*, 39–56; Axtell, *Invasion Within*, 196–99.

18. *Boston Post Boy*, no. 246, Sept. 3, 1739, p. 3, col. 2; Wheeler, *To Live upon Hope*, 59–60; Frazier, *Mohicans of Stockbridge*, 54.

19. Wheeler, *To Live upon Hope*, 197.

20. Lynch Collection, box 4, folder 21, Stockbridge Library Historical Room, Stockbridge, Mass.; Wheeler, *To Live upon Hope*, 60.

21. Wheeler, *To Live upon Hope*, 195.

22. The literature on these themes is enormous. Among many works, see Thomas S. Kidd, *The Great Awakening: The Roots of Evangelical Christianity in Colonial America* (New Haven, 2007); Frank Lambert, *Inventing the "Great Awakening"* (Princeton, N.J., 1999); Richard L. Bushman, *From Puritan to Yankee: Character and the Social Order in Connecticut, 1690–1765* (Cambridge, Mass., 1965); Patricia U. Bonomi, *Under the Cope of Heaven: Religion,*

Society, and Politics in Colonial America (New York, 1986); Jon Butler, *Awash in a Sea of Faith: Christianizing the American People* (Cambridge, Mass., 1990).

23. The best study of Brainerd is John Grigg, "The Lives of David Brainerd" (Ph.D. diss., University of Kansas, 2002).

24. Jonathan Edwards, *The Life of David Brainerd,* ed. Norman Pettit (1749; New Haven, Conn., 1985), 155.

25. Grigg, "Lives of David Brainerd," 114.

26. Ibid., 117–18; Edwards, *Life of David Brainerd,* 202–50.

27. Grigg, "Lives of David Brainerd," 118; Frazier, *Mohicans of Stockbridge,* 58–59.

28. Francis Jennings, *The Ambiguous Iroquois Empire: The Covenant Chain Confederation of Indian Tribes with the English Colonies* (New York, 1984), 332–46; Schutt, *Peoples of the River Valleys,* 87–93.

29. James H. Merrell, "Shamokin: 'the very seat of the Prince of darkness': Unsettling the Early American Frontier," in *Contact Points: American Frontiers from the Mohawk Valley to the Mississippi, 1750–1830* ed. Andrew R. L. Cayton and Fredrika J. Teute (Chapel Hill, N.C., 1998), 16–59; Jane T. Merritt, *At the Crossroads: Indians and Empires on a Mid-Atlantic Frontier* (Chapel Hill, N.C., 2003), 28–36; Laurence M. Hauptman, "Refugee Havens: The Iroquois Villages of the Eighteenth Century," in *American Indian Environments: Ecological Issues in Native American History,* ed. Christopher Vecsey and Robert W. Venables (Syracuse, N.Y., 1980), 128–39; Francis Jennings, "'Pennsylvania Indians' and the Iroquois," in *Beyond the Covenant Chain: The Iroquois and Their Neighbors in Indian North America, 1600–1800* ed. Daniel K. Richter and James H. Merrell (Syracuse, N.Y., 1987), 75–92.

30. David Brainerd, *Mirabilia Dei inter Indicos, or the Rise and Progress of a Remarkable Work of Grace Amongst a Number of Indians in the Provinces of New-Jersey and Pennsylvania* (Philadelphia, 1746), 231.

31. John Brainerd to Ebenezer Pemberton, Aug. 30, 1751, in Thomas Brainerd, *The Life of John Brainerd, the Brother of David Brainerd, and his Successor as Missionary to the Indians of New Jersey* (Philadelphia, 1865), 235.

32. Aaron S. Fogleman, "From Slaves, Convicts, and Servants to Free Passengers: The Transformation of Immigration in the Era of the American Revolution," *Journal of American History* 85, no. 1 (1998), 43–76; Michael Zuckerman, ed., *Friends and Neighbors: Group Life in America's First Plural Society* (Philadelphia, 1982); Sally Schwartz, *A Mixed Multitude: The Struggle for Toleration in Colonial Pennsylvania* (New York, 1989).

33. Schutt, *Peoples of the River Valleys,* 40–51, 63, 94; C. A. Weslager, *The Delaware Indians: A History* (New Brunswick, N.J., 1972), 261–62.

34. Grigg, "Lives of David Brainerd," 169.

35. Ibid., 163.

36. Brainerd, *Mirabilia Dei inter Indicos,* 68–69.

37. Brainerd, *The Life of John Brainerd; John Brainerd's Journal, 1761–1762,* reprint ed., Transcriptions of Early Church Records of New Jersey (Newark, N.J., 1941).

38. Occom, "Autobiographical Narrative, Second Draft [Sept. 17, 1768], *Occom Writings,* 53.

39. Kidd, *Great Awakening,* 111–16, 138–55; Harry S. Stout and Peter Onuf, "James Davenport and the Great Awakening in New London," *Journal of American History* 70, no. 3

(Dec. 1983), 556–78; Richard Warch, "The Shepherd's Tent: Education and Enthusiasm in the Great Awakening," *American Quarterly* 30 (1978), 177–98; Douglas Winiarski, "Pentecost and Protest," unpublished manuscript.

40. The Rev. Joseph Fish, quoted in William S. Simmons, "Red Yankees: Narragansett Conversion in the Great Awakening," *American Ethnologist* 10 (1983), 255.

41. The Rev. James Park, quoted in Simmons, "Red Yankees," 261.

42. Kidd, *Great Awakening*, 107–8.

43. Quoted in Trudy Lamb Richmond and Amy E. Den Ouden, "Recovering Gendered Political Histories: Local Struggles and Native Women's Resistance in Colonial Southern New England," in *Reinterpreting New England Indians and the Colonial Experience,* ed. Colin Calloway and Neal Salisbury (Charlottesville, Va., 2003), 203.

44. Conn. Indian Series, 1st ser., vol. 2, p. 252a.

45. For these sorts of problems among the Mashantucket Pequots, see ibid., 1st ser., vol. 1, pp. 139a, 139b, 147, 148, 227, 231; 1st ser., vol. 2, pp. 11, 13, 51–52, 53a, 54a–b, 55, 57a–b, 111–12, 114a–114, 116a–k, 118a–g, 119, 123, 246b, 247; *Connecticut Records*, 5:366–67, 398, 431, 7:325, 411–12, 8:397, 411, 9:306–7, 446, 494, 574, 523–24, 10:20–21, 137. Among the Stonington Pequots, see Conn. Indian Series, 1st ser., vol. 2, pp. 40, 41a–c, 44a–b, 45a, 46a–b, 48a–b, 250; *Connecticut Records,* 9:446, 494, 574. Among the Lyme Niantics, see Conn. Indian Series, 1st ser., vol. 2, p. 124a. Among the Farmington Tunxis, see Conn. Indian Series, 1st ser., vol. 2, pp. 173a, 174, 176, 178a–d, 180a, 182a, 183a, 184a, 185a, 186a, 187a, 188a, 189a, 190a, 190b; *Connecticut Records,* 7:176, 13:192–39. Among the Montauketts, see Stone, ed., *History and Archaeology of the Montauk,* 2d ed., vol. 3., pp. 133–34.

46. In 1725, Connecticut authorities counted 351 Mohegans, 321 Mashantucket Pequots, and 218 Pawcatuck Pequots. They did not give numbers for the Western Niantics and Tunxis. Though these figures are probably low given the numbers of Indians, especially men, who were away from the reservation at a given time, they are likely within range of the actual population. Talcott to Robert Ashurst, Sept. 1725, *The Talcott Papers, Correspondence and Documents (Chiefly Official) during Joseph Talcott's Governorship of the Colony of Connecticut, 1724–1741, Collections of the Connecticut Historical Society,* vol. 5 (Hartford, 1829), 400–402.

47. Conn. Indian Series, 1st ser., vol. 2, pp. 17–17b. On the origins of Indians claiming the status of royal subjects to use as leverage against colonists, see Jenny Hale Pulsipher, *Subjects unto the Same King: Indians, English, and the Contest for Authority in Colonial New England* (Philadelphia, 2005). On Indians reminding the English of their military service performed in the spirit of reciprocal friendship, see Lisa Brooks, *The Common Pot: The Recovery of Native Space in the Northeast* (Minneapolis, 2008), 51, 64, 70, 75, 86.

48. These themes are addressed at length in Amy E. Den Ouden, *Beyond Conquest: Native People and the Struggle for History in New England* (Norman, Okla., 2005). On Indian economic adjustments to land loss, see Kevin A. McBride, "'Ancient and Crazie': Pequot Lifeways during the Historic Period," in *Algonkians of New England,* ed. Peter Benes, Annual Proceedings of the Dublin Seminar for New England Folklife, 1991 (Boston, 1993), 63–75; McBride, "The Historical Archaeology of the Mashantucket Pequots, 1637–1900," in *The Pequots in Southern New England: The Fall and Rise of An American Indian Nation* Laurence E. Hauptman and James D. Wherry (Norman, Okla., 1990), 96–116, 239–41; Strong, *Algonquian Peoples of Long Island,* chs. 10–11; David J. Silverman, "'We chuse to be bounded': Native American

Animal Husbandry in Colonial New England," *WMQ*, vol. 60, no. 3 (Jul. 2003), 511–48. For examples of these petitions, see Conn. Indian Series, 1st ser., vol. 1, pp. 52, 73, 75, 95a, 132–33, 168, 171a, 225, 227, 254a–c, 255; vol. 2, pp. 11, 17–17b, 41a–c, 51–52, 57a–b, 99, 172a, 248–49; Stone, ed., *History and Archaeology of the Montauk*, 2d ed., vol. 3, pp. 133–34; Petition of the Pequot Indians, Sept. 22, 1735, Declaration of Nine of the Prime Mohegan Indians, Apr. 17, 1736, and Petition of Mahomet to the King, *Talcott Papers* vol. 4, 320–21, 365, 368–72; Petition from Sachems and councilors against the taking of Indians' lands, folder 3, and Petition of Sarah Ninigret vs. Indian Trustees, Jun. 1747, folder 6, Narragansett Indian Documents, 1731–1842, Rhode Island State Archives, Providence, R.I.

49. For the Mashantucket Pequots, see Conn. Indian Series, 1st ser., vol. 2, pp. 123, 243a–b, 246a–c, 247. For the Pawcatuck Pequots, see Conn. Indian Series, 1st ser., vol. 2, pp. 46a–b; 48a–b, 49, 50; *Connecticut Records*, 10:18–19. For the Lyme Niantics, see Conn. Indian Series, 1st ser., vol. 2, pp. 124a; *Connecticut Records*, 12:115–16. For the Farmington Tunxis, see Conn. Indian Series, 1st ser., vol. 2, pp. 190a, 190b, 192a.

50. Ouden, *Beyond Conquest*, 7.

51. Ibid., 91–141; Brooks, *Common Pot*, 51–105; Wendy B. St. Jean, "Inventing Guardianship: The Mohegan Indians and their 'Protectors,'" *New England Quarterly* 72, no. 3 (Sept. 1999), 362–87; David W. Conroy, "The Defense of Indian Land Rights: William Bolan and the Mohegan Case in 1743," *Proceedings of the American Antiquarian Society* 103 (1993), 395–424; John W. DeForest, *History of the Indians of Connecticut* (Hartford, 1852), 290–97, 303–15, 320–42; Laura J. Murray's introductory comments to *Writings of Joseph Johnson*, 33–36; Michael Leroy Oberg, *Uncas: First of the Mohegans* (Ithaca, N.Y., 2003), 154–56, 166; Love, *Samson Occom*, 119–23; Fisher, "'Traditionary Religion,'" 81–132.

52. See, for instance, the account of the Narragansett preacher, Samuel Niles, in William S. Simmons and Cheryl L. Simmons, eds., *Old Light on Separate Ways: The Narragansett Diary of Joseph Fish, 1765–1772* (Hanover, N.H., 1982), 5.

53. Joseph Park, "An Account of the late Propagation of Religion at Westerly and Charlestown in Rhode-Island Colony," in *The Christian History: Containing Accounts of the Propagation and Revival of Religion in England, Scotland, and America*, no. 26, Aug. 27, 1743, p. 208; Simmons and Simmons, eds., *Old Light on Separate Ways*, 68, 87; Love, *Samson Occom*, 32–33; Brad Devin Edward Jarvis, "Preserving the Brothertown Nation of Indians: Exploring Relationships amongst Land, Sovereignty, and Identity, 1740–1840" (Ph.D. diss., University of Minnesota, 2006), 98.

54. Benjamin Colman quoted in Jarvis, "Preserving the Brothertown Nation of Indians," 78–79.

55. Joseph Park, "Westerly and Charlestown in Rhode Island Colony, &c., February the 6th, 1743/44," *The Christian History*, no. 55 (Mar. 17, 1744), 22.

56. Conn. Indian Series, 1st ser., vol. 1, pp. 251a–b. See also the petition of Cuish from Farmington in ibid., 2d ser., vol. 1, p.14.

57. "The Rev. Mr. Park's Account of the Progress of Religion at Westerly," *The Christian History*, no. 56 (Mar. 24, 1744), 26. For a similar assessment of the Narragansetts some twenty years later, see Simmons and Simmons, eds., *Old Light on Separate Ways*, 3.

58. Kevin A. McBride, "Transformation by Degree: Eighteenth Century Native American Land Use," in *Eighteenth Century Native Communities of New England in Colonial Context*,

ed. Jack Campisi (Mashantucket, Conn., 2005), 51–56; McBride, "Ancient and Crazie'"; McBride, "Historical Archaeology of the Mashantucket Pequots."

59. Conn. Indian Series, 1st ser., vol. 2, pp. 54b, 118ff., 326b; *Diary of David McClure,* 137, 191.

60. Silverman, "'We chuse to be bounded'"; Daniel R. Mandell, *Tribe, Race, History: Native Americans in Southern New England, 1780-1880* (Baltimore, 2008), 10–15.

61. Fisher, "'Traditionary Religion,'" 81.

62. Correspondence with Douglas Winiarski, Jul. 3, 2008. See also Fisher, "'Traditionary Religion,'" 159–60, 194; John W. DeForest, *History of the Indians of Connecticut* (Hartford, 1852), 384; Kidd, *Great Awakening,* 107–8.

63. George Griswold, "Account of the Revival of Religion at Lyme, East Parish, in Connecticut, *The Christian History,* no. 67, Jun. 9, 1744, 113.

64. "The Remainder of Mr. Park's Account," *The Christian History,* no. 27, Sept. 3, 1743, 209.

65. Simmons and Simmons, eds., *Old Light on Separate Ways,* xxxii–xxxiii.

66. Simmons, "Red Yankees," 262.

67. Franklin Bowditch Dexter, ed. *The Literary Diary of Ezra Stiles, D.D., LL.D.,* 3 vols. (New York, 1901), 1:232–33. See also Simmons, "Red Yankees"; Jarvis, "Preserving the Brothertown Nation of Indians," 98.

68. Franklin B. Dexter, ed., *Diary of David McClure...1740-1820* (New York, 1899), 190. For descriptions of the Narragansett congregation, see Joseph Fish to Eleazar Wheelock, Jul. 30, 1766, *Wheelock Papers,* 766430; Edward Deake to Wheelock, Apr. 25, 1767, *Wheelock Papers,* 767275.1.

69. Fisher, "'Traditionary Religion,'" 146–48.

70. Conn. Indian Series, vol. 1, pp. 251a–b.

71. Fisher, "'Traditionary Religion,'" 257.

72. Love, *Samson Occom,* 22. See also Brooks, *Common Pot,* 78–83.

73. Ouden, *Beyond Conquest,* 1–2, 7–8, 126–41.

74. Love, *Samson Occom,* 75–76; Fisher, "'Traditionary Religion,'" 236–37.

75. James Dow McCallum, *The Letters of Eleazar Wheelock's Indians* (Hanover, N.H., 1932), 142–43.

76. Occom, "Autobiographical Narrative, Second Draft," *Occom Writings,* 54.

77. Axtell, *Invasion Within,* 211.

78. Eleazar Wheelock, *A plan and faithful Narrative of the Original Design, Rise, Progress and the present State of the Indian Charity-School at Lebanon, in Connecticut* (Boston, 1763), 25. See also Wheelock, *A Continuation of the Narrative of the Indian Charity-School, in Lebanon, in Connecticut; from the Year 1768, to the Incorporation of it with Dartmouth-College, And Removal and Settlement of it in Hanover, in the Province of New-Hampshire, 1771* (Boston, 1771), 21.

79. Tammy Schneider, "'This Once Savage Heart of Mine': Joseph Johnson, Wheelock's Indians, the Construction of a Christian Indian Identity, 1774–1776," in *Reinterpreting New England Indians,* ed. Calloway and Salisbury, 236–39.

80. *Occom Writings,* 68, 69, 70, 73.

81. Joseph Johnson to Eleazar Wheelock, Apr. 20, 1768, *Writings of Joseph Johnson,* 69. On hierarchical wordplay in Wheelock's correspondence with Indians, see Laura J. Murray, "'Pray Sir, Consider a Little': Rituals of Subordination and Strategies of Resistance in the

Letters of Hezekiah Calvin and David Fowler to Eleazar Wheelock," and Dana D. Nelson, "'(I Speak Like a Fool but I am Constrained)': Samson Occom's Short Narrative and Economies of the Racial Self," in *Early Native American Writing: New Critical Essays,* ed. Helen Jaskoski (New York, 1996), 15–41, 42–65; Murray, "What did Christianity do for Joseph Johnson? A Mohegan Preacher and his Community," in *Possible Pasts: Becoming Colonial in Early America* ed. Robert Blair St. George (Ithaca, 2000), 160–80.

82. James Axtell, *The School upon a Hill: Education and Society in Colonial New England* (New Haven, Conn., 1974); E. Jennifer Monaghan, *Learning to Read and Write in Colonial America* (Amherst, Mass., 2005); Bernd C. Peyer, *The Tutor'd Mind: Indian Missionary-Writers in Antebellum America* (Amherst, Mass., 1997), 66.

83. For a parallel example, see Michael D. McNally, *Ojibwe Singers: Hymns, Grief, and a Native Culture in Motion* (New York, 2000).

84. Solomon Williams to?, May 4, 1752, *Wheelock Papers,* 752304. See also Andrew Oliver to Eleazar Wheelock, Apr. 26, 1750, *Wheelock Papers,* 750266; Benjamin Pomeroy to Solomon Williams, Jul. 24, 1751, *Wheelock Papers,* 751424. On Occom's methods, see his "Autobiographical Narrative, Second Draft, Sept. 17, 1768," in *Occom Writings,* 56; and Peyer, *Tutor'd Mind,* 66.

85. Andrew Oliver to Eleazar Wheelock, Apr. 26, 1750, Wheelock Papers, 750266. See also Samuel Buell and James Brown to Eleazar Wheelock, Mar. 21, 1758, *Wheelock Papers,* 758221.

86. On Horton, see Kidd, *Great Awakening,* 190–92; the Rev. Earnest Edward Eells, "Indian Missions on Long Island: Part IV: Azariah Horton," and John Strong, "Azariah Horton's Mission to the Montauk, 1741–44," in *History and Archaeology of the Montauk,* ed. Stone, 2d ed., vol. 2, pp. 170–76, 191–94.

87. Occom, "Autobiographical Narrative, Second Draft," *Occom Writings,* 58.

88. See, for instance, *Occom Writings,* 251–52.

89. On Hannah Garret, see Love, *Samson Occom,* 26, 72, 113. On the Poquiantups, see Kevin McBride, "'Desirous to Improve after the European Manner': The Mashantucket Pequots in the Brotherton Indian Movement," 16, ms. in the author's possession.

90. Samuel Buell, *A Sermon Preached at East-Hampton, August 29, 1759, at the Ordination of Mr. Samson Occum, A Missionary among the Indians* (New York, 1761), ix.

91. William B. Sprague, *Annals of the American Pulpit, or, Commemorative Notices of Distinguished American Clergymen of Various Denominations,* 4 vols. (New York, 1857–59), 3:195.

92. On this organization, see Kellaway, *New England Company.*

93. Occom, "Autobiographical Narrative, Second Draft," *Occom Writings,* 55.

94. Wheelock? to Col. Henchmen and the Commissioners in Boston, *Wheelock Papers,* 756190; Wheelock to Dennis DeBerdt, Jul. 22, 1758, *Wheelock Papers,* 758422; Wheelock to Moses Peck, Mar. 25, 1761, *Wheelock Papers,* 761225.

95. Occom, "Autobiographical Narrative, Second Draft," *Occom Writings,* 55.

96. Ibid., 57.

97. Ibid., 58.

98. Quoted in Love, *Samson Occom*, 53. On discussions about sending Occom to Cherokee country, see Samuel Buell to Eleazar Wheelock, Oct. 17, 1758, *Wheelock Papers*, 758567.1; Buell to Wheelock, May 7, 1759, *Wheelock Papers*, 759307; Wheelock to George Whitefield, Nov. 3, 1759, *Wheelock Papers*, 759603. On talk of sending him to the Forks and the Susquehanna, see Solomon Williams to Andrew Oliver, Oct. 7, 1751, *Wheelock Papers*, 751557; Minutes of the Correspondent Commissioners of the Scottish Society meeting at Nassau Hall, Sept. 27, 1758, *Wheelock Papers*, 758554.

99. Wheelock, *Plain and Faithful Narrative*, 16.

100. Wheelock, *Plain and Faithful Narrative*, 26.

101. Wheelock to William Hyslop, Dec. 1, 1760, *Wheelock Papers*, 760651.2; Margaret Connell Szasz, "'Poor Richard' Meets the Native American: Schooling for Young Indian Women in Eighteenth-Century Connecticut," *Pacific Historical Review* 49 (1990), 215–35.

102. Love, *Samson Occom*, 68–70; Brainerd, *Life of John Brainerd*, 331–32. The figures come from Axtell, *Invasion Within*, 207.

103. David McClure to Eleazar Wheelock, Sept. 25, 1765, *Wheelock Papers*, 765525.2.

104. On British missions of the early to mid-eighteenth century, see Axtell, *Invasion Within*, 191–93, 247–63.

105. Wheelock to DeBerndt, Jul. 5, 1763, *Wheelock Papers*, 763407.1. See also Wheelock to George Whitefield, Sept. 18, 1758, *Wheelock Papers*, 758518; Hopkins, *Historical Memoirs*, 165–66.

106. Solomon Williams to Andrew Oliver, Oct. 7, 1751, *Wheelock Papers*, 751557; Minutes of the Correspondent Commissioners of the Scottish Society meeting at Nassau Hall, Sept. 27, 1758, *Wheelock Papers*, 758554; Corporation for the Propagation of the Gospel in New England, Commissioners Meeting Minutes, entry for Nov. 14, 1758, NEHGS; Love, *Samson Occom*, 48; Kidd, *Great Awakening*, 203–4.

107. Peyer, *Tutor'd Mind*, 69.

108. Samuel Buell to Eleazar Wheelock, Oct. 17, 1758, and May 7, 1759, *Wheelock Papers*, 758567.1 and 759307; Tom Hatley, *The Dividing Paths: Cherokees and South Carolinians through the Revolutionary Era* (New York, 1995), 105–60.

109. William Tryon, "Report ... on the State of the Province of New York, 1774," *DHSNY*, 1:766.

110. Karim Tiro, "The People of the Standing Stone: The Oneida Indian Nation from Revolution through Removal" (Ph.D. diss., University of Pennsylvania, 1999), 50.

111. Colin G. Calloway, *The American Revolution in Indian Country: Crisis and Diversity in Native American Communities* (New York, 1995), 110–11; Tiro, "People of the Standing Stone," 41.

112. Calloway, *American Revolution in Indian Country*, 110–11; and Kidd, *Great Awakening*, 205–6.

113. Marjory B. Hinman, *Onaquaga: Early Missionary Outpost, 1748-1777* (Old Onaquaga, N.Y., 1968), 1.

114. Ibid., 1–2.

115. Calloway, *American Revolution in Indian Country*, 113–14.

116. Hinman, *Onaquaga*, 3–4.

117. Eleazar Wheelock to Gideon Hawley, Jun. 10, 1761, *Wheelock Papers*, 761360.2; William M. Beauchamp, ed., *Moravian Journals Relating to Central New York, 1745–1766* (Syracuse, N.Y., 1916), 226; Love, *Samson Occom*, 75–76.

118. Hawley to Eleazar Wheelock, Nov. 26, 1761, *Wheelock Papers*, 767626. (The *Wheelock Papers* editors mistakenly date this letter as 1767.) See Jean Fitz Hankins, "Bringing the Good News: Protestant Missions to the Indians of New England and New York" (Ph.D. diss., University of Connecticut, 1993), 315n39.

119. Calloway, *American Revolution in Indian Country*, 115.

120. Eleazar Wheelock to George Whitefield, Nov. 25, 1761, *Wheelock Papers*, 761625.1.

121. Bishop A. G. Spangenberg's Journal of a Journey to Onondaga in 1745, Beauchamp, ed., *Moravian Journals*, 7.

122. Samuel Kirkland, *The Journals of Samuel Kirkland: 18th Century Missionary to the Iroquois, Government Agent, Father of Hamilton College*, ed. Walter Pilkington (Clinton, N.Y., 1980), 23–24.

123. Gregory Evans Dowd, *A Spirited Resistance: The North American Indian Struggle for Unity, 1745–1815* (Baltimore, 1992), 27–33; Alfred A. Cave, *Prophets of the Great Spirit: Native American Revitalization Movements in Eastern North America* (Lincoln, Neb., 2006), 11–22.

124. Nancy Shoemaker, "How Indians Got to Be Red," *American Historical Review* 102 (1997), 625–44.

125. *Johnson Papers*, 2:702.

126. Book of a Journal after my mission in the Country of the Six Nations, January 27 to May 31, 1754, vol. 1, Gideon Hawley Journal and Letters, 4 vols., Congregational Library, Boston, Mass. See also Diary of Brother Zeisberger's and Henry Freey's Journey and Stay in Onondaga from April 23d to November 12th, 1753, in Beauchamp, ed., *Moravian Journals*, 179.

127. Wheelock to?, Feb. 3, 1761, *Wheelock Papers*, 761153.

128. Hezekiah Calvin to Eleazar Wheelock, Aug. 14, 1767, *Wheelock Papers*, 767464.

129. Quoted in Jarvis, "Preserving the Brothertown Nation of Indians," 92–93.

130. David Fowler to Eleazar Wheelock, Jun. 24, 1765, *Wheelock Papers*, 765374.2; Fowler to Wheelock, Nov. 28, 1766, *Wheelock Papers*, 766628.1.

131. David Fowler to Eleazar Wheelock, May 28, 1767, *Wheelock Papers*, 767328.1.

132. David Fowler to Eleazar Wheelock, Jun. 15, 1765, *Wheelock Papers*, 765360.3.

133. Axtell, *School upon a Hill*, 96; Hart, "For the Good of our Souls," 275–85.

134. Eleazar Wheelock to B. Forsett, Sept. 8, 1763, *Wheelock Papers*, 763508.1.

135. On Kirkland's early missionary work, see Christine Sternberg Patrick, "The Life and Times of Samuel Kirkland, 1741–1808: Missionary to the Oneida Indians, American Patriot, and Founder of Hamilton College" (Ph.D. diss., State University of New York at Buffalo, 1993), 43–149.

136. Eleazar Wheelock to H. Sherburne, Dec. 31, 1765, *Wheelock Papers*, 765681; Eleazar Wheelock to Nathaniel Whitaker, Dec. 8, 1766, *Wheelock Papers*, 766658; Jarvis, "Preserving the Brothertown Nation of Indians," 89.

137. Hawley to Wheelock, Nov. 26, 1767, *Wheelock Papers*, 767626.

138. Occom to Samuel Buel, Feb. 1786?, *Occom Writings*, 127.

Chapter 3. Betrayals

1. The letter appears in *Occom Writings*, 98–100.

2. Joanna Brooks, "Working Definitions: Race, Ethnic Studies, and Early American Literature," *Early American Literature* 41, no. 2 (2006), 315; Brooks, *American Lazarus Religion and the Rise of African-American and Native American Literatures* (New York, 2003).

3. On the Moravians, see Aaron Spencer Fogelman, *Jesus Is Female: Moravians and Radical Religion in Early America* (Philadelphia, 2007). On this meeting, see Rachel Wheeler, *To Live upon Hope: Mohicans and Missionaries in the Eighteenth-Century Northeast* (Ithaca, N.Y., 2008), 67–72.

4. Jane T. Merritt, *At the Crossroads: Indians and Empires on a mid-Atlantic Frontier, 1700–1763* (Chapel Hill, N.C., 2003).

5. This discussion draws on Wheeler, *To Live upon Hope*; Corinna Dally-Starna and William A. Starna, "American Indians and Moravians in Southern New England," in *Germans and Indians: Fantasies, Encounters, Projections*, ed. Colon G. Calloway, Gerd Gemünden, and Susanne Zantop (Lincoln, Neb., 2002), 83–96; and Merritt, "Dreaming of the Savior's Blood: Moravians and the Indian Great Awakening in Pennsylvania," *WMQ* 54 (1997), 723–46.

6. Quoted in Wheeler, *To Live upon Hope*, 91.

7. Ibid., 67–134, 145–74.

8. Lion G. Miles, "The Red Man Dispossessed: The Williams Family and the Alienation of Indian Land in Stockbridge, Massachusetts, 1736–1818," *New England Quarterly* 67, no. 1 (Mar. 1994), 46–76.

9. This paragraph draws on James Axtell, "The Scholastic Frontier in Western Massachusetts," in his *After Columbus: Essays in the Ethnohistory of Colonial North America* (New York, 1988), 47–57; Wheeler, *To Live upon Hope*, esp. 180–86, 206–12; Patrick Frazier, *The Mohicans of Stockbridge* (Lincoln, Neb., 1992), 82–104. On the falling out of Edwards and his Northampton parish, see Patricia J. Tracy, *Jonathan Edwards, Pastor: Religion and Society in Eighteenth-Century Northampton* (New York, 1979); Christopher Grasso, *A Speaking Aristocracy: Transforming Public Discourse in Eighteenth-Century Connecticut* (Chapel Hill, N.C., 1999), 86–143.

10. Review of the Trade and Affairs of the Indians in the Northern District of America, *NYCD*, 7:960.

11. *Early American Indian Documents: Treaties and Laws, 1607–1789*, gen. ed. Alden T. Vaughan, vol. 20, *New England Treaties, North and West, 1650–1676*, vol. ed. Daniel R. Mandell (Bethesda, Md., 2003), 544–45, 546, 588, 591, 596.

12. *Early American Indian Documents, North and West*, 588, 591, 596; Frazier, *Mohicans of Stockbridge*, 105–23.

13. Earl of Shelburne to William Johnson, Oct. 11, 1766, *Johnson Papers*, 5:394; Report of the Lords of Trade on the Petition of the Wappinger Indians, Aug. 30, 1766, *NYCD*, 7:869–70; Alden T. Vaughan, *Transatlantic Encounters: American Indians in Britain, 1500–1776* (New York, 2006), 177–79; Frazier, *Mohicans of Stockbridge*, 160–64; Thomas J. Humphrey, *Land and Liberty: Hudson Valley Riots in the Age of Revolution* (DeKalb, Ill., 2004), 55–56, 64–68, 78–81. Figure calculated from data in Miles, "Red Man Dispossessed," 68.

14. Frazier, *Mohicans of Stockbridge*, 176–77.

15. "A Letter from Gideon Hawley," *MHSC*, 1st ser., 4 (1795), 55.

16. Thomas Brainerd, *The Life of John Brainerd, the Brother of David Brainerd, and his Successor as Missionary to the Indians of New Jersey* (Philadelphia, 1865), 118–20.

17. Ibid., 246.

18. Ibid., 154–56; and George D. Flemming, *Brotherton: New Jersey's First and Only Indian Reservation and the Communities of Shamong and Tabernacle that Followed* (Medford, N.J., 2005), 37.

19. *Life of John Brainerd*, 268–69.

20. Ibid., 273.

21. Fleming, *Brotherton*, 38.

22. *Life of John Brainerd*, 302.

23. *New Jersey Archives*, 1st ser., 42 vols. (Newark, N.J., 1880–1949), 16:565.

24. *Early American Indian Documents: Treaties and Laws, 1607–1789*, gen. ed. Alden T. Vaughan, vol. 10: *New York and New Jersey Treaties, 1754–1775*, vol. ed. Barbara Graymont (Bethesda, Md., 2001), 283–84.

25. *Early American Indian Documents, New York and New Jersey Treaties*, 285–86.

26. Testimony of Samuel Davis, Constable of Montaugue, and his assistants, *Johnson Papers*, 5:171. For more on this incident, see ibid., 5:169–70, 171, 172, 180, 182, 201; Sir William Johnson to the Lords of Trade, Jun. 28, 1766, in *NYCD*, 7:837; Governor Franklin to the Early of Sherlburne, Dec. 16, 1766, *New Jersey Archives*, 9:575–76.

27. George Croghan to Sir William Johnson, Apr. 18, 1766, *Johnson Papers*, 5:181–82.

28. *New Jersey Archives*, vol. 16, *Journal of the Governor and Council, 1748–1755*, 16:568, 571–73.

29. Gov. Francis Bernard to the Lords of Trade, Oct. 13, 1758, *New Jersey Archives*, 9:140–41; *An Act to impower certain Persons to purchase the Claims of the Indians to Land in this Colony* (Woodbridge, N.J., 1758); C. A. Weslager, *The Delaware Indians: A History* (New Brunswick, N.J., 1972), 264–71; Fleming, *Brotherton*, 43.

30. Francis Bernard to the Lords of Trade, Jun. 15, 1759, *New Jersey Archives*, 9:174–75.

31. John Brainerd, Brotherton, to Elizabeth Smith, Aug. 24, 1761, in Graymont, ed., *New York and New Jersey Treaties*, 360.

32. Heads of Enquiry relative to the present State & Condition of His Majesty's Province of New Jersey in America and the Governor's Answers thereto, *New Jersey Archives*, 10:447; *Early American Indian Documents, New York and New Jersey Treaties*, 360; Fleming, *Brotherton*, 43.

33. Samson Occom to Eleazar Wheelock, May 7, 1764, *Occom Writings*, 71.

34. Robert Clelland to Eleazar Wheelock, Mar. 12, 1762, *Wheelock Papers*, 762212; Robert Clelland to Eleazar Wheelock, Aug. 31, 1762, *Wheelock Papers*, 762481; Eleazar Wheelock to Henry Whitefield, Oct. 10, 1764, *Wheelock Papers*, 764560.2; David Jewett to Eleazar Wheelock, Jun. 26, 1765, *Wheelock Papers*, 765376.2; William DeLoss Love, *Samson Occom and the Christian Indians of New England* (1899; Syracuse, N.Y., 2000), 119–29; Bernd C. Peyer, *The Tutor'd Mind: Indian Missionary-Writers in Antebellum America* (Amherst, Mass., 1997), 72–74.

35. Samson Occom to Robert Clelland, 1768, *Occom Writings*, 85.

36. David Jewett to Eleazar Wheelock, Jun. 26, 1765, *Wheelock Papers*, 765376.2.

37. Samson Occom to Robert Clelland, 1768, *Occom Writings*, 85.

38. Racially charged violence committed by colonists against the Iroquois, and the Oneidas in particular, is detailed in *Johnson Papers*, 5:169–70, 171, 172, 180, 182, 201; Sir William Johnson to the Lords of Trade, Jun. 28, 1766, in *NYCD*, 7:837; Governor Franklin to the Early of Sherlburne, Dec. 16, 1766, *New Jersey Archives*, 9:575–76; Andrew Burnaby, *Travels through the Middle Settlements in North-America, in the Years 1759 and 1760* (London, 1775), 18. Generally, see Alden T. Vaughan, "Frontier Banditti and the Indians: The Paxton Boys' Legacy, 1763–1775," *Pennsylvania History* 51 (1984), 1–29; Krista Camenzind, "Violence, Race, and the Paxton Boys," in *Friends and Enemies in Penn's Woods: Indians, Colonists, and the Racial Construction of Pennsylvania*, ed. William A. Pencak and Daniel K. Richter (University Park, Pa., 2004), 201–20; Richard White, *The Middle Ground: Indians, Empires, and Republics in the Great Lakes Region* (Cambridge, Mass., 1991), 366–412; Peter Silver, *Our Savage Neighbors: How Indian War Transformed Early America* (New York, 2008).

39. Address of Capt. Cordon at Ft. St. George, *Boston News-Letter*, no. 2947, Dec. 25, 1760. See also the letter of Virginia Lt. Gov. Robert Dinwiddie in *Boston News-Letter*, no. 2699, Mar. 28, 1754; reprinted article from the *New York Mercury* in *Boston News-Letter*, no. 2773, Aug. 29, 1755.

40. Eleazar Wheelock to Rev. Dr. Gifford, Oct. 31, 1763, *Wheelock Papers*, 763581.

41. David Crosby to Eleazar Wheelock, Nov. 4, 1767, *Wheelock Papers*, 767604.1.

42. Occom to Wheelock, Feb. 12, 1767, *Occom Writings*, 79.

43. Solomon Williams to Eleazar Wheelock, Jan. 9, 1765, Eleazar Wheelock to John Brainerd, Jan. 14, 1765, and Eleazar Wheelock to Samson Occom, in Leon Burr Richardson, ed., *An Indian Preacher in England* (Hanover, N.H., 1933), 24, 26, 119.

44. Samson Occom to Eleazar Wheelock, Dec. 16, 1765, *Occom Writings*, 265.

45. "They don't want the Indians to go to Heaven with them" (1768), *Occom Writings*, 86.

46. Saying What Think Ye of Christ," Matthew 22:42, *Occom Writings*, 174.

47. Journal of Nov. 21, 1765–Jul. 22, 1766, *Occom Writings*, 266.

48. Dr. Wood to Nathaniel Whitaker, Sept. 28, 1767, in Richardson, ed., *Indian Preacher in England*, 303–4.

49. T. Ponty to Samson Occom, Occom Papers, folder 3. See also Joseph Green to Occom, Apr. 15, 1767, Occom Papers, folder 4.

50. "Saying What Think Ye of Christ."

51. Occom Journal of Nov. 21, 1765–Jul. 22, 1766, *Occom Writings*, 269.

52. Ibid.

53. Ibid., 267.

54. Occom to Mary Fowler Occom, 1767, *Occom Writings*, 80–81.

55. Ibid.

56. Nathaniel Whitaker to Eleazar Wheelock, undated; Whitaker to Wheelock, Mar. 19, 1766; and Whitaker to Wheelock, Jun. 27, 1766, in Richardson, ed., *An Indian Preacher in England*, 94, 114, 134.

57. Timothy Woodbridge to Wheelock, Dec. 30, 1768, *Wheelock Papers*, 768676.

58. Wheelock, *A Continuation of the Narrative of the Indian Charity-School in Lebanon in Connecticut; from the Year 1768, to the Incorporation of it with Dartmouth-College, and Removal*

and Settlement of it in Hanover, in the Province of New-Hampshire, 1771 (Hartford, Conn., 1771), 19.

59. Samuel Kirkland to Eleazar Wheelock, Dec. 29, 1768, *Wheelock Papers,* 768679.

60. Hezekiah Calvin to Eleazar Wheelock, Dec. 26, 1767, *Wheelock Papers,* 767676.2: Calvin to Wheelock, Jan. 29, 1768, *Wheelock Papers,* 768129; Edward Deake, Charlestown, Jun. 21, 1768, *Wheelock Papers,* 768371.2; Wheelock to Occom, Mar. 9, 1769, *Wheelock Papers,* 769209.2.

61. Wheelock, *A Continuation of the Narrative of the Indian Charity-School,* 18–22.

62. James Axtell, *The School upon a Hill: Education and Society in Colonial New England* (New Haven, Conn., 1974), 104.

63. Edward Deake to Wheelock, Jun. 21, 1768, *Wheelock Papers,* 768371.2.

64. John Daniel to Wheelock, Nov. 30, 1767, *Wheelock Papers,* 767630.3.

65. Fowler to Wheelock, Feb. 17, 1766, *Wheelock Papers,* 766167.1.

66. Board of Correspondents, Connecticut, Records, 1764–1769, entry for Jan. 4, 1769, Papers of the Society for Propagating Christian Knowledge, 1764–1893, box 1, folder 1, Rauner Library. See also Love, *Samson Occom,* 162–66.

67. *Occom Writings,* 21. See also Sir William Johnson to Daniel Burton, Apr. 26, 1770, *Johnson Papers,* 7:589.

68. Franklin Bowditch Dexter, ed., *The Literary Diary of Ezra Stiles,* 3 vols. (New York, 1901), 2:338.

69. On the Narragansetts, see James N. Arnold, comp., *A Statement of the Case of the Narragansett Tribe of Indians, As Shown in the Manuscript Collection of Sir William Johnson* (Newport, R.I., 1896), 34, 41, 43, 50–52; John R. Bartlet, ed., *Records of the Colony of Rhode Island and Providence Plantations in New England,* 10 vols. (Providence, R.I., 1856–1865), 6:357, 8:173–74; *Johnson Papers,* 5:92–95; Tobias Shattock to Sir William Johnson, 1767, *Johnson Papers,* 6:59; Matthew Graves to Sir William Johnson, Feb. 1, 1768, *Johnson Papers,* 6:88; Eleazar Wheelock to Sir William Johnson, *Johnson Papers,* 12:349. On the Niantics, see Arnold, ed., *Statement of the Case of the Narragansett Tribe,* 51; Matt Graves to Sir William Johnson, Feb. 23, 1767, *Johnson Papers,* 5:502. On the Pequots, see *Early American Indian Documents: Treaties and Laws, 1607–1789,* gen. ed. Alden T. Vaughan, vol. 17, *New England and Middle Atlantic Laws,* vol. eds. Alden T. Vaughan and Deborah Rosen (Bethesda, Md., 2004), 177–78. On the Montauketts, see Gaynell Stone, ed., *The History and Archaeology of the Montauk,* Readings in Long Island Archaeology and Ethnohistory, 2d ed., vol. 3 (Mattituck, N.Y., 1993), 133–34. On the Mohegans, see Meetings of Mohegan Indians, Mar. 24, 1764, *Johnson Papers,* 4:375–76; Mohegan Tribe to Sir William Johnson, 1765, *Johnson Papers,* 4:727–28; Mohegan Tribe to Sir William Johnson, 1764, *Occom Writings,* 144–45.

70. William S. Simmons and Cheryl L. Simmons, eds., *Old Light on Separate Ways: The Narragansett Diary of Joseph Fish, 1765–1772* (Hanover, N.H., 1982), xxxv; John Wood Sweet, *Bodies Politic: Negotiating Race in the American North, 1730–1830* (Baltimore, 2003), 51.

71. These petitions can be found in the *Johnson Papers* as follows: Stockbridge (4:25, 4:654), Narragansetts (4:152–54, 589–91, 659–60, 691–92, 693, 756–58; 5:92–95, 491, 588; 6:58–61; 11:408, 413, 476, 483, 639; 12:299–300), Pequots (4:679–80); Mohegans (4:727–28); Niantics (5:425). See also Eleazar Wheelock to Sir William Johnson, *Wheelock Papers,* 763571.1; Wheelock to Johnson, Apr. 23, 1767, *Wheelock Papers,* 767723.

72. Tobias Shattock to Col. Joseph Hazzard, Dec. 8, 1767, in Gertrude Selwyn Kimball, ed., *The Correspondence of the Colonial Governors of Rhode Island, 1723–1775*, 2 vols. (Boston, 1902), 398–99.

73. Tobias Shattock to Eleazar Wheelock, Nov. 30, 1767, *Wheelock Papers*, 767630.2; Vaughan, *Transatlantic Encounters*, 179–81; Love, *Samson Occom*, 70–72.

74. Occom to Buell, 1773, *Occom Writings*, 103.

75. *DHSNY*, 3:236–37.

76. "A Sermon, Preached at the Execution of Moses Paul, an Indian" [1772], *Occom Writings*, 188.

77. Ibid., 192.

78. Ibid., 194.

Chapter 4. Out from Under the Burdens

1. Michael D. McNally, *Ojibwe Singers: Hymns, Grief, and a Native Culture in Motion* (New York, 2000).

2. Joanna Brooks, *American Lazarus Religion and the Rise of African-American and Native American Literatures* (New York, 2003), 66–83; Brooks, "Six Hymns by Samson Occom," *Early American Literature* 38, no. 1 (2003), 66–87.

3. William S. Simmons and Cheryl L. Simmons, eds., *Old Light on Separate Ways: The Narragansett Diary of Joseph Fish, 1765–1772* (Hanover, N.H., 1982), 8n3, 31; Joseph Johnson Diary, entries for Nov. 14, 15, 16, 20, Dec. 8, 1771; Feb. 2, Nov. 18, 27, 29, Dec. 1, 3, 4, 6, 10, 12, 15, 18, 1772; Jan. 24, 30, 1773, *Writings of Joseph Johnson*, 105–6, 107, 117, 133, 151, 153, 154, 155, 156, 157, 158, 159, 161, 164.

4. Brooks, *American Lazarus*, 66.

5. Johnson, Journal entry of Dec. 17, 1772, *Writings of Joseph Johnson*, 160.

6. Robert A. Williams Jr., *Linking Arms Together: American Indian Treaty Visions of Law and Peace, 1600–1800* (New York, 1999), 85–87; Joshua A. Piker, "'White and Clean' and Contested: Creek Towns and Trading Paths in the Aftermath of the Seven Years' War," *Ethnohistory* 50, no. 2 (Spring 2003), 315–47.

7. Thomas Commuck, "Sketch of the Brothertown Indians," *WHC* 4 (1859), 292.

8. Tobias Shattock to Wheelock, Oct. 16, 1765, *Wheelock Papers*, 765566.1.

9. Shattock to Wheelock, Oct. 16, 1765, *Wheelock Papers*, 765566.1; *Johnson Papers*, 4:25, 152–54, 589–91, 654, 659–60, 679–80, 691–92, 693, 727–28, 756–58; 5:92–95, 425, 491, 588; 6:58–61; 11:408, 413, 476, 483, 639; 12:299–300.

10. Tobias Shattock to Eleazar Wheelock, Nov. 30, 1767, *Wheelock Papers*, 767630.2.

11. *Johnson Papers*, 12:645.

12. See the overview of this literature in Franz Laurens Wojciechowski, "Actors and Actions of the Brothertown Indian Genesis: A Tale of Contradictory Accounts, and a Proposed Solution," *Yumtzilob* 10, no. 4 (1998), 391–412.

13. On this point too, see ibid.

14. William DeLoss Love, *Samson Occom and the Christian Indians of New England* (1899; Syracuse, N.Y., 2000), 157; Christine Sternberg Patrick, "The Life and Times of Samuel Kirkland, 1741–1808: Missionary to the Oneida Indians, American Patriot, and

Founder of Hamilton College" (Ph.D. diss., State University of New York at Buffalo, 1993), 159–65.

15. Shattock to Wheelock, Oct. 2, 1767, *Wheelock Papers*, 767552.

16. Wheelock to Robert Keen, Nov. 2, 1767, *Wheelock Papers*, 767602.1.

17. Timothy Woodbridge, Stockbridge, to Wheelock, Dec. 30, 1768, *Wheelock Papers*, 768676.

18. *Connecticut Gazette*, no. 310, Oct. 20, 1769.

19. Eleazar Wheelock to Sir William Johnson, Aug. 14, 1769, *Wheelock Papers*, 769464; John C. Guzzardo, "The Superintendent and the Ministers: The Battle for Oneida Allegiances, 1761–75," *New York History* 57 (1976), 267–68; David J. Norton, "Rebellious Younger Brother: Oneida Leadership and Diplomacy, 1750–1800" (Ph.D. dissertation, University of Western Ontario, 2004), 141–42, 147; Patrick, "Life and Times of Samuel Kirkland," 176–86.

20. Alan Taylor, *The Divided Ground: Indians, Settlers, and the Northern Borderland of the American Revolution* (New York, 2007), 61.

21. Wheelock to Occom, Jan. 25, 1769, *Wheelock Papers*, 769125. See also Edward Deake to Wheelock, Dec. 20, 1768, *Wheelock Papers*, 768670.

22. Occom to Wheelock, Jan. 15, 1770, Boston Public Library Special Collections.

23. Samuel Kirkland to Eleazar Wheelock, Dec. 29, 1768, *Wheelock Papers*, 768679.

24. Joseph Johnson to All Enquiring Friends [1772 or 1773], *Writings of Joseph Johnson*, 178.

25. Joseph Johnson to the Connecticut Assembly, Jun. 2, 1774, *Writings of Joseph Johnson*, 234.

26. Gregory Evans Dowd, *War under Heaven: Pontiac, the Indian Nations, and the British Empire* (Baltimore, 2002); Howard H. Peckham, *Pontiac and the Indian Uprising* (Princeton, N.J., 1947); Richard White, *The Middle Ground: Indians, Empires, and Republics in the Great Lakes Region, 1650–1815* (New York, 1991), 269–314.

27. Kirkland to Eleazar Wheelock, Oct. 9, 1770, Kirkland Papers 12b; Kirkland to John Thornton, Feb. 6, 1771, Kirkland Papers 15a. See also Kirkland to Wheelock, Oct. 29, 1773, Kirkland Papers 44a.

28. Kirkland to Wheelock, Oct. 29, 1773, Kirkland Papers 44a.

29. Colin G. Calloway, *The American Revolution in Indian Country: Crisis and Diversity in Native American Communities* (New York, 1995), 120–21.

30. Norton, "Rebellious Younger Brother," 216–18; Anthony Wonderly, "An Oneida Community in 1780: Study of an Inventory of Iroquois Property Losses during the Revolutionary War," *Man in the Northeast* 56 (Fall 1998), 19–42.

31. Kirkland to Andrew Elliot, Oct. 24, 1774, Kirkland Papers 51a.

32. On these points, see Taylor, *Divided Ground*, 61.

33. Guzzardo, "Superintendent and the Ministers," 269–72; Taylor, *Divided Ground*, 54; Norton, "Rebellious Younger Brother," 313–14.

34. Laurence M. Hauptman, "Refugee Havens: The Iroquois Villages of the Eighteenth Century," in *American Indian Environments: Ecological Issues in Native American History*, ed. Christopher Vecsey and Robert W. Venables (Syracuse, N.Y., 1980), 128–39; Francis

Jennings, "'Pennsylvania Indians' and the Iroquois," in *Beyond the Covenant Chain: The Iroquois and Their Neighbors in Indian North America, 1600–1800,* ed. Daniel K. Richter and James H. Merrell (Syracuse, N.Y., 1987), 75–92.

35. Colin G. Calloway, *The Scratch of a Pen: 1763 and the Transformation of North America* (New York, 2006), 35.

36. Bernard Bailyn, *Voyagers to the West: A Passage in the Peopling of America on the Eve of the Revolution* (New York, 1986); Peter C. Mancall, *Valley of Opportunity: Economic Culture Along the Upper Susquehanna, 1700–1800* (Ithaca, N.Y., 1991); Aaron S. Fogleman, "From Slaves, Convicts, and Servants to Free Passengers: The Transformation of Immigration in the Era of the American Revolution," *Journal of American History* 85, no. 1 (1998), 43–76.

37. Frontier violence against Iroquois, and the Oneidas in particular, is detailed in *Johnson Papers,* 5:169–70, 171, 172, 180, 182, 201; Sir William Johnson to the Lords of Trade, Jun. 28, 1766, in *NY Colonial Docs.,* 7:837; Governor Franklin to the Early of Sherlburne, Dec. 16, 1766, *New Jersey Archives,* 1st ser., 42 vols. (Newark, N.J., 1880–1949), 9:575–76; Karim Tiro, "The People of the Standing Stone: The Oneida Indian Nation from Revolution through Removal" (Ph.D. diss., University of Pennsylvania, 1999), 57–67.

38. Tiro, "People of the Standing Stone," 67–79; Norton, "Rebellious Younger Brother," 122–208.

39. Sir William Johnson Conference with the Six Nations and the Delawares, Apr. 29–May 22, 1765, *NYCD* 7:725; Proceedings at Treaty of Fort Stanwix, Oct. 22–Nov. 6, 1768, *Iroquois Indians,* reel 29.

40. Tiro, "People of the Standing Stone," 84.

41. Samson Occom to the New York Presbytery, Nov. 10, 1773, folder 7, Occom Papers.

42. Joseph Johnson to New York Congress, Aug. 26, 1775, *Writings of Joseph Johnson,* 276.

43. Joseph Johnson to the Connecticut Assembly, Jun. 2, 1774, *Writings of Joseph Johnson,* 235.

44. Joseph Johnson to Eleazar Wheelock, Oct. 17, 1774, *Writings of Joseph Johnson,* 244.

45. Ibid.; Occom to Wheelock, Jan. 6, 1774, *Occom Writings,* 109.

46. Sermon of Joseph Johnson, Farmington, May 7, 1774, Occom Papers, folder 22. See also *Occom Writings,* 376.

47. "An Account of some Extraordinary Charges attending the Mission of Saml. Kirkland...from October 6th, 1770 to October 6, 1771," Kirkland Papers, 21g.

48. Occom to the Officers of the English Trust for Moor's Indian Charity School, Nov. 10, 1773; Occom to Wheelock, Mar. 14, 1774, in *Occom Writings,* 107, 110.

49. *Johnson Papers,* 8:1094, 12:1037–38, 1060; Occom to Wheelock, Jan. 6, 1774, *Occom Writings,* 109–10; *NYCD,* 8:476; Joseph Johnson to Eleazar Wheelock, May 2, 1774, *Wheelock Papers,* 774302; *Early American Indian Documents, New York and New Jersey Treaties,* 671.

50. "To the Indians Concerning Oneida Lands," *Writings of Joseph Johnson,* 204; *Early American Indian Documents, New York and New Jersey Treaties,* 660–61.

51. Occom to Wheelock, Jan. 6, 1774, *Occom Writings,* 109–10.

52. William N. Fenton, *The Great Law and the Longhouse: A Political History of the Iroquois Confederacy* (Norman, Okla., 1998), 493.

53. Ibid.; Williams, *Linking Arms Together*, 62–82; Mary Druke Becker, "Linking Arms: The Structure of Iroquois Intertribal Diplomacy," in *Beyond the Covenant Chain*, ed. Richter and Merrell, 29–39.

54. See the discussion of Oneida settlements in Tiro, "People of the Standing Stone," 40–47.

55. "Joseph Johnson's Speech to the Oneidas, January 20, 1774," and "Joseph Johnson's Second Speech to the Oneidas," *Writings of Joseph Johnson*, 206, 221. For more on this metaphor, see Nancy Shoemaker, *A Strange Likeness: Becoming Red and White in Eighteenth-Century North America* (New York, 2004), 126.

56. "An Account of some Extraordinary Charges attending the Mission of Saml. Kirkland...from October 6th, 1770 to October 6, 1771," Kirkland Papers, 21g.

57. "Joseph Johnson's Speech to the Oneidas, January 20, 1774," *Writings of Joseph Johnson*, 206.

58. "Oneidas Second Answer to Joseph Johnson, January 22, 1774," *Writings of Joseph Johnson*, 216.

59. Ibid., 219.

60. Joseph Johnson to Eleazar Wheelock, Oct. 17, 1774, *Writings of Joseph Johnson*, 243; English Minutes of Indian Affairs, Oct. 1–4, 1774, in *Iroquois Indians*, reel 31.

61. Certificate of the Oneidas, Grant of a Tract of Land to the New England Indians, Oct. 4, 1774, *Johnson Papers*, 13:683–84.

62. Thomas N. Ingersoll, *To Intermix with our White Brothers: Indian Mixed Bloods in the United States from the Earliest Times to the Indian Removals* (Albuquerque, N.M., 2005), 108–9; William B. Hart, "Black 'Go-Betweens' and the Mutability of 'Race,' Status, and Identity on New York's Pre-Revolutionary Frontier," in *Contact Points: American Frontiers from the Mohawk Valley to the Mississippi, 1750–1830*, ed. Andrew R. L. Cayton and Fredrika J. Teute (Chapel Hill, N.C., 1998), 88–113.

63. "Agreement Respecting Strange Indians Living at Montauk, 1754," typescript, Indian Deeds of Montauk, accession no. F129.E13 I53 1900Z, Brooklyn Historical Society, Brooklyn, N.Y.

64. Simmons and Simmons, eds., *Old Light on Separate Ways*, 22.

65. William Samuel Johnson Papers, vol. 3, docs. 72–73.

66. Russell Lawrence Barsh, "'Colored' Seamen in the New England Whaling Industry: An Afro-Indian Consortium," in *Confounding the Color Line: The Indian-Black Experience in North America*, ed. James Brooks (Lincoln, Neb., 2002), 76–108; Daniel R. Mandell, "Shifting Boundaries of Race and Ethnicity: Indian-Black Intermarriage in Southern New England, 1760–1880," *Journal of American History* 85 (1998–99), 468–69.

67. Love, *Samson Occom*, xxix.

68. Patrick Wolfe, "Land, Labor, and Difference: Elementary Structures of Race," *American Historical Review* 106, no. 3 (Jun. 2001), 866–905; Pauline Turner Strong and Barrik Van Winkle: "'Indian Blood': Reflections on the Reckoning and Refiguring of Native North American Identity," *Cultural Anthropology* 11, no. 4 (Nov. 1996), 547–76.

69. These nineteenth-developments are skillfully treated in Daniel R. Mandell, *Tribe, Race, History: Native Americans in Southern New England, 1780–1880* (Baltimore, 2007).

70. Ann Marie Plane, *Colonial Intimacies: Indian Marriage in Early New England* (Ithaca, N.Y., 2000), 153–77.

71. Conn. Indian Series, 1st ser., vol. 2, pp. 310, 311, 312a; Report of a Committee on Mohegan affairs appointed on Petition of Zachary Johnson and Others, Oct. 1774, Learned Hebard, comp., *Papers Relating to the Mohegan Indians, 1699–1861* (n.p.), Connecticut State Archives. See also the discussion of these matters in *Writings of Joseph Johnson*, 39.

72. List of the Mohegan Indians, agreable to the Minds of Zachary Simon and Noah Samuell Dantaquigin, Sept. 1, 1774, Conn. Indian Series, 1st ser., vol. 2, p. 314. Also in Hebard, comp., *Papers Relating to the Mohegan Indians* (n.p.), Conn. State Archives, Sept. 1, 1774. See also Conn. Indian Series, 1st ser., vol. 2, p. 293b.

73. Conn. Indian Series, 1st ser., vol. 2, pp. 287a–b, 290, 293a–b, 310a–b, 312a–b.

74. Ibid., p. 312b.

75. Ibid.

76. Ibid., p. 260.

77. Johnson to Trumbull, 1773, *Writings of Joseph Johnson*, 185.

78. Samson Occom to Rev. John Moorhead, Apr. 10, 1773, *Occom Writings*, 104. See also David Fowler to Samson Occom, Feb. 24, 1774, Occom Papers, folder 8.

79. Joseph Johnson to Sir William Johnson, Jul. 8, 1774, *Johnson Papers*, 12:1117–18.

80. Ibid.

Chapter 5. Exodus

1. Occom to Eleazar Wheelock, Jul. 1, 1769, and Occom to John Bailey, [Jun. or Jul.] 1783, *Occom Writings*, 90, 118.

2. *Occom Writings*, 118

3. Occom to Benoni Occom, Jun. 24, 1780, *Occom Writings*, 117.

4. Mary Occom to Eleazar Wheelock, Nov. 8, 1766, and Samson Occom to Eleazar Wheelock, Feb. 10, 1767, in Leon Burr Richardson, ed., *An Indian Preacher in England* (Hanover, N.H., 1933), 182, 222.

5. Occom to John Bailey, [Jun. or Jul.] 1783, *Occom Writings*, 120.

6. Mohican-Stockbridge and Brothertown Tribes to All Benevolent Gentlemen, Nov. 28 and 29, 1787, *Occom Writings*, 155.

7. Occom to John Bailey, May 1783.

8. It is entirely possible that Johnson died violently. Yet in one of his last letters Johnson mentioned that his wife, Tabitha, was terribly ill. Thus, he might very well have died from disease. See Johnson to John Phillips, Mar. 19, 1776, *Writings of Joseph Johnson*, 282.

9. Kirkland to Philip Schuyler, Mar. 11, 1776, Kirkland Papers, 64b.

10. Conn. Indian Series, 1st ser., vol. 2, p. 193.

11. Ibid., pp. 194–199b; *Connecticut Records*, 14:292.

12. Johnson to Wheelock, Feb. 14, 1775, *Writings of Joseph Johnson*, 252. See also David McClure to Wheelock, Feb. 2, 1775, *Wheelock Papers*, 774152.

13. Joseph Johnson to John Rodgers, Feb. 15, 1775, *Writings of Joseph Johnson*, 253.

14. Joseph Johnson to Guy Johnson, Mar. 25, 1775, *Writings of Joseph Johnson*, 255–56. All of the following quotations in this paragraph come from the same letter. For a similar

incident involving Indian students from Wheelock's school, see Eleazar Wheelock to Gov. Trumbull [1775], *American Archives*, ser. 4, vol. 2, pp. 528–83, copy in *Iroquois Indians*, reel 31.

15. David Fowler to Colonel Guy Johnson, Apr. 8, 1775, *Writings of Joseph Johnson*, 260.

16. Ibid., 259–60; Samuel W. Durant, *History of Oneida County, New York, with Illustrations and Biographical Sketches of Some of its Prominent Men and Pioneers* (Philadelphia, 1878), 483–84.

17. Joseph Johnson to Guy Johnson, Mar. 25, 1775, *Writings of Joseph Johnson*, 257.

18. Occom to Joseph Johnson, Apr. 14, 1775, *Writings of Joseph Johnson*, 260.

19. Oneidas to the New England Provinces, Jun. 19, 1775; Joseph Johnson to the New York Congress, Jun. 21, 1775, *Writings of Joseph Johnson*, 262, 265.

20. Joseph Johnson to Sir William Johnson, Jul. 8, 1774, *Writings of Joseph Johnson*, 238.

21. Occom to the Oneidas, 1775, *Occom Writings*, 111–12.

22. Occom to John Bailey, [Jun. or Jul.] 1783, *Occom Writings*, 120.

23. Oneidas to the New England Provinces, *Writings of Joseph Johnson*, 263.

24. George Washington to Joseph Johnson, Feb. 20, 1776, *Writings of Joseph Johnson*, 281; Brad Devin Edward Jarvis, "Preserving the Brothertown Nation of Indians: Exploring Relationships amongst Land, Sovereignty, and Identity, 1740–1840" (Ph.D. diss., University of Minnesota, 2006), 136.

25. Joseph Johnson to New York Congress, Aug. 26, 1775, *Writings of Joseph Johnson*, 275.

26. David Fowler to Colonel Guy Johnson, Apr. 8, 1775, *Writings of Joseph Johnson*, 261.

27. Joseph Johnson to New York Congress, Jul. 5, 1775, Joseph Johnson to Connecticut Assembly, Jul. 5, 1775, and Connecticut's Exoneration of Joseph Johnson, Jul. 1775, *Writings of Joseph Johnson*, 266–68, 269–72.

28. Report of a Committee on Mohegan affairs appointed on Petition of Zachary Johnson and Others, Oct. 1774, Learned Hubbard, comp., *Papers Relating to the Mohegan Indians, 1699–1861* (n.p.), Connecticut State Archives, Hartford. See also the discussion of these matters in *Writings of Joseph Johnson*, 39.

29. Zachary Johnson to Richard Law, May 30, 1781, in Occom Papers, folder 10, and Ayer Ms. 459 ("Indians and disorderly white people"; "certain Indian Minister"); Petition to the Committe for Indian Affairs by Zachary Johnson, Aug. 1782, in Hubbard, comp., *Papers Relating to the Mohegan Indians* ("Indians and Negros"); Conn. Indian Series, 1st ser., vol. 2, p. 314 ("is determined . . ."). See also the competing lists of Mohegans in Conn. Indian Series, 1st ser., vol. 2, pp. 315a, 315b, 316, 317; William Samuel Johnson Papers, vol. 3, pp. 78, 84a, 93–94, CHS; *Early American Indian Documents: Treaties and Laws, 1607–1789*, vol. 17, *New England and Middle Atlantic States*, 381–82, and other Johnson complaints in Conn. Indian Series, 1st ser., vol. 2, pp. 319, 320a, 322a–b.

30. Kathleen J. Bragdon, *Native People of Southern New England, 1500–1650* (Norman, Okla., 1996), 140–55.

31. Bragdon, *Native People of Southern New England*, 143.

32. Conn. Indian Series, 1st ser., vol. 2, pp. 103a–b, see also p. 286b.

33. John Wood Sweet, *Bodies Politic: Negotiating Race in the American North, 1730–1830* (Baltimore, 2003), esp. 183–267; Joanne Pope Melish, *Disowning Slavery: Gradual Emancipation and 'Race' in New England, 1680–1860* (Ithaca, N.Y., 1998); Gary B. Nash, *The Unknown American Revolution: The Unruly Birth of Democracy and the Struggle to Create America* (New York, 2005), 151–66, 320–39; William Dillon Pierson, *Black Yankees: The Development of an Afro-American Subculture in Eighteenth-Century New England* (Amherst, Mass., 1988), ch. 2; Leon F. Litwack, *North of Slavery: The Negro in the Free States, 1790–1860* (Chicago, 1961).

34. Barbara Graymont, *The Iroquois in the American Revolution* (Syracuse, N.Y., 1972), 86–128.

35. Quoted in Alan Taylor, *The Divided Ground: Indians, Settlers, and the Northern Borderland of the American Revolution* (New York, 2006), 80. See also Isabel Thompson Kelsay, *Joseph Brant, 1743–1807: A Man of Two Worlds* (Syracuse, N.Y., 1984).

36. Taylor, *Divided Ground*, 81–83; Karim M. Tiro, "James Dean in Iroquoia," *New York History* 80 (1999), 402–5; Tiro, "People of the Standing Stone," 103–12; Christine Sternberg Patrick, "The Life and Times of Samuel Kirkland, 1741–1808: Missionary to the Oneida Indians, American Patriot, and Founder of Hamilton College" (Ph.D. diss., State University of New York at Buffalo, 1993), 273–305.

37. Joseph T. Glatthaar, and James Kirby Martin, *Forgotten Allies: The Oneida Indians and the American Revolution* (New York, 2006), 110–11.

38. Ibid., 118, 125, 129

39. On the events below, see Graymont, *Iroquois in the American Revolution*, 129–56.

40. Glatthaar and Martin, *Forgotten Allies*, 176; David Levinson, "An Explanation for the Oneida-Colonist Alliance in the American Revolution," *Ethnohistory* 23 (1976), 273; William T. Hagan, *Longhouse Diplomacy and Frontier Warfare: The Iroquois Confederacy in the American Revolution* (Albany, N.Y., 1975), 23–24; Taylor, *Divided Ground*, 92

41. Karim M. Tiro, "A 'Civil' War? Rethinking Iroquois Participation in the American Revolution," *Explorations in Early American Culture* 4 (2000), 148–65.

42. Graymont, *Iroquois in the American Revolution*, 174–79, 181, 187–89; Glatthaar and Martin, *Forgotten Allies*, 221–25, 230–31, 255.

43. Glatthaar and Martin, *Forgotten Allies*, 255.

44. Graymont, *Iroquois in the American Revolution*, 208–19; Glatthaar and Martin, *Forgotten Allies*, 256.

45. Oneidas to George Clinton, Jun. 24, 1780, *Public Papers of George Clinton, First Governor of New York, 1777–1795, 1801–1804*, 10 vols. (New York and Albany, 1899), 5:883–84.

46. Graymont, *Iroquois in the American Revolution*, 235, 242; Glatthaar and Martin, *Forgotten Allies*, 270–74; Taylor, *Divided Ground*, 100; Levinson, "An Explanation for the Oneida-Colonist Alliance," 276; Laurence A. Hauptman, "The Oneida Nation: A Composite Portrait, 1784–1816," in *The Oneida Indian Journey: From New York to Wisconsin, 1784–1860*, ed. Hauptman and L. Gordon McLester III (Madison, Wisc., 1999), 21.

47. Tiro, "People of the Standing Stone," 137; Hagan, *Longhouse Diplomacy*, 47–48; Glatthaar and Martin, *Forgotten Allies*, 283–84, 289–90.

48. Tiro, "People of the Standing Stone," 140–41.

49. Daniel R. Mandell, "'The times are exceedingly altered': The Revolution and Southern New England Indians," in *Eighteenth Century Native Communities of New England in Colonial Context*, ed. Jack Campisi (Mashantucket, Conn., 2005), 170–71.

50. Estimates of the Mohegans' size during these years range from thirty to sixty families. See *The Literary Diary of Ezra Stiles, D.D., LL.D.*, ed. Franklin Bowditch Dexter, 3 vols. (New York, 1901), 3:263; John S. Ezell, ed., *The New Democracy in America: Travels of Francisco de Miranda in the United States, 1783–84*, trans. Judson P. Wood (Norman, Okla., 1963), 124. The numbers of war dead are from Mandell, "'The times are exceedingly altered,'" 171.

51. William Samuel Johnson Papers, 3:78, CHS. See also Conn. Indian Series, 1st ser., vol. 2, p. 326b.

52. Mandell, "'The times are exceedingly altered,'" 171, 181.

53. Jarvis, "Preserving the Brothertown Nation of Indians," 138–39.

54. Colin G. Calloway, *The American Revolution in Indian Country: Crisis and Diversity in Native American Communities* (New York, 1995), 93–94.

55. Patrick Frazier, *The Mohicans of Stockbridge* (Lincoln, Neb., 1992), 198–26; Calloway, *American Revolution in Indian Country*, 95–96. See also Provincial Congress regarding Stockbridge Enlistments, Apr. 1, 1775, *Early American Indian Documents: Treaties and Laws, 1607–1789*, gen. ed. Alden T. Vaughan, vol. 20, *New England Treaties: North and West, 1650–1776*, vol. ed. Daniel R. Mandell (Bethesda, Md., 2003), 602; Meeting of the Albany Commissioners for Indian Affairs, Jun. 13, 1776, Philip Schuyler Papers, Box 13, Indian Papers, New York Public Library; John Sergeant to Eleazar Wheelock, Aug. 6, 1777, *Wheelock Papers*, 777456; List of the Warriors of the Muhhekunuk Tribe killed in Battle during the War with Great Britain, Pickering Papers, vol. 62, p. 167, MHS.

56. Joseph P. Tustin, ed., *Diary of the American War, A Hessian Journal: Captain Johann Ewald, Field Jager Corps* (New Haven, Conn., 1979), 145; Ted J. Brasser, *Riding on the Frontier's Crest: Mahican Indian Culture and Culture Change*, National Museum of Man Ethnology Division, Paper No. 13 (Ottawa, 1974), 36; "The Indian Company of 1778," Teacher Resource Sheet No. 4.2, courtesy of Stockbridge-Munsee Education Committee.

57. Calloway, *American Revolution in Indian Country*, 99–101.

58. *At a meeting of the Governor and Council, Convened at Hartford, the second Day of November, Anno. Domini, 1780* (Hartford, 1780), Early American Imprints, 1st ser., no. 43781; Daniel Simon to Eleazar Wheelock, Oct. 7, 1778, in James Dow McCallum, ed., *The Letters of Eleazar Wheelock's Indians* (Hanover, N.H., 1932), 219–24; Conn. Indian Series, 1st ser., vol. 2, pp. 226-b, 227a-b.

59. Indian Proprietors Minutes, 1749–1790, pp. 55, 57, 69, 70, Stockbridge Town Clerk's Office, Stockbridge, Mass.; Frazier, *Mohicans of Stockbridge*, 124–30; Calloway, *American Revolution in Indian Country*, 90–91.

60. Frazier, *Mohicans of Stockbridge*, 191–92.

61. Ibid., 176–77.

62. Conn. Indian Series, 1st ser., vol. 2, p. 227a.

63. Samuel Kirkland to James Bowdoin, Mar. 10, 1784, Kirkland Papers, 85c.

64. To the Senators and wise Men of the Commonwealth of the Massachusetts who are about to Smoke their Pipes together in doing the great Business of the State [ca. 1783], Stockbridge Indian Collection, box 1, folder 7, Stockbridge Public Library, Stockbridge, Mass.

65. Samuel Kirkland to James Bowdoin, Mar. 10, 1784, Kirkland Papers, 85c.

66. Ibid.; *Massachusetts Spy: Or, Worcester Gazette*, Oct. 12, 1784, vol. 14, no. 694, p. 3.

67. Samson Occom Journal, entries for Sept. 23 and Sept. 29, 1785, *Occom Writings*, 299, 300.

68. Samuel Kirkland to James Bowdoin, Mar. 10, 1784, Kirkland Papers, 85c; Edward Wigglesworth to John McFarlan, Nov. 13, 1787, Rauner Ms. 787613; Numbers of the Six Nations, 1792, Jasper Parish Papers, box 2, folder 99, Vassar College Special Collections, Poughkeepsie, N.Y.; Jeremy Belknap and Jedidah Morse, *Report on the Oneida, Stockbridge, and Brotherton Indians*, 1796, Indian Notes and Monographs, no. 54 (New York: Museum of the American Indian, Heye Foundation, 1955), 7; Thomas Eddy and Edmund Prior to John Jay, Aug. 31, 1799, Brothertown Records, pp. 83–85, WSHS.

69. Muheacunnuck Tribe to Samson Occom, Aug. 27, 1787, folder 11, Occom Papers.

70. Occom Journal, Entry for Oct. 24, 1785, *Occom Writings*, 306.

71. *Kirkland Journals*, 126.

72. Muheacunnuck Tribe to Samson Occom, Aug. 27, 1787, folder 11, Occom Papers.

73. *Occom Writings*, 339 (journal entry for June 30, 1786), 381 (journal entry for Oct. 14, 1787), 402–3 (journal entries for July 18 and 20, 1788).

74. John Sergeant Journal, 1793–94, entries for Jan. 19, 23, 25, Feb. 7, 1794, WHS; Journals of John Sergeant, 1789–1809, entries for Mar. 14, 1790, Apr. 10, 25, May 1, Jul. 19, 1790; Dec. 3, 1793; Jan. 10, Feb. 7, Jul. 26, 1794, Harvard Grants; Journals of John Sergeant, Entries for Jul. 8, 1814; Sept. 13, 28, Oct. 7, 1815; Nov. 2, 1817, NYHS.; *Kirkland Journals*, 126–27, 128, 132, 134–35, 159, 161–62, 168, 172, 200, 204, 211, 224, 252, 254, 257, 296, 410; Occom Journal, Entry for Jun. 30, 1786, *Occom Writings*, 339.

75. "Extracts from the Journals of the Indians along with the 6th speech delivere'd the Delaware nation residing at Waupehaummhuhk or White River on the 15th of April, 1803," Sergeant Journals, entry for Aug. 4, 1803, Harvard Grants. On Auapumut's travels see Rachel Wheeler, "Hendrick Aupaumut: Christian-Mahican Prophet," *Journal of the Early Republic* 25 (2005), 187–220; Alan Taylor, "Captain Hendrick Aupaumut: The Dilemmas of an Intercultural Broker," *Ethnohistory* 43 (1996), 431–57.

76. Occom to ?, Dec. 26, 1791, *Occom Writings*, 136; Superintendents of Brothertown to John Jay, 1795, Brothertown Records, p. 16, Hamilton College Special Collections.

77. Sergeant Journals, entry for Jul. 20, 1794, Harvard Grants.

78. Belknap and Morse, *Report on the Oneida, Stockbridge, and Brotherton Indians*, 21–22.

79. Thomas Eddy to the Philadelphia Yearly Meeting Indian Committee, Sept. 26, 1797, AA41, Box 3, PYMICR.

80. Edmund Prior and Thomas Eddy to John Jay, Sept. 1, 1797, Brothertown Records, Hamilton College, 56; William Floyd, Edmund Prior, and Thomas Eddy to John Jay, Oct. 15, 1796, Brothertown Records, p. 46, WHS.

81. Jonathan Thomas, Jacob Taylor, and Henry Simmons Jr., at Oneida, to the Philadelphia Yearly Meeting Indian Committee, Apr. 3, 1797, PYMICR; Minutes of the Indian Committee, 1795–1815, p. 37, PYMICR.

Chapter 6. Cursed

1. All quotations are from Autograph of Samson Occom, Mohegan Indian [1784?], William Griswold Lane Papers, box 2, Yale University Manuscripts and Archives, Sterling Library, Yale University, New Haven, Conn. On the Fort Stanwix Treaty conference, see Alan Taylor, *The Divided Ground: Indians, Settlers, and the Northern Borderland of the American Revolution* (New York, 2006), 154–62. On Iroquois symbolism, see William N. Fenton, *The Great Law of the Longhouse: A Political History of the Iroquois Confederacy* (Norman, Okla., 1998); Francis Jennings, ed., *The History and Culture of Iroquois Diplomacy: An Interdisciplinary Guide to the Treaties of the Six Nations and Their League* (Syracuse, N.Y., 1995); Robert Williams Jr., *Linking Arms Together: American Indian Treaty Visions of Law and Peace, 1600–1800* (New York, 1995).

2. Quoted in Taylor, *Divided Ground*, 145. Generally on these jurisdictional disputes, see Peter Onuf, *The Origins of the Federal Republic: Jurisdictional Controversies in the United States, 1775–1787* (Philadelphia, 1983). As they applied to Iroquois country, see Taylor, *Divided Ground*; and J. David Lehman, "The End of the Iroquois Mystique: The Oneida Land Cession Treaties of the 1780s," *WMQ* 47, no. 4 (1990), 531–34, 539.

3. Alan Taylor, "'The Hungry Year': 1789 on the Northern Border of Evolutionary America," in *Dreadful Visitations: Confronting Natural Catastrophe in the Age of Enlightenment*, ed. Alessa Johns (New York: Routledge, 1999), 145–81.

4. Extracts from the Proceedings of the Treaty at Fort Herkimer between New York and the Oneidas and the Tuscaroras, Jun. 23, 1784, in *Early American Indian Documents: Laws and Treaties*, gen. ed. Alden T. Vaughan, vol. 18, *Revolution and Confederation*, vol. ed. Colin G. Calloway (Frederick, Md., 1994), 333–36; Taylor, *Divided Ground*, 165.

5. Karim M. Tiro, "James Dean in Iroquoia," *New York History* 80 (1999), 413–14; Laurence W. Hauptman, *Conspiracy of Interests: Iroquois Dispossession and the Rise of New York State* (Syracuse, N.Y., 1999), 73–74; Taylor, *Divided Ground*, 147; Lehman, "End of the Iroquois Mystique," 540–41.

6. *Early American Indian Documents, Revolution and Confederation*, 472–73.

7. Tiro, "James Dean," 412–13.

8. Occom journal entries for Oct. 17 and 18, 1786, *Occom Writings*, 344–45.

9. Occom Journal, entry of Oct. 24, 1787, *Occom Writings*, 382.

10. Treaty of Fort Schuyler, Sept. 22, 1788, in *Iroquois Indians*, reel 39. Also printed in *Early American Indian Documents, Revolution and Confederation*, 472–73; Brothertown Records, pp. 3–7, WHS; Brothertown Records, p. 2, Hamilton College.

11. "An Act for the Sale and Disposition of Lands, Belonging to the People of this State, Feb. 25, 1789," *Laws of the State of New York Passed at the Sessions of the Legislature Held in the Years 1789, 1790, 1791, 1792, 1793, 1795, and 1796, Inclusive...* (Albany, N.Y., 1887), 3:70; William DeLoss Love, *Samson Occom and the Christian Indians of New England*, introduction by Margaret Connell Szasz (1899; Syracuse, N.Y., 2000), 286; John Wood Sweet, *Bodies Politic: Negotiating Race in the American North, 1730–1830* (Baltimore, 2003), 323; Brad Devin

Edward Jarvis, "Preserving the Brothertown Nation of Indians: Exploring Relationships amongst Land, Sovereignty, and Identity, 1740–1840" (Ph.D. diss., University of Minnesota, 2006), 163.

12. Proceedings of the Commissioners appointed by the State of New York to hold treaties with the Indians within that State, under statute passed March 1, 1788, *Iroquois Indians*, reel 39; Franklin B. Hough, ed., *Proceedings of the Commissioners of the Indian Affairs, Appointed by Law for the Extinguishment of Indian Titles in the State of New York* (Albany, N.Y., 1861), 1:230.

13. Brothertown Tribe to New York State [Jan. 1791], *Occom Writings*, 157.

14. Taylor, *Divided Ground*, 385.

15. Occom Journal, Entry of Oct. 10, 1787, *Occom Writings*, 380.

16. Taylor, *Divided Ground*, 183–84.

17. Samuel Kirkland to Peter Thacher, Stockbridge, Jan. 14, 1791, Kirkland Papers, 132b. See also *Kirkland Journals*, 167; Thomas Eddy and Edmund Prior to John Jay, Dec. 12, 1798, Brothertown Records, pp. 24–25, Hamilton College; Taylor, "'The Hungry Year.'"

18. In 1785, the Narragansett "King's Council Party" petitioned the Rhode Island Assembly against leases by the "Tribe's Council Party." Forty different surnames appeared on that petition. Of them, just nine appeared at Brothertown in the 1790s and early 1800s (Charles, Hammer, Harry, Paul, Robin, Simon, Simond, Skeesuck, and Wappy). At a Meeting of a Number of the Indians in Charlestown, Feb. 20, 1785, Paul Campbell Research Notes, box 2, folder 1770–1779, RIHS. See also *Early American Indian Documents: Treaties and Laws, 1607–1789*, gen. ed. Alden T. Vaughan, vol. 17, *New England and Middle Atlantic Laws*, vol. eds. Alden T. Vaughan and Deborah Rosen (Bethesda, Md., 2004), 473–74; Daniel R. Mandell, *Tribe, Race, History: Native Americans in Southern New England, 1780–1880* (Baltimore, 2007), 6, 17.

19. Report of a Committee of Indian Affairs, Dec. 17, 1792, Shepley Papers, vol. 9, p. 31, RIHS. See also *Early American Indian Documents: New England and Middle Atlantic Laws*, 479–80.

20. Petition of John Skesuck to Committee to Transact Indian Affairs, May 24, 1792, box 2, folder 1770–1779, Paul Campbell Papers, RIHS.

21. Conn. Indian Series, ser. 1, vol. 2, p. 330a, 329, and 331. See also Conn. Indian Series, ser. 2, vol. 1, pp. 39, 41, 42, 45, 48.

22. "An Act for the Sale and disposition of Lands belonging to the People of this State, Feb. 25, 1789," Brothertown Records, WHS, p. 7.

23. Brothertown Tribe to the New York State Assembly, Jan. 1791, *Occom Writings*, 158.

24. Occom Journal, Entries for Jul. 16, 1788, 402.

25. *Kirkland Journals*, 251 ("rent & torn"; "divisions & animosities"); 257 ("methodists ...").

26. Dorothy Ripley, *Bank of Faith and Works United* (Philadelphia, 1819), 101.

27. Brothertown Tribe to the New York State Assembly, Jan. 1791, *Occom Writings*, 157.

28. Rebecca Kugel, *To be the Main Leaders of Our People: A History of Minnesota Ojibwe Politics, 1825–1898* (East Lansing, Mich., 1998); Melissa L. Meyer, *The White Earth Tragedy: Ethnicity and Dispossession at a Minnesota Anishinaabe Reservation, 1889–1920* (Lincoln, Neb., 1994).

29. On Pechaker, see Jerome D. Segal and R. Andrew Pierce, *The Wampanoag Genealogical Dictionary of Martha's Vineyard, Massachusetts* (Baltimore, 2003), 220, 258.

30. Occom to George Clinton [1792?], *Occom Writings*, 137–38.

31. An Act for the Relief of the Indians residing in Brothertown and New Stockbridge, Feb. 21, 1791, *Laws of the State of New York, Passed at the Fifteenth Session of the Legislature*, in *Laws of the State of New York Passed at the Sessions of the Legislature Held in the Years 1789, 1790, 1791, 1792, 1793, 1795, and 1796, Inclusive*...(Albany, N.Y., 1887), 212–13.

32. Ibid., 370–72.

33. Samson Occom to George Clinton [1792?], *Occom Writings*, 137. See also reports of Wimpey's petition in *The Federal Gazette, and Philadelphia Evening Post*, Feb. 22, 1792, p. 3; *Columbia Centenial*, Feb. 25, 1792, vol. 16, no. 48, p. 190; and *Windham Herald*, Mar. 10, 1792, vol. 2, no. 53, p. 53. These newspapers reported that the petitioners asked "to be put on the footing of free white citizens, except that they do not wish to the priviledge of selling their lands." I am assuming that they did not ask for the vote or for the responsibility of paying taxes, for such issues never arose in any other documents from this period. The request to become "citizens" probably meant the right to hold and manage land individually.

34. Love, *Samson Occom*, 290–91.

35. William Colbrath to George Clinton, Dec. 15, 1795, New York Assembly Papers, box 2, folder 35, NYSA.

36. George Clinton to Hugh White, Amos Whitmore, Jonas Platt, Arthur Breeze, Elizier Mosely, and Thomas R. Gould, Dec. 30, 1795, William Pierrepoint White Papers, Special Collections, Cornell University Library.

37. *The Federal Gazette, and Philadelphia Evening Post*, Feb. 22, 1792, p. 3.

38. Petition of the Magistrates and other Inhabitants of the county of Herkimer, New York Assembly Papers, box 2, folder 30.

39. Petition of the Brothertown Lessees, Feb. 17, 1794, New York Assembly Papers, box 1, folder 28.

40. John Sergeant to Timothy Pickering, Jan. 3, 1795, Pickering Papers, vol. 62, p. 200, MHS.

41. "Act Relative to the lands at Brothertown, passed March 31, 1795," and "Act for the Relief of the Indians who are Intitled to Lands in Brothertown, Passed March 4, 1796," *Laws of the State of New York, Passed at the Eighteenth Session of the Legislature*, in *Laws of the State of New York Passed at the Sessions of the Legislature Held in the Years 1789, 1790, 1791, 1792, 1793, 1795, and 1796, Inclusive*...(Albany, N.Y., 1887), 585–88, 655–62.

42. John Sergeant to Samuel Kirkland, Mar. 22, 1791, Kirkland Papers, 124c; Stockbridge Indians to Samuel Kirkland, Jun. 22, 1792, Kirkland Papers, 149L; Samuel Kirkland to Thomas Pickering, May 31, 1792, Kirkland Papers, 148j; Samuel Kirkland to Israel Chapin, May 31, 1792, Kirkland Papers, 148i; Entry for Mar. 15, 1791, Journals of Samuel Kirkland...from Feb. 16 to May 30, 1791, box 1, folder 7, SPGNA Recs.; John Konkapot to Timothy Pickering [ca. 1792], Pickering Papers, vol. 62, pp. 73–74, MHS; Samuel Kirkland to Timothy Pickering, May 12, 1792 and Jun. 5, 1792, Pickering Papers, vol. 62, pp. 46–48a, 52; John Sergeant to Peter Thatcher, May 19, 1793, Rauner Ms. 788319.

43. Hendrick Aupaumut to Timothy Pickering, Mar. 21, 1796, Pickering Papers, vol. 62, p. 244, MHS; Jeremy Belknap and Jedidah Morse, *Report on the Oneida, Stockbridge, and Brotherton Indians, 1796*, Indian Notes and Monographs, no. 54 (New York, 1955), 8. On Konkapot, see *Diary of William Bentley, D.D., Pastor of the East Church of Salem, Mass.*, vol. 3 (Salem, Mass., 1911), 41; Love, *Samson Occom*, 239–40.

44. Entry of Aug. 7, 1794, Journals of John Sergeant, 1789–1809, Harvard Grants. See also Report of the Committee to whom was referred several Petitions of the Oneida, of the Male, of the Female of New Stockbridge, and of the Tuscarora Indians, New York Assembly Papers, box 5, folder 40.

45. Hendrick Aupaumut to Timothy Pickering, Mar. 21, 1796, Pickering Papers, vol. 62, p. 244, MHS. See also Stockbridge Sachems and Counselors to New York, Feb. 3, 1794, New York Assembly Papers, box 2, folder 18.

46. Journals of John Sergeant, "April 23 to July 26, 1794" folder, Harvard Grants.

47. Kirkland to James Bowdoin, Mar. 10, 1784, Kirkland Papers, 85c.

48. *Kirkland Journals*, 162, emphasis in original.

49. Speech of the Oneida Sachems, Aug. 8, 1795, Indian Papers, 1710–1797, box 15 of the Peter Schuyler Papers, New York Public Library, New York, N.Y.

50. Quoted in Jack Campisi and William A. Starna, "On the Road to Canandaigua: The Treaty of 1794," *American Indian Quarterly* 19 (1995), 474. For an example of these conversations, see Good Peter's Narrative of Several Transaction Respecting Indian Land, Apr. 1792, Pickering Papers, vol. 60, p. 128, MHS.

51. *Kirkland Journals*, 390–91. Reprinted in Dorothy Ripley, *Bank of Faith and Works United* (Philadelphia, 1819), 120–22.

52. "Though Shalt Love thy Neighbor as Thyself, Luke 10:26–27," *Occom Writings*, 199–207.

53. "The Most Remarkable and Strange State Situation and Appearance of Indian Tribes in this Great Continent" [1783] and "Though Shalt Love thy Neighbor as Thyself" [1787?], *Occom Writings*, 58, 206.

54. Kirkland to Israel Chapin, May 31, 1792, Kirkland Papers, 148i; Kirkland to Timothy Pickering, May 12, 1792, vol. 62, pp. 46–48a, Pickering Papers, MHS.

55. Stockbridge Indians to Samuel Kirkland, Jun. 22, 1792, Kirkland Papers, 149L; Hendrick Aupaumut to Timothy Pickering, Mar. 21, 1796, Pickering Papers, vol. 62, p. 244, MHS. See also Kirkland to Israel Chapin, May 3, 1792, Kirkland Papers, 148i.

56. Quoted in Taylor, *Divided Ground*, 182–83.

57. Sachem and Counsellors of the Muhheconnuk or Stockbridge, to Isaiah Roland, John Pierce, Joseph Sansom, and James Cooper, Sept. 9, 1797, PYMICR, Box 1. For a similar statement by the Oneida chief, Blacksmith, see Ripley, *Bank of Faith and Works United*, 80, 115.

58. Oneidas, Muhheconnuck, and Tuscarora Sachems and Chiefs to the New York Assembly, Feb. 4, 1799, New York Assembly Papers, box 3, folder 13; Stockbridge to New York Assembly, Jul. 1, 1800, New York Assembly Papers, box 3, folder 15.

59. Entry of Jan. 6, 1797, Journals of John Sergeant, 1789–1809, Harvard Grants.

60. Stockbridge to New York Assembly, Jul. 1, 1800, New York Assembly Papers, box 3, folder 15; *Kirkland Journal*, 390–91. See also "Oneidas, Tuscaroras, and Stockbridges to the

Great Sachem and Chiefs of the State of New York," reprinted in Samuel L. Knapp, *The Life of Thomas Eddy* (New York, 1834), 112–15.

61. "Indians Must Have Teachers of Their Own Coular or Nation" [Nov. 1791], *Occom Writings*, 134.

62. Thomas N. Ingersoll, *To Intermix with Our White Brothers: Indian Mixed Bloods in the United States from Earliest Times to the Indian Removal* (Albuquerque, N.M., 2005), 170.

63. Letter from a Gentleman recently returned from Niagara, Aug. 8, 1792, Kirkland Papers, 151a.

64. *American Mercury* (Hartford, Conn.), Feb. 2, 1795, vol. 11, no. 552, p. 2.

65. Ripley, *Bank of Faith and Works United*, 87.

66. *Kirkland Journals*, 171–72.

67. Ibid.

68. Kirkland to Jerusha Kirkland, Jan. 14, 1787, Kirkland Papers, 101a; Belknap and Morse, *Report on the Oneida, Stockbridge, and Brotherton Indians*, 21, 22; Brothertown Superintendents to Lewis Morgan, Feb. 25, 1804, Brothertown Records, Hamilton College; Thomas Eddy to Philadelphia Yearly Meeting Indian Committee, Sept. 26, 1797, box 3, PYMICR; A Statistical Account of the Brothertown, Stockbridge, South Settlement of the Oneida, and Onondaga Tribes of Indians, taken in the year 1819," box 5, folder 32, Record Series A1823–78, 8 boxes, vols. 40–41, Petitions, Correspondence, and Reports Regarding Indians, NYSA.

69. Christopher Grasso, *A Speaking Aristocracy: Transforming Public Discourse in Eighteenth-Century Connecticut* (Chapel Hill, N.C., 1999), 30–40.

70. Entries for Aug. 14, 1794, and Jan. 18, 1795, Sergeant Journals, Harvard Grants.

71. Gregory Evans Dowd, *A Spirited Resistance: The North American Indian Struggle for Unity, 1745–1815* (Baltimore, 1992); R. David Edmunds, *The Shawnee Prophet* (Lincoln, Neb., 1983); Alfred A. Cave, *Prophets of the Great Spirit: Native American Revitalization Movements in Eastern North America* (Lincoln, Neb., 2006).

72. "The Most Remarkable and Strange State, Situation, and Appearance of Indian Tribes in this Great Continent" (1783), *Occom Writings*, 58–59.

73. Samson Occom to John Bailey, 1784, *Occom Writings*, 121.

74. Indians Must Have Teachers of Their Own Coular or Nation, [Nov. 1791], *Occom Writings*, 134.

75. Entry of Sept. 19, 1791, Journal of John Sergeant...from the 27th of July to the 7th of October, 1791, SPGNA Recs.

76. *Kirkland Journals*, 167, 171–72, 260–61; Entry of Aug. 12, 1794, Sergeant Journals, Harvard Grants.

77. Oneida Indians to the Regents of New York, Apr. 27, 1793, Kirkland Papers, 159b.

78. Journal of Samuel Kirkland...from June 13th to October 1791, SPGNA Recs., box 1, folder 7.

79. "Some Account of the Labours of Friends of New York Yearly Meeting, on Behalf of the Indians, from 1795 to 1843," in Clifford Gene Snyder, comp. and ed., *The Brotherton*

Indians: A Collection of Historical Writings on the Brotherton or Brothertown Band of Northeastern Indians (N. Hollywood, Calif., 1994), 47.

80. Entry for Aug. 15, 1791, Sergeant Journal, Harvard Grants.

81. Address by David Avery to Oneidas to mark his departure, Jun. 20, 1772, Kirkland Papers, 30d; Samuel Kirkland to Alexander Miller, May 24, 1800, Kirkland Papers, 211c.

82. *Kirkland Journals*, 169–70, 260.

83. The demoralized state of these communities is evident in Karim Tiro, "The People of the Standing Stone: The Oneida Indian Nation from Revolution through Removal" (Ph.D. diss., University of Pennsylvania, 1999), ch. 4. For the superintendents' complaints about liquor abuse at Brothertown, see Thomas Eddy to John Tukie, Jun. 13, 1797, Thomas Eddy to Morgan Lewis, ca. 1804, Thomas Eddy to Henry McNeil, Nov. 20, 1805, Thomas Eddy to Azra L. Mommediue, Feb. 5, 1808, Brothertown Records, p. 55 and unpaginated, WHS. See also parallel developments among the Senecas in Anthony F. C. Wallace, *The Death and Rebirth of the Seneca* (New York, 1969), ch. 7. Some of the murders can be traced in *Albany Centinel*, Jun. 30, 1801, vol. 5, no. 1, p. 3; *Commercial Advertiser* (New York), Jun. 24, 1817, vol. 20, no. 7670, p. 2, and Oct. 1, 1817, vol. 20, no. 7702, p. 2; *Alexandria Gazette and Daily Advertiser*, Jun. 30, 1817, vol. 17, no. 4955, p. 2; *Utica Gazette*, Sept. 16, 1818, vol. 1, no. 140; *Pittsfield Sun*, Oct. 5, 1818, vol. 18, no. 933, p. 3; *The Life and Confession of John Tuhi, An Indian of the Brothertown Tribe, while under the Sentence of Death for the Murder of his Brother, Joseph Tuhi…* [1817].

84. *Kirkland Journals*, 255–56, 373; *Albany Centinel*, Jun. 30, 1801, vol. 5, no. 1, p. 3; New York Correction History Society, "Timeline on Executions by Hanging in New York State," available at www.correctionhistory.org/hanngings/hangdates4.html, accessed Jan. 22, 2010.

85. *Commercial Advertiser*, Jun. 24, 1817, vol. 20, no. 7670, p. 2; *Life and Confession of John Tuhi*.

86. *Kirkland Journals*, 103, 311–12, 339, 393.

87. On Agwelondongwas see Hauptman, *Conspiracy of Interests*, 39–43.

88. Samuel Kirkland to John Thornton, Sept. 29, 1772, Kirkland Papers, 32b.

89. Quoted in Taylor, *Divided Ground*, 208.

90. Christine Sternberg Patrick, "The Life and Times of Samuel Kirkland, 1741–1808: Missionary to the Oneida Indians, American Patriot, and Founder of Hamilton College" (Ph.D. diss., State University of New York at Buffalo, 1993), 484–88, 519–22, 531, 532, 542–43; Taylor, *Divided Ground*, 226, 366–69; Petition of Hendrick Aupaumut and the Oneida Chiefs, Jan. 29 and 30, 1794, Pickering Papers, vol. 62, pp. 83–85.

91. Stockbridge Indians to Samuel Kirkland, June 22, 1792, Kirkland Papers, 149L; Entry of Aug. 2, 1791, Journal of Samuel Kirkland…from June 13 to October, 1791, box 1, folder 7, SPGNA Recs.

92. *Kirkland Journals*, 222–24; *New Jersey Journal*, Oct. 8, 1795, vol. 9, no. 460, p. 3.

93. Lisa Brooks, *The Common Pot: The Recovery of Native Space in the Northeast* (Minneapolis, Minn., 2008).

94. John Sergeant Jr., Letter of Aug. 7, 1792, in "John Sergeant, 1792–1808" folder, Harvard Grants.

Chapter 7. Red Brethren

1. Brothertown Peacemakers' Records, 1797–1840, pp. 174, 176, 177, 178, 189, 196, 202, 204. Photostats of private collection in author's possession. See also John Dean Daybook, Dean Family Papers, box 1, folder 12.

2. Indian Comptroller's Records, A0832–77, NYSA.

3. Brothertown Indians to President James Monroe, the Senate, and the H of R, Brothertown, Feb. 8, 1825, and Petition of the Brothertown Tribe to President Jackson, Dec. 27, 1830, LROIA, Six Nations Agency, reel 832.

4. Samuel W. Durant, *History of Oneida Country, New York, with Illustrations and Biographical Sketches of Some of its Prominent Men and Pioneers* (Philadelphia, 1878), 485; Love, *Samson Occom*, 343.

5. Minutes of the Indian Committee, 1795–1815, pp. 62, 65, 66, PYMICR; Some Expressions of the Stockbridge People, to Henry Drinker, David Bacon, Ellis Garnall, and Thomas Wister, Oct. 14, 1801, PYMICR, AA41, box 1; Minutes of the Indian Committee, 1795–1815, p. 158, PYMICR; Joseph Clark, *Travels among the Indians, 1797* (Doyletown, Pa., 1968), 28–42. Doxtater appears under her maiden name, Peters, in these documents.

6. Constitution of the Female Cent Society, Dec. 4, 1817, Dean Family Papers, box 1, folder 9; also in Brotherton Indian Collection, box 39, folder 17, R. Stanton Avery Special Collections Department, NEHGS; Christopher Densmore, "New York Quakers among the Brotherton, Stockbridge, Oneida, and Onondaga, 1795–1834," *Man in the Northeast* 44 (1992), 87.

7. David Butler to Lt. Gov. Taylor, Mar. 17, 1818, Ayer Ms. 127.

8. *Journal of the Life, Labours, and Travels of Thomas Shillitoe*, 2 vols. (London, 1839), 2:181.

9. Dick's business can be traced in Brothertown Fieldbook, pp. 25–27, Hamilton College Special Collections. Doxtater's business is mentioned in Catherine Littleman, Elizabeth Paulquhke, Eunice Jordan, et al., to Thomas Dean, Aug. 12, 1828, Dean Family Papers, box 2, folder 1.

10. For Doxtater, see Stockbridge Power of Attorney, Jan. 18, 1825, Brothertown Indian Collection, box 39, folder 29, NEHGS. Also in Dean Family Papers, box 1, folder 12. For Dick, see New York State Archives, Original Indian Deeds/Treaties, A4609–97, vol. 1, p. 5, NYSA.

11. *Journal of the Life, Labours, and Travels of Thomas Shillitoe*, 2:181.

12. A List of the Inhabitance of the Brothertowns who wish to remove to Wisconsin Territory this ensuing season, Oct. 3, 1841, Original Indian Deeds/Treaties, A4609–97, vol. 1, pp. 29–34, NYSA.

13. Carol Sheriff, *The Artificial River: The Erie Canal and the Paradox of Progress, 1817–1862* (New York, 1996).

14. Data culled from; and www.census.gov/history/www/1830/010950.html. http://www2.census.gov/prod2/decennial/documents/1790g-01.pdf; and http://www2.census.gov/prod2/decennial/documents/1830a-01.pdf, accessed Feb. 8, 2010.

15. Laurence M. Hauptman, *Conspiracy of Interests: Iroquois Dispossession and the Rise of New York State* (Syracuse, N.Y., 1999), 5, 8, 15–16, 68; Philip Lord Jr., "The Mohawk/Oneida

Corridor: The Geography of Inland Navigation Across New York," in *The Sixty Years' War for the Great Lakes, 1754–1814,* ed. David Curtis Skaggs and Larry L. Nelson (East Lansing, Mich., 2001), 275–85.

16. Hauptman, *Conspiracy of Interests,* page 6, table 1.

17. Numbers of the Six Nations, 1792, Jasper Parrish Papers, box 2, folder 99, Vassar College Library Archives and Special Collections; Jeremy Belknap and Jedidiah Morse, *Report on the Oneida, Stockbridge, and Brotherton Indians, 1796,* Indian Notes and Monographs, no. 54 (New York, 1955), 6–7; A Statistical Account of the Brothertown, Stockbridge, South Settlement of the Oneida, and Onondaga Tribes of Indians, Taken in the year 1819, New York Assembly Papers, box 5, folder 32.

18. Quoted in Hauptman, *Conspiracy of Interests,* 19.

19. Ibid., 20.

20. Vivian C. Hopkins, "DeWitt Clinton and the Iroquois," *Ethnohistory* 8, no. 2 (Spring 1961), 115, 135.

21. Ibid., 115.

22. Memorial of the subscribers, inhabitants of the counties of Oneida and Madison and residing in the vicinity of New Stockbridge, Dec. 20, 1820, New York Assembly Papers, box 6, folder 37.

23. Alan Taylor, *The Divided Ground: Indians, Settlers, and the Northern Borderland of the American Revolution* (New York, 2006), 252–53, 302–8.

24. Taylor, *Divided Ground,* 308, 391.

25. Report of the Superintendents of Brothertown and new Stockbridge Indians for 1818, New York Assembly Papers, box 5, folder 20.

26. *Republican Watch-Tower,* Sept. 15, 1807, vol. 8, no. 603, p. 3.

27. John Murray to Henry McNeil, Jun. 7, 1810, Dean Family Papers, box 1, folder 7.

28. Brad Devin Edward Jarvis, "Preserving the Brothertown Nation of Indians: Exploring Relationships amongst Land, Sovereignty, and Identity, 1740–1840" (Ph.D. diss., University of Minnesota, 2006), 203.

29. Russell Lawrence Barsh, "'Colored' Seamen in the New England Whaling Industry: An Afro-Indian Consortium," in *Confounding the Color Line: The Indian-Black Experience in North America,* ed. James F. Brooks (Lincoln, Neb., 2002), 81.

30. Thomas Eddy to the Brothertown Peacemakers, Brothertown Records, pp. 96–97, WHS.

31. Brothertown Records, pp. 11–12, Hamilton College; Brothertown Records, Sept. 25, 1796, and Oct. 15, 1796, WHS.

32. Thomas Eddy to Samuel Jones, Dec. 17, 1795, Thomas Eddy to J. Kirkland, Dec. 17, 1795, Edmund Prior to Brothertown Peacemakers, Oct. 4, 1799, Brothertown Records, pp. 72–73, 77, WHS.

33. Thomas Eddy to Edmund Prior, Brothertown Records, p. 78, and Meeting of the Superintendents of the Brothertown Indians, Jul. 24, 1804, WHS.

34. On the Mohawk prophet, see Samuel Kirkland to the Rev. Alexander Miller, May 24, 1800, Kirkland Papers, 21c; Report of Samuel Kirkland, May 24, 1800, box 1, folder 12, Harvard Grants; *Kirkland Journals,* 364–66; Ripley, *Bank of Faith and Works United,* 80;

Elisabeth Tooker, "The Iroquois White Dog Sacrifice in the Latter Part of the Eighteenth Century," *Ethnohistory* 12 (1965), 129–40. On Handsome Lake, see the classic work by Anthony F. C. Wallace, *The Death and Rebirth of the Seneca* (New York, 1969). See also Elisabeth Tooker, "On the Development of the Handsome Lake Religion," *Proceedings of the American Philosophical Society* 133, no. 1 (Mar. 1989), 35–50; Gregory Evans Dowd, *A Spirited Resistance: The North American Indian Struggle for Unity, 1745–1815* (Baltimore, 1992), 124–29; Alfred A. Cave, *Prophets of the Great Spirit: Native American Revitalization Movements in Eastern North America* (Lincoln, Neb., 2006), 183–224. On Handsome Lake's influence among the Oneidas, see Hauptman, "The Oneida Nation," 29–30.

35. Hopkins, "Clinton and the Iroquois," 119.

36. *Kirkland Journals,* 265–66; Karim Tiro, "The People of the Standing Stone: The Oneida Indian Nation from Revolution through Removal" (Ph.D. diss., University of Pennsylvania, 1999), 198–99; Hauptman, *Conspiracy of Interests,* 47; Taylor, *Divided Ground,* 390; Alex F. Ricciardelli, "The Adoption of White Agriculture by the Oneida Indians," *Ethnohistory* 10, no. 4 (Fall 1963), 313.

37. These conversations appear in Journals of John Sergeant, 1789–1809, entries for Jun. 30, 1803; Jun. 30, Aug. 10, Sept. 2, and Oct. 20, 1805, Harvard Grants.

38. Samson Occom to ?, Dec. 26, 1791, and "Indians Must Have Teachers of Their Own Coular or Nation" [Nov. 1791], *Occom Writings,* 134, 136.

39. See, for instance, the Delaware statement in Grand Council at Onondaga, Jun. 3–Jun. 19, 1756, *Early American Indian Documents, Treaties and Laws, 1607–1789,* gen. ed. Alden T. Vaughan, vol. 10, *New York and New Jersey Treaties, 1754–1775,* vol. ed. Barbara Graymont (Bethesda, Md., 2001), 196.

40. "A Speech delivered to Col. Pickering, at a Treaty at New Town Point, June 20th, 1791, by Capt. Hendrick of the Mohukunnuk Indians," vol. 61, Pickering Papers, MHS; Letter of John Sergeant, May 14, 1739, John Sergeant Letters, Ayer MS 800; Indian Conference, Nov. 7–24, 1763, *Johnson Papers,* 10:931. See also Hendrick Aupaumut, "Indian History," in Electa F. Jones, *Stockbridge, Past and Present; or, Records of an Old Mission Station* (Springfield, Mass., 1854), 16–17; Ted J. Brasser, *Riding on the Frontier's Crest: Mahican Indian Culture and Culture Change* (Ottawa, 1974), 24.

41. Hendrick Aupaumut, "A Short Narration of my Journey to the Western country," *Iroquois Indians,* reel 33.

42. On the history of the Miami offer, see Statement of the Claims of the Stockbridge Indians to a tract of land at White River, State of Indiana, O'Reilly Papers, vol. 14, no. 60, NYHS; John Sergeant Jr. to H. R. Storrs, Jan. 31, 1820, O'Reilly Papers, vol. 14, no. 67, NYHS; *Federal Gazette, and Philadelphia Evening Post,* Sept. 7, 1791, p. 3; "At a Council, New Stockbridge, Dec. 5, 1794," Pickering Papers, vol. 62, pp. 113–a, MHS; "Heads of Capt. Hendrick's Speech at Mohhekonnuk, New Stockbridge, Dec. 5, 1794," Pickering Papers, vol. 62, p. 117, MHS; Petition of Jacob Konkapot and Robert Nimham of New Stockbridge, 1796, New York Assembly Papers, box 3, folder 3.

43. Hendrick Aupaumut, "A Short Narration of my Journey to the Western Country," *Iroquois Indians,* reel 33; Narrative of Capt. Hendrick, Jul.–Oct. 1791, Kirkland Papers, 138d.

44. C. A. Weslager, *The Delaware Indians: A History* (New Brunswick, N.J., 1972), 332–38; Helen Hornbeck Tanner, *Atlas of Great Lakes History* (Norman, Okla., 1987), 90, 102.

45. "Extracts from the Journals of the Indians along with the 6th speech delivere'd the Delaware nation residing at Waupehaummhuhk or White River on the 15th of April, 1803," Sergeant Journals, Entry for Aug. 4, 1803, Harvard Grants.

46. Ibid.

47. Robert S. Grumet, "The Selling of Lenapehoking," *Bulletin of the Archaeological Society of New Jersey* 44 (1989), 1–6; Grumet, "The Nimhams of the Colonial Hudson Valley, 1667–1783," *Hudson Valley Regional Review* 9 (Sept. 1992), 80–101.

48. W. DeLoss Love, *Samson Occom and the Christian Indians of New England,* introduction by Margaret Connell Szasz (1899; Syracuse, N.Y., 2000), 242–43.

49. *The Centinel of Freedom* (Newark, N.J.), Mar. 1, 1797, vol. 1, no. 22, p. 2; *New Jersey Journal,* Feb. 27, 1798, vol. 5, no. 750, p. 2.

50. Sergeant Journals, entries for May 10, Jul. 29, and Aug. 18, 1802, Harvard Grants; *New Jersey Journal,* Dec. 14, 1802, vol. 20, no. 998, p. 1.

51. Memorial of the Delaware Indians, New Stockbridge, Nov. 25, 1819, O'Reilly Papers, vol. 14, no. 545, NYHS.

52. Packet entitled "Acct. and Vouchers, Supers. for Brothertown Indians, 1809," box 17, and Stockbridge to the Brothertown Peacemakers, Jul. 8, 1808, box 18, Records of the New York Comptroller's Office, Onondaga Historical Association, Syracuse, N.Y.; Speech of the Brothertown Indians to the Delawares, by vote of the town, Apr. 4, 1809, reprinted from the town records, in Pomeroy Jones, *Annals and Recollections of Oneida County* (n.p., 1851), 267–70.

53. Journal of John Sergeant Missionary to the New Stockbridge Indians from the Society in Scotland for Propagating Christian Knowledge from the first of January to the first of July 1809, NYHS; Thomas Jefferson, Deposition, Dec. 21, 1808, *Letter Book of the Indian Agency at Fort Wayne, 1809–1815,* ed. Gayle Thornbrough, Indiana Historical Society Publications, no. 22 (Indianapolis, 1961), 53–54.

54. William Wells to the Secretary of War, Dec. 31, 1807, *Territorial Papers of the United States,* ed. Clarence Edwin Carter, 28 vols., vol. 7: *The Territory of Indiana, 1800–1810* (Washington, D.C., 1939), 510–11; Henry Dearborn to Capt. Hendrick, Dec. 27, 1808, *Letter Book of the Indian Agency at Fort Wayne, 1809–1815,* ed. Gayle Thornbrough, Indiana Historical Society Publications, no. 22 (Indianapolis, 1961), 54–55; John Sergeant Jr. to Jedidah Morse, Jun. 17, 1811, Rauner, Ms. 811367.1; Sergeant Journals, entry for Jun. 25, 1809, Harvard Grants; Jedidiah Morse, *Signs of the Times: A Sermon Preached before the Society for Propagating the Gospel...Nov. 1, 1810* (Charlestown, Mass., 1810), 53–54; Hendrick Aupaumut to John Sergeant Jr., Jan. 3, 1809, Dean Family Papers, box 1, folder 6; "Extracts from Hendrick's Letter from White River, July 7, 1809," Journal of John Sergeant Missionary to the New Stockbridge Indians from the Society in Scotland for Propagating Christian Knowledge from the first of January to the first of July 1809, NYHS.

55. John Sergeant Jr. to Jedidah Morse, Jun. 29, 1813, Papers of the Society for Propagating Christian Knowledge, 1764–1893, box 1, folder 2, Rauner Library; Report of the

Superintendents of Brothertown and New Stockbridge Indians for 1818, New York Assembly Papers, box 5, folder 20; Stockbridge to the New York Assembly, Winter 1819, New York Assembly Papers, box 6, folder 6; Committee Report on Stockbridge Lands, New York Assembly Papers, box 6, folder 34; Oneida and Stockbridge Indians to John Taylor, Feb. 27, 1806, Ayer MS, folder 12.

56. Sergeant Journals, entry of Jun. 26, 1808, Harvard Grants.

57. John Sergeant Jr. to John P. Therwood, Jan. 5, 1820, O'Reilly Papers, vol. 14, no. 61, NYHS; Muster roll of the Indian Warriors of the Six Nations Invited in the Service of the United States by the Secretary of War, Feb. 14, 1814, Jasper Parish Papers, box 2, folder 102, Vassar College Archives and Special Collections; Tiro, "People of the Standings Stone," 212, 214; Laurence M. Hauptman and L. Gordon McLester, *Chief Daniel Bread and the Oneida Indians of Wisconsin* (Norman, Okla., 2002), 3–5; Hauptman, *Conspiracy of Interests*, 37.

58. Journal of a Voyage to Indiana, 1817, Dean Family Papers, box 11, folder 3.

59. Ibid.; Testimony of Jonathan Johnstoy, Oct. 2, 1817, Dean Papers, WHS.

60. Journal of John Sergeant Jr., summary comments for journal of Jul. 1, 1817–Jan. 1, 1818, NYHS; New York Assembly Papers, box 5, folder 20.

61. John Sergeant Jr. to Thomas Dean, Feb. 26, 1818, Dean Family Papers, box 1, folder 10. See also "Memorial of the Stockbridge Indians, Jan. 29, 1818," New York Assembly Papers, box 5, folder 22; New York Department of Transportation, Surveyor General Maps and Field Books, series no. 10424, map 790, NYSA.

62. John Sergeant to H. R. Storrs, Feb. 8, 1820, O'Reilly Papers, vol. 14, no. 63; John Sergeant Jr. to H. R. Storrs, Jan. 31, 1820, O'Reilly Papers, vol. 14, no. 67, NYHS.

63. John Sergeant to H. R. Storrs, Feb. 8, 1820, O'Reilly Papers, vol. 14, no. 63, NYHS.

64. The figure comes from Stockbridge to the New York Assembly, Jan. 16, 1821, New York Assembly Papers, box 6, folder 31. See also John Sergeant to Jedidah Morse, Apr. 4, 1821, Ayer MS 317, folder 3; *Providence Gazette,* Dec. 12, vol. 54, no. 2686, p. 1.

65. John Sergeant Journals, entries for Jul. 24, Aug. 2, Aug. 15, 1818, SPGNA Recs., box 4, folder 12. See also the letter from John Metoxen, May 6, 1819, and Sergeant's commentary Journal of John Sergeant, Missionary to the New Stockbridge Indians, from the Society in Scotland and from the Society in Boston for Propagating the Gospel among the Indians from the 1st of January to the 1st of July 1819, typescript, Rauner Library.

66. Charles J. Kappler, ed., *Indian Affairs: Laws and Treaties,* 7 vols., vol. 2: *Treaties* (Washington, D.C., 1904), 170–71; Stockbridge Indians to James Monroe, Nov. 16, 1819, Stockbridge Indian Papers; Weslager, *Delawares,* 351–52.

67. John B. Dillon, *A History of Indiana: From its Earliest Exploration by Europeans to the Close of the Territory Government in 1816* (Indianapolis, 1816), 418, 563.

68. John Sergeant Jr. to H. R. Storrs, Jan. 27, 1820, O'Reilly Papers, vol. 14, no. 58, NYHS.

69. Jonathan Johnston to Capt. Hendrick and the Chiefs of New Stockbridge, Aug. 17, 1818, Misc. Ms., NYHS.

70. Stockbridge Indians to James Monroe, Nov. 16, 1819, and John Sergeant Jr. to Jedidiah Morse, Oct. 20, 1819, Stockbridge Indian Papers.

71. Isaac Wobby to Thomas Dean, Oct. 3, 1818, Dean Family Papers, box 1, folder 10; Thomas Dean to John C. Calhoun, Feb. 24, 1825, LROIA, Green Bay Agency, reel 315, frames 16–18. See also Thomas Dean to John C. Calhoun, Feb. 24, 1825, LROIA, Green Bay Agency, reel 315, frames 16–18; Isaac McCoy to Thomas Dean, Sept. 2, 1822, Dean Family Papers, box 1, folder 11.

72. Cutting Marsh to John Codman, Aug. 1, 1833, Rauner Ms. 833451.

73. *New Hampshire Gazette*, Feb. 22, 1820, vol. 65, no. 13, p. 1.

74. Hauptman and McLester, *Chief Daniel Bread*, 32.

75. On these themes and those that immediately follow, see Patrick J. Jung, *The Black Hawk War of 1832* (Norman, Okla., 2007), 16–31; Lucy Eldersveld Murphy, *A Gathering of Rivers: Indians, Métis, and Mining in the Western Great Lakes, 1737–1832* (Lincoln, Neb., 2000), 30–31, 45, 95–97; Louise Phelps Kellogg, *The French Regime in Wisconsin and the Northwest* (Madison, Wisc., 1925); Kellogg, *The British Regime in Wisconsin and the Northwest* (Madison, Wisc., 1935); Felix M. Keesing, *The Menomini Indians of Wisconsin: A Study of Three Centuries of Cultural Contact and Change* (1939; Madison, Wisc., 1987), 53–126; David R. M. Beck, *Siege and Survival: History of the Menominee Indians, 1634–1856* (Lincoln, Neb., 2002), 25–95.

76. John C. Calhoun to Lewis Cass, May 16, 1818, and Calhoun to Cass, Aug. 19, 1818, in R. L. Meriwether, W. E. Hemphill, and C. N. Wilson, eds., *The Papers of John C. Calhoun*, 26 vols. (Charleston, S.C., 1959–2001), 2:296, 3:42.

77. The life of Eleazar Williams is traced in Geoffrey E. Buerger, "Eleazar Williams: Elitism and Multiple Identity on Two Frontiers," in *Being and Becoming Indian: Biographical Studies of North American Frontiers*, ed. James A. Clifton (Chicago, Ill., 1989), 112–36; Albert G. Ellis, "Recollections of Rev. Eleazar Williams," *WHC* 8 (1879), 322–52; Ellis, "Advent of the New York Indians into Wisconsin," *WHC* 2 (1856), 418–20; John H. Hanson, *The Lost Prince: Facts Tending to Prove the Identity of Louis the Seventeenth of France and the Rev. Eleazar Williams, Missionary among the Indians of North America* (New York, 1858).

78. Reginald Horsman, "The Origins of Oneida Removal to Wisconsin, 1815–1822," in *Oneida Indian Journey*, ed. Hauptman and McLester, 61.

79. "Rev. Cutting Marsh on the Stockbridges, March 25, 1857," *WHC* 4 (1859), 299–301. For a contemporary source crediting Morse with the idea, see John Sergeant Jr. to H. R. Storrs, Nov. 20, 1820, O'Reilly Papers, vol. 14, no. 70, NYHS.

80. Shirley W. Dunn, *The Mohican World, 1680–1750* (Fleischmanns, N.Y., 1997), 53–54, 101.

81. Stockbridge Tribe to the St. Regis Tribe, Jan. 13, 1825, Dean Family Papers, box 1, folder 2.

82. Petition of the Chiefs and Warriors of those tribes of Indians that have emigrated from New York to Green Bay, Dec. 4th, 1829, LROIA, Green Bay Agency, reel 315.

83. "Sergeant to Rev. Mr. Codman, June 24, 1821," Papers of the Society for Propagating the Christian Knowledge, 1764–1893, folder 3, Rauner Library. See also Sergeant to Jedidiah Morse, Nov. 19, 1821, Ayer MS 31b7.

84. Communication of the New York Indians, ca. 1831, LROIA, Green Bay Agency, reel 315.

85. Affidavit of Thomas Dean, Jan. 1832, Dean Family Papers, box 2, folder 7; Journal entry of Sept. 6, 1824, Thomas Dean Papers, 1814–1836, WHS.

86. Journal of C. C. Trowbridge's Trip to Green Bay in Company with the Representatives of the Oneida Indians of New York, Jul. 11–Sept. 1, 1821, *Iroquois Indians,* reel 46.

87. Beck, *Siege and Survival,* 66, 113.

88. Horsman, "The Origins of Oneida Removal to Wisconsin, 1815–1822," 64; Jarvis, "Preserving the Brothertown Nation of Indians," 243–44.

89. David Butler to Lt. Gov. Taylor, Mar. 17, 1818, Ayer Ms. 127 ("wilderness"); John Sergeant to Jedidiah Morse, Apr. 4, 1821, Ayer Ms. 317 ("whites and liquor").

90. Oneida and Stockbridge Indians to John Taylor, Feb. 27, 1806, Ayer Ms., folder 12.

91. Report of the Superintendents of Brothertown and New Stockbridge Indians for 1818, New York Assembly Papers, box 5, folder 20.

92. Tiro, "People of the Standing Stone," 232.

93. Ibid., 234.

Chapter 8. More Than They Know How to Endure

1. Report of the Superintendents of the Brothertown and Stockbridge Indians, Jan. 15, 1825, New York Assembly Papers, box 7, folder 8. See also Chiefs of Part of the New Stockbridge Indians to the Society for the Propagation of the Gospel, Dept. 6, 187, SPGNA Recs., box 3; Thomas Dean to DeWitt Clinton, Jan. 4, 1824, Dean Family Papers, box 1, folder 12

2. S. C. Stambaugh to the Sec. of War, Nov. 8, 1831, LROIA, Green Bay Agency, reel 315, frame 571.

3. David Green's Report, Aug. 22, 1829, Stockbridge Indian Papers, item 9B.

4. James W. Oberly, *A Nation of Statesmen: The Political Culture of the Stockbridge-Munsee Mohicans, 1815–1972* (Norman, Okla., 2005), 38–39.

5. Cutting Marsh to David Green, Jan. 10, 1833, Marsh Papers, p. 12 of the letter.

6. Report of Commissioners Erastus Root, and James McCall, Sept. 20, 1830, LROIA, Green Bay Agency, reel 315, frames 133–43.

7. G. Troup, T. L. Ogden, and B.N. Rogers, to James Barbour, Oct. 16, 1827, LROIA, Six Nations Agency, reel 832, slides 238–40.

8. Albert G. Ellis, "Some Account of the Advent of the New York Indians into Wisconsin," *WHC* 2 (1856), 418; Oberly, *Nation of Statesmen,* 27.

9. Solomon U. Hendrick to?, Jun. 3, 1825, Papers of the Society for Propagating Christian Knowledge, 1764–1893, box 1, folder 3, Rauner Library; Jasper Parish to Thomas L. McKinney, Feb. 26, 1827, LROIA, Six Nations Agency, reel 832, slide 178; Lewis Cass to Jasper Parish, Jan. 14, 1828, and Jasper Parish to Thomas L. McKinney, Apr. 30, 1829, LROIA, Six Nations Agency, reel 832, slides 295, 359–60; *Memorial of John W. Quinney, to the Honorable the Senate and House of Representatives of the United States in Congress Assembled* (Washington, D.C., 1852), appendix D; Oberly, *Nation of Statesmen,* 44.

10. On these kinds of expenses, see Solomon U. Hendricks to John C. Calhoun, Jun. 9, 1821, LRSW, 1800–1823, microfilm 271, reel 3, slides 942–44; John Sergeant to Jedidiah Morse, Jan. 6, 1824, Ayer MS 31b7; John Sergeant to Jedidiah Morse, Feb. 16, 1824, and Solomon Hendrick to J. C. Calhoun, Feb. 11, 1825, LROIA, Six Nations

Agency, reel 832, slides 49–50, 62–63; Brothertown Indians' Preparation in New York Comptroller's Office, Indian Annuity Claims and Receipts, box 1, folder 3, RG A0832–77, NYSA; Thomas Dean Thomas Dean Journal, entry for Sept. 6, 1824, Thomas Dean Papers, 1814–1836, WHS; Affidavit of Thomas Dean, Jan. 1832, Dean Family Papers, box 2, folder 7; Thomas Dean Journal, entries for Aug.–Sept. 1826, Dean Family Papers, box 11, folder 5; Journal of C. C. Trowbridge's trip to Green Bay in company with the representatives of the Oneida Indian, Jul. 11–Sept. 1, 1821, *Iroquois Indians,* reel 46.

11. Report of the Superintendents of the Brothertown and Stockbridge Indians, Joseph Stebbins, Austin Mygatt, and Samuel L. Hibbins, Jan. 15, 1825, New York Assembly Papers, box 7, folder 8.

12. Dean to Clinton, Jan. 4, 1824, Dean Family Papers, box 1, folder 12.

13. S. C. Stambaugh to the Secretary of War, Nov. 8, 1831, LROIA, Green Bay Agency, reel 315, frames 566–607; Samuel Stambaugh, "Report on the Quality and Condition of Wisconsin Territory, 1831," *WHC* 15 (1900), 407.

14. Memorial of the Stockbridge, Oneida, St. Regis, and Brothertown Indians to President Monroe relative to their Lands at Green Bay, 1823, LRSW, reel 4, slide 756; Solomon Hendrick to John C. Calhoun, Feb. 11, 1825, LROIA, Six Nations Agency, reel 832, frames 62–63; Memorial to Congress from inhabitants of Green Bay to the Honorable the Senate of the United States [1823], Secretary William Woodbridge to the Secretary of State, Feb. 4, 1824, Thomas L. McKenney to Henry B. Brevoort, Mar. 8, 1825, James Barbour to Lewis Cass and Thomas L. McKenney, Mar. 27, 1827, *Territorial Papers of the United States,* vol. 11: *The Territory of Michigan, 1820–1829* (Washington, D.C., 1943), 334–39, 507, 657–58, 1064.

15. Journal of George B. Porter, Joshua Boyer Papers, WHS, p. 26.

16. Green's Report, Aug. 22, 1829, Stockbridge Indian Papers, item 9B; Samuel Stambaugh to Lewis Cass, Sept. 25, 1830, LROIA, Green Bay Agency, reel 315, frame 309.

17. Journal of the Proceedings of a Board of Commissions appointed by the President … to locate a District of Country at Green Bay, and establish the boundaries thereof for the accommodation and settlement of the New York Indians," LROIA, Green Bay Agency, reel 315, frames 395–469.

18. S. C. Stambaugh to the Secretary of War, Nov. 8, 1831, LROIA, Green Bay Agency, reel 315, frames 566–607.

19. David J. Silverman, "'Natural inhabitants, time out of Mind': Sachem Rights and the Struggle for Wampanoag Land in Colonial New England," *Northeast Anthropology* 70 (2005), 4–10.

20. Journal of George B. Potter, Joshua Boyer Papers, 31.

21. Oberly, *Nation of Statesmen,* 42–43; Patrick J. Jung, *The Black Hawk War of 1832* (Norman, Okla., 2002), 43–44; Murphy, *Gathering of Rivers,* 101–33, esp. 128–29.

22. Francis Paul Prucha, *The Great Father: The United States Government and the American Indians* (Lincoln, Neb., 1995), 258–64.

23. Oberly, *Nation of Statesmen,* 42–43.

24. Prucha, *Great Father,* 245.

25. Report of A. G. Ellis, Sept. 24, 1830, LROIA, Green Bay Agency, reel 315, frames 159–75.

26. Brad Devin Edward Jarvis, "Preserving the Brothertown Nation of Indians: Exploring Relationships amongst Land, Sovereignty, and Identity, 1740–1840" (Ph.D., diss., University of Minnesota, 2006), 264; Thomas Dean Journal, Jan.–Feb. 1831, Thomas Dean Papers, WHS; Ellis, "Some Account of the Advent of the New York Indians into Wisconsin," 432–33; Laurence M. Hauptman and L. Gordon McLester III, *Chief Daniel Bread and the Oneida Indians of Wisconsin* (Norman, Okla., 2002), 70–73; Oberly, *Nation of Statesmen*, 48–49.

27. Thomas Dean to John C. Calhoun, Feb. 24, 1825, LROIA, Green Bay Agency, microfilm 234, reel 315, frames 16–18. See also the list of documents mentioned in Thomas Dean to James Barber, Nov. 24, 1827, LROIA, Six Nations Agency, reel 832, frames 141–42; Solomon U. Hendricks to John C. Calhoun, Jun. 9, 1821, LRSW, microfilm 271, reel 3, frames 942–44; John C. Calhoun to the Chiefs of the Onondaga, Seneca, Tuscarora, Oneida, and Stockbridge Tribes of New York, Oct. 27, 1823, LRSW, reel 4, frames 767–71; Brothertown Indians to John Quincy Adams, Jan. 17, 1827, LROIA, Six Nations Agency, reel 832, frames 134–35; John C. Calhoun to Lewis Cass, Jun. 21, 1821, and Calhoun to Solomon U. Hendricks, Feb. 13, 1822, *Papers of John C. Calhoun*, vol. 6, *1821–22* (Columbia, S.C., 1971) 205, 696; Ellis, "Account of the Advent of the New York Indians into Wisconsin," 422–23.

28. Jedidiah Morse to John C. Calhoun, Aug. 15, 1820, *Papers of John C. Calhoun*, vol. 5, *1820–21*, ed. W. Edwin Hemphill (Columbia, S.C., 1971), 332; Governor Cass to the Secretary of War, Nov. 11, 1820, *Territorial Papers of the United States*, vol. 11, *Territory of Michigan, 1820–1829* (Washington, D.C., 1943), 69–70.

29. Oberly, *Nation of Statesmen*, 43. See also Statement of Daniel Bread to the Commissioners, Jan. 1832, Dean Family Papers, box 2, folder 7.

30. John Ridge to Thomas Dean, Mar. 18, 1831, Dean Family Papers, box 2, folder 6.

31. Lewis Cass to William B. Lewis, Nov. 30, 1830, *Territorial Papers of the United States*, vol. 22, *Territory of Michigan, 1827–1837* (Washington, D.C., 1945), 215–16. See also J. Stambaugh to Andrew Jackson, Sept. 8, 1830, LROIA, microfilm 234, Green Bay Agency, reel 315, frames 293–99.

32. Daniel Fowler, John Quinney, and Daniel Bread to Enos Throop, Apr. 13, 1831, Dean Papers, WHS; Communication of the New York Indians, ca. 1831, LROIA, Green Bay Agency, reel 315; Deposition of Thomas Dean, [1832], Thomas Dean Papers, WHS; Affidavit of Thomas Dean, Jan. 1832, Dean Family Papers, box 2, folder 7.

33. Reply of the New York Indians to Judge Doty, Sept. 3, 1830, LROIA, Green Bay Agency, reel 315, frames 261–64. Generally on these differing interpretations of the New York Indians' purchase, see Robert W. Venables, "Victim versus Victim: The Irony of the New York Indians' Removal to Wisconsin," in *American Indian Environments: Ecological Issues in Native American History*, eds. Christopher Vecsey and Robert W. Venables (Syracuse, N.Y., 1980), 140–51.

34. Reply of the New York Indians to Judge Doty, Sept. 3?, 1830, LROIA, Green Bay Agency, reel 315, frames 261–64.

35. Brothertown Indians to Andrew Jackson, Dec. 27, 1830, Dean Papers, WHS.

36. Memorial of the delegates from the Stockbridge, Munsee, Oneida, St. Regis, and Brothertown Indians, to the President of the United States, Jan. 20, 1831, LROIA, Green Bay

Agency, reel 315, frames 200–203. See also Brothertown Indians to James Barber, Jan. 17, 1827, LROIA, Six Nations Agency, reel 832, frames 130–32.

37. Petition of the Chiefs and Warriors of those tribes of Indians that have emigrated from New York to Green Bay, Dec. 4, 1829, LROIA, Green Bay Agency, reel 315.

38. *Correspondence on the Subject of the emigration of Indians between the 30th November, 1831, and 27th December, 1833…*, vol. 2, serial set no. 245, session no. 8, 23d Congress, 1st session.

39. Daniel Fowler, John Quinney, and Daniel Bread to Enos Throop, Apr. 13, 1831, Dean Papers, WHS; Communication of the New York Indians, ca. 1831, LROIA, Green Bay Agency, reel 315. See also Thomas Dean to Eleazar Williams, Jul. 21, 1829, Den Family Papers, box 2, folder 3.

40. Memorial of John M. Quinney to the President, Dec. 14, 1830, LROIA, Microfilm 234, Green Bay Agency, reel 315, frames 204–5.

41. Communication of the New York Indians, in *Correspondence on the Subject of the emigration of Indians, between the 30th November, 1831, and 27th December, 1833…*, vol. 2, serial set vol. no. 245, session vol. no. 8, 23d Congress, 1st session. S. Doc. 512, pt. 2., pp. 151–59, LROIA, Green Bay Agency, 315, frames 266–85.

42. S. C. Stambaugh to the Sec. of War, Nov. 8, 1831, LROIA, Green Bay Agency, reel 315, frame 596.

43. Petition of the Chiefs and Warriors of those tribes of Indians that have emigrated from New York to Green Bay… 1829, LROIA, Green Bay Agency, reel 315, frame 191.

44. On this settlement, see Report of A. G. Ellis, Surveyor, to Erastus Root, James McCall, and John T. Mason, U.S. Commissioners, Sept. 24, 1830, LROIA, Green Bay Agency, reel 315, frames 159–75; Ellis, "Advent of the New York Indians into Wisconsin," 429–30; Haputman and McLester, *Chief Daniel Bread*, 43–62.

45. George B. Porter to Lewis Cass, Feb. 3, 1832, LROIA, Green Bay Agency, reel 315, frames 711–43.

46. Thomas Dean to George Boyd, Aug. 18, 1834, LROIA, Green Bay Agency, reel 316, frame 188.

47. Cutting Marsh to Jeremiah Everts, Sept. 9, 1830, p. 99, Marsh Papers.

48. Marsh to B. B. Wisner, R. Ander, and D. Greene, Jul. 8, 1833, Marsh Papers, p. 113.

49. Marsh to David Greene, Jan. 10, 1833, Marsh Papers; Marsh to John Codman, Aug. 1, 1832, Loose Manuscripts, 832451.2, Rauner Library, Dartmouth College.

50. Brothertown Indian Nation, Supporting Documentation for the 1995 Petition for Federal Acknowledgment as an American Indian Tribe in Accordance with 25 CFR Part 83, pp. 55–56. Ms. in possession of the author courtesy of the Brothertown Indian Nation.

51. J. N. Davidson, *Muh-he-ka-ne-ok* (Milwaukee, 1893), 30–31.

52. Cutting Marsh to John Codman, Apr. 1831, Misc. Ms. 831290, Rauner Library, Dartmouth College.

53. Jung, *Black Hawk War of 1832*; Murphy, *Gathering of Rivers*, 161–65, 168; Cutting Marsh, Expedition to the Sacs and Foxes (Jun.–Sept. 1834), entry for Jun. 29, p. 18, Marsh

Papers; Marsh, Expedition to the Sacs and Foxes, entry for Aug. 16, 1834, p. 168. See also entry for Aug. 19, 1834, p. 190.

54. Jung, *Black Hawk War of 1832*, 46.

55. John P. Bowles, *Exiles and Pioneers: Eastern Indians in the Trans-Mississippi West* (New York, 2007); Stephen Warren, "The Ohio Shawnees' Struggle against Removal, 1814–1830," in *Enduring Nations,* ed. Edmunds, 72–93.

56. Available at http://www2.census.gov/prod2/decennial/documents/1840b-07.pdf, accessed Jan. 22, 2010.

57. George B. Porter to Lewis Cass, Feb. 3, 1832, LROIA, Green Bay Agency, reel 315, frames 714–15.

Chapter 9. Indians or Citizens, White Men or Red?

1. Generally, see Eric Foner, *The Story of American Freedom* (New York, 1998).

2. Argument by atty. J. W. Quinney, 1846, Stockbridge Tribe of Indians, Recs., Ayer Ms. 836, folder 10.

3. Memorial of the Stockbridge Tribe, Jan. 29, 1844, House Report on Stockbridge Indians, 9th Congress, 1st session, report no. 447 (1846), serial set vol. 1, 489.

4. *Stockbridge Indians. Memorial of the chiefs and sachems of the "Indian Party" of the Stockbridge Indians, praying for the repeal of the law of Congress for 1842 for their relief. February 17, 1846.* Serial set vol. no. 483, session vol. no. 4, 29th Congress, 1st session, H.Doc. 128.

5. William Dickinson to George Boyd, Nov. 15, 1834, LROIA, Green Bay Agency, reel 316; Survey Report on the Military Road from Fort Crawford, by Winnebago, to Fort Howard, at Green Bay, *Message from the President of the United States, to the two Houses of Congress, at the commencement of the Twenty-sixth Congress,* Dec. 24, 1839, serial set vol. no. 363, session vol. no. 1, 26th Congress, 1st session, House Doc. 2, p. 650; Thomas Commuck, "Sketch of Calumet County," *WHC* 1 (1854), 104; William Wallace Wright, Diary and Reminiscence, 1841–1842, WHS.

6. *Message from the President,* 650; Rev. P. S. Bennet, *History of Methodism in Wisconsin* (Cincinnati, Oh., 1890), 15, 42, 56–57, 62.

7. Thomas Dick to Thomas Dean, Jan. 20, 1835, Dean Family Papers, box 2, folder 9.

8. Randal Abner to Thomas Dean, Jan. 13, 1835, and William Fowler to Thomas Dean, Mar. 2, 1838, Dean Family Papers, box 2, folder 9.

9. Dean Family Papers, box 2, folder 2; Reports of Elkanah Dick and Asa Dick, Jun. 8, 1841, Original Indian Deeds/Treaties, 1:23, A4609–97, NYSA; H. Gillet to C. A. Harris, Dec. 29, 1837, LROIA, New York Agency, reel 583; Paul R. Campbell and Glenn W. LaFantasie, "Scattered to the Winds of Heaven: Narragansett Indians, 1676–1800," *Rhode Island History* 37, no. 3 (1978), 77; Brothertown Indian Nation, Supporting Documentation for the 1995 Petition for Federal Acknowledgment as an American Indian Tribe in Accordance with 25 CFR Part 83, p. 12, Ms. in possession of the author courtesy of the Brothertown Indian Nation.

10. Cutting Marsh to B. B. Wisner, R. Anderson, and D. Greene, Jul. 8, 1833, Marsh Papers; James Stryker Census of New York Indians, Mar. 13, 1834, LROIA, Six Nations Agency, reel 832, Frames 669–71. Note that in 1837 J. F. Schermerhorn put the population

of Stockbridge at "about" 250 and that of Brothertown at 360, but the citations above suggest that he mistakenly reversed those figures. Report of J. F. Schermerhorn, Jan. 10, 1837, LROIA, New York Agency, reel 583, frames 325–38.

11. *Wisconsin Enquirer,* vol. 1, no. 43, Sept. 7, 1839, p. 3, col. 1.

12. Cutting Marsh to David Greene, Sept. 21, 1836, Marsh Papers, p. 142.

13. Cutting Marsh to David Greene, May 11, 1836, Marsh Papers, p. 136.

14. J. F. Schermerhorn, to Elbert Harring, Nov. 12, 1833, LROIA, Six Nations Agency, reel 832, frames 574–77.

15. Cutting Marsh to David Greene, Sept. 21, 1836, Cutting Marsh Papers, p. 142; Report of J. F. Schermerhorn, LROIA, New York Agency, reel 583, frames 173–88.

16. James W. Oberly, *A Nation of Statesmen: The Political Culture of the Stockbridge-Munsee Mohicans, 1815–1972* (Norman, Okla., 2005), 64.

17. Oneida Chiefs to the President of the United States, Aug. 1837, LROIA, New York Agency, reel 538, frames 300–303.

18. Treaty with the Stockbridge and Munsee Indians convened at Green Bay, Sept. 17, 1836, LROIA, New York Agency, reel 538, frames 205–9.

19. Arlinda Locklear, "The Buffalo Creek Treaty of 1838 and its Legal Implications for Oneida Indian Land Claims," in *The Oneida Indian Journey: From New York to Wisconsin, 1784–1860,* ed. Laurence M. Hauptman and L. Gordon McLester III (Madison, Wisc., 1999), 85–104.

20. Council of Aug. 31, 1836, LROIA, Green Bay Agency, reel 316, frames 424–25.

21. Council with the Oneidas, LROIA, Green Bay Agency, reel 316, frames 435–40.

22. Brothertown Peacemakers to Thomas Dean, Nov. 30, 1836, Dean Family Papers, box 2, folder 9.

23. Council with the Brothertowns, LROIA, Green Bay Agency, reel 316, frames 430–32.

24. Thomas Commuck to Thomas Dean, Nov. 1, 1836, Dean Papers, box 2, folder 9. See also Marsh to David Greene, Sept. 21, 1836, p. 142, Marsh Papers.

25. *Journal of the Senate of the United State of America: Being the second session of the Twenty-fifty Congress, begun and held at the City of Washington, December 4, 1837, and in the sixty-second year of the independence of the United States,* serial set vol. no. 313, 25th Congress, 2d session; Thomas Dean to the Committee on Public Lands of the Senate, Apr. 14, 1838, Dean Papers, box 2, folder 9. Generally, see John A. Turchenekse Jr., "Federal Indian Policy and the Brotherton Indians," in William Cowan, ed., *Papers of the Sixteenth Algonquian Conference* (Ottawa, 1985), 205–7; Brad Devin Edward Jarvis, "Preserving the Brothertown Nation of Indians: Exploring Relationships amongst Land, Sovereignty, and Identity, 1740–1840" (Ph.D. diss., University of Minnesota, 2006), 303.

26. Letter of Thomas Commuck, Randal Abner, Charles Anthony, and Alonzo Dick to C. C. Shorles, May 16, 1839, in an article entitled "Brothertown Indians," in *Wisconsin Enquirer,* vol. 1, no. 31, Jun. 15, 1839, p. 3, cols. 1–2.

27. James Duane Doty to Mr. Clay, Oct. 10, 1826, *Territorial Papers of the United States,* ed. Clarence Edwin Carter, 28 vols., vol. 22, *The Territory of Michigan, 1827–1837* (Washington, D.C., 1945), 113.

28. "Odd Wisconsin: Tribal Sovereignty Outlined in 1830 Murder Trial," *Wisconsin State Journal*, Sept. 3, 2008; J. W. Beall to Thomas Dean, Jul. 28, 1830, Dean Family Papers, box 2, folder 4.

29. Cutting Marsh Journal for Aug. 1836, Marsh Papers, p. 139.

30. Cutting Marsh Journal for Aug. 1836, Marsh to David Greene, Jun. 30, 1837, and Marsh to John Codman, Jan. 15, 1838, Marsh Papers, pp. 139, 144, and unpaginated, respectively; Thomas Dean Daybook, entry for Sept. 9–14, 1836, Dean Family Papers, box 12, folder 2.

31. *Brothertown Indians—Wisconsin (To accompany Bill H.R. No. 1112) February 6, 1839*, serial set no. 351, session vol. no. 1, 25th Congress, 3d session, H. rpt. 244.

32. James H. Kettner, *The Development of American Citizenship, 1608–1870* (Chapel Hill, N.C., 1984), 292–93; Alexander Keysar, *The Right to Vote: The Contested History of Democracy in the United States* (New York, 2000), 59.

33. Mary E. Young, *Redskins, Ruffleshirts, and Rednecks: Indian Allotments in Alabama and Mississippi, 1830–1860* (Norman, Okla., 1961); Michael D. Green, *The Politics of Indian Removal: Creek Government and Society in Crisis* (Lincoln, Neb., 1982); and J. Leitch Wright Jr., *Creeks and Seminoles: The Destruction and Regeneration of the Muscogulge People* (Lincoln, Neb., 1986), 245–80; Alfred A. Cave, "Abuse of Power: Andrew Jackson and the Indian Removal Act of 1830," *Historian* 65 (Winter 2003), 1330–53.

34. *Wisconsin Enquirer*, vol. 1, no. 13, Feb. 9, 1839, p. 3, col. 3.

35. "Brothertown Indians," *Wisconsin Enquirer*, vol. 1, no. 31, Jun. 15, 1839, p. 3, cols. 1–2.

36. Report on the Petition of the Brothertown Indians by the Committee on Territories, Brothertown Indians, Records, 1839, 1 folder, WHS. See also *Brothertown Indians—Wisconsin (To accompany H.R. No. 1112) February 6, 1839*, serial set no. 351, session vol. no. 1, 25th Congress, 3d session, H. rpt. 244.

37. Brotherton and Stockbridge Indian Records, 1839–1945, 1 reel, pp. 1–10, 27–31, WHS. See also John S. Horner to Martin Van Buren, Jul. 2, 1839, pp. 4–10 of the same collection.

38. Jarvis, "Preserving the Brothertown Nation of Indians," 310–12; Brothertown Indian Nation, Supporting Documentation for the 1995 Petition, 66.

39. *Wisconsin Enquirer*, Feb. 6, 1841, vol. 3, no. 11, p. 1, cols. 3–5, and p. 3, cols. 1–2; Moses M. Strong, *History of the Territory of Wisconsin* (Madison, Wisc., 1885), 327, 329.

40. *Milwaukee Courier*, Dec. 30, 1846, vol. 6, no. 42, col. 5; Strong, *History of the Territory of Wisconsin*, 426.

41. On these Munsee Delaware bands, see C. A. Weslager, *The Delaware Indians: A History* (New Brunswick, N.J., 1972), 352–53, 369; John P. Bowes, *Exiles and Pioneers: Eastern Indians in the Trans-Mississippi West* (New York, 2007), 99–103.

42. Petition to President Van Buren, Dec. 5, 1838, LROIA, Green Bay Agency, reel 317, frames 610–15.

43. Marsh to David Greene, Dec. 13, 1837, Marsh Papers, p. 176.

44. Marsh to David Greene, Jun. 17, 1836, Marsh Papers, p. 137.

45. Oberly, *Nation of Statesmen*, 52–53, 69–70.

46. Stockbridge Declaration of Rights and Frame of Government, Feb. 17, 1837, LROIA, Green Bay Agency, reel 317, frames 704–13. See also Stockbridge to Col. George Boyd, Jun. 11, 1838, and Austin E. Quinney and Jonathan W. Quinney to the Secretary of War, Mar. 7, 1839, LROIA, Green Bay Agency, M234, reel 317, frames 108–11, 545–52; Oberly, *Nation of Statesmen,* 62.

47. Marsh to David Greene, Dec. 13, 1837, Marsh Papers, p. 176.

48. Austin Quinney to Henry Dodge, Mar. 20, 1838, *Territorial Papers of the United States,* vol. 27, *The Territory of Wisconsin, Executive Journal, 1836–1848; Papers, 1836–1839* (Washington, D.C., 1969), 969.

49. Munsees to Martin Van Buren, Aug. 28, 1839, LROIA, Green Bay Agency, reel 317, frame 464–68; Austin Quinney to Henry Dodge, Mar. 20, 1838, *Territorial Papers of the United States,* vol. 27, *The Territory of Wisconsin, Executive Journal, 1836–1848; Papers, 1836–1839* (Washington, D.C., 1969), 969; Marsh to Green, Dec. 13, 1837, Marsh Papers, p. 176.

50. Austin E. Quinney and Jonathan W. Quinney to the Secretary of War, Mar. 7, 1839, LROIA, Green Bay Agency, reel 317, frames 545–52.

51. Stockbridge and Munsee Indians to Henry Dodge, Dec. 5, 1838, LROIA, Green Bay Agency, reel 317, frames 616–19.

52. Stockbridge to Martin Van Buren, Dec. 5, 1838, LROIA, Green Bay Agency, reel 317, frames 610–15. See also Stockbridge and Munsee Indians to Gov. Dodge, Dec. 5, 1838, reel 317, frames 616–19.

53. Nathan Pendleton, John Baldwin, Jonathan Johnston, George Cook, Charles Toussey, and Joshua Pendleton to the New York Legislature, Feb. 9, 1826, New York Assembly Papers, box 7, folder 20.

54. Stockbridge to DeWitt Clinton, Jan. 26, 1821, New York Assembly Papers, box 6, folder 39; Field Book of the Indian Lands in New Stockbridge (1825), box 34, folder 4, RG 4019, NYSA; Entry of Mar. 2, 1826, Indian Annuity Claims and Receipts, New York Comptroller's Office, box 3, folder 1, RG A0832–77, NYSA; Survey of New Guinea Tract, New York Assembly Papers, box 6, folder 23.

55. Cutting Marsh to David Greene, Jul. 31, Nov. 29, 1838; and May 15, 1839, Marsh Papers.

56. Thomas Hendrick and others to J. H. Crawford, Aug. 1, 1839, LROIA, Green Bay Agency, reel 317, frames 477–79.

57. Marsh to David Greene, May 28, 1838, Marsh Papers. See also entries for Jul. 31, 1838 and Nov. 29, 1838.

58. Quoted in Oberly, *Nation of Statesmen,* 66.

59. Ayer Ms., Folio E95.U69 1825, vol. 2, no. 83–149.

60. List of Persons who Separated and Agreed to Emigrate under the Treaty of 1839, Stockbridge Indian Papers, reel 1, item no. 24; *Letter from the Secretary of War, to the Chairman of the Committee on Indian Affairs, recommending an appropriation for the removal and subsistence of a number of Stockbridge and Munsee Indians, January 7, 1840,* serial set vol. no. 355, session vol. no. 2, 26th Congress, 1st session, S. Doc. 42T; Henry Crawford to J. R. Pouiett, Jul. 1, 1840, LROIA, Green Bay Agency, reel 318, frames 360–62; Austin E. Quinney and John W. Quinney to Henry Crawford, Feb. 19, 1839, *Territorial Papers of the United States,* vol.

27, *The Territory of Wisconsin, Executive Journal, 1836–1848; Papers, 1836–1839* (Washington, D.C., 1969), 1199; Commissioner Crawford to the Secretary of War, Jul. 1, 1840, *Territorial Papers of the United States*, vol. 28, *The Territory of Wisconsin, 1839–1848* (Washington, D.C., 1975), 201; Eliot Hendrick, et al., to James Polk, Dec. 29, 1847, LROIA, Green Bay Agency, reel 320, frames 124–25. See also Oberly, *Nation of Statesmen*, 67; Bowes, *Exiles and Pioneers*, 53–55, 82. Stockbridge-Munsee religious life in Kansas can be traced in "Two Minute Books of Kansas Missions in the Forties," *Kansas Historical Quarterly* 2, no. 3 (Aug. 1933), 227–50.

61. Marsh to David Greene, Oct. 2, 1839, Marsh Papers.

62. Oberly, *Nation of Statesmen*, 74.

63. *Wisconsin Enquirer*, Mar. 25, 1840, vol. 2, no. 18, p. 3, col. 5; Marsh to David Greene, Feb. 24, 1840, and Jun. 8, 1840, Marsh Papers.

64. *Stockbridge Indians. (To accompany Bill H.R. No. 559.) July 30, 1842.* serial set vol. no. 411, session vol. no. 5. 27th Congress, 2d session, H.R. rpt. 961; J. D. Doty to the Secretary of War, Jun. 20, 1842, *Territorial Papers of the United States*, vol. 28, *The Territory of Wisconsin, 1839–1848*, 449–50. See also Marsh to John Codman, Jun. 1, 1842, Rauner Ms., 842351.1.

65. Stockbridge to James Duane Doty, Jun. 6, 1842, LROIA, Green Bay Agency, reel 320, frames 177–78.

66. *Stockbridge Indians. (To accompany Bill H.R. No. 559.) July 30, 1842.* serial set vol. no. 411, session vol. no. 5. 27th Congress, 2d session, H.R. rpt. 961.

67. Austin E. Quinney and Jonathan W. Quinney to the Secretary of War, LROIA, Green Bay Agency, reel 319, frames 116–17. See also Cutting Marsh to Robert Stuart, Jun. 5, 1843, LROIA, Green Bay Agency, reel 318, frames 885–88.

68. A List of lots and parcels of land sold by the Stockbridge Indians in the County of Calumet since the 3d of March 1843, LROIA, Green Bay Agency, reel 319, frame 811.

69. Stockbridge Tribe to James Duane Doty, Jan. 19, 1839, and Indian Party to James Doty, May 11, 1843, LROIA, Green Bay Agency, reel 318, frames 895–98, 922–23.

70. *Stockbridge Indians, Memorial of the chiefs and sachems of the "Indian Party" of the Stockbridge Indians, praying for the repeal of the law of Congress for 1842 for their relief. February 17, 1846,* serial set vol. no. 483, session vol. no. 4, 29th Congress, 1st session, H.Doc. 128.

71. Marsh to David Greene, Jun. 24, 1844 and Aug. 12, 1844, Marsh Papers; Oberly, *Nation of Statesmen*, 72.

72. Memorial to Congress by Stockbridge Indian Citizens, Jan. 22, 1845, *Territorial Papers of the United States*, vol. 28, *The Territory of Wisconsin, 1839–1848* (Washington, D.C., 1975), 780.

73. Quinney to J. Slingerland, Jul. 10, 1844, Stockbridge Indian Papers, reel 1.

74. John W. Quinney to J. Slingerland, Jul. 10, 1844, Stockbridge Indian Papers, roll 1.

75. Statement of the Sachem and Counsellors of the Stockbridge Tribe of Indians...to the Hon. Commissioner of Indian Affairs, Jul. 7, 1847, Green Bay Agency, reel 319, frames 825–29.

76. House Report on Stockbridge Indians, 9th Congress, 1st session, report no. 447 (1846), by Jacob Thompson from the Committee on Indian Affairs, serial set vol. no. 489.

77. Marsh to David Greene, Apr. 1, 1845, Marsh Papers.

78. Marsh to David Greene, Oct. 19, 1842, Marsh Papers.

79. *Stockbridge Indians, Memorial of the chiefs and sachems of the "Indian Party"...*, serial set vol. no. 483, session vol. no. 4, 29th Congress, 1st session, H.Doc. 128; House Report on Stockbridge Indians, 9th Congress, 1st session, report no. 447 (1846), by Jacob Thompson from the Committee on Indian Affairs, serial set vol. no. 489; Oberly, *Nation of Statesmen*, 74.

80. Statement of the Sachem and Counsellors of the Stockbridge Tribe of Indians...to the Hon. Commissioner of Indian Affairs, Jul. 7, 1847, Green Bay Agency, reel 319, frames 825–29.

81. Ibid.

82. Speech of John Metoxen, Austin Quinney, John W. Quinney, and Simon S. Metoxen, on behalf of the Stockbridges of Wisconsin, to the Delawares, May 11, 1842, LROIA, Green Bay Agency, reel 318, frames 912–15. See also Austin E. Quinney and Jonathan W. Quinney to T. H. Crawford, Feb. 19, 1839, LROIA, Green Bay Agency, reel 317, frames 539–40; J. D. Doty to T. H. Crawford, May 14, 1843, LROIA, Green Bay Agency, reel 318, frames 920–21; Marsh to David Greene, May 19, 1843, Marsh Papers.

83. Stockbridge to William Mills, Nov. 20, 1846, *Territorial Papers of the United States*, vol. 28, *The Territory of Wisconsin, 1839–1848* (Washington, D.C., 1975), 1018.

84. John N. Chicks, John W. Abrams, Daniel David, Timothy Jourdan, and Joseph L. Chicks to the Secretary of War, Dec. 10, 1845, LROIA, Green Bay Agency, reel 319, frames 455–57. See also the letter of Mar. 9, 1844, in frames 113–13 of the same reel.

85. House Report on Stockbridge Indians, 9th Congress, 1st session, report no. 447 (1846), by Jacob Thompson from the Committee on Indian Affairs, serial set vol. no. 489; Oberly, *Nation of Statesmen*, 74.

86. Cutting Marsh to David Greene, Apr. 1, 1847, Marsh Papers; A. G. Ellis to Henry Dodge, Jan. 14, 1847, LROIA, Green Bay Agency, reel 319, frames 764–66; *Oshkosh City Times* excerpts in George A. Hyer, news clippings, 1820–1824, 1830–1860, part 10, WHS.

87. Stockbridge to New York Assembly, Nov. 16, 1847, Ayer Ms. 836.

88. Marsh to David Greene, Oct. 18, 1847, Marsh Papers.

89. *Annual Report of the Commissioner of Indian Affairs, Transmitted with the Message of the President at the Opening of the First Session of the Thirtieth Congress* (Washington, 1848), 57.

90. *Annual Report of the Commissioner of Indian Affairs...1853* (Washington, D.C., 1853), 50; *Annual Report of the Commissioner of Indian Affairs...1854* (Washington, D.C., 1854), 39; Oberly, *Nation of Statesmen*, 83.

91. Treaty Between the United States of America and the Stockbridge and Munsee Indians, Feb. 5, 1856, Ayer Ms. Folio E 95.U69 1825 v. 2, no. 83–149; Electa F. Jones, *Stockbridge, Past and Present; or, Records of an Old Mission Station* (Springfield, Mass., 1854), 114–15; Oberly, *Nation of Statesmen*, 79–95; Bill for the Relief of the Stockbridge and Munsee Tribe of Indians in Wisconsin, U.S. House of Representatives Misc. Doc. No. 14, 46th Congress, 3d session, Accompanying Bill H.R. 3678, Brotherton Collections, folder 79, NEHGS.

92. "Brothertown Indian," *Wisconsin Enquirer* (Madison), vol. 1, no. 31, Jun. 15, 1839, p. 3, cols. 1–2.

93. *Annual Report of the Commissioner of Indian Affairs...1854* (Washington, D.C., 1854), 38.

94. T. J. Brasser, "Mahican," *Handbook of North American Indians: Northeast*, vol. 15, ser. ed. William C. Sturtevant, vol. ed. Bruce G. Trigger (Washington, D.C., 1978), 210; Oberly, *Nation of Statesmen*, 86–167.

95. Records of the Bureau of Indian Affairs, Records of the Finance Division, Records Relating to the Kansas Claims of New York Indians, RG 75, Reports of Special Agent Guion Miler, 1903–05, 7 boxes, box 4, folder 11, National Archives, Washington, D.C.

96. Bowes, *Exiles and Pioneers*, 187–260; Weslager, *Delaware Indians*, 399–439, esp. 399–410; H. Craig Miner and William E. Unrau, *The End of Indian Kansas: A Study of Cultural Revolution, 1854–1871* (Lawrence, Kans., 1978); and Paul Wallace Gates, "A Fragment of Kansas Land History: The Disposal of the Christian Indian Tract," *Kansas Historical Quarterly* 6, no. 3 (Aug. 1937), 227–40. On specific events and developments, see *Annual Report of the Commissioner of Indian Affairs...1854* (Washington, D.C., 1854), 8–10; *Annual Report of the Commissioner of Indian Affairs...1855* (Washington, D.C., 1855), 7–9, 92; *Annual Report of the Commissioner of Indian Affairs...1856* (Washington, D.C., 1856), 120; *Annual Report of the Commissioner of Indian Affairs...1857* (Washington, D.C., 1857), 109–10.

97. Thomas Commuck, "Sketch of the Brothertown Indians," *WHC* 4 (1859), 297–98.

98. Patrick Wolfe, "Land, Labor, and Difference: Elementary Structures of Race," *American Historical Review* 106, no. 3 (Jun. 2001), 866–905; and Pauline Turner Strong and Barrik Van Winkle, "'Indian Blood': Reflections on the Reckoning and Refiguring of Native North American Identity," *Cultural Anthropology* 11, no. 4 (Nov. 1996), 547–76.

99. Brothertown Indian Nation, Supporting Documentation for the 1995 Petition, passim.

Epilogue

1. "Celebration of the Fourth of July 1854, at Reidsville New York. Interesting Speech of John W. Quinney, Chief of the Stockbridge Tribe of Indians," *WHC* 4 (1859), 314–20.

2. James Clifford, *The Predicament of Culture: Twentieth-Century Ethnography, Literature, and Art* (Cambridge, Mass., 1988), 277–346.

3. Brothertown Indian Nation, Supporting Documentation for the 1995 Petition for Federal Acknowledgment as an American Indian Tribe in Accordance with 25 CFR Part 83, pp. 8–18; Krista Ackley "Renewing Haudenosaunee Ties: Laura Cornelius Kellogg and the Idea of Unity in the Oneida Land Claim," *American Indian Culture and Research Journal* 32, no. 1 (2008), 57–81; Laurence M. Hauptman, "Designing Woman: Minnie Kellog, Iroquois Leader," in *Indian Lives: Essays on Nineteenth- and Twentieth-Century Native American Leaders*, ed. L. G. Moses and R. Wilson (Albuquerque, N.M., 1985), 159–88.

Index

CPSIA information can be obtained at www.ICGtesting.com
Printed in the USA
LVOW06s0318190915

454798LV00014B/39/P